# EUROPEAN INTEGRATION THEORY

**ANTJE WIENER**

*Professor of International Relations and Jean Monnet Professor*
*Queen's University*
*Belfast*
*Northern Ireland*

AND

**THOMAS DIEZ**

*Senior Lecturer in International Relations Theory*
*University of Birmingham*
*UK*

OXFORD
UNIVERSITY PRESS

# OXFORD

UNIVERSITY PRESS

Great Clarendon Street, Oxford OX2 6DP

Oxford University Press is a department of the University of Oxford.
It furthers the University's objective of excellence in research, scholarship,
and education by publishing worldwide in

Oxford New York

Auckland Bangkok Buenos Aires Cape Town Chennai
Dar es Salaam Delhi Hong Kong Istanbul Karachi Kolkata
Kuala Lumpur Madrid Melbourne Mexico City Mumbai Nairobi
São Paulo Shanghai Taipei Tokyo Toronto

Oxford is a registered trade mark of Oxford University Press
in the UK and in certain other countries

Published in the United States
by Oxford University Press Inc., New York

© the several contributors and in this collection Oxford University Press 2004

The moral rights of the authors have been asserted

Database right Oxford University Press (maker)

First published 2004

A catalogue record for this title is available from the British Library

British Library Cataloguing in Publication Data
Data available

ISBN 0–19–925248–3

10 9 8 7 6 5 4 3 2 1

Typeset by Graphicraft Limited, Hong Kong
Printed in Great Britain
on acid-free paper by
Biddles Ltd., Guildford and King's Lynn

# EUROPEAN INTEGRATION THEORY

# Dedication

In memoriam of Ernst Haas who so greatly inspired generations of integration scholars.

We dedicate this book to our students in Belfast and Birmingham.

Antje Wiener
Thomas Diez

## PART II  ANALYSING EUROPEAN GOVERNANCE

## PART III  CONSTRUCTING THE EUROPEAN UNION

# Notes on Contributors

**Michael Burgess** is Professor of Politics and the Director of the Centre for European Union Studies at the University of Hull. Among his publications are *Federalism and the European Union: The Building of Europe 1950–2000* (UCL Press, 2000) and *Comparative Federalism and Federation* (Harvester Wheatsheaf, 1993; edited with Alain C. Gagnon).

**Thomas Diez** is Senior Lecturer in International Relations Theory at the Department of Political Science and International Studies, University of Birmingham (UK). His publications include *The European Union and the Cyprus Conflict* (Manchester University Press, 2002) and *Die EU lesen* (Leske und Budrich, 1999).

**Ulrich Haltern** is *Privatdozent* at the law faculty of Humboldt University Berlin. He teaches European, international, and comparative law at St Gallen University. His publications include *Verfassungsgerichtsbarkeit, Demokratie und Misstrauen* (Duncker und Humblot, 1998).

**Catherine Hoskyns** is Emeritus Professor of European Studies at Coventry University and a visiting fellow at the Centre for the Study of Globalization and Regionalization at the University of Warwick. She is the author of *Integrating Gender—Women, Law and Politics in the European Union* (Verso, 1996) and the editor (with Michael Newman) of *Democratizing the European Union—Issues for the Twenty-first Century* (Manchester University Press, 2000).

**Markus Jachtenfuchs** is Professor of Political Science at the International University Bremen. He is the author of *Die Konstruktion Europas: Verfassungsideen und institutionelle Entwicklung* (Nomos, 2002) and co-editor, with Beate Kohler-Koch, of *Europäische Integration* (Leske und Budrich, second edn., 2003).

**Beate Kohler-Koch** holds the chair of Political Science and International Relations at the University of Mannheim, Germany, and is the coordinator of a national research programme on European Governance, funded by the German Science Council. Her recent book publications include *Linking EU and National Governance* (Oxford University Press, 2003) and *The Transformation of Governance in the European Union* (co-edited with Rainer Eising; Routledge, 1999).

**John Peterson** is Jean Monnet Professor of Politics at the University of Glasgow. Recent publications include *Integration in an Expanding European Union* (co-edited with Joseph Weiler and Iain Begg; Blackwell, 2003), and *The Institutions of the European Union* (co-edited with Michael Shackleton; Oxford University Press, 2001).

**Mark Pollack** is Associate Professor of Political Science at the University of Wisconsin-Madison. He is the author of *The Engines of European Integration: Delegation, Agency, and Agenda Setting in the European Union* (Oxford University Press, 2003), and co-editor (with John Peterson) of *Europe, America, Bush: Transatlantic Relations in the Twenty-first Century* (Routledge, 2003).

**Thomas Risse** holds the Chair in International Politics at the Free University of Berlin's Otto Suhr Institute of Political Science. He is co-editor of the *Handbook of International Relations* (Sage, 2002) and of *Transforming Europe. Europeanization and Domestic Change* (Cornell University Press, 2001).

**Frank Schimmelfennig** is a Fellow of the Mannheim Centre for European Social Research (Germany). His publications include *The EU, NATO, and the Integration of Europe* (Cambridge University Press, 2003) and *European Union Enlargement—Theoretical and Comparative Approaches* (special issue of *Journal of European Public Policy* vol. 9 (2002) no. 4, co-edited with Ulrich Sedelmeier).

**Philippe C. Schmitter** is a Professor of Political Science at the European University Institute (EUI). Among his publications on the EU are *Governance in the European Union* (with Gary Marks, Fritz Scharpf, and Wolfgang Streeck; Sage, 1996) and *How to Democratize the European Union . . . and Why Bother?* (Rowman and Littlefield, 2000).

**Ole Wæver** is Professor of International Relations at the University of Copenhagen. He is co-author of *Security: A New Framework for Analysis* (Lynne Rienner, 1998; with Barry Buzan and Jaap de Wilde) and *Regions and Powers: The Structure of International Security* (Cambridge University Press, 2003).

**Antje Wiener** holds a Chair in International Relations and a Jean Monnet Chair at the School of Politics and International Studies, at Queen's University Belfast. Her recent publications include *The Social Construction of Europe* (co-edited with Thomas Christiansen and Knud Erik Jørgensen; Sage, 2001) and *'European' Citizenship Practice —Building Institutions of a None-State* (Westview, 1998).

# 1

# Introducing the Mosaic of Integration Theory

*Thomas Diez and Antje Wiener*

## The relevance of integration theory

### The dual purpose of this book

There is surely no shortage of books on European integration. This is a booming field, and readers will know better than anyone else the difficulties in choosing the appropriate literature. But it is all the more surprising then that very few of these books are dedicated to the theory of European integration. Most of them deal with the history of the integration process and its main actors, with the European Union's formal institutions and particular policies, or with present and future member states' policies. This is not to say that there is no work done on integration theory. Indeed, this is in many respects a vibrant field that has overcome the impasses of the past. Yet, except for a few notable exceptions that we will return to in the course of this introduction, concise overviews of the field of integration theory remain rare.

This is therefore what we set out to do in this book: first, to provide an introduction to integration theory, its various approaches and how they have developed to those who have started to study European integration, and are interested (as, we argue below, anyone studying European integration should be) in the theories of their field; second, to provide an overview of the field and take stock of its achievements to date, but also its problems, for those who are involved in the development of European integration theory, and who want to make sense of the sometimes confusing array of approaches that have been proliferating since the 1960s.[1]

To this end, we have invited ten eminent scholars who have contributed significantly to the development of a particular theoretical approach, to take part in this 'stock-taking'.[2] We have asked them to reflect upon the development, achievements, and problems of 'their' approach according to a set pattern, which we will introduce below and which will allow for comparing and relating individual approaches to each other. In this introduction, we want first to make the case for the relevance of theory when studying European integration, which will be our concern in the remainder of this first section. The second section then proceeds to give a broad overview of the phases of theorizing European integration, thereby surveying the theoretical approaches that we have included in this volume and providing our rationale for this particular selection. The third section introduces the comparative framework that provided the guide for the chapters. This will include a discussion of the nature of the relationships between theories, a theme that we return to in the conclusion of this book. Finally, building on this discussion, the last section introduces the pattern of each chapter and provides an overview of the book.

We should add that the process of stocktaking would make no sense if it did not lead to the further development of theory. To that extent, we would not want to see this book read purely to understand and replicate existing theories, but rather as the starting point for criticizing and reformulating existing approaches, bringing them together in novel ways, and to move beyond them. And we would like to see both colleagues and students involved in this project—it is probably fair to say that without the critical engagement of their students, none of the authors of this book could have made the contribution they did to European integration theory.

## What is integration theory?

In order to talk meaningfully about integration theory, its two constitutive terms 'integration' and 'theory' need to be defined. This is less straightforward than it may at first seem, since both terms are heavily contested.

Let us turn to *integration* first. Ernst Haas, one of the most influential neofunctionalist integration theorists (see also Schmitter in chapter 3), once defined integration as the process 'whereby political actors in several, distinct national settings are persuaded to shift their loyalties, expectations and political activities toward a new centre, whose institutions process or demand jurisdiction over the pre-existing national states' (Haas 1958: 16). This is a broad definition, which includes both a social process (the shifting of loyalties) and a political process (negotiation and decision-making about the construction of new political institutions above the participating member states with a direct say in at least a part of the member states' affairs). Not all theorists would include both aspects in their definition, and there are reasons why Haas, from his perspective, emphasized the social element of integration: as will become clear in chapter 3, functionally defined actors are core promoters of integration in neofunctionalism. A less demanding definition preferred by intergovernmentalists, coming from a different angle within the spectrum of integration theory, focuses instead on political processes, although this may then be qualified as 'political integration'. While we agree with the societal focus in the neofunctionalist account, we will for the purposes of this book nonetheless adopt the latter, minimalist definition, as we would otherwise exclude some of the more prominent approaches.

While this may seem broad enough as a common denominator for most of traditional integration theory, it is nonetheless too restrictive to account for some of the later developments in what may broadly be seen as the field of integration theory. In both of the definitions above, integration is first and foremost a *process*: both neofunctionalists and intergovernmentalists are more concerned with the process of integration than with the political system to which that integration leads. However, more recently various authors have focused specifically on the shape of what they call a new system of governance emerging in the EU. While they are more concerned with the *outcome* than the process of integration (see Marks et al. 1996a, 1996b), their work is included in our understanding of integration theory, because it now undeniably forms an important part of that field.

Secondly, what is *theory*? Again, understandings differ, and as above, we endorse a broad rather than a narrow definition. Narrowly defined, theory is understood as a causal argument of universal, transhistorical validity and nomothetic quality, which can be tested through the falsification of a series of hypotheses (King, Keohane, and Verba 1994; Przeworski and Teune 1982). Some of the chapters discussed in this book will stick to this narrow definition, many however will not. Instead, they use theory in a rather loose sense of abstract reflection, which despite its abstract nature can nonetheless be context-specific, for instance by taking its point of departure in the consideration of a particular policy field of the EU. To make this point clearer, it helps to consider that theories serve different purposes. Some explain outcomes, behaviour, or decision-making rationales, others criticize general trends on the basis of abstract considerations; some fit particular developments into a larger scheme, others seek to provide normative guidance (see, e.g. Woods 1996). In each case, theory means something else. As we will argue later, different theoretical approaches to European integration are informed by different understandings of the meaning and purpose of theorizing.

To distinguish these different understandings from the narrow definition of theory outlined above, we will speak of 'integration theory' when we mean the *field* of theorizing the process and outcome of (European) integration, while we use the term 'theoretical approaches' when we refer to the *individual* ways of dealing with integration (see also Figure 3.1 in chapter 3), some, but not all of which may be classified as theories in the narrow sense of the term. What they all share, however, is that they are not primarily concerned with the development of particular policies, but with the abstract reflection on European integration.

European integration theory is thus the field of systematic reflection on the process of intensifying political cooperation in Europe and the development of common political institutions, as well as on its outcome. It also includes the theorization of changing constructions of identities and interests of social actors in the context of this process.

## Why study integration theory?

For many, the main purpose of studying integration is to gain a better understanding of the EU's formal institutions. To do so, students require first and foremost knowledge about how these institutions are set up and how they work so as to identify organizational competences, the role and function of a particular institution according to the

Treaties, or access points for lobbying activities. From this perspective, the value-added of theory is not immediately obvious—instead, empirical facts appear to provide sufficient information. Why then study integration theory? There are, at least, three reasons.

First, theories in the narrow sense of the term help us to explain processes and outcomes of integration, which not only leads to a better understanding of the current set of institutions, but may also help to formulate expectations about future developments and institutional behaviour.

Second, apart from the set up, role, and function of formal institutions, many readers will, for example, be concerned with questions of democratic reform and legitimacy. On the one hand, these *do* require detailed knowledge about the EU's institutions. Yet, on the other hand, they also require a deeper understanding of the normative issues at stake, such as: What should legitimacy be based on? Or: What form of democracy is appropriate for a polity beyond the nation state? Many approaches that do not fit the narrow scientific definition of theory address such issues and assist and encourage further reflections upon them.

Third, and arguably more importantly, 'pure' empirical knowledge of how institutions work is impossible and thus not very meaningful. It is *impossible* since the representation of empirical facts is always based on particular concerns, and assumptions about the nature of the EU and the finality of the integration process, which often remain unreflected. Integration theory helps to highlight and problematize these concerns and assumptions. 'Pure' empirical knowledge is *not very meaningful* in the sense that since any empirical representation is imbued with such assumptions, to concentrate on the 'facts' provides only a superficial understanding that disregards at least some of the political disputes 'underneath' the surface. To sum this point up, analysing integration is not only a 'technical' matter, but involves particular understandings and conceptualizations of integration and the EU, for which we need integration theory.

Two examples illustrate this point. The first one concerns the nature of foreign policy decision-making within the EU. To observers who base their assessment on the idiosyncratic organizational design, the EU's Common Foreign and Security Policy (CFSP) is by and large identified as a matter of the Council and therefore intergovernmentally organized. Not quite so, argue some more recent studies (see Jørgensen 1997; Glarbo 2001; Øhrgaard 1997). While it is true that formally, CFSP is primarily a matter between governments and does not fall within the scope of the Commission, this characterization misses some of the informal, 'societal' developments that have created a dense web of consultation with integrative effects, which are not captured by the intergovernmentalist picture. These take place on the 'social' level through the creation of a 'diplomatic community' within the EU (Glarbo 2001), or the projection of normative power in international politics on the basis of common values and norms (Manners 2002), and they have political consequences, such as the so-called 'co-ordination reflex', the wide-spread tendency to co-ordinate foreign policy with other member states rather than going it alone. The extent to which this is true is a matter of empirical analysis, but the important point is that these studies employ a particular theoretical approach that allows them to bring to the fore the social dimension of the integration process, even in areas formally characterized by intergovernmentalism (see also Risse on social constructivism in chapter 8).

The second example concerns the development of citizenship in the EU. Here, formal institutional approaches would find that Union citizenship was 'invented' at the intergovernmental conference that prepared the treaty revisions at Maastricht. As such, it is often seen as a 'thin' institution with little substantive importance. Yet, some authors have pointed out that elements of (market-) citizenship, i.e. fundamental rights of working citizens, had been included in the treaties before, and that the way European citizenship emerged at Maastricht was in fact conditioned by previous legal cases, rulings, and provisions (O'Leary 1996; Kostakopoulou 2001; Kadelbach 2002). Others have pointed out that previous 'citizenship practice', i.e. the policies and political processes that forge the institutionalized terms of citizenship within a particular context, had constructed elements of citizenship rights, access, and belonging that shaped the formulation of Union citizenship later on (Wiener 1998; see also Meehan 1993). The citizenship case demonstrates that the assessment of an institution's meaning depends on the type of theoretical approach chosen to study the problem. Whether one regards the institutionalization of EU citizenship with the Maastricht Treaty as an important development will, for instance, depend on the theoretical assumptions about context, institutional role, and function, i.e. whether citizenship is approached from a normative, liberal or, indeed, dogmatic legal perspective. Furthermore, the process of integration raises questions about theoretical assumptions and contested concepts, for example, the question of whether such citizenship undermines the familiar concept of modern (national) citizenship. All of these are questions that are ultimately of a theoretical nature in the sense of this book, and the theoretical vantage point one takes is crucial to how one answers them.

Reviewing the history of European integration demonstrates that there have been a number of occasions that are hotly debated in the integration literature, mostly due to analysts approaching them from different theoretical angles. The following is just a brief selection of controversies, some of which we will get back to in more detail later on:

- *The role of state interests in the founding years*: From a 'realist' perspective,[3] integration and especially the developments in the founding years are largely down to interests and power of big member states, during that phase particularly France and Germany, with France wanting to control Germany and Germany having an interest in getting back onto the international stage (see, e.g. Pedersen 1998). Against this, neofunctionalists have emphasized the role of private and sectorial interests (see chapter 3).

- *The lack of major institutional developments in the 1970s*: The 1970s are often labelled the 'doldrum years' of integration (and, as it were, integration theory), because political integration seemed to stagnate. But others have argued that 'below the surface' a lot of changes took place that would prepare for the 'reinvigoration' of integration and integration theory in the latter half of the 1980s (Caporaso and Keeler 1995). Furthermore, outside Political Science, legal scholars have advanced the argument of 'integration through law', focusing on increasing legal interdependencies and corresponding shifts in the meaning of sovereignty (see chapter 9).

- *The agreement on the Single European Act (1986)*: The agreement on institutional change introduced with the SEA raised a number of new questions for integration theory. Having been forged at an intergovernmental conference, it led to a re-launch of the theoretical debate discussing the role and formation of state preferences in the negotiations towards the SEA (Moravcsik 1991, 1993, see chapter 4), on the one hand, and emphasizing the role of the Commission, informal processes within the Committee of Permanent Representatives (COREPER), and the influence of private actors such as the European Round-Table of Industrialists, on the other (Wincott, 1995; Hayes-Renshaw, Lequesne, and Mayor Lopez 1992; Ross 1995; Bornschier 2000).

All of these controversies need to be investigated empirically, but they cannot be reduced to a simple testing of alternative hypothesis, nor can they be addressed purely by 'thick description' (Wallace 1996). Instead, seemingly competing theories often shed a different light on the issue that is enabled by a particular theoretical perspective.

# Integration theory: a broad overview

## Phases of European integration theory

Having established the relevance of integration theory, we will in the following provide a first overview of its development. This places the theoretical approaches in their historical disciplinary context.

We suggest that the development of integration theory can be divided into three broad phases (see also Wiener 2003). These are preceded by a normative proto-integration theory period. We identify the three phases as explanatory, analytical, and constructive, respectively. A note of caution is in order, however. Since most approaches combine various dimensions of theory, the distinction among the respective phases is not as clear-cut as analytically suggested. The phases are therefore meant to identify the emergence, development, and, at times, dominance of particular theoretical tendencies, but it is by no means meant to suggest that these were the only (and sometimes not even the dominant) ones. In Table 1.1, we have left the endpoints of these phases open, since work in one tradition tends to continue after the emergence of new tendencies in theorizing. However, when we mention end dates in the following text, these are to signify a shift within European integration theory towards new approaches.

Similarly, although perhaps to a lesser extent, the dates provided for the beginnings of our three phases are also problematic. In 1970, Haas (1970: 635), for instance, had already conceptualized the then European Community as an 'anarchoid image of a myriad of unity' with significant 'asymmetrical overlapping' and 'infinitely tiered

**Table 1.1** Three phases in integration theory

| Phase | When? | Main themes |
|---|---|---|
| Explaining integration | 1960s onwards | How can integration outcomes be explained? |
| | | Why does European integration take place? |
| Analysing governance | 1980s onwards | What kind of political system is the EU? |
| | | How can the political processes within the EU be described? |
| | | How does the EU's regulatory policy work? |
| Constructing the EU | 1990s onwards | How and with which social and political consequences does integration develop? |
| | | How are integration and governance conceptualized? How should they be? |

multiple loyalties', and Lindberg and Scheingold (1970) analysed the EC as a 'would-be polity'. Both of these works address issues characteristic of the phase of 'Analysing Governance' in European integration theory, which we will further develop below, yet they had been published at least a decade before. We would nonetheless argue that our three phases identify the major tendencies in the development of European integration theory. They are also significant as the general self-image of the discipline, although not everyone would agree with our identification of a third phase in particular.

The normative proto-integration period predates the actual development of political integration in Europe. It is an important pre-cursor of the three phases of integration theory building. Functionalism is typical of this normative period. Popular in the inter-war years, with David Mitrany's *A Working Peace System* (Mitrany 1943) as the core publication, it had a strong normative agenda, namely how, through a network of transnational organizations on a functional basis, one could constrain states and prevent future war. This was a global concern and had no direct relation to European integration—as a matter of fact, Mitrany was an opponent of regional integration that he saw as undermining his global concerns and replicating rather than transcending a state-model (Mitrany 1966; see Rosamond 2000: 36–38). Early federalism, too, can be located in this period. As a political movement it was more directly related to particular developments in Europe, for example in the form of calls for a European federation made during the inter-war years by actors as different as the German Social Democrats (see Schneider 1977; Hrbek 1972) and the conservative Hungarian Count Coudenhove-Kalergi (1971).

With the *first phase* roughly lasting from the signing of the Treaty of Rome until the early 1980s, we enter European integration theory proper. Despite the realist attempts to integrate them into their worldview, the early successes of integration challenged the existence of the territorial state system, which is at the core of realist assumptions. Accordingly, integration theories initially sought to explain the processes of institution-building above the state. Two theoretical approaches came to dominate the debate. Both were based on rational actor assumptions, while locating the push and pull for the integration process on different levels and in different societal realms. Thus, neofunctionalists, in line with their broad definition of integration, explained the move away from the anarchic state system and towards supranational institution-building by depicting particular societal and market patterns as pushing for élite behaviour towards common market building.

Because of the functional interconnectedness of policy areas, these shared policy initiatives in so-called 'low politics' areas were seen as having potential for 'spilling over' into other policy areas, at first to those closely related to market policy, but ultimately beyond (*functional spill-over*). In addition to this, to the extent that actors shifted their loyalties and redefined their identities, they were expected to actively demand further integration (*political spill-over*). Neofunctionalists built on functionalism and kept part of its normative agenda (especially 'political' neofunctionalists, such as Jean Monnet), yet they also introduced both a stronger emphasis on actors with an interest in, and therefore promoting further integration—primarily the Commission—and an explicit social scientific interest in creating a general theory of regional integration that was applicable beyond the singular case of Europe (see in particular Ernst Haas's as well as Philippe Schmitter's work; Haas 1961, 1967, 1970; Haas and Schmitter 1964; and Schmitter in chapter 3 of this book). In a different but not dissimilar way, Karl W. Deutsch (1957) saw integration coming about through the increased communication and interaction across borders, which gave his theoretical approach the name 'transactionalism'.

These arguments were opposed by intergovernmentalists who explained supranational institution-building as the result of rational decision-making within a historical context that was conducive to strong and clearly defined interests of the nation state governments involved (Hoffmann 1966). The debate between supporters of integration as 'the rescue of the nation state' (Milward 1992), on the one hand, and as the overcoming of the nation state, on the other, which began in this first phase of integration theory, has remained a consistent factor in social science analysis to this day. While especially more recent additions to this strand of theorizing, in particular liberal intergovernmentalism, have not denied the societal impact on supranational institution-building, as the theorization of societal preference formation in Moravcsik's work demonstrates (see Schimmelfennig in chapter 4), their focus has been on governmental actors whose capacity for decisions were enhanced by supranational institutions, but not constrained by them. Institutions, according to this view, are designed for particular purposes and under control of the actors who created them. They therefore remain potentially reversible or changeable at any point in time.

For a new generation of integration theorists, however, institutions were not mere tools in the hands of their creators, but had themselves an important impact on both the integration process and the development of European governance. As neoinstitutionalists have demonstrated, institutions can cause 'unintended consequences' (North 1990), making the process of institution-building less easily reversible than the intergovernmentalists would have it (Pierson 1996). A particularly dramatic example of unintended consequences was the largely underestimated push to further integration by the Single European Act (Weiler 1999). In terms of European integration theory, as indicated above, this led to the revival and revision of classic integration theories in the form of liberal intergovernmentalism (Moravcsik 1991) and (neo-)neofunctionalism (Stone Sweet 2002; Sandholtz and Zysman 1989; Tranholm-Mikkelsen 1991). It also marks the starting point for a shift of focus in theoretical approaches to European integration away from International Relations Theory towards Comparative Politics, not least out of a recognition that the EU's complex institutional set-up seemed to be here to stay. This *second phase* considerably broadened the scope of empirical research and theoretical reflection on European integration, and introduced a greater degree of interdisciplinarity. It brought comparative and institutionalist approaches to the foreground of integration theory, following questions of what kind of polity the EU really is and how it operates—as Thomas Risse-Kappen (1996) famously put it, to 'explore the nature of the beast'. Among the concepts developed during this phase to answer these questions are the EU as a system of 'multi-level' (Marks et al. 1996a) or 'network governance' (Jachtenfuchs and Kohler-Koch 1996), or as a 'multi-perspectival polity' (Ruggie 1993). Others focused on the way in which policies are made through the analysis of policy networks (Peterson 1995; Peterson and Bomberg 1999). A key process analysed was the 'Europeanisation' of governance rules, institutions, and practices across the EU (Cowles et al. 2001). Questions of institutional adaptation and 'misfit' and of 'good governance' including legitimacy, democracy, and transparency are other issues addressed by works in this second phase of integration theories.

To some extent, the *third phase* of integration theory is marked by the return of International Relations Theory, although of a different kind. During the 1980s and 1990s, International Relations Theory was characterized by the rise of a variety of critical and constructivist approaches, which drew their inspiration from developments in other fields of social theory. Scholars questioned both the ontological and epistemological assumptions on which traditional approaches had been built. Social constructivists, for instance, demonstrated the relevance of ideas, norms, institutions, and identities for international politics and pointed to the interdependence of the structure of the state system, on the one hand, and the agency of those involved in international politics, on the other. Post-structuralists problematized core concepts of International Relations Theory and drew attention to the discursive construction of our understanding of international politics. Critical Theorists and feminists not only developed important critiques of the contemporary international system, but also often offered alternatives paths towards what they saw as a more just world.

These developments coincided with the move towards political union in the 1991 Maastricht and the 1996 Amsterdam Treaties. Under the pressure of massive enlargement and constitutional revision, integration theory faced the challenge of analysing and problematizing the interrelated processes of widening and deepening. Different from the first two phases, which sought to explain or analyse either institution-building on the supranational level, or institutional change on the meso- and sub-state levels, this third phase of integration theory thus faced the more encompassing task of theorizing the goal or finality of European integration, the competing ideas and discourses about European governance, and the normative implications of particular EU policies. Accordingly, apart from problem-oriented theorizing, works during this phase have been concerned with questions about our understanding of integration, how particular policy areas have been defined and developed in the way they did, and what political effects these definitions and historical processes have had.

This third phase therefore focuses on substantial questions about 'constructing' (and limiting) European integration. It is in answering these questions that the critical and constructivist approaches in International Relations Theory were taken up,[4] alongside or combined with insights from the 'constitutional turn' later in the second phase, which, sparked by the Maastricht and Amsterdam Treaties and the increased public debate about the legitimacy of European governance, brought normative questions about the EU's constitution to the heart of the analysis of governance. Social constructivism, especially, has in some respects drawn on, and in turn contributed to insights of governance approaches. In particular, it has addressed issues of the development of the EU's formal and informal institutions, as well as processes of Europeanization, although as far as the latter are concerned, its focus has been on the Europeanization of identities rather than institutions and policies (see Risse in chapter 8).

## Approaches covered in this book

The theoretical approaches discussed in this book cover the three phases of integration theory, including their normative pre-cursor. We have therefore divided the book into three corresponding parts, 'Explaining European Integration', 'Analysing European Governance', and 'Constructing the European Union'.

Part I Explaining European Integration, contains firstly a chapter on federalism. While federalism is first and foremost a normative theory, it has been used more recently in a comparative fashion to explain, analyse, or devise particular features of the Euro-polity (Koslowski 2001). Furthermore, scholars such as Moravcsik (1998) have derived hypotheses about the particular institutional choices made in intergovernmental conferences for European governance from federalism. Together with neofunctionalism and intergovernmentalism, federalism can be seen as a triad of theories that are often, although problematically so, as we will argue below, presented as competing with each other. Accordingly, chapter 3 is devoted to neofunctionalism and chapter 4 to intergovernmentalism, both of which we regard as explanatory approaches.

In Part II Analysing European Governance, we turn our focus to those approaches that try to understand and analyse the EU as a type of political system. Chapter 5 reflects on the development of governance theory, and suggests that this could provide an encompassing framework to address normative, analytical, and explanatory questions. Focusing more on the analysis of policy-making processes and drawing on a different set of Political Science literature, chapter 6 discusses the policy network approach to the analysis of European governance, at the core of which is the explanation of particular policy-decisions with the configuration of the respective policy-field. Finally, chapter 7 looks at the contribution that various 'new institutionalisms' have made to the study of European governance, analysing in particular the impact of institutions on policy-making and the overall development of governance, as well as the shaping of those institutions by political actors. The focus in this chapter is on rationalist and historical institutionalism, whereas sociological institutionalism is discussed as part of social constructivism in chapter 8.

Finally, Part III Constructing the European Union deals with those more recent approaches that stress the constructed dimension of European integration and governance and add a critical dimension to studying the European Union. This part includes firstly, a discussion of social constructivist approaches in chapter 8. Similar to the development of social constructivism in other social sciences, these approaches come in various forms and with different purposes, but maintain an ambition to understand or explain integration outcomes. Chapter 9 charts the development of legal approaches in the opposite direction by critically recalling the 'integration through law' approach (Cappelletti et al. 1986) that sought to explain integrative progression in the EEC based on the ECJ's rulings and then opening the scope of integration theory towards legal studies, which, while often overlooked in the theoretical debates of European Studies, have long had a key role in assessing the progress, scope, and constructive force of the integration process, and, in line with our three phases, have since the 1980s moved from explanatory to more critical and normative analyses (Shaw and More 1995; Bellamy and Castiglione 1996; Weiler, Haltern, and Mayer 1996). Gender perspectives, which are covered in chapter 10, follow a critical and problematizing line throughout, building in part on the advances of feminist approaches in other disciplines. Finally, chapter 11 reviews discursive approaches to the analysis of European integration, some of which have used post-structuralist concepts taken mostly from International Relations Theory to problematize particular conceptions of European integration and governance, while others have tried to use those concepts to develop an explanatory framework for the analysis of the European policies of member states.

The list of approaches covered in this book is obviously not exhaustive of all the approaches available to the student of European integration. We have included what we believe are the currently most salient and influential approaches in European integration theory, and by including some of the more recent developments, we will have already expanded the scope of what is conventionally taught as the core of the discipline. Nonetheless some of the omissions may prove more controversial than others. Three require particular justification.

Firstly, we have not included a chapter on transactionalism. While we agree with those who would like to see this approach given much more attention than it currently receives, because it would refocus our attention to the social, rather than the political integration process, we cannot ignore that, a few exceptions aside, hardly anyone has followed the lead of Karl Deutsch in this respect. In addition to this, Deutsch's focus was on NATO and the transatlantic 'security community', rather than on European integration *per se* (but see Deutsch et al. 1967). It is telling that one of the few recent pieces that comes close to transactionalism subsumes Deutsch's work under neofunctionalism, and focuses on transnational exchange as one of the independent variables influencing the form of supranational organization, rather than on different forms of community as a result of communication across borders (Stone-Sweet and Sandholtz 1997).

Secondly, we have not included a chapter on Critical Theory, which would have included approaches that build on the work of Jürgen Habermas on legitimacy, discourse, and democracy beyond the nation state, and on the work of critical international political economists such as Robert Cox or Steven Gill, who try to conceptualize the struggles of transnational social forces in a globalizing world. Both of these strands of Critical Theory have been used to analyse European integration. Studies that draw on Habermas are gaining influence particularly in interdisciplinary assessments of democratic or good governance (Eriksen and Fossum 2000; Joerges and Neyer 1997; Joerges 2002; Maduro 2002). Members of what may be called the 'Amsterdam School' have offered critical analyses of EU economic policies and the impact of economic interests on the integration process, building on the work done by Cox and others in International Relations Theory (Cafruny and Ryner 2003; Ryner et al. 1998; van Apeldoorn 2002). Particularly the latter's impact on integration theory has so far been relatively limited compared to gender perspectives and discursive approaches, although this may well change in the future.

The relative neglect of Critical Theory, particularly its political economy variety, brings us to a third omission in this book, that of economic theories of integration. In this respect, we do not believe that there can be a purely economic theory of European integration as defined above, which is above all a political and social process. To the extent that economic theories exist in this field, they are looking at particular aspects and especially the effects of economic integration, and are thus not theories of European integration as such (see Balassa 1962; El-Agraa 1982). Economic theories have, however, found their way into some of the approaches covered, such as liberal intergovernmentalism, where predictions about the outcome of domestic bargains over national interests are made on the basis of economic theorems, and they are therefore discussed within these contexts. But we do not think that an economic theory as such is currently playing a major part in the integration theory debates, nor are we convinced that it should be.

Last but not least, the approaches included in this book have in their majority been formulated by scholars working in English, and within the Anglo-Saxon scholarly community. This is a problem to the extent that we are thereby imposing a narrative of the development of European integration theory on scientific communities that may have had a very different experience, and we may have overlooked important and exciting theoretical developments in that process—European integration theory outside the Anglo-Saxon boundaries may indeed be 'the best kept secret' (see Jørgensen 2000 for International Relations Theory). Having said that, not all of our approaches have their stronghold in English-speaking universities, as the discussion of national differences below will illustrate. At the same time, the success of approaches beyond national boundaries requires its formulation in what is increasingly becoming the *lingua franca* of academia. This is not to say that there are no interesting developments outside what is accessible in English. It is also true that there are particular academic styles that differ between national academic communities, and that translating from another language into English does not always properly convey the meaning of the original. But as an overview and a stock-taking exercise, we had to base our selection on what we regarded as success across borders, and English-speaking publications remain in many ways the yardstick for such an exercise, even if this is problematic.

# Studying integration theory

## Contexts of theoretical development

The story of integration theory can be told from a chronological angle or with a focus on theoretical debates and the specific issues covered. Our account above combined a chronological perspective with a perspective on debates because there are distinct themes and controversies to particular *phases* of European integration theory. Telling the story of integration theory in these terms is not uncommon (cf. the overviews by Caporaso and Keeler 1995; Bache and George 2001; Rosamond 2000). More contested is the question of how the theoretical approaches relate to each other. There are two aspects to this issue. The first relates to the emergence of theories and the movement from one dominant approach to another, and can therefore be seen as a contribution to the history and sociology of European integration studies. The second is concerned with the 'fit' of theories, (e.g. are they compatible or competing?), and is therefore a contribution to theory-building in itself.

Starting with the historical-sociological approach, there are two factors that are often seen as influencing the development of theories, the academic and the socio-political context (cf. Rosamond 2000: 9). The academic context consists of debates and problems that are pursued in the wider scientific context of a particular field as well as the legacies of previous debates in the field itself. Of particular importance in this context are particular 'paradigms' that provide researchers with guideposts about how to conduct and present their studies (see Kuhn 1964). The socio-political context, in contrast, consists of factors outside of academia, such as the development of the object under analysis, the influence of sponsors on research agendas, or the discursive restrictions set by a particular political climate. In addition, both of these contexts can be coloured by national differences.

Our account of the three phases of European integration theory above provides plenty of examples for how the study of European integration has followed the ups and downs of its subject. The rise, fall, and comeback of neofunctionalism in the 1950s, following the Empty Chair crisis and the Single European Act respectively, is the most obvious one. The relation between the socio-political context and the development of theory is, however, not a one-way street. Thus, not only was neofunctionalism developed on the basis of what happened in Western Europe in the 1950s, neofunctionalism itself also became the quasi-official ideology in the Commission and other parts of the EC institutions. Ironically, as George and Bache (2001: 15) point out, it is today often used by so-called Eurosceptics to increase fears of a technocratic, centralized, and undemocratic super-state, whereas governments supportive of further integration tend to resort to the intergovernmentalist rhetoric of sovereignty being only 'pooled' in order to alleviate these fears.

While the influence of the EU's development on integration theory may be obvious, the academic context has been no less forceful in shaping the way in which integration has been conceptualized and analysed. As Rosamond (1995: 394) argues, theoretical approaches to the analysis of European integration 'have arisen in the context of dominant perspectives in the broad arena of social scientific inquiry' and are 'bound up with intellectual fashion and debates between and within different theoretical paradigms'. Thus, if we had included a list of major works in other social sciences and neighbouring fields in this introduction, we would have seen that theoretical movements in European integration studies are often preceded by or run in parallel with developments in disciplines such as International Relations, Political Science, or Legal Studies. Neofunctionalism provides yet again a good example with its social-scientific turn against earlier versions of functionalism (see Caporaso and Keeler 1995: 32–4; Kelstrup 1998: 24).

European integration also became an instrument for the pursuit of academic controversies in that it served as ammunition for the critique of the dominant, state-centred realist paradigm (George and Bache 2001: 19). Thereby, the neofunctionalism versus intergovernmentalism debate became embedded in a discourse in which the model of the state remained at the core, either on the national or on the European level (see Rosamond 1995), which in turn hindered the development of a debate about legitimacy 'beyond the state' (Kelstrup and Williams 2000: 8). That such a debate eventually became possible is not only due to the acceptance of the EU as a polity discussed above (see Hix 1994: 10), but also to the development of normative, critical, and constructivist approaches in other social sciences that could be imported into the third phase of European integration theory (Kelstrup and Williams 2000: 1, 9). Similarly, the comparativist project of the second phase benefited greatly from the previous development of neoinstitutionalist research in sociology, which provided comparativists with new concepts to analyse political institutions as an important influence on politics in their own right.

Interestingly, it is the academic context where national differences seem to matter most, rather than the socio-political context, and the problem of language discussed earlier plays a crucial part in this. It is perhaps ironic that most of the classic integration theories have been developed in the United States, rather than within Europe. This, however, can be explained by the dominance of theory-driven American Social Science in International Relations (see Wæver 1998a), from which the approaches in the crucial first phase of integration theory developed. 'European' approaches have traditionally tended to be much more historically or normatively oriented, or have been engaged in detailed empirical studies of particular policies (Smith and Ray 1993). Only with the advent of the second and the third phase of integration theory are there more clearly audible European voices—most of them advocating a form of social inquiry that is different from the American social science model. Among these voices, there is also a certain degree of differentiation along national or regional lines, although whether this is more than coincidental would require further analysis. To give but two examples, discursive studies of the EU have by and large emerged from a Scandinavian context (e.g. Hansen and Wæver 2002; Larsen 1997; Neumann 1999; Wæver 1998b), whereas two major studies on ideas and European governance have originated in Germany (Jachtenfuchs et al. 1998; Marcussen et al. 2001). Further research would have to be done to substantiate these initial findings, but they are striking enough to suggest that particular approaches often have a regional 'centre'.

## Competing or complementary approaches?

The importance of socio-political and academic contexts for the development of integration theory raises fundamental questions about the relationship of individual approaches to each other. Does the discussion in the last section imply that instead of moving to one unified theory, these approaches offer different perspectives that are largely determined by the contexts in which they are developed? Are these perspectives mutually exclusive, and can the arguments they put forward be tested against each other? How, in short, is one to compare the different theoretical approaches?

   At the extremes of this debate are, on the one hand, the notion of scientific progress, where through falsification our knowledge of (in this case) integration advances, and, on the other hand, the notion of incommensurable paradigms, which, in effect, construct and talk about different realities, and between which dialogue is hardly possible. If we take the different understandings of theory advanced above, the more scientifically minded will generally tend towards the former, those with a broader understanding of theory towards the latter pole. Consequently, Moravcsik (1998) for instance, in his major contribution to the development of European integration theory, tests different theories against each other in order to establish a (liberal-inter governmentalist) ground on which future theory can build. His exchange with Diez as well as with Risse and Wiener on the value of this contribution, however, can serve as an example for talking past each other because of very different agendas, concepts, and definitions that emerge from very different contexts (see Diez 1999; Moravcsik 1999, 2001; Risse and Wiener 2001).

   While we agree that scientific progress is ultimately influenced by its academic and socio-political context, we nonetheless find the argument of incommensurability problematic. Most integration theories have been developed within the context of Western academia, and although their pedigree differs, and consequently their ontological and epistemological foundations, they share quite a lot of common ground, as will become more obvious when reading through the chapters of this book. To the extent that they are incompatible, this is a consequence not of their inherent incommensurability, but of the claims they make about their scope. In other words, many theorists make broader claims such as 'explaining integration', when what they really do is a much more limited enterprise, for instance explaining results of intergovernmental conferences, criticizing a particular conceptualization of integration, or seeking to understand the historical development of a particular aspect of integration. This problem, as well as the criticism of it, is not new. Puchala already remarked in 1972 that 'different schools of researchers have exalted different parts of the integration "elephant". They have claimed either that their parts were in fact whole beasts, or that their parts were the most important ones, the others being of marginal interest' (Puchala 1972: 268).

Inappropriate scope claims take an ontological and an epistemological form. Ontologically, approaches often explicitly or implicitly claim to provide a theoretical approach to (European) integration as such, while they in fact focus on a particular process or outcome. If this claim is relaxed, it should be possible to combine different approaches depending on the subject of analysis. Epistemologically, approaches would only be incommensurable if they claimed to have the same purpose and if they were directly related to reality. If, however, we assume that approaches can have different purposes, and if, perhaps more controversially, we further assume that our under-standing of reality is always mediated by particular discursive contexts, which seems particularly opportune in the face of the 'multi-perspectival' character of the European Union (Ruggie 1993), then it is possible to see different approaches adding to a larger picture without being combined into a single, grand theory.

Even if two approaches agree on the aim of explaining integration, for instance, they might still be difficult to compare if what they mean by integration (ontological scope claim) are two different things. Moravcsik, for instance, focuses on political integration and the role of intergovernmental bargains, whereas neofunctionalists such as e.g. Stone Sweet and Sandholtz (1997) see integration as a much more social process happening in part through what they call 'transnational exchange' between member states soci-eties (see also Branch and Øhrgaard 1999; on liberal intergovernmentalism see also Rosamond 1995: 398). All of these are respectable accomplishments in their own right, and hardly testable against each other (see also Hix 1994: 3). Yet, at the same time, this does not necessarily make them incommensurable once there is a certain modesty in-troduced regarding the scope of the argument made.

The approaches in this book therefore can be seen as providing different perspectives on the subject of integration, each contributing to our overall understanding of the subject. They cannot easily be lumped together to form a grand theory of integration because one needs to adopt one's own viewpoint in order to 'make them work' (see also Figure 3.1 in chapter 3), and we therefore differ in this respect from the project of developing an overarching framework as it was eventually pursued even by Puchala (1972) and is suggested by Jachtenfuchs and Kohler-Koch in chapter 5. However, they are not always direct competitors either, although some of them will indeed formulate hypotheses that can be tested against each other. Instead, one might see them as stones in an always-incomplete mosaic. The picture of integration that emerges from them is a multi-faceted one—a point we will have to revisit in the conclusion to this volume, together with some of the questions this raises about the advancement and value of theory.

For now, it is important to develop an understanding of the main dimensions along which these approaches differ. We consider two such dimensions as particularly important. One is about the functions of theory briefly referred to above; the other is about the areas (developed below) that the approaches analyse.

## The functions of theory

There are three main functions of theory (broadly understood), and these run parallel with the three main phases of integration theory identified above.

1. *Theory as explanation or understanding.* Although explaining and understanding approaches differ widely in the epistemological claims they make, and consequently in the methodologies they apply (see Hollis and Smith 1990), they share a common purpose in the sense that they ask why (explaining) or how (understanding) an event has come about. To that extent, they ask for reasons and/or causes for something to happen (on reasons and causes, see the discussion in Wendt 1999 and Smith 2000). The approaches in the first phase of integration theory have asked these sorts of questions, and most of them have leaned towards the 'explanation' variant. More recent approaches such as Social Constructivism have sometimes asked similar questions, and while most Social Constructivists would see themselves in the 'understanding business', at least some of them have leaned towards 'explaining'.

2. *Theory as description and analysis.* This might at first seem like a waste-bin category, but it is not. Approaches in this category focus on the development of definitions and concepts with which to grasp particular developments, practices, and institutions. In that sense, explaining and understanding approaches have to presuppose descriptive and analytical approaches because the latter provide the former with the concepts on the basis of which events can be explained or understood. In the second phase of integration theory, we would expect a focus on description and analysis because one of the aims of these approaches was to provide a vocabulary with which to capture 'the nature of the beast'.

3. *Theory as critique and normative intervention.* While approaches in the first two categories take the development of integration more or less as a given, other approaches question the route that the integration process, or a particular policy, has taken, or develop norms and principles for the future of integration. Approaches in this category therefore either problematize a given development, or they develop alternatives. Theory in this understanding is often much closer to what one might call philosophy, or perhaps only 'abstract reflection', but in the form of normative theory, it has always had its rightful place in the canon of Political Theory, and many critical theories have recently been added to this. At least some of the approaches included in our third phase of integration theory fall into this category.

If theory has such different purposes, it would be unfair and not even valid to hold one approach accountable on the basis of criteria set by another one. Evaluating and weighing theoretical approaches against each other therefore always has to take account of the principal function or purpose that the approach assigns to itself, unless we want to impose one common purpose on all theoretical approaches.

## The areas of theory

It is, however, not only the purpose of theory that varies, but also the area, or the 'object' of particular approaches. Analysing member states' integration policy is different from, although related to, reflecting on the best institutional set-up for the EU, and consequently may require a different methodology. These areas of theory are a second, independent dimension on which theoretical approaches can differ from each other. Again, we propose three different areas, which we have delineated along the triad of polity, policy, and politics.

1. *Theory dealing with polity.* 'Polity' refers to the political community and its institutions. Approaches falling into this category would be those analysing the 'nature of the beast', those explaining how the EU's institutional structure came about, or those trying to find constitutional alternatives on the basis of normative considerations, to give examples taken from all three functions of theory.

2. *Theory dealing with policy.* 'Policy' includes the actual measures taken to tackle concrete problems, and theoretical approaches in this area analyse and compare their content, or critically reflect upon them. This includes aspects such as 'policy style, the general problem-solving approach, the policy instruments used, and the policy standards set' (Börzel and Risse 2000: 3). However, to qualify as theory according to our definition above, such analyses need to be brought onto an abstract level, for instance by drawing out general patterns of policy content, or reflecting on the normative underpinnings within a policy field.

3. *Theory dealing with politics.* 'Politics' comprises the process of policy-making and the daily struggles and strategies of political actors dealing with each other. It is about the bargaining between governments, the influence of particular interest groups, or the dominance of a specific style of how decisions are reached. Approaches concerned with politics look at such issues as why technocratic governance prevails over participatory governance, how interest groups try to influence the policy-making process, or how particular groups are systematically disadvantaged by the dominant political style.

As these definitions have illustrated, it would empirically be rather difficult to stick strictly to one of these areas. Any discussion of polity is likely to involve constitutional frames in which policy-making takes place, or which restrict the content of policy, as well as the implication of constitutional arrangements for politics. Nonetheless, approaches are likely to emphasize one or the other, and not deal with all three poles of the triad in equal measure. Moreover, to the extent that they want to explain, they will use polity, policy, and politics either as the *explanandum* (what is to be explained) or the *explanans* (the explaining factor). However, a theoretical approach such as neofunctionalism might aim at explaining integration outcomes (here polity), while focusing on their explanation (here politics). Therefore, one has to specify how the areas of theory figure within each approach. Furthermore, to say that an approach 'deals with polity', does not necessarily mean that the other two areas are excluded from all other considerations, but that they are of less importance within the works of this approach.

## The mosaic of integration theory

Combining these two dimensions, we arrive at what we call the 'mosaic of integration theory'. Keeping the caveats raised above in mind, theoretical approaches can be located in the nine cells of Table 1.2. Its 'mosaicness' comes from the fact that each approach can be seen as a stone that adds to the picture that we gain of the EU. This picture is likely to remain unfinished, as new approaches will add new stones to change the picture. To reiterate, our point is that rather than directly competing with each other, each approach contributes to the emerging picture in its own limited way. The contributions can be ambiguous—as is the EU itself in many ways. But they are not necessarily mutually exclusive and incommensurable, as is often assumed. Placing an approach in a particular part of the mosaic therefore clarifies with which approaches it actually competes in a rather narrow field.

Even if this is the case, however, any two approaches may still not be directly testable against each other. The example of liberal intergovernmentalism v. neo-neofunctionalism illustrates this. In this case, while both approaches want to explain the political process of reaching a decision, and to some extent the outcome of that process in terms of its effects on the polity, they analyse different aspects of the decision-making process because they start from a different definition of integration. The distinction of various analytical areas is therefore a rather general one that always needs to be supplemented by a closer look at the basic concepts and definitions that approaches use within their area. This is not only true for the area- but also for the function-dimension. Because we have lumped together 'explaining' and 'understanding', 'analytical' and 'descriptive', 'critical' and 'normative', approaches even within one cell are not necessarily directly comparable, as the epistemological claims they make differ widely, and thus the scope of their argument.

**Table 1.2** The functions and areas of (integration) theory

|  | POLITY | POLICY | POLITICS |
|---|---|---|---|
| EXPLANATORY/UNDERSTANDING |  |  |  |
| ANALYTICAL/DESCRIPTIVE |  |  |  |
| CRITICAL/NORMATIVE |  |  |  |

As we have pointed out above, approaches will usually find themselves in more than one category. The mosaic should not be seen as an exercise in compartmentalization. Instead, it is a heuristic device that allows us to move beyond fruitless debates in which approaches operating in different areas and pursuing different purposes talk past each other. Besides, even though approaches will cross the imaginary boundaries of the identified fields, they will tend to focus on one or the other—life is too short, and book space too restricted to deal with everything.

# Reviewing integration theory

## The structure of the chapters

Although the structure of individual chapters varies, they all address a set of questions that will help in the comparison between theoretical approaches and the assessment of their compatibility or incommensurability. Each author was asked to summarize the origins of the approach covered, its main arguments, and development over time. As the majority of the authors were substantially involved in the development of 'their' approach, these sections are to be seen not only as an introduction, but also as a reflection on the current state-of-the-art of each approach in relation to earlier work. Chapters also include an overview of the main debates surrounding approaches, including the criticism raised from the perspective of other approaches, the main current questions facing authors, and potential ways forwards.

However, in order to answer our main questions regarding the comparison of the approaches, we have asked authors to include a section in which they provide an example of a specific puzzle that they think 'their' approach is particularly apt to address, and which in the past has been a focus of many works written in this tradition. If our argument about European integration theory as a mosaic holds, we expect approaches to differ in their 'best case', or in the area that they focus upon. We have furthermore asked authors to include a section in which they summarize, or speculate, how works written from 'their' approach have, or would address the issue of enlargement as a 'test case'. Again, we expect the contributions to focus on different areas of, but also to ask different types of questions about enlargement, illustrating the different functions of theory.

On the basis of these two sections where authors provide examples of how 'their' approaches deal with concrete issues, we will return in the conclusion to the questions raised in this introduction, but we also invite readers to make their own comparisons when reading this book, and to use these sections as a starting point for critical reflections on the past or ongoing debates summarized in each chapter, and thereby pushing European integration theory forward.

## Past, present, and future

'Past, present, and future' is the—invisible—subtitle of this book. It provides an organizing theme in a double sense. Firstly, each chapter, by reflecting on the origins and development of each approach, on the main puzzles addressed and state-of-the-art, and on the current challenges and ways forward, addresses the past, present, and future of each approach. Secondly, the three parts of this volume reflecting the three phases of European integration theory can be seen as an expression of 'past, present, and future': 'past' in the sense of a set of approaches that have been with us since the early days of integration theory, have been developed to a considerable degree, and have influenced subsequent generations of integration scholars; 'present' in the sense that a lot of theoretical work today has shifted towards questions of governance that combine International Relations and Comparative Politics; and 'future' in the sense that a set of novel approaches raises a number of issues which, although unlikely to dominate theoretical development in the future, will have to be taken into account, as they are now taken into account in other Social Sciences.

We have already made clear that we do not wish to reinforce some of the fault(y) lines along which the field of European integration theory was divided in the past. Instead, we see in the present a healthy trend towards a proliferation of approaches that contribute to an ever more faceted and nuanced picture of the European Union, its history and its development. What we would like to see in the future is neither the development of one single grand theory, nor the isolation and non-communication between approaches. The following chapters should help to clarify from where each approach comes, and the scope of its argument, so that a critical but constructive and open debate can thrive.

## Notes

1. Previous versions of this chapter were presented at the 1st Pan-European Conference on European Union Politics in Bordeux, September 2002, the Biennial Convention of the European Union Studies Association in Nashville, March 2003 and at seminars at Koç, Sabançi, and Boğaziçi Universities Istanbul. We are grateful to Knud Erik Jørgensen, Daniel Wincott, the co-panellists and audiences, and our students in Belfast and Birmingham.

2. The exception is Andrew Moravcsik, whom we had invited to write the chapter on Liberal Intergovernmentalism. Although in the end he did not do so, he did comment extensively on earlier drafts of Frank Schimmelfennig's chapter on this approach.

3. When we use the term 'realism' in this chapter, we refer to realism as a particular tradition in International Relations Theory, rather than as an epistemological position.

4. There have of course been critical approaches to European integration all along. See for example, International Political Economy approaches, informed by Marxism and Post-Marxism (e.g. Deppe 1976; Holland 1980), posed themselves as alternatives to the mainstream in the 1970s and 1980s, but they were always confined to a few niches, and did not gain as much popularity as the more recent approaches covered here, although there has over the past decade or so been a resurgence of related approaches in the form of what one could call the 'Amsterdam School' (see below).

# PART I

# EXPLAINING EUROPEAN INTEGRATION

# 2

# Federalism

*Michael Burgess*

## Introduction

In this chapter I want to explore the relationship between federalism and European integration in order to demonstrate the relevance of the federal idea to the building of Europe. It is imperative at the outset to begin with a preliminary caution. This is that federalism is a word that has been used to describe different phenomena. In practice it can excite and arouse passionate political controversy as well as exerting a calm moderating influence simply because it means different things to different people in different contexts at different times. Small wonder, then, that it has been used and abused in equal measure. Consequently, any meaningful analysis of federalism must take account of what I shall call 'empirical context'. Put simply, the word 'federalism' has different connotations in different political contexts: it suggests disunity and fragmentation in India and in the United Kingdom (UK), while it implies the exact opposite in Germany and the United States of America (USA). So even in established federations there are widely varying perspectives about the word 'federal' or 'federalism'.

When we focus upon European integration, the empirical context looms particularly large because it has transcended the familiar level of the nation state to the level of an unknown 'ever closer union among the peoples of Europe' that currently includes intergovernmental, supranational, federal, confederal, and functional elements. This hybrid Europe, with its complex institutions, structures, and procedures that defy precise definition and categorization in conventional political science terms, is widely deemed today to be moving toward that *finalité politique* that looks increasingly like a federal destination. Step by step, in piecemeal, incremental fashion, the European Community (EC) has evolved into the European Union (EU), which is now on the threshold of a constitutional and political Europe that is nothing less than a federal Europe, but not necessarily a federal state as we know it.

For those who advocate a federal Europe, the gradual evolution of a 'Community' into a 'Union' during the last half-century is a firm vindication of the continuing strength and vitality of the federal idea. The relations between states and peoples in the voluntary union that was first created in 1951 by the Treaty of Paris with the European Coal and Steel Community (ECSC) and then extended in 1957 to include both the

European Economic Community (EEC) and the European Atomic Energy Community (EAEC) in the Treaties of Rome, continue to widen and deepen. One consequence of this unending process of economic and political integration is that in many important respects the 'peoples' of the European member states have now become 'citizens' of the EU.

Given the empirical reality that is the contemporary EU, with its unique institutional framework and its conspicuous policy outputs that increasingly resemble an emergent federal polity, it comes as little surprise to learn that federalism, sometimes referred to as the 'f' word, has acquired much more credibility today than at any time since its heyday in the early post-war years. Indeed, the sheer pace of European integration since the ratification of the Single European Act (SEA) in 1987 has unquestionably revived the fortunes of the federal idea. Consequently, a political idea that historically and philosophically has always been about different forms of human association and organization, and that antedates the modern state in Europe, is also now representative of a particular theoretical approach to the analysis of European integration. Federalism seeks to explain political integration—the building of Europe—as a conscious and perfectly rational goal of European nation states that continue to pursue their national interests in a world of turbulent international change.

Historically, federalism has been associated with the conventional processes of state-building and national integration. It has been construed as a particular way of bringing together previously separate, autonomous, or independent territorial units to constitute a new form of union based upon principles that, broadly speaking, can be summarized in the dictum 'unity in diversity'. This dictum refers to a union of states and peoples, but it is a particular kind of union. It is a voluntary union whose principal purpose is to recognize, preserve, and formally accommodate distinct interests, identities, and cultures according to the Latin term *foedus*—from which the term 'federal' derives—meaning covenant, compact, bargain, or contract. This formal agreement is rooted in the idea of an equal partnership between the respective partners to the bargain based upon the notion of mutual reciprocity: the idea that participants will not only make decisions for the general welfare of the whole, but that they will also refrain from taking decisions that knowingly do harm either to other members or to the union as a whole. There is a sense, then, of a moral commitment to the community of the membership that constitutes the union.

Past federations have been founded upon distinct territorial identities and interests as well as upon minority cultures, sub-state nationalisms, religious differences, and a range of socio-economic factors that served to underline societal cleavages having political salience. The unity of federations therefore has traditionally been based upon the preservation and promotion of certain federal values that together allow these differences and diversities to breathe and flourish. And federal values are enshrined in written constitutions that entrench these diversities in order to sustain the original purpose of the union. Later on, during the course of the federation's constitutional and political evolution, new bargains or agreements might be struck between new interests and identities that emerge and these enable the union to adapt and adjust to contemporary change in order to maintain political legitimacy, order, and stability. Established federations in Europe that have been highly successful in this process of conflict management include Switzerland, Germany, Austria, and, more recently, Belgium, while the USA, Canada, Australia, India, and Malaysia have also achieved different forms and levels of unity and integration outside Europe. Indeed, Switzerland and India stand out as remarkable examples of how multinational, multilingual, and multicultural federal unions can survive and sustain impressive levels of unity built upon federal principles. It is no accident therefore that Switzerland, in particular, is frequently singled out as a model for the future evolution of the EU (McKay 2001).

Federal models, of course, have their limitations. The EU is not intended to become either the USA or a Switzerland writ large. There is no historical precedent for the kind of union that Europe is busy constructing. The road to federal union along which the EU seems to be travelling has no signposts or footprints to follow. Previous federations have emerged as a result of conscious political actions that first created a written constitution as the foundation of the new state whereas the EU has evolved uniquely as the result of concrete economic steps based upon international treaties whose goals have been rooted, at best, in ambiguity. There can be no doubt, however, that while the means to building Europe have been principally economic, the underlying imperative of post-war European integration has been political. There has, in short, been a complex interaction between economics and politics in the pursuit of national self-interest by the member states of the EU that has resulted in a new kind of federal union the like of which has never before been seen.

# Federalism and European integration

I will begin with a short survey of the origins of the federal idea together with a sketch outline of its relationship to the modern state in Europe. This historical and philosophical background context is crucial to a basic understanding of the relevant contemporary concepts and their interrelationships. Consequently there is a need to define our fundamental concepts first, such as federalism, federation, confederation, the modern state, and European integration, before our exploration can proceed.

## The federal idea

The origin of the federal idea, in the words of Davis (1978: 2), is 'wreathed in mist' and it has evolved over several centuries long before the emergence of the modern state in Europe, but for our purposes in this chapter it is worth noting that the meaning of *foedus* constituted the first serious challenge to Jean Bodin's classic conception of the state almost as soon as his *Les Six Livres de la Republique* was first published in 1576 and quickly became the standard rationalization of the unitary monarchical state (Tooley 1955). The rise of the modern state in Renaissance Europe during the sixteenth and early seventeenth centuries went hand in hand with the emergence of sovereignty as a conceptual instrument for the organization of power in the state. The seventeenth and eighteenth centuries witnessed the gradual development and consolidation of the modern territorial state as the sole legitimate source of public order and political authority. And the state was 'sovereign' in the sense that it admitted no rival or competing authority within its own territorially demarcated boundaries. The modern territorial sovereign nation state—the *Westphalian* state—was predicated upon the assumption that there was a final and absolute political authority in the political community.

The significance of Bodin for the emergence of the federal idea about the organization of the state resided in the imperative to refute his rigid, unyielding conception of the state and sovereignty. As Davis observed (1978: 46–7), it might initially seem paradoxical to include Bodin in a survey of the federal idea and Europe but to omit him completely would actually be 'a grave error' for:

whether by the force of repulsion or resistance, his catalytic influence on federal theory cannot be ignored ... other jurists could no more evade Bodin than successive generations of political jurists could free themselves from the questions—who commands, and how many masters can there be in a stable state, one, two, three or more?

Bodin's legacy was enduring. For two centuries up until the American colonists challenged the constitutional, political, and ultimately the military might of the British empire in the War of Independence in 1776, and substituted the federal idea for its imperial counterpart as a form of political organization, the notion of the independent sovereign state as centralized, absolute, and indivisible with the supreme power resident in a monarch answerable only to God and natural law dominated political and diplomatic discourse in continental Europe. Indeed, even as the reformist idea of a contractual limit placed upon the supreme power—a constitutional monarchy—gradually gained currency in England in the seventeenth century, traces of the Bodinian conception of the state survived in the European mindset until well into the twentieth century.

What, then, do we mean by the federal idea and how is it related to European integration? We have already noted that the term 'federal' derives from the old Latin word *foedus* meaning some kind of covenant, contract, or bargain. But it is also important to remember that the act of forming such a covenant is rooted in the core principles of equality, partnership, reciprocity, mutuality, toleration, recognition, and respect. Davis (1978: 3) refers to the cognate term *fides* meaning faith and trust so that covenantal federalism has evolved over the centuries to refer to a voluntary union of entities, be they persons, a people, communities, or states. In short, it is a 'vital bonding device of civilisation'. However, while this description tells us something about the nature of this kind of union, it does not explain how it must be structured nor does it identify the principles that shape such unions.

When we refer to terms such as reciprocity, mutuality, equality, recognition, and respect, we already have a sense of what is at stake here. In the memorable language of Albert Venn Dicey (1915: 75), the fundamental pre-requisite that always underpins this form of association is the sentiment of *union*, but not *unity*. In other words, the purpose of the union is to integrate different entities but not to assimilate them. The presumption of a federal union, then, is that it is a union based upon the formal constitutional recognition of difference and diversity. Previously discrete, distinct, or independent entities come together to form a new whole—a union—in which they merge part of their autonomous selves while retaining certain powers, functions, and competences fundamental to the preservation and promotion of their particular cultures, interests, identities, and sense of self-definition. The usual shorthand expression of this peculiar trait is Daniel Elazar's (1987: 12) reference to 'self-rule and shared rule'. Typically a federal union can be said to have two faces: it is both a unifying force and a means of maintaining difference and diversity. And it is precisely this inherent ambiguity in the federal concept that periodically has been the root cause of genuine confusion and mis-understanding. Conventionally people have used the term to describe both the process of political unification—the building of a state by aggregation—and the diffusion of power within an established state, or the process of disaggregation. But federalism is directly related to both unity and diversity and expresses both of these simultaneously.

## Federalism, federation, and confederation

In this very brief outline, the basic appeal of the federal state lies precisely in its institutional and structural capacity both to accommodate and reconcile different kinds of union with different kinds of diversity. Federations exist because they formally acknowledge, via constitutional entrenchment, the sorts of identities and diversities that constitute that sense of difference so essential to a pluralist social and political order. But it is important to understand that the federal principles identified above can be structured and institutionalized collectively in a variety of different ways. No federation is identical to another. The way that salient differences and diversities are incorporated in each federal state and how they adjust and adapt to changing circumstances will be shaped and determined by unique historical factors. And the formal constitutional expression of federal principles might require only that a union be a confederation—a union of states—rather than a single state—a federation. As we shall see, the EU represents a new kind of federal order.

Let us consider some definitions in order to clarify what has been surveyed so far. Recent research on the subject of federalism has established a firm conceptual distinction between *federalism* and *federation*, originally introduced into the mainstream literature by Preston King in 1982, where the former is identified as the original and persistent driving-force of the latter. Accordingly federalism can be construed as political ideology and/or political philosophy and it comprises the assorted identities and interests that are grouped around historical, cultural, social, economic, ideological, intellectual, and philosophical factors, making it effectively the sustaining dynamic that was the federation's original *raison d'être*. Federation is therefore defined by King (1982: 77) as 'an institutional arrangement, taking the form of a sovereign state, and distinguished from other such states solely by the fact that its central government incorporates regional units in its decision procedure on some constitutionally entrenched basis'. The relationship between these two concepts is clearly complex. Federalism informs federation and *vice versa*. Moreover, while it is perfectly possible to have federalism without federation, 'there can be no federation without some matching variety of federalism' (1982: 76). Diversity notwithstanding, all federations are composite states that constitute a single people.

Confederation, however, is something that is conceptually distinct from both federalism and federation but is often either ignored or overlooked in the mainstream literature on the federal idea and European integration. This is a mistake because confederation is significant for a deeper understanding of what is meant by a federal Europe. Murray Forsyth (1981) has defined confederation as a union of *states* in a body politic in contrast to a federation that is a union of *individuals* in a body politic, suggesting the unity of one people or nation. Conceptually, of course, the matter is neither as simple nor as straightforward as these definitions would imply because the distinctions between federation and confederation are in practice sometimes rather blurred and imprecise, but they do nonetheless convey the basic historical differences between these phenomena.

Federalism in the context of the EU is the application of federal principles to the process of European integration where the term 'integration' refers to the sense of a coming together of previously separate or independent parts to form a new whole. Charles Pentland (1973: 21) defined integration as 'a process whereby a group of people, organized initially in two or more independent nation states, come to constitute a political whole which can in some sense be described as a community'. The point is that a new totality of relations between states and peoples is created and the utility of the term depends upon which particular approach to integration is adopted. Before we leave this section, let us summarize briefly what we mean by the federal idea and European integration.

We have seen that at the core of the federal idea is the principle of association. In the context of our subject, it is based upon the notion of a voluntary union of states and peoples—the result of a bargain, treaty, contract, or covenant freely entered into—that is binding upon its members and rooted in mutual respect, recognition, reciprocity, tolerance, consent, and equality. The shape and structure of this federal union are determined by the declared goals of the covenant and the historical circumstances that brought it into being. And since it is integration and not assimilation that is the main goal of the EU, the federal principles identified above suggest that it will be founded upon self-rule and shared rule. The federal idea is also an organizing concept that is essentially anti-absolutist and anti-centralist, its watchwords being autonomy, solidarity, pluralism, citizenship, and a subsidiarity that has implications for the building of a union from the bottom upwards rather than a hierarchical top-down approach (European Commission 1992; Burgess 2000).

Unions, however, are not confined by their origins. They evolve in both size and scope, and new bargains are formulated and agreed based upon changing circumstances. New policy agenda constantly emerge that allow for adjustment and adaptation so that federal unions are subject to an endless debate about the principles of governance and interminable disputes about rival teleologies. This is as it should be, but as we shall see, there is a price to be paid for the relentless pursuit of the perfect union. One of the main problems for students of European integration is how to explain and understand the nature of this curious union that has evolved principally from a series of economic steps and is wholly unprecedented. We can begin to appreciate its significance by looking more closely at federalist theory and practice.

## Federalist theory and practice

### Three strands of federalism after the Second World War

It is often claimed that in terms of political practice the federalist movement had its heyday in the early post-war years that were remembered chiefly for the Hague Congress of May 1948 in which the federalists were particularly active and influential. It is certainly true that the federalist movement was conspicuous during these years and that its political influence was seriously underestimated by British political élites, but it is not the case, as some observers have claimed, that it petered out in 1954 when the pioneering projects for a European Defence Community (EDC) and a European Political Community (EPC) abruptly collapsed. To accept this interpretation would be to distort the history of the post-war federalist movement. It suggests that their influence was merely transitory when in reality it displayed a strong continuity of thought and practice throughout the subsequent half-century.

Recent research has demonstrated that the appeal of the federal idea to many Europeans can be located in both the threat of war and the practical experience of World War II itself (Burgess 1989). It was largely among the members of the anti-fascist European Resistance that the federal idea was originally nurtured as the answer to Europe's post-war destiny. For them the defeat of Hitler was only the first step. It offered a golden opportunity for Europeans to return to fundamental questions and the ferment of political ideas and discussions about the role of federalism in post-war European integration was clearly established in the various plans for European union that were drawn up in the years between 1939 and 1945 (Wilkinson 1981; Lipgens 1985). Of course it is very important to note that while the crystallization of the federal idea was essentially part of the *intellectual* Resistance to Hitler and was tantamount to a *spiritual* revolution of ideas, federalism also comprised many radically different conceptions of Europe and divergent political strategies about how to achieve what was broadly conceived of as a 'federal' Europe.

Probably the most famous federalist document to emerge during the war years was the Ventotene Manifesto of 1941. Drawn up by a small nucleus of Italian federalists led by Altiero Spinelli and Ernesto Rossi, federal ideas, attitudes, and assumptions were lucidly expressed in what was one of the first Resistance declarations devoted to European integration (Lipgens 1982; Pinder 1998). It remained, however, a monument to an idea that was never implemented. Immediately after the war, the European nation states regrouped and re-established themselves, thus effectively rejecting federation as the solution to European unity. Nonetheless, if it is true that the Resistance programme—and the spiritual revolution that it symbolized—was effectively defeated and abandoned by the conservative restoration of the immediate post-war years, the federal idea did not disappear with it. On the contrary, it survived in the plethora of influential interest groups that sprouted across Western Europe after 1945 and it was vigorously sustained in the European Union of Federalists (EUF) founded in Basle in December 1946. Indeed, one scholar has noted that in 1948 in France alone there were seventeen European federalist groups, each with between fifty and 4,000 members (Greilsammer 1979). And it was during the late 1940s that renowned federalists like Alexander Marc, Henri Brugmans, and Denis De Rougemont began to formulate highly elaborate federalist doctrines which were eventually to play a part in the ideological split in the EUF during 1955–56.

From a practical policy-making standpoint, the impact of the federalists upon the EDC and EPC projects of the early 1950s was incontestable. Indeed, the attempt to launch them was made 'largely as a result of federalist pressure' and 'federalist ideas also contributed a great deal to the content of the proposals' (Cardozo 1987). Spinelli's role in this episode was particularly noteworthy (Burgess 2000). As Secretary-General of the Italian Movimento Federalista Europeo (MFE), it was he who was instrumental in channelling the Italian government's support toward a federal solution for the EPC which was to have a directly elected European assembly, powers of taxation, and a joint decision-making structure. Spinelli's federalist strategy was what he called 'democratic radicalism', being built upon the idea of a major role for a parliamentary assembly in drafting a new treaty for Europe. This came to be known as 'the constitutional method' whereby an elected European assembly would act as the embryonic constituent voice of the European peoples and serve to mobilize a dynamic European public opinion in the quest to establish a popular European federation. As we shall see, it departed sharply from the competing political strategy of Jean Monnet who became Spinelli's great rival in the concerted post-war drive to champion a federal Europe. Monnet was the first President of the supranational High Authority of the ECSC during 1951–55 and he led the Europe-wide Action Committee for a United States of Europe up until 1975, always believing that the political strategy of small, concrete, economic steps would *culminate* in a federal Europe. In complete contrast, Spinelli's own radical strategy meant *starting* with the political institutions and a popularly-endorsed treaty that would be quickly translated into the familiar statist language of a constitution. It was a fundamental strategic difference founded upon competing conceptions of a federal Europe that has served indelibly to characterize both the theory and the practice of European integration up until the present day (Burgess 2000).

In addition to Monnet's 'federalism by instalments' and Spinelli's self-styled 'democratic radicalism' (for a more detailed discussion, see below), there existed another important strand of federalist thought that merits inclusion in our survey. This is what is variously labelled 'integral', 'personalist', or Proudhonian federalism and encapsulates a fairly broad range of political and sociological ideas based upon the notion of a European society and the spread of federalist values across the established boundaries of European states. Derived mainly from the philosophical writings of Marc, Brugmans, and de Rougemont, mentioned above, the pantheon of personalist writers would also include Robert Aron, Emmanuel Mounier, and Daniel Rops. Put simply, the basic intellectual position of the personalists revolves around the dignity of the human person and it involves a highly searching critique of advanced capitalism. Its normative, prescriptive predisposition is to restore man as a whole person by rescuing him from the modern capitalist state whose mass society has effectively cut him off from his family, neighbours, and local associations, reducing him to the isolation of anonymity in a monist world where he finds himself confronted by global society. As an isolated individual, man is ultimately cut off from himself. Personalism, in bringing man back in touch with society, seeks also to bring political authority back to human beings as complex, responsible members of society. And it does this by active citizen participation in decision-making processes, decentralization to the grassroots, local autonomy, and respect for personal differences. The upshot of this personalist federalism is a quite elaborate, sophisticated way of looking at European integration, but while it has retained its ideological distinctiveness it has suffered from the problem of how precisely to translate these ideas into practical action. It is no easy task to try to change attitudes and mentalities among mass publics (Kinsky 1979, 1991). In this respect, federal theory and practice seem to have been decidedly decoupled and it is therefore easy to understand why many federalists describe the personalists as Utopian federalists (Burgess 2000).

The three strands of federalism identified above underline the rich tradition of philosophical, ideological, and empirical ideas, influences, and strategies that have been developed in response to the drive for European integration. Rival federalists with competing perspectives in the post-war years have been constantly engaged in the contest for practical relevance and if it is true that Monnet's approach to the building of Europe has been the most successful of these political strategies, this does not imply that the others have become redundant. Indeed, many of Spinelli's assumptions and beliefs about the need for a constitutional and political Europe to build upon Monnet's economic foundations have been vindicated since the ratification of the Single European Act (SEA) in 1987. The implications of this ideological and strategic contest for federalism and European integration strongly suggest that the role of EU member states as propulsive forces in helping to build a federal Europe has actually been underestimated by federalists themselves and should be much more effectively integrated into federalist theory. While certainly not wishing to construct a federal Europe that follows traditional processes of state-building and national integration which have produced the nation states of today, the relevance of existing federal models as 'comparators' is nonetheless well worth more than a moment's reflection (Sbragia 1992; McKay 2001). Clearly, different aspects of *both* comparative politics and IR can be comfortably accommodated in the quest to explain and understand European integration. However, students of European integration theory should be cautious about recent theoretical trends and developments that have spawned a new model, dubbed 'Liberal Inter-governmentalism' (LI) by its author, Andrew Moravcsik, who, in a series of seminal articles published in the 1990s, has produced probably the most elaborate of the current explanations for the building of Europe (Moravcsik 1991, 1993, 1997, 1998).

## Liberal intergovernmentalism and federalism

The implications of LI for federalism are both serious and damaging because it is relegated to the margins of serious analytical discussion. For those who seek to reinstate federalism as a perfectly rational approach to European integration, however, LI is a model that is fundamentally flawed. Moravcsik's important contribution to the intellectual debate about European integration is obviously to be welcomed, but it has never effectively come to terms with why and how the contemporary EU has evolved in such a strong federal direction. The biggest stumbling-block to a meeting of minds on this question seems to hinge upon the way he construes federalism itself. His early articles simply failed to incorporate federalism in his analysis at all, while he was successively able to dismiss it as irrelevant merely by subsuming it within neofunctionalism so that it was rendered virtually invisible. His more recent contributions (1998, 2001) have witnessed a significant willingness to confront what many observers see self-evidently as a federal Europe, but even here there is some evidence of serious intellectual discomfort.

Moravcsik has begun to remove federalism from the shadow of neofunctionalism but its recognition has still not extended much beyond that of a subordinate category labelled 'the geopolitical explanation of national preferences' (1998: 70). Moreover, the claim made for different kinds of 'institutional choice', based upon the 'pooling and delegation of sovereignty', being reduced to 'federalist versus nationalist ideology' appears superficially plausible but is actually over-simplified and assumes what needs to be proved. For example, the assumption that federalism predicts 'systematic variation across countries rather than across issues' is highly questionable. So-called 'federalist' countries do not consistently favour 'delegation and pooling' independently of 'substantive consequences of cooperation' nor is it convincing to claim that 'pro-European' groups will always favour 'pooling and delegation' independently of 'substantive concerns' (1998: 70).

In a recent essay that finally confronts the question about whether or not European integration has evolved to such an extent in social, economic, political, legal, and constitutional terms that we can now make claims to have a federal Europe, Moravcsik has described the EU as 'an exceptionally weak federation' (2001: 186). He is, however, clearly uncomfortable with this description, adding that it might well be thought of 'as something qualitatively different from existing federal systems' and much preferring to refer to it as 'a particular sort of limited, multi-level constitutional polity designed within a specific social and historical context' (2001: 186–7). Considering his established concern for analytical rigour and methodological prowess, these are surprisingly equivocal conclusions derived from his own assessment of the EU's current policy and institutional capacity which he construes as weak. Clearly it is one thing to seek to derive 'standardized hypotheses' leading to the 'generalizability of conclusions' about European integration (2001: 2), but it is quite another to explain why the evolution from a *community* to a *union* has been a federal evolution.

Moravcsik's construction of federalism is conceptually shallow and incomplete. His failure to give it the detailed attention it deserves means that instead of explaining federalism he *explains it away*. Yet there is clearly some scope for applying his methods to federal evolution in the same way that he uses them to explain and understand supra-national developments. Without wishing to labour the point about Moravcsik's most recent detailed work, it might assist toward a deeper understanding and appreciation of the nature of the debate between federalism and LI if we take a closer look at one par-ticular area where both schools of thought entertain strong but divergent viewpoints and interpretations. This pertains to the constitutional evolution of the EU and it has been chosen for inclusion in this chapter precisely because it serves as a convenient example or case study to demonstrate how federalism can be effectively used to explain the building of political Europe. By its very nature, this case study propels us into the area of history and theory or, more accurately, historical revisionism and its theoretical implications for European integration. Let us return, then, to the conceptual world of federalism and the shift from Monnet's 'functionalism' to Spinelli's 'constitutionalism'.

## Federalism and the constitutional evolution of the EU

In practice, the question of a constitution for Europe has never been at the forefront of the public debate about European integration. It has never been on the official policy agenda of the EU member states simply because such a commitment was never required. As we shall see, Monnet's peculiar approach to the building of Europe rendered such a requirement redundant. Consequently it has been deliberately eschewed as irrelevant to the nebulous goal of an 'ever closer union among the peoples of Europe'. Indeed, in hindsight, such a strategy at any time in the post-war evolution of the European project would have been tantamount to suicide. Member state governments were neither will-ing nor able even to contemplate, let alone introduce, such a proposal that would have been peremptorily rejected as chimerical.

In these circumstances, then, it might seem strange to refer to the *constitutional* evolution of the EU. However, this is not the case. Monnet's own political strategy for the construction of a federal Europe lay in what we might call 'issue avoidance'. He sought to build Europe by avoiding a damaging confrontation with issues that might conceiv-ably call national sovereignty directly into question. The constitutional evolution of the European project would occur, as it were, almost imperceptibly by adding institutional pieces to the larger jigsaw in incremental fashion. The process was made crystal clear in the famous public speech of 9 May 1950 in which the French Foreign Minister, Robert Schuman, declared the goal of a united Europe:

Europe will not be made all at once, or according to a single plan. It will be built through concrete achievements which first create a de facto concrete solidarity. The coming together of
the nations of Europe requires the elimination of the age-old opposition of France and
Germany. Any action taken must in the first place concern these two countries. . . . The pooling of coal and steel production should immediately provide for the setting up of common
foundations for economic development as a first step in the federation of Europe . . . this proposal will lead to the realization of the first concrete foundation of a European federation
indispensable to the preservation of peace (Nelsen and Stubb 1998: 11–12).

The Schuman Declaration was silent about a European constitution. This was something that, if it occurred at all, would arrive in its own time as the logical result of a
highly successful pioneering experiment in economic integration. Let us explore this
apparent conundrum a little further.

It is the argument of this chapter that history and theory are the key to understanding the relationship between federalism and European integration. And integral to this
relationship are the ubiquitous role of Jean Monnet and the nature of Monnet's Europe.
This refers to Monnet's own unique approach to the building of post-war Europe that
relied, as we have seen, upon piecemeal, cumulative concrete steps leading to a federal
Europe. By forging specific functional links between states in a way that did not directly
challenge national sovereignty, Monnet believed that the door to federation would
gradually be opened. These so-called 'functional' links were primarily economic activities and they were perfectly expressed in the ECSC initiative of the early 1950s. This
novel form of sectoral supranational organization would be the foundation of the
European federation that would evolve only slowly to engage national élites in a process of mutual economic interest. These concrete benefits would gradually form that
crucial solidarity—the common interest—which Monnet believed indispensable for
the removal of physical and mental barriers.

If we glance at a preliminary sketch outline of what became the Schuman Plan, this
continuity in Monnet's thinking is quite striking. Since Franco-German union could
not be achieved at once, a start would have to be made by 'the establishment of common bases for economic development' (Monnet: 295). The goal of a federal Europe
would be attained via Franco-German union that would itself be realized 'through the
interplay of economics and institutions' necessitating 'new structures on a European
scale' (Monnet: 295). The approach to federation, which Monnet called 'the ECSC
method' of establishing 'the greatest solidarity among peoples', implied that gradually
other tasks and other people would become subject to the same common rules and
institutions—or perhaps to new institutions—and this experience would 'gradually
spread by osmosis' (Monnet: 392–3). No time limits were imposed on what was clearly
deemed to be a long, slow, almost organic, process of economic and political integration. The following extract from Monnet's *Memoirs* is worth quoting at length:

We believed in starting with limited achievements, establishing de facto solidarity, from which
a federation would gradually emerge. I have never believed that one fine day Europe would be
created by some great political mutation, and I thought it wrong to consult the peoples of
Europe about the structure of a Community of which they had no practical experience. It was

another matter, however, to ensure that in their limited field the new institutions were thoroughly democratic; and in this direction there was still progress to be made ... the pragmatic method we had adopted would ... lead to a federation validated by the people's vote; but that federation would be the culmination of an existing economic and political reality, already put to the test ... it was bringing together men and practical matters (Monnet: 367).

This exceptionally lucid account of how Monnet viewed the path to federation not only underlines the authenticity of his federalist credentials, but it also confirms the European project as quintessentially a federal project that would need to engage the constitutional question only at some distant, undefined date in the future. Monnet's 'method' was based upon the bold assumption that 'political' Europe would be the 'culminating point of a gradual process' so that Europe would experience a qualitative change in the constitutional and political relations between states and citizens. But this metamorphosis would happen only when 'the force of necessity' made it 'seem natural in the eyes of Europeans' (Monnet: 394–5). Consequently Monnet's approach to a federal Europe rendered constitutionalism—the building of political Europe—contingent upon cumulative functional achievements.

It was precisely at this juncture—in the interaction between politics and economics—that Altiero Spinelli entered the theoretical debate. The mistake that Spinelli attributed to Monnet was inherent in the functional approach which neglected to deal with 'the organization of political power at the European level'.[1] This meant that the political centre remained weak and largely impotent, lacking the capacity to go much beyond what already existed and unable to adapt to new forces and problems encountered at the European level. Here the focus shifted to the role of the European institutions. For Monnet, institutions were crucial but his conception differed significantly from Spinelli's in the extent to which he viewed their development as akin to organic growth arising directly out of functional performance. Spinelli, in contrast, had a much more positive conception of institutions. As the bedrock of political integration, they had to be solid. He believed that Europe could not afford the 'wait and see' policy of Monnet: what was urgently required if Europe was not to suffer political immobilism and stagnation was institutional reform.

In summary, then, Spinelli believed that Monnet's Europe was vulnerable to paralysis at some point in the future because it failed to confront the realities of organized political power. The central institutions would remain weak and the predicted shift from *quantity* to *quality* would not occur precisely because of Monnet's excessive reliance upon functionalist logic. Consequently the constitutional and political evolution of Europe would simply be stunted. This fervent conviction prompted Spinelli to confront the political implications of Monnet's Europe by engaging the difficult and controversial task of attempting to forge ahead in the 1980s with building 'political' Europe (Burgess 2000). Since the SEA in 1987, therefore, the public debate about the future of Europe—its institutional architecture, policy scope, and membership size—has become so controversial precisely because it is at heart a 'constitutional' debate, that is, a debate about constitutionalizing the European construction.

The conceptual and strategic differences between the two major protagonists in the federal cause had enormous theoretical implications for the building of Europe. Today there appears to be an emerging consensus among informed commentators on the EU that we have now reached the limits of Monnet's conception of European integration. It is now time for statesmen and politicians to address Spinelli's concerns. Europeans have to recognize and deal with the emerging federal reality that is staring them in the face. Together the Maastricht, Amsterdam, and Nice Treaties have combined to build upon Monnet's Europe by accelerating and accentuating its federal direction. And with the recent commitment of the fifteen member states to work together to forge a written constitution for the EU at the next intergovernmental conference (IGC) in 2004, considerable institutional and policy evidence has accumulated to substantiate the claim that the EU already constitutes a federal Europe.

The historical and theoretical background context sketched out above, then, suggests a number of things. First, we have reached a new crossroads in the EU's economic and political evolution that has enormous empirical and theoretical implications for federalism and European integration. Secondly, the increasing public concern and controversy about the future of Europe indicates the heightened engagement of mass publics in the integration process largely, but not solely, because this crossroads represents the shift from Monnet's functionalism to Spinelli's constitutionalism that is implicit in the building of political Europe. Thirdly, the EU is about to move from the formal language of treaty to the discourse of constitution that is indicative of the member states' collective perception of the union as more than just an intergovernmental reality. But the LI model of European integration seems to be out of step with these contemporaneous developments. It has recently evolved to subsume 'European federalist thinking' in the larger category of 'geopolitical considerations' where the federal idea is, once again, relegated to the margins of analytical explanation as merely playing a 'secondary role', yet Moravcsik (1998: 501) nonetheless concludes that 'European integration was no accident' and that it 'continues to advance despite a series of obstacles'. It is a sentiment of which Monnet would have approved. A plausible meeting of minds might be that the primacy of economic interests over ideological factors is entirely consistent with Monnet's political strategy or approach to European integration. And the paradox that follows from this reasoning is that LI must explain why it is that member state governments have been and continue to be predominantly responsible not only for *supranational* developments but also for building a *federal* Europe.

## Federalism and the enlargement of the EU

The enlargement of the EU was always a part of the 'Community psyche'. Article 237 of the Rome Treaty makes it clear that 'any European state may apply to become a member of the Community' (Treaty of Rome 1957). And according to Article 240, the Treaty was also concluded 'for an unlimited period' so that here was the institutional and policy framework for a voluntary union of states and citizens that was pledged to infinite membership expansion in Europe for an indefinite period. Moreover, the basis for a *federal* union, though never explicitly established, was always at least a distinct *possibility* given the institutional implications of Article 138 concerning direct elections to the European Parliament (EP) together with those of Articles 171–7 relating to the powers of the European Court of Justice; the principle of Qualified Majority Voting (QMV); and, finally, the establishment of an executive body (the European Commission) in Article 155 that, once appointed, was independent of the member state governments and accountable to the EP.

The current EU of fifteen constituent units has grown in size from the original six founding members via a series of piecemeal, incremental steps that has no discernible pattern and no inherent logic beyond the fact of expansion. Each enlargement in 1973 (the UK, Denmark, and Ireland), 1981 (Greece), 1986 (Spain and Portugal), and 1995 (Sweden, Finland, and Austria) has been the result of ad hoc individual negotiations and a series of compromises carefully designed to accommodate the specific needs and requirements of both the evolving EU and its applicant states. The end of the Cold War and the sudden and dramatic collapse of communism throughout eastern Europe, however, ushered in a completely new era—a stable disorder—with a distinctly different dynamic in terms of European integration. The sight of twelve or thirteen countries *en masse* beating a path to the EU's door in what has sometimes seemed to be an undignified scramble for membership posed unprecedented problems for the European project. The so-called 'Copenhagen criteria', confirmed in June 1993, specified three main economic and political preconditions which can be summarized as the following: the acceptance of liberal democratic institutions based on the rule of law, respect for human rights, and the protection of minorities; the existence of a functioning market economy; and the ability to take on the obligations of membership, including political, economic, and monetary union. But even with these formidable admission criteria, the socio-economic, political, legal, and financial implications for the EU remain colossal.

From a federalist perspective, the overriding imperative is clearly to seek to accommodate all of the applicants without seriously damaging the *acquis communautaire* and to continue to pursue an agenda for wide-ranging reform that already existed but has become much more urgent since 1989–90. And the range of reforms is extensive. Its general focus would be to enhance the federal and confederal elements that the EU already exhibits at both the institutional and policy levels. The battery of reforms includes inter alia the following proposals: further extensions of Qualified Majority Voting (QMV) in the Council of Ministers (CM); more accountability and transparency of decision-making in the CM; the election of the President of the European Commission from the EP; the power of the EP to force the resignation of individual commissioners; the extension of the co-decision procedure to the remaining legislative areas that it does not cover; a larger EU budget, with extended EP scrutiny; and enhanced Commission participation in the emerging European Security and Defence Policy (ESDP). Federalists would also like to see the series of opt-outs originally negotiated by the UK, Sweden, and Denmark that included EMU, the CFSP, defence, and citizenship become opt-ins in order to allow the EU to function more efficiently and democratically, and to buttress its external role as a unitary actor that can speak with a single voice in world affairs. A federal Europe that works would be one that utilized to the full the dictum 'common solutions to common problems' and the fulfilment of all of the conditions identified above would certainly be sufficient to justify calling the EU federal (Pinder: 1992).

The questions that the challenge of enlargement poses for federalism are related to the maintenance of unity and diversity in both institutions and the policies. Some of these have already been identified above, but institutional reform concerns the strengthening of the central supranational institutions—the Commission, EP, and the ECJ—in the wake of the relatively recent emergence of the intergovernmental conference method (1985–2004) of union-building, while policy matters are essentially about enhancing the EU's policy capacity and implementation, such as in the fields of ESDP, labour markets in the SEM, and energy policy. It is important to note that the promotion of federalist values and principles—reciprocity, mutual respect, recognition, tolerance, and consent—can still be pursued if they are conducted through the existing institutional channels of the EU that represent the member state governments, such as the Council of Ministers and the European Council that constitute the confederal dimension of the European project. The EU, we are reminded, is a political, economic, social, and legal hybrid that is characterized by a combination of federal, confederal, supranational, and intergovernmental features.

Enlargement of the EU, then, does not necessarily mean that the federal and confederal elements in its future evolution will be attenuated. On the contrary, the accentuation of difference and diversity will be counterbalanced by protection of the *acquis* and the commitment of applicant states to EMU and the SEM. The main threat to the EU is likely to be the practicability of existing decision-making processes and perhaps policy implementation. But some of these matters have been, or are already being, addressed. The Nice Treaty symbolized the current limits to integration imposed by an intergovernmental institution based upon consensus-building that is inherently fragile and ephemeral, but the indecent haste with which the big powers sought to institutionalize their national interests in the revised decision-making processes will ultimately have to connect with the federal reality of how to divide and share power and competences equitably in the union. The EU, we are reminded, has evolved in a series of incremental steps that have gradually enhanced the federal and confederal characteristics in European integration so that 'self-rule and shared rule' is its shorthand definition.

Enlargement must be construed not solely as a challenge or threat to the union but also as an opportunity to strengthen it. And this is how we should view the meetings of the so-called 'Constitutional Convention' agreed by member states at Laeken, Belgium in December 2001.[2] This, too, symbolizes yet another crossroads in the overall process of building Europe and it furnishes one of those periodic moments to pause for reflection, reappraisal, and revision in order to adapt and adjust to changing circumstances.

New bargains are struck, fresh impetus is given to integration, and the EU's institutional mechanisms, its decision-making procedures and its policy capacity are all buttressed to meet the challenges of an expanding union. And the larger the union becomes, the more that federal and confederal principles and values will act as the operative means to achieve the goal of 'an ever closer union' among European states and peoples.

## Conclusion

This chapter has explored the conceptual relationship between federalism, federation, confederation, and European integration. It has defined the basic terms and looked at some of the problems and pitfalls involved in theory and practice, taking the opportunity to make some brief comparisons and contrasts with functionalism, neofunctionalism, and liberal intergovernmentalism. The relevance of the federal idea to European integration has been examined by a series of brief excursions into history and theory, a short case study of the EU's constitutional evolution, and a concise assessment of the enlargement issue from the standpoint of federalist perspectives. Each of these areas has confirmed the significance of federalism and the federalists to the post-war historical evolution of the European project.

One outstanding contemporary change that already has colossal implications not only for federalism, but also for theories of European integration in general is the engagement of mass publics in the future direction of the EU. The increasing use of referenda to obtain political legitimacy for new treaty arrangements suggests a veritable sea change in integration theories. The building of Europe can no longer progress according to a permissive consensus. Member state governments can no longer rely upon their electorates for automatic confirmation of élite decisions and there is clear evidence that a chasm has opened up in élite-mass relationships concerning the future of Europe. The implication of this increasing reliance upon intergovernmental conferences for new treaties that must be ratified by parliaments and peoples harbours many problems for federal political strategies in national arenas where the 'f' word remains extremely sensitive in mainstream political discourse, but these strategic problems are likely to be overtaken by events if the current intention to introduce an EU constitution is successful. A constitution for the EU will probably render the current use of intergovernmental conferences largely redundant in the future.

If we turn to the question of theoretical convergence, there would appear to be some evidence of an intellectual *rapprochement* in many important respects between federalism, neofunctionalism, and liberal intergovernmentalism. There is, for example, an increasing tendency to be more realistic and less fanciful about theories of European integration than in the past and this has resulted in a much lower level of intellectual expectations. But all three approaches acknowledge, admittedly to differing degrees, the reality of supranational actors and institutions, the significance of selective contributions to European integration made by individual statesmen, the impact of changing national policy preferences, the interaction of intra- and extra-EU events and circumstances, the complex interrelationship between economics and politics, the relevance of path dependency, and the intellectual sensitivities to both International Relations and Comparative Politics methodologies. Of course federalism and a revised neo-functionalism both have normative as well as empirical properties absent from liberal intergovernmentalism and, as already mentioned above, there is some evidence of a willingness to be more open-minded about recommending comparative federalism as a useful benchmark for identifying various pathways to the building of Europe. Alberta Sbragia (1992: 262–3), for example, implicitly accepted the conceptual distinction between federalism and federation when she noted that 'one can have what might be called segmented federalism, that is, treaty-based federal arrangements in certain policy arenas, without having a formal, constitutionally based federation'. Or again, 'a federal-type organization could evolve without becoming a constitutionally based federation in the traditional sense'. This would make 'the study of federations useful in thinking about the Community's future'. In this chapter, the wheel, it would appear, has come full circle.

## Notes

1. Interviews with Altiero Spinelli, 15 September 1983 and 14 February 1985 in the European Parliament, Strasbourg, France.

2. It should be noted that there is some minor confusion over the terminology used to refer to the Convention. I have used the term 'Constitutional Convention', but the EU website refers to 'European Convention'. See http://european-convention.eu.int.

## Guide to further reading

*Key primary works*

ELAZAR, D.J. (1995), 'From Statism to Federalism: a paradigm shift', *Publius: The Journal of Federalism* 25(2), 5–18. This is an important federalist perspective on the shift from the Westphalian state to new forms of federal union that have drawn their inspiration from the post-war evolution of the EU.

LISTER, F.K. (1996), *The European Union, the United Nations and the Revival of Confederal Governance* (London: Greenwood Press). This is a very interesting and thought-provoking thesis about the revival of confederal principles in the world of states.

PINDER, J. (1986), 'European community and nation state: a case for a neo-federalism?' *International Affairs* 62(1), 41–54. This is now a classic article on the arguments for a new kind of federal Europe.

ROSSITER, C. (ed.) (1961), *The Federalist Papers* (New York: The New York American Library). This is the classic collection of papers written by Hamilton, Jay, and Madison in defence of the proposed new American constitution that has subsequently become a philosophical treatise on government and is frequently alluded to in contemporary analyses of European integration.

*Other important primary works*

BURGESS, M. (ed.) (1996), 'Federalism and the European Union', Special Issue of *Publius: The Journal of Federalism* 26(4), 1–162. This is an important collection of contemporary essays on various dimensions of the subject.

CARNEY, F.S. (ed.) (1995), *Politica: Johannes Althusius* (Indianapolis: Liberty Fund). This is the best translation and survey of the political ideas of Althusius.

HUEGLIN, T.O. (1999), *Early Modern Concepts for a Late Modern World: Althusius on Community and Federalism* (Waterloo, ON.: Wilfrid Laurier University Press). This survey has become important for the contemporary debate about the revival of the federalist ideas of Althusius in the context of European integration.

KING, P. and BOSCO, A. (eds.) (1991), *A Constitution for Europe: A Comparative Study of Federal Constitutions and Plans for the United States of Europe* (London: Lothian Foundation Press). This is important for the range of material germane to the emergence of ideas about a federal constitution for Europe.

PINDER, J. (1993), 'The New European Federalism: The Idea and the Achievements', in Burgess, M. and Gagnon, A.-G. (eds.), *Comparative Federalism and Federation: Competing Traditions and Future Directions* (Hemel Hempstead: Harvester Wheatsheaf), 45–66. This is now a classic chapter on the emergence of 'incremental federalism' in European integration.

ROSS, G. (1995), *Jacques Delors and European Integration* (Oxford: Polity Press). This is indispensable for an understanding of the federal ideas, influences, and strategies of the former President of the European Commission during the period 1985–95.

VERNON, R. (ed.) (1979), *The Principle of Federation by P.-J. Proudhon* (Toronto: University of Toronto Press). The best survey of Proudhonian ideas of federalism and their continuing practical significance.

# 3

# Neo-Neofunctionalism

*Philippe C. Schmitter*

## Introduction: déjà vu, all over again?

No theory of regional integration has been as misunderstood, caricatured, pilloried, proven wrong, and rejected as often as neofunctionalism. Numerous scholars have rejoiced at having 'overcome' the much-decried antagonism between it and inter-governmentalism, presumably by adhering to some version or another of the latter. So much so, that with very few exceptions, virtually no one currently working on European integration openly admits to being a neofunctionalist. Its own creator has even declared it obsolescent—on two occasions![1] So, why bother to flog this dead horse? Why not celebrate its demise and move on to a more promising and up-to-date approach? There is certainly no shortage of self-proclaimed candidates for the job. Especially since its *relancement* in the mid-1980s, European integration has become once again a very lively site for theoretical speculation. Hardly a year passes without someone coming up with a new theory and, even more surprisingly, managing to con-vince a group of other scholars to produce a collective volume extolling its virtues. 'International regime analysis', 'the regulatory approach', 'liberal intergovernmental-ism', 'the policy-network approach', 'the Fusion-Thesis', 'multi-lateral governance', 'institutionalism', 'rationalism', 'constructivism', 'reflectivism', and 'post-modernism' have all followed each other over the past years onto the bookshelves that I reserve for integration theory.

The editors of this volume asked me to review and reflect upon these more recent efforts, presumably from the perspective of a senior scholar whose youthful flirtation with neofunctionalism had long since past. I found this impossible to do. Most of these 'novelties' turned out not to be theories at all, but just more or less elaborate languages for describing what the authors thought had taken place in the recent past—devoid of any discrete and falsifiable hypotheses about where the process might be heading in the future. And when there was some theoretical core it often sounded quite familiar to me.[2] Real-live neofunctionalists may be an endangered species, but neofunctionalist thinking turned out to be very much alive, even if it was usually being re-branded as a different animal.[3]

**Neofunctionalism:** a theory of regional integration that places major emphasis on the role of non-state actors—especially, the 'secretariat' of the regional organization involved and those interest associations and social movements that form at the level of the region—in providing the dynamic for further integration. Member states remain important actors in the process. They set the terms of the initial agreement, but they do not exclusively determine the direction and extent of subsequent change. Rather, regional bureaucrats in league with a shifting set of self-organized interests and passions seek to exploit the inevitable 'spill-overs' and 'unintended consequences' that occur when states agree to assign some degree of supra-national responsibility for accomplishing a limited task and then discover that satisfying that function has external effects upon other of their interdependent activities. According to this theory, regional integration is an intrinsically sporadic and conflictual process, but one in which, under conditions of democracy and pluralistic representation, national governments will find themselves increasingly entangled in regional pressures and end up resolving their conflicts by conceding a wider scope and devolving more authority to the regional organizations they have created. Eventually, their citizens will begin shifting more and more of their expectations to the region and satisfying them will increase the likelihood that economic-social integration will 'spill-over' into political integration.

So, with apologies for reviving a moribund theory that everyone was so pleased to have long since buried, I will try to make the case that its root assumptions, concepts, and hypotheses are still worth considering—overtly and not just covertly. Needless to say, this will take a bit of adjusting. Contrary to the caricatural accounts, neofunctionalism has always been a reflexive theory. It did not spring forth mature and complete from the brain of its founder, Ernst B. Haas. Indeed, his initial work came out of a critical encounter with its precursor, the functionalism of David Mitrany. During its golden age from the 1960s to the mid-1970s, the theory underwent further substantial modification, largely as the result of efforts to apply it comparatively outside Western Europe. This made its proponents increasingly aware of factors that made this region of the world so much more propitious for moving ahead with integration. Parametric variables such as the fact that all of the member polities were democratic, that their citizens enjoyed the freedom to organize collectively within and across national borders, that the distribution of the benefits from integration were both dispersed and variable across time and units, that the issues relating to the external security of the region were being taken care of by another international organization, that changes in national ruling élites and the socio-economic coalitions that brought them to power could block and even reverse agreements already reached, that levels of development, size of country and product mix cut across each other, and so forth, had to be incorporated within the theory, not left outside it. The result was a vastly more complex vision of the integration process and one that quite explicitly predicted a wider range of possible outcomes—not only across regional settings but within the same region depending on the evolution over time of institutions, policies, and payoffs.

## Neofunctionalism in relation to other theories of integration

Some critics of neofunctionalism mourned the loss of its original faith in automaticity and uni-directionality and complained about the proliferation of potential trajectories, but this was a logical and desirable result of its comparative application and its conversion of 'taken-for-granted' constants into 'should-be-taken-into-consideration' variables. **Any comprehensive theory of integration should potentially be a theory of disintegration**. It should not only explain why countries decide to coordinate their efforts across a wider range of tasks and delegate more authority to common institutions, but also why they do not do so or why, having done so, they decide to defect from such arrangements. Unfortunately, almost all of the other so-called theories of regional integration are only theories of European integration and this has deprived them of most of their capacity for self-reflexivity—except to the extent that inter-temporal comparisons of the same case allows for some questioning of the endogenous and exogenous status of explanatory variables and causal processes.[4]

Before I offer an updated target for criticism, I propose to try to place neo-functionalism within the present context of contending theories of regional/European integration. In my opinion, all these theories can be placed within a two-dimensional property space.

(1) Ontology: whether the theory presumes a process that **reproduces** the existing characteristics of its member-state participants and the interstate system of which they are a part, or presumes a process that **transforms** the nature of these sovereign national actors and their relations with each other; and

(2) Epistemology: whether the evidence gathered to monitor these processes focuses primarily on **dramatic political events**, or upon **prosaic socio-economic-cultural exchanges**.

Figure 3.1 represents my first attempt at filling that property space with real-live 'isms'. Since I am confident that individual contemporary theorists of regional integration will not agree with where I would have placed them, I have prudently not done so.

Appropriately, we find functionalism with its neo- and neo-neo-versions in the bottom right-hand corner of the plot. Its ontology is transformative in that it assumes that both actors and the 'games they play' will change significantly in the course of the integration process; its epistemology is rooted in the observation of gradual, normal, and (by and large) unobtrusive exchanges among a wide range of actors. Its historic opponent, realism with its pure intergovernmental and liberal intergovernmental modifications, is diametrically opposite since its key assumptions are that dominant actors remain sovereign national states pursuing their unitary national interests and controlling the pace and outcome through periodic revisions of their mutual treaty obligations. Federalism is another transformative option, but it too relies on episodic 'moments' at which a multitude of actors (and not just their governments) agree upon a new constitutional format. Its diametrical opposite is what I have labelled 'regulation-ism,' as best exemplified in the work of Giandomenico Majone. It shares with intergovernmentalism

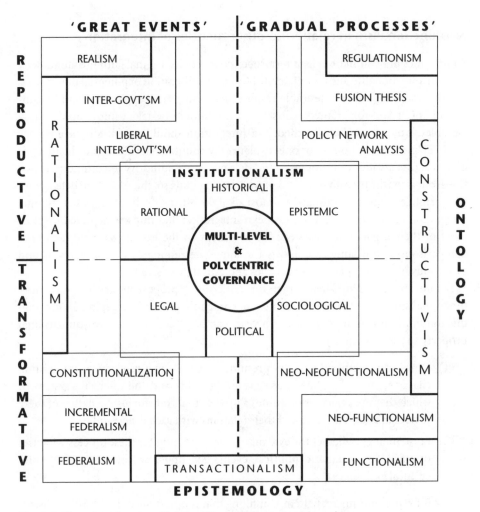

**Fig. 3.1** Theories of regional integration: ontology x epistemology

the presumption of fundamental continuity in actors with only a shift upward in the level at which regulation occurs. The member states, however, remain the same as does their motivation and their predominant influence over the process. The empirical focus differs in that, like functionalism, it emphasizes almost exclusively socio-economic exchanges and the 'normal' management of their consequences.

In the centre of the property space of Figure 3.1, we find an enormous and amorphous thing called 'institutionalism'. Most of the growth in recent theorizing about European and regional integration proudly proclaims itself as such—and then immediately alerts the reader to the fact that there are many different versions of 'it'. By my account, there are six: (1) a 'rational' one that overlaps loosely with liberal intergovernmentalism in its insistence on unitary actors, marginalist calculations, and credible commitments; (2) a 'legal' one that stresses the gradual but intrusively federalist role of juridical decisions and precedents; (3) an 'historical' one that emphasizes the 'stickiness' of identities and the 'path-dependency' of institutions, but is not insensitive to less obtrusive processes of change; (4) an 'epistemic' one that focuses on the normative and professional communities that cluster around specific issues-arenas and influence the making and implementing of regulations; (5) a 'political' one that locates a source of potential transformation in the interpersonal networking of key politicians and their relative autonomy from followers; and, finally, (6) a 'sociological' one that overlaps with neo-neofunctionalism in its emphasis on the formation of transnational class, sectoral and professional associations, and the contestation generated by global and regional social movements. Whether any or all of these deserve the prestigious title of 'theory' is a matter of dispute. Institutionalism, as such, has only minimal content ('institutions matter' seems to capture and exhaust it), but some of its sub-types at least deserve the label of an approach.

In the very centre of that amorphous thing in Figure 3.1 called 'institutionalism' comes '**Multi-Level Governance**'. MLG can be defined as an arrangement for making binding decisions that engages a multiplicity of politically independent but otherwise interdependent actors—private and public—at different levels of territorial aggregation in more-or-less continuous negotiation/deliberation/implementation, and that does not assign exclusive policy *compétence* or assert a stable hierarchy of political authority to any of these levels.

I prefer to stress the 'poly-centric' as well as the 'multi-level' nature of the EU in order to include the functional dimension along with the territorial one. A system of Polycentric Governance (PCG) can be defined as an arrangement for making binding decisions over a multiplicity of actors that delegates authority over functional tasks to a set of dispersed and relatively autonomous agencies that are not controlled—*de jure* or *de facto*—by a single collective institution.[5]

MLG has become the most omnipresent and acceptable label one can stick on the contemporary EU. Even its own politicians use it! My hunch is that its popularity among theorists can be attributable to its descriptive neutrality and, hence, its putative compatibility with virtually any of the institutionalist theories and even several of their more extreme predecessors. For politicians, it has the singular advantage of avoiding the controversial term: 'state' (especially, 'supra-national state') and, therefore, sounds a lot less forbidding and threatening. For example, the emergence of the MLG and PCG from the process of European integration can be explained (in part) by almost all of the theories in Figure 3.1. The EU (and, if they existed, all analogous arrangements for the integration of previously sovereign states) became and will remain an ML and PC polity for the following reasons:

1. It is the product of successive treaties between formally (and formerly) sovereign national-states.
   1.1. *Ergo*, it is the outcome of a gradual and incremental process whose institutions were not modelled on any previous polity and, hence, whose eventual configuration could not be imagined in advance.

*1.2. Ergo*, since formal revision of treaties requires unanimity, their provisions are virtually impossible to change and tend to accumulate over time—creating overlaps and inconsistencies that can only be revised by informal negotiations—which in turn reinforces MLG and PCG.

*1.3. Ergo*, if it were to be 'constitutionalized' and, thereby, its *finalité politique* defined, it would have to transform its MLG and PCG properties and become a polity more similar to an orthodox federal state with a democratic government—probably of the parliamentary/consociational *genus*.

2. The actors/principals (i.e. the member states) that form the EU do not trust each other to respect mutual agreements faithfully and accurately.

   *2.1. Ergo*, they require an authoritative and independent agent to monitor and, when necessary, enforce these agreements—hence, the intrinsic role for a supranational secretariat and judiciary, i.e. the Commission and the ECJ.

   *2.2.* But, they are wary of delegating too much authority to this supranational agent, hence, the dispersion of these monitoring and enforcing tasks to multiple sites (and the reluctance to provide it with the two key independent powers of any state, namely, taxation and security).

   *2.3.* And, even when they delegate this authority, they surround it with mechanisms of 'inter-level' representation/accountability that restrict its autonomy.

   *2.4.* But, the actors/principals do trust that none of the others will use force or the threat of force to impose an arrangement/outcome, hence, they are less concerned with relative benefits than in a traditional intergovernmental system.

3. The actors/principals that form the EU do not have a common identity or politico-administrative culture.

   *3.1. Ergo*, these actors will be unwilling/unable to impose a single *modus operandi* on their common institutions and, therefore, will tend to disperse them to multiple sites.

   *3.2. Ergo*, the principals will only be capable of exercising a limited amount of solidarity among themselves, i.e. redistributing wealth from the more to the less well-endowed, and this leads to *lottizzazione* of benefits across both territories and functions.

   *3.3. Ergo*, the member states will reciprocally defend each other's distinctive identity (out of fear of losing their own) and, therefore, prefer institutions that 'build-in' multi-level accountability—even at the cost of lower efficacy/efficiency.

4. The tasks/functions independently assigned to the set of common EU institutions are sufficiently interdependent in their effects that they cannot be performed alone without incurring increasing costs or diminishing returns.

   *4.1. Ergo*, whatever the initial intentions, there will be a tendency to 'spill-over' within each function, as well as across them, and, hence, an (uneven) trend toward task expansion in both scope and level of authority.

*4.2.* *Ergo*, the principals will resist this trend as much as they can, at least until awareness of the unintended and unwanted consequences begins to affect key domestic publics or the wider national citizenry who will mobilize collectively—both for and against the integration process—and, thereby, threaten what has already been accomplished.

*4.3.* When this politicization reaches the level that it jeopardizes their tenure in office, the national governments/principals will prefer greater task expansion to contraction, but will seek to disperse its effects across a multiplicity of EU institutions—each with its surrounding system of inter-level negotiation.

5. The member states of the EU were of uneven size, varying capability, and different socio-economic composition at its point of departure and, thanks to enlargement, this diversity has increased over time—despite considerable convergence in their macro-economic performances.

*5.1.* *Ergo*, their initial governance arrangements reflected this diversity, as have subsequent ones—only more so.

*5.2.* *Ergo*, the main consequence of this is the systematic over-representation of smaller member states—and the average member state has tended to get even smaller over time.

*5.3.* *Ergo*, smaller (and, to a lesser extent, less developed) member states tend to prefer greater delegation of authority to common institutions in general (and the Commission, in particular), but they also insist on their (disproportionately) 'fair share' of voting weights, structural funds, institution sites, etc.

6. The integration strategy initially chosen (the so-called Monnet Method and the only viable one at the time) was based on segmented interaction between a privileged set of actors—mostly, upper-level national bureaucrats, Commission officials, and business interest representatives.

*6.1.* *Ergo*, those institutions that might have represented larger numbers of citizens and a wider range of their interests were excluded from the process and have subsequently found it difficult to gain access.

*6.2.* *Ergo*, those most closely involved tended to represent highly specialized (and relatively less visible) constituencies and this was reflected in a highly compartmentalized decision-making structure within and across EU institutions.

*6.3.* *Ergo*, those political mechanisms that led to the break-up of MLG and PCG in previous federations or confederations—namely, the formation of national party systems and comprehensive nationalist ideologies (not to mention, revolutions)—have had little opportunity to emerge in the EU.

*6.4.* Also, the non-decision to include security issues from the initial (and, so far, subsequent) stages of the integration process, deprived the emerging EU-polity of the coercive mechanisms that elsewhere promoted greater administrative uniformity and concentration of governmental authority at the national level—namely, military mobilization and centralized taxation.

7. The EU may be unique as a polity—precisely, because of its extreme reliance on MLG and PCG—but it is sensitive to broader trends in government and governance that are affecting the 'domestic democracies' of its member states. Indeed, one could describe the EU as the *reductio ad absurdum* of such trends.

    *7.1. Ergo*, the trend toward delegating tasks to 'guardian institutions' (central banks, regulatory commissions, autonomous agencies, etc.) at the national and sub-national levels of member states will be imitated at the supranational level.

    *7.2. Ergo*, the observed decline in partisan identification and electoral turnout in its member states will make it even more difficult to create a viable party system in the EU.

    *7.3. Ergo*, the national trends toward decline in political trust, loyalty to traditional institutions, and symbols of legitimacy will not only be reflected at the supranational level but magnified—given that the EU has never had a historical 'stock' of these properties to draw upon.

## The basic assumptions of neo-neofunctionalism

In the following (and at the risk of self-referential anachronism), I will take a text that I wrote in 1969 and revise it in the light of over forty years of European integration.[6] To differentiate the revised from the original, I will indicate with an ellipsis ( . . .) when I have exorcised something, and use italics when I am citing directly from the old text.

    (1) *The integration of formally independent political entities engages—in the contemporary world—basically the same variables and processes. These can be specified by induction from existing empirical research and can be understood in a probabilistic sense by means of a single analytical model. Variable values will . . . differ, as will outcomes; but the integration process is structurally similar in all such settings. (a) This does not mean that in all contexts variables will produce 'the same effect, marginal or absolute. . . . (b) Nor does it imply necessarily that the same variable will be equally consequential throughout the integration process . . . (c) The specification of operative variables in the form of a model does not mean that only these are relevant to understanding integration outcomes. Variation in other variables can also cause variation in the caused variable without falsifying the causal law. Any given dependent variable may be involved in a large number of causal laws.[7] . . .*

    *With these caveats protecting me I would, however, readily concede that if the specified operative conditions were to prove irrelevant in a given integrative context (for example, if transactions increased but were not associated with any change in perceived inequalities or the formation of regional interest groups) or that if actor strategies were to change significantly in the absence of variation in the specified variables (such as would occur if regional institutions were permitted to augment their authoritative control over member policies without any prior variation in perceived inequalities, regional group activity, common identitive appeal, deliberate manipulative attempts by regional technocrats, or sensitivity to deterioration in international status), something is very likely wrong with the model!*

(2)  *The theory proposed herein is—like all social theories—composed of variables and hypotheses about variable relationships. A variable is a concept which can have various values and which is defined in such a way that one can tell by means of observations which value it has in a particular occurrence.*[8] *As such, variables are observer-invented orderings of facts and perceptions, not the physical occurrences themselves. Nor are they necessarily the categories with which actors order and explain their behaviour. . . . Even more confusingly, these concepts are usually summations or aggregate evaluations of complex, interrelated behaviours. Such classifications, rankings or scorings pose a major operational difficulty for this (and many other) theories. Unclear definitions and failure to specify how the multiple observations are to be collapsed into a single assessment have plagued comparative research and made intersubjective reliability poor* and my perception is that this problem has gotten worse rather than better as the integration process itself has become more complex.

(3)  *The basic causal imagery . . . is functionalist. As Arthur Stinchcombe has so cogently exposed, the structure of such an explanation is one in which 'the consequences of some behavior or social arrangement are essential elements of the causes of that behavior'.*[9] *In this conception of the integration process national units originally adopt strategies of action which converge in the establishment of some permanent regional institution(s) for the purpose of attaining certain common objectives. The attainment of these objectives is made difficult by the presence of certain tensions or, better, contradictions. The latter are a specific sort of tension-producing conditions that are generated by the integration process itself, i.e. by the collective attempt to obtain the initial objectives. Summarizing (and hypothesizing), these basic contradictions are:*

(a)  *uncertainty with regard to the capacity to guarantee relative equality of perceived benefits once new productive and distributive forces are unleashed (**equity**);*

(b)  *impossibility of maintaining prolonged separability of different issue areas in a complex, interdependent policy matrix (**engrenage**);*

(c)  *difficulty in isolating joint regional deliberations from a context of global socioeconomic dependence (**externalization**);*

(d)  *heightened sensitivity to the comparative performance of one's 'partners' generated by higher transactions and available information (**envy**).*

*The consequences produced by this 'competition' between regional institutions and exogenous tensions or process-generated contradictions 'feeds back' to the regional institutions. In the event that the policy-making forum originally established is sufficiently resourceful and flexible to handle the consequences and sustain satisfactory performance toward the attainment of common objectives, a self-maintaining international subsystem is likely to emerge. I have labelled this integrative outcome: 'encapsulation'.* In other words, the normal outcome of international cooperation between consenting adult states to resolve common problems should be a self-contained 'service-oriented' organization that neither expands its tasks nor changes the 'sovereign stateness' of its members. The contemporary international system is replete with hundreds, if not thousands, of such 'regimes' at the regional and global levels. Only in exceptional circumstances will such an initial convergence produce a collectivity that will succeed in breaking out of its capsule and it is the function of a theory of regional integration to specify what these are.

*If . . . as a result of the consequences of trying to reach these initial objectives, the performance of the regional organization is inadequate, actors may be forced to revise their strategies and to consider alternative integrative obligations, i.e. they may re-evaluate the level and/or scope of their commitment to regional institutions and they may even come adopt a new set of common objectives*, e.g. change from economic to political integration. 'Transcendence' has been accomplished in the exotic lexicon of this theory. This particular 'success syndrome' is only one of several possible outcomes . . . and not a very probable one at that. They might just as well have chosen to 'spill-back' . . . and withdraw from their original objective, downgrading their commitment to mutual cooperation. What makes the difference is what neo- and neo-neofunctionalism tries to specify. Its answer to whether 'spill-over' into new tasks or level of authority will occur is: it depends! Not that it has to happen or that it will automatically happen.

*. . . This functionalist imagery can . . . be falsified. For example, if the role of a regional organization changes in the absence of a prior increase in tensions, it hardly seems warranted to classify it as a functional consequence. Or, if one or more of the contradictions listed should appear and there is forthcoming neither more 'compensatory' activity . . . nor some alternative search behaviour, the basic functionalist assumption is false.* The above discussion should make clear one of *the major . . . options of this theory: the selection of the dependent variable. All its effort focuses upon an attempt to specify for the past and predict for the future the conditions under which the consequences generated by prior joint decisions will lead to* **a redefinition of actor strategies vis-à-vis the scope and level of regional decision-making.** *Whether member states will expand or contract the type of issues to be resolved jointly (scope) or whether they will increase or decrease the authority for regional institutions to allocate values (level) are the two basic dimensions of the dependent variable, and . . . they are by no means always covariant.*

Neofunctionalism (and neo-neofunctionalism) . . . *is an eminently political theory of integration which asks not whether 'artificial' barriers to exchange are decreasing, resources being more efficiently distributed, or peoples growing to like each other more and more, but what kind of a strategy politically relevant actors are likely to adopt in a given context. These other conditions of economic and social integration do, of course, form important elements in the model, but as independent and intervening, not dependent, variables.*

*(4) Certain variables have been deliberately excluded. These have been historically operative in integration processes and, in fact, play a prominent role in other theoretical formulations.*[10] *Their presence is regarded to be either unlikely in contemporary settings or so disturbing as to call for a very different conceptual formulation.*

(a) *The first of these is the postulated or assumed absence of conquest or organized physical violence on the part of one member or group of members to enforce compliance with regional decisions or to compel changes in the strategy of other participants. This, in other words, is a model pertaining to the peaceful and voluntary transformation of international systems. It does not, of course, exclude the relevance of 'bluff, bombast and brinkmanship' in actor styles, but physical coercion to enforce regional decisions would make the model irrelevant.*

(b) *'Irrational' postures or strategies—whether for dogmatic/ideological or personal/ emotive reasons—are never absent from social action, even at the international level, but they are from this theory. They fit very uncomfortably within it. 'Instant brotherhood' as a motive and 'all or nothing' as a strategy make its operation exceedingly difficult. Unless some policy area can initially be separated out as jointly manipulable and unless some possibility of subsequent compromise involving tradeoffs or side payments exists, international integration, as conceived herein, is not likely to occur. The model assumes that integration is basically (but not exclusively) a rational process whereby actors calculate anticipated returns from various alternative strategies of participation in joint decision-making structures.* More recently, this has been called the 'soft rationality' assumption by Ernst B. Haas.[11]

(c) *None of this excludes integration movements from 'infringing' upon the symbolic and emotional areas of so-called 'high politics'. Nevertheless, . . . the margin for peaceful manoeuvrability in these 'indivisible' arenas is very limited and most international organizations . . . are likely to get encapsulated long before they reach such sensitive issues.*

## Some critical afterthoughts

Now that we have almost fifty years of experience with European integration, i.e. since the founding of the Coal and Steel Community in 1952, it is possible to discern where specific neofunctionalist assumptions proved weaker than expected and where 'non-assumptions' were made about phenomena that nonetheless contributed to the outcome as we know it today:

(1) The processes of functional interdependence took more time to emerge and, especially, to assert themselves than initially anticipated.

(2) One reason for this is that collective organization across national borders proved more difficult and uneven from sector to sector and class to class than expected —and some of this had (ironically) to do with the corporatist rather than pluralist nature of the national systems involved.

(3) The activist role 'assigned' to the secretariat of regional institutions, i.e. the EU Commission, was only sporadically filled and more contingent upon personal factors, i.e. who occupied its presidency and how much support he received from key member states, than originally thought.

(4) Moreover, it was erroneous to presume that all extensions of policy scope and authoritative *compétences* would accrue to the Commission and that, therefore, this institution would provide the nucleus of a future supranational state.

(5) One major reason for several of these misunderstandings was the completely 'un-theorized' and, nevertheless, significant impact of enlargement to include new member states whose entry inevitably imposed changes in decision-making rules and upset prevailing informal practices.

(6) Although the neo-version paid more attention to it, the external context sur-rounding the process of regional integration had more of an effect than was initially specified—whether due to 'exogenous shocks' that had little or nothing to do with exchanges within the region, or to gradual shifts in policy paradigms that came from the United States, i.e. the displacement of Keynesianism by neo-liberalism.

(7) By concentrating so exclusively on interdependencies rooted in production and exchange and, hence, on the role of European interest politics, neofunctionalists tended to discount the significance of decisions taken and precedents set by the European Court of Justice. This court's assertion of the primacy of Community law—in effect, converting the Treaty of Rome into a proto-Constitution for Europe—and its imaginative interpretations of specific treaty provisions made a major (if unexpected) contribution to the assertion of EU supra-nationality.[12]

(8) Although they anticipated resistance from national authorities, neofunctionalists may have underestimated its strength in some cases and they definitely failed to anticipate the extent to which Heads of State and Government would play an increasingly direct role by creating the European Council.

(9) Finally, neofunctionalism misjudged the role of politicization. Not only did it come much later than it 'should' have, but when it did, it proved to be more anti- than pro-integration. Moreover, instead of strengthening the role of pan-European political parties, it has weakened them and had a disintegrative impact upon national party systems. Needless to say, if this theoretical approach is to be updated and re-equipped to deal with the contemporary EU, the neo-neo-version will have to take a serious look at these issues.

## The ontology of neo-neofunctionalism

As befits a transformative theory, functionalism and its neo-versions are themselves transformative, that is to say, they specify conditions under which the identity of actors and their relationships change in the course of the integration process. When these conditions are favourable (admittedly, not often the case), it even predicts its own 'obsolescence', i.e. its transformation into a revised version of itself.[13]

In the early Mitrany version, the model was quite simple. As the result of expert cooperation across borders to solve a growing set of common problems, the loyalty of beneficiaries would shift—thereby, making cooperation easier and more efficient over time. Eventually, there would come a moment of 'transcendence' in which the sum of loyalties and expectations in transnational functional arrangements would greatly exceed those lodged in national political authorities and a new global (for Mitrany) or regional (for his successors) polity would assert its supremacy.

The neo- and the neo-neo-versions insert many more stages or levels of transformation and are much more sensitive to the likely resistance of national politicians and citizens whose careers and loyalties are at least as determined by emotions and symbols as by functional satisfactions. Nevertheless, these neo-versions postulate an underlying sequence (admittedly of indeterminate length) whereby organizational roles, efforts at collective action, and actor conceptions of interest shift from the national to the supranational level. This does not happen 'automatically', as in the original model, but requires a considerable amount of political action and that is usually associated with a crisis in the integration process. Its previous functioning has failed to meet expectations, generated a distribution of benefits that is not voluntarily acceptable, and/or produced negative externalities that can no longer be ignored. Regardless of their initial intentions (and what they have placed in the documentary record), the national actors have to reassess the level and scope of their regional institutions. They can, of course, decide to withdraw from joint obligations ('spill-back') or they could try to survive without changing institutions ('muddle-about'), but the macro-hypothesis of neo- and neo-neofunctionalist theory is that, under certain conditions, they will prefer to resolve these crises by expanding their mutual obligations ('spill-over'), rather than contracting or just reasserting them.

From such a perspective, *the process whereby an emerging regional centre gains or loses in the scope or level of its authority vis-à-vis pre-existent national centres is best conceived as involving a series of crisis-provoked decisional cycles.* These recurrent cycles of activity, generated by endogenous contradictions and/or exogenous tensions, compel national and regional authorities to revise their respective strategies and, collectively, to determine whether the new joint institution(s) will expand or contract. The basic structure of the neo-neo-model, therefore, *consists not of a single continuum or even of a multitude of continua, nor does it involve any assumptions about automatic, cumulative and irreversible progress toward a single goal. Successive cycles of induced decision-making may involve complex movements 'upward' and 'downward' simultaneously in different issue areas. Various strategies, national and regional, may be adopted and various outcomes or endpoints are possible and even likely. Once, however, a given regional process of regional integration fails to generate or respond to crises, it has disintegrated; if it responds by reasserting previous strategies, it has reached a state of stable self-maintenance ('encapsulation').*

## The macro-hypotheses of neo-neofunctionalism

*The following macro-hypotheses should be relevant (and potentially falsifiable) throughout the integration process, i.e. during all of its decision-making cycles. The first two . . . are derived from the basic functionalist causal imagery discussed above.*

(1) *Tensions from the global environment and/or contradictions generated by past performance give rise to unexpected performance in the pursuit of agreed-upon common objectives. These frustrations and/or dissatisfactions are likely to result in the search for alternative means for reaching the same goals, i.e. to induce actors to revise their respective strategies vis-à-vis the scope and level of regional decision-making. This is the basic functionalist proposition, called 'the spill-over hypothesis' by me in a previous article.[14] . . .*

(2) *In their search among alternatives, national actors will tend to arrive at that institutional solution (in terms of scope and level) which will meet minimal common objectives despite prevailing tensions and will subsequently seek to seal the regional organization off as much as possible from its environment, thereby adopting a self-maintaining set of institutional norms. This 'hypothesis of natural entropy' suggests that all integration processes will tend toward a state of rest or stagnation—unless disturbed by exceptional (i.e. unintended) endogenous outcomes or exogenous conditions not present in the original convergence or . . . institutions themselves. Expressed in terms of strategies, the highest probability is that in any decisional cycle the actors will opt for encapsulation rather than spill-over, spill-around, buildup, or spill-back.*

(3) *In those cases where strong exogenous tensions and/or powerful internal contradictions (the independent variables in the model seek to predict these conditions) force successive 'upward' evaluations of strategy, i.e. tend to involve more national actors in an expanding variety of policy areas and increasing degree of joint decision-making, costs and resistances are likely to increase. The 'politicization hypothesis' refers . . . to this process whereby the controversiality of joint decision-making goes up.*

(4) *This in turn is likely to lead to a widening of the audience or clientele interested and active in integration. Somewhere along the line, a manifest redefinition of mutual objectives will probably occur (transcendence) . . . Ultimately, one could hypothesize that there will be a shift in actor expectations and loyalty toward the new regional centre. Nevertheless, it seems worth repeating that only in exceptional, i.e. high scoring, circumstances is such a cumulative process to be anticipated. Normally, the response by established national officials to higher costs and wider publics will be entropy.*

(5) *The integration process begins with a large number of unspecified exogenous conditions that are very important in determining outcomes. Idiosyncratic and random variables play their most important roles before the consequences of regional decisions have begun to affect national structures and values. . . . The model is, therefore, a very poor predictor of the initiation of integration movements and of the consequences of their first decisional cycles. It does not purport to synthesize such sufficient causes. If, however, it has any analytical validity, the residual proportion of variance attributable to these idiosyncratic and random events should decline. In other words, predictability should increase with successive 'upward-grading' cycles*

*as the movement approaches a political community. I grant that when applied to integration schemes which encapsulate early and/or whose decisions are so limited in scope or ineffectual in authority that they have little or no impact upon changes at the national or regional level, the model may never prove very predictive of changes in actor strategy. One might call this: the 'hypothesis of increasing mutual determination'.*

(6) *External conditions begin, as do all the independent ('background') variables, as 'givens'. While the changes in national structures and values become at least partially predictable as consequences of regional decisions, the global position and the dependent client status of member states and regions as a whole continue to be exogenously determined for a longer time. Nevertheless, integrating units will find themselves increasingly compelled—regardless of original intentions—to adopt common policies vis-à-vis non-participant third parties. This 'externalization hypothesis' predicts that external conditions will become less exogenously determined if integrative rather than disintegrative strategies are commonly adopted. The 'independent' role of these conditions should decline as integration proceeds until joint negotiation vis-à-vis outsiders has become such an integral part of the decisional process that the international system accords the new unit full participant status.*

(7) *At each decisional cycle, actors will be induced to reconsider their respective strategies of participation. What influences (and predicts) the result of these 'policy reconsiderations' is a central concern of the neo-neo-model. Of equal interest are the questions of how these conditions combine and what sort of a formula is used in weighing their marginal contribution to the position finally adopted. As a first guess, I would advance 'the hypothesis of additivity', namely, that actor perceptions of the impact of regional processes enter into their calculations of interest, as do variables in a stepwise multiple regression equation,—one at a 'time with—each successive one contributing (positively or negatively) to the prediction of a remaining portion of the variance. Frankly, I suspect this to be an excessive simplification in that the simultaneous presence of certain variables, e.g. strong perceptions of inequality coupled with low rates of transnational group formation, is likely to have an interactive or multiplicative effect on the type of strategy chosen—in this case, to make it much more likely to opt for one of the disintegrative strategies. . . .*

(8) *One must never forget that international integration is an innovative and experimental process. It takes place in an ambiance of considerable uncertainty and trepidation in which negotiating actors can rarely be sure of the probable effect of their joint 'solutions' on established interests and statuses. In some cases they are venturing into policy areas not previously handled at the national level; in all cases they are creating new channels of influence and new reward systems. Under these conditions even 'good' performance, e.g. more transactions, greater equality, more internal pluralism, etc., can become upsetting when it outruns expectations and the capacity to absorb change gradually.*

(9) *Another way of stating this is that the relationship between indicators of change at the national and regional level is likely to be curvilinear or, better, parabolic. Up to a point, the relation between change processes and integrative strategies is probably linear, e.g. increases in commercial transactions are positively associated with increases in regional group formation or mutual identity. When, however, changes are so rapid and large in magnitude as to clog existing channels of communication or confound existing categories of evaluation, then actors are liable to react defensively, if not negatively. They are getting too much of a good thing but not knowing what to do with it or how to react to it. My field work on integration among less developed countries convinced me that the parabolic effect of independent and dependent variables is particularly crucial there, as the whole governing system has a very limited capacity for absorbing change, even 'good' change. This 'hypothesis of curvilinearity' complicates the model-building exercise but, I would argue, is a necessary concession to reality.*

# A self-transforming neo-neofunctionalism model

The neo-neofunctionalist model . . . *constitutes an open system of explanation in the sense that antecedent conditions are not perfect or even exclusive predictors of subsequent ones. Error variables—some exogenous, others random values of endogenous variables— are present throughout the model although according to the 'hypothesis of increasing mutual determination', these should decline with successive positive resolutions of decisional crises.* By now, the process of European integration should have reached this stage and, therefore, if the variables specified in this model produce no effect or an effect contrary to the expected one, then, the theory would be false. *For example, the model hypothesizes that the combined effect of changes in relative size/power, changes in the rate of transactions, and changes in internal pluralism plus some external factors should 'predict' the perceived equity in the distribution of benefits. This intermediate outcome . . . in turn helps predict . . . changes in national actor strategies. In each case the prediction is probabilistic, i.e. it estimates a mean change in the dependent variable, and incomplete, i.e. it includes an . . . error variable.*

## The notion of 'decision cycles'

In the earlier version, I began with so-called 'initiation cycles' that are present at the very beginning of an integration process. Needless to say, the present European Union has passed through these and has long since gone into what I called the 'priming cycles'. By my calculation as many as five of these have already occurred. So far, however, none has produced self-encapsulation. Some long periods of stasis, yes, but always followed by a wider and sometimes deeper commitment to common objectives. Each cycle has generated further imbalances and contradictions, and the institutional equilibrium that presumably lies at the end is not yet in sight. It is possible that the so-called 'Convention' might generate such an outcome, i.e. delimit definitively the territorial scope of the Euro-polity, define the nature and scope of common institutions, and assign these functions (*compétences*) to specific levels of governance. If the EU were at this point in its evolution (which I doubt), it would presently be in what I will call below: a 'transforming cycle'.

In this abbreviated version, I will only discuss the 'priming' and 'transforming' models. The reader is reminded that most of this text was written in 1969—long before the actual controversies were in sight. Those who are interested in applying neo-neofunctionalism to more recent and uncertain integration arrangements outside Europe, e.g. MERCOSUL, ASEAN, and even the African Union that was created only a very short time ago, should consult the original article in *International Organization* where the earlier models of 'initiating cycles' are specified.

## Priming cycle(s)

Analysis of a priming cycle first depends on an assessment of changes at the level of national member states since the last decision cycle. Presumably, these define the context of the crisis that is compelling actors to change their strategies.

(1) *Differences in Relative Size/Power: changes (since last cycle) in relative rankings or subsequent deviations from the regional mean for individual units, as well as changes in overall rank incongruence across all units for the region. . . .*

(2) *Differences in Rates of Transactions: changes in extent of interdependence of member states in economic, social, and cultural exchanges within, as contrasted to outside, the region. . . .*

(3) *Differences in Member Internal Pluralism: changes either in the number and coverage of interest associations or in their freedom to articulate demands. . . .*

(4) *Differences in Élite Value Complementarity: differences in the mobilization of group expectations and evaluations (pro and con) vis-à-vis regional integration on the part of newly affected groups and/or previously engaged élites. . . .*

(5) *Differences in Extra-regional Dependence: changes in the extent to which member states and the region as a whole are subjected to asymmetric constraints by actors outside the region that reduce their capacity for independent, national, decision-making. . . .*

The major difference between 'initiating' and 'priming' cycles, however, comes from the rising importance of distinctive regional processes. With each successive crisis resolved as the common institutions emerge from the initiation cycles, regional-level rules and distributions gain in significance to the point that they begin to overshadow the opinions and actions of national governments, associations, and individuals.

These variables can be summarized as follows:

(1) *Equitable Distribution of Benefits: change in the extent to which costs and benefits accruing from regionally induced transactions are perceived as being reciprocally distributed among participants. . . .*

(2) *Regional Group Formation:* pattern of *formation and active participation of new non-governmental or quasi-governmental organizations representing some or all members* across national borders *and designed explicitly to promote the interest of classes, sectors, professions, and causes at the regional . . . levels. . . .*

(3) *Development of Regional Identity: extent to which participants in regional processes come to regard such activity as rewarding due to material inducements, emotional-fraternal-symbolic ties, status satisfactions, etc., and, thereby, acquire a larger sense of loyalty. . . .*

(4) *Regional Reform-mongering: degree to which actors employed by or closely associated with the new regional institutions engage actively and deliberately in the promotion of new policies by anticipation, i.e. on the basis of an intellectual or technical calculation before such measures are demanded or opposed by aroused interest representatives, or politicians. . . .*

(5) *International Status Effect: extent to which the relative standing of individual countries or the region as a whole is perceived as dependent upon the performance of regional institutions. . . .*

## Bivariate hypotheses concerning the priming cycle(s)

(1) *The less change in the relative size and power of national actors (vis-à-vis each other), the more likely that perception of benefits will be equitable.*

(2) *The greater and more varied the changes in rates of transaction, the higher is the likely rate of regional group formation and the more rapid is the development of a distinctive regional identity likely to be.*

(3) *The greater the increase in internal pluralism within and across member states, the more likely are transnational groups to form and are regional identities to emerge.*

(4) *The more complementary élites come to acquire similar expectations and attitudes toward the integration process, the easier it will be to form transnational associations and to accept regional identities. Similarly, their joint sensitivity to variations in international status is likely to become stronger.*

(5) *The greater the previous scope and level of regional institutions and the more 'upward-grading' their decisional style, the more likely are regional bureaucrats to engage in reform-mongering. . . .*

(6) *The effect of changes in extra-regional dependence seems particularly paradoxical or parabolic. Both the marked rise or decline in global economic dependence may heighten sensitivity to international status. In the former case new regional institutions may come to be regarded as the only bulwark of defence against further*

*deterioration; in the latter they may be at least partially credited with the relative success. Specific attempts by extra-regional authorities to influence the integration process likewise may have a dual effect.*

(7) *Actors who perceive their returns from integration as equitable—in line with anticipated returns and in proportion to those of others—will not re-evaluate their integrative strategies (unless forced to do so by less satisfied actors) and eventually will opt for encapsulation. Only actors dissatisfied with the equity of returns will promote or reconsider alternative strategies. Within a certain negative range the most likely response is a positive one—push the process into new areas or provide central decision-makers with more resources or authority to redistribute returns. Beyond that negative range, the response will probably be negative in either scope or level or both.*

(8) *The greater the coverage, density, participation, vitality, and autonomy of regional interest associations, the greater the propensity for overcoming national resistance to expansions in scope and/or level.*

(9) *The greater the development of a distinctive regional identity and the wider its distribution across classes and corporate groups, the more likely national actors will be able to build supportive coalitions for pro-integrative strategies.*

(10) *The greater the reform-mongering activism of regional bureaucrats, the greater the likelihood of pro-integrative strategies being adopted. . . .*

(11) *The greater the perceived effect of participation in a regional organization upon enhancing international status, the greater the propensity for devolving new obligations upon that organization.*

These have been a selection of the most obvious bivariate relationships in the model during the priming cycle(s). All seem to be at least potentially falsifiable, and many probably would be falsified if one could only examine them in such a discrete, bivariate setting. Given the limited number of cases and the tendency for everything to be changing at once, this condition seems difficult to satisfy.[15] A more productive research strategy would seem to be to pass directly to multivariate, interactive relationships, i.e. to admit the intrinsic complexity of the subject matter.

## Multivariate hypotheses concerning the priming cycle(s)

(1) *Prior changes in national structures/values jointly influence the extent of variation in regional processes, but they do so in different respective proportions. Some, in other words, contribute more to understanding or predicting subsequent changes at the transnational level than others, but their marginal contribution will vary in different regional settings (for example, among less rather than more developed countries). . . .*

(2) *If no changes in the specific national structures/values are forthcoming or, . . . if the scores are asynchronic, . . . there should be no change in the regional processes and, subsequently, no inducement to change national actor strategies. The model*

*would continue to cycle until this entropic condition stabilized (encapsulation) or until new national structures/values were . . . sufficient . . . to induce strategic redefinitions.*

(3) *Asynchrony in rates of change at the national level sets up—due to their differing marginal impacts—asynchrony in rates of regional change. This, in turn, enhances the probability that less convergent, and possibly divergent, actor strategies will be promoted and this makes the adoption of a joint policy vector more and more difficult.*

(4) *Also, asynchronic change at the regional level . . . enhances politicization, i.e. greater controversiality among already involved actors and the mobilization of wider audiences. Particularly crucial to this is the generally very slow rate with which a distinctive regional identity emerges.*

(5) *The 'peculiar' configuration in the model of Regional Reform-mongering intro- duces the possibility that anticipating, calculating Eurocrats will be able to promote a disparity between changes at the two levels—the national and the regional. During these priming cycles, their activities are limited, on the one hand, by the reduced authority and resources of regional institutions and, on the other, by the relatively undifferentiated nature of national actors. Of course, . . . they may be aided and abetted in their efforts by extra-regional support.*

(6) *During one of these priming cycles, . . . one should be able to discern the first signs of externalization—of conscious attempts by regional 'partners' to bring . . . Extra- Regional Dependence under their partial . . . control. The greater the initial scope and level and the more 'progressive' the decision-making style, the more intensive will be the effect of regional decisions on external dependence. The success or failure of these efforts will in turn have an important impact on the international status of the movement.*

(7) *Regional change processes 'inter-determine' national actor strategies or better, they set certain parameters within which alternative strategies are selected. . . .* Contrary to intergovernmentalism which postulates that these strategies for pursuing the (allegedly) unitary national interest will only be determined by 'domestic actors', this theory stresses the extent to which such strategies may come to be influenced by transnational (regional or global) actors.

(8) *During the initiation cycle(s), the probability that a given national actor will push a spill-over policy is relatively low . . . if only because initial insecurity and mistrust of partners is likely to make all negotiators more cautious.* Outside Western Europe, the scores are likely to be so low and so asynchronic that they never manage to generate much change in regional processes and, therefore, sufficient 'steam' for a simultaneous leap forward in the level and scope of common institutions. This was a conclusion I drew from research in Central America (CACOM) and Latin America (ALALC) during the 1960s and I find no reason to expect anything different from more recent experiences in Africa.

This probability changes, however, during the priming cycles. As regional processes begin to have a greater effect, *national actors may become more receptive to changing the authority and compétences of regional institutions. 'Spill-around'*—the proliferation of functionally specialized, independent, but strictly intergovernmental organizations—*is a particularly attractive and easy strategy . . . due to the ready availability of a large number of unexploited and relatively non-controversial policy areas. 'Build-up'*—the concession by member states of greater authority to a regional organization without expanding its mandate—*is more difficult . . . because of the 'untried' capacity of such a newly formed organization. It may prove more attractive where a competent but encapsulated one already exists and where its members are strongly but unequally affected by regional changes in a single sector. Disintegrative ('spill-back') strategies are, of course, less costly early in the process due to lower sunken costs, less entrenched patterns of benefit and weaker symbolic engagement. It is the most likely strategy for an actor weakly affected by regional group formation, the development of regional identity and the international status effect, but highly sensitive to perceptions of inequity on comparative rate of return.* Characteristically, this takes the form of a single country defecting and, thereby, bringing the entire process of regional integration to a halt.

But the most likely strategy to prevail, once the priming cycles have kicked in, is 'spill-over'. Herein lies the core dynamic of neo- (and neo-neo-) functionalism —namely, that the regional processes mentioned above will dispose national actors to resolve their inevitable dissatisfactions by increasing both the level and the scope of common institutions.

*Most international/regional integration arrangements will not make it this far. Limited in initial scope to narrow policy areas or grudgingly conceded very modest authoritative competence, their activities . . . will have little subsequent impact. Some reciprocal distribution of benefits will eventually be established; . . . a cluster of surrounding clients will become satisfied with the existing level of services performed and grow wary of risking that for possibly greater but less certain future returns; socialization effects will be confined to a small bureaucratic clique, itself devoted to avoiding change in established procedures; extra-regional actors accommodate and come to regard the arrangement as an unobjectionable given.* Large numbers of these encapsulated functionalist organizations persist in the international environment. By 'doing their own thing' and providing marginal, but often important, services to their clients, they contribute more to reproducing than transforming the existing nation state system.

## Transformative cycle(s)

Only regional integration experiments that make it through the priming cycles are likely to transform themselves into something qualitatively different. They will have exhausted the potentialities inherent in functionally integrating their economies and dedicate more and more of their efforts to functionally integrating their polities. In the jargon of Mitrany's functionalism, they will 'transcend' their initial commitment. In the jargon of Euro-speak, they will, at long last, define their *finalité politique*.

Needless to say, any theory about how (not to mention, when) this happens has to be purely speculative. No existing nation state integrated itself in this fashion. They all used other means: war, revolution, dynastic marriage, anti-colonial struggle, and so forth. The European Union is, at the present moment, the only plausible candidate for entering this transformative cycle by cultivating complex interdependence, negotiating a sequence of voluntary (and unanimous) agreements, and foregoing even the threat of using force to produce a successful outcome.

And it is debatable whether the EU has yet arrived at this threshold. *Pace* numerous journalistic (and a few scholarly) accounts, it is not in that deep a crisis. The margin for the further exploitation of functional interdependencies has not been exhausted—just think of the potential spill-overs inherent in such fields as energy, communications, financial services, transport, air traffic control, *e così via*. Politicization at the national and sub-national level has undoubtedly made it difficult to reach agreement on these (and other) issues and even more difficult to ratify the subsequent treaties, but there is virtually no sign that groups mobilized for and against further integration are clamouring for a comprehensive political solution. Admittedly, Eastern enlargement will be a tough nut to crack and will upset many existing decision rules and substantive policies, but will it be sufficient to trigger a major reform in EU institutions, *pace* the Convention? Academics have been complaining about the 'democracy deficit' for some time, but mass publics still seem quite indifferent (if not hostile) to the prospect of extending democratic practices to the scale of Europe as a whole.

If (and I repeat, if ) the European Union has already entered or is about to enter into a transformative cycle, what processes might operate to bring this about? The higher order hypothesis of neo-neofunctionalism is that this will not come from below, i.e. from a convergence of changes in national institutions and interests, but from above, i.e. from innovations in exchanges and power relations at the regional level.

(1) *The first major innovation would be an increase in the 'reform-mongering' role of regional bureaucrats within the EU institutions. Their capacity and resources augmented by previous re-definitions of scope and level, they are more likely to step up their efforts at directly influencing regional processes, even bypassing intervening changes at the national level. By negotiating directly with regional NGOs (and sub-national governments), by inventing and promoting new symbols of regional identity, and by bargaining as representatives for the region as a whole with outsiders, they could begin to affect virtually all these processes rather than, as during the priming cycles, being confined to a few of them.*

(2) *Regional institutions are also most likely during this cycle to begin in earnest their attempts at externalization. Their extended scope and level plus the previously recorded and consolidated strength of regional change processes provide the internal resources for such an effort; the impact of regional discrimination on*

*non-participants is likely to provide the external stimulus. These outsiders are going to begin to insist on treating the region as a new international bargaining unit* and may even insist that it shoulder additional responsibilities in such areas as defence and security. . . .

(3) *A new regional change process could well emerge. Let us call it, the Domestic Status Effect. The redefined scope/level of regional institutions will tend to affect relative status and influence in the domestic politics of its member states. Ministries, autonomous agencies, associations and parties that have 'gotten in on' the earlier rounds of regional decision-making will have acquired more resources (proportion of the budget, regulatory capacity, international status, votes, etc.). This should cause other national institutions to try to 'get in on' the operation, although not necessarily in support of it. A good deal of this 'fall-out,' as I have called this process elsewhere, may be purely symbolic, but at some point virtually all political and administrative organizations at the national level will have to have their respective 'integration policies'.*

(4) *The most important structural transformation in the model during this stage should occur in the nature of national actors. Up to this point, they have been treated as units with a single integrative or disintegrative strategy during any crisis. Now they begin to appear as differentiated actors, as a plurality of negotiating units (classes, status groups, sub-regions, clientelas, bureaucratic agencies, ideological clusters, etc.). This fragmentation depends, in large measure, upon the degree of prior change in regional group formation and the emergence of a new, superimposed wider identity.*

(5) *These fragmented actors will begin to form stable 'transnational coalitions' of support and opposition for particular measures. The policy that emerges at the EU level becomes the product of alliances that cut across national boundaries (and, perhaps, historic national cleavages). National governmental actors will, no doubt, continue to play the formally preponderant role in the concatenation of strategies at the regional level, but increasingly they can be circumscribed, if not circumvented, by coalitions of other governmental and non-governmental actors with regional officials.*

(6) *The combination of increased activism by Eurocrats, their efforts at trying to gain full actor status in the international domain, the spread of interest by 'fall-out', the emerging . . . fragmentation of national actors, and the formation of stable transnational coalitions—all make the transforming cycle the most controversial and complex moment in the process of supranational integration. Moreover, these changes are likely to be asynchronic. The bypassing of prior changes at the national level (especially at the level of loyalty and legitimacy), the resistance to activism on the part of regional bureaucrats unaccountable to the citizenry, the reaction of governmental decision-makers to the erosion of their monopolistic control over certain policy areas . . . have an enormous potential for generating conflict (and encouraging defection by particular countries).*[16]

(7) *In terms of joint strategies, spill-over seems increasingly likely to occur either as the result of package deals designed to appeal to a broad transnational coalition of interests or as necessary accommodation to the region's new status as a 'global player'.* Such a compromised solution with its simultaneous payoffs in terms of both new policy arenas and additional authority for regional institutions may be the only 'peaceful' way to deal with the increased conflict potential— without jeopardizing what has already been accomplished and what no one wishes to give up.

(8) *The intervening role of changes in national institutions and values that played such a crucial role during the initiating and priming cycles should decline in importance. It should become more and more possible to predict changes at the regional level as a direct, not as a mediated, consequence of decisions* taken by the EU. *Actors (now multiple and diverse) at the national level have become less sensitive to variation in relative size and power within their country and have begun to calculate more in terms of transnational classes, status groups, sub-regions, etc. Transactions across national boundaries become less important than inter-sectorial flows of labour, capital, and management. The political role of regional NGOs begins to eclipse that of national interest associations, the latter becoming subsections or branch offices of the former. Élite values are now more focused on regional symbols and loyalties, although national ones are unlikely to wither away entirely.*

(9) *Extra-regional dependence becomes partly endogenous and is no longer exclusively determined by exogenous forces.* Some of this may simply be due to increase in the number of member states since neighbouring countries will want to join such a successful venture. But much of it will be *because Europe will bargain routinely across almost the whole range of issues with outsiders and, in return, will make effective its full recognition as a new actor in the global international system.*

(10) *Eventually, one should expect the formation of a regional, i.e. European, system of political parties which will serve to aggregate national and regional NGOs into a more unified system of representation, to provide a permanent intermediary focus for the diffuse sense of regional loyalty and identity, and, most importantly, to link the crisis issues to the broader concerns of the citizenry on a territorial, and not just a functional, basis.*

(11) The previous point brings up a concept that played no explicit role in neofunctionalism, namely, **democracy**. The theory assumed its presence at the national level, but never envisaged the need for it at the supranational level.[17] It would not be an exaggeration to say that the process it analyzed (and prescribed) was nothing less than a conspiracy to advance as far as possible on the path to regional integration without engaging mass publics or party politicians. The quantum leap in controversiality intrinsic to the 'transformative cycle', makes this manifestly untenable. Moreover, it is difficult to imagine that the

formation of a regional party system with competitive elections and legislative institutions capable of holding regional leaders accountable could come about merely by the mechanism of functional spill-over and that Europeans would simply wake up one morning to find themselves supranationally democratic! Such a 'transcendent' action will require explicit and unanimous voluntary agreement—and only after a long process of deliberating and compromising over institutions.

What sort of crisis might bring this about (and whether Eastern Enlargement is sufficient for the purpose) and what sort of political effort should be envisaged (and whether constitutionalization is desirable for this purpose) are issues presently on the EU table.[18]

(12) Finally, I would also like to bring up another concept that has yet to be mentioned: the **state**. Neofunctionalism has always been about 'process' not 'product'. It quite conscientiously avoided specifying exactly what these hypothesized changes in the scope and level of regional institutions would produce—although I think it fair to say that its practitioners did presume that eventually this would be a supranational state with most of the generic features of the national states it was supposed to transform. At the core of this presumption lay another presumption, namely, that the successive spill-overs would accrue to the same regional institution, i.e. the EU Commission. Once, however, in the neo-neo-version one seriously entertains a much wider range of intermediate outcomes as the result of crises of differing intensity and cycles of differing nature, it becomes possible (even probable) to envisage other end-states. A 'Multi-level and Poly-centric System of Governance' is one such candidate, but it is hardly unique to neofunctionalism (as we have seen in Figure 3.1). Elsewhere, in terms more explicitly intended to be compatible with this theory, I have 'modelled' two outcomes, the '*consortio*' and the '*condominio*' that differ from the '*confederatio*' presumed by intergovernmentalists and the '*federatio*' implied by previous neofunctionalists and wished by so many federalists.[19]

# Conclusion

I think that all students of regional integration—first and foremost, those working on the European Union—now understand that no single theory will be capable of explaining its dynamics and predicting its outcome. The EU is already the most complex polity ever created by human artifice and it is going to become even more so before it reaches its end-state—whatever that will be. Efforts to select out specific events, policies, or institutions and subject them to simplified assumptions may produce momentary 'confirmations' of a specific theory, but often at the expense of contrary evidence and countervailing trends. I can think of no better way of concluding but by re-iterating what I said at the end of my 1969 article: *understanding and explanation in this field of inquiry are . . . best served not by the dominance of a single 'accepted' grand model or paradigm, but by the simultaneous presence of antithetic and conflictive ones which—while they may converge in certain aspects—diverge in so many others. If this sort of dialectic of incompleteness, unevenness, and partial frustration propels integration processes forward, why shouldn't it do the same for the scholarship that accompanies them?*

## An *excursus* on 'enlargement'

As suggested above, neither functionalism nor neofunctionalism nor neo-neofunctionalism has or had anything to say about enlargement. Expansion into additional functional tasks, yes; extension into additional territorial units, no. Had their basic assumptions been taken seriously, they would have been immediately proven wrong in predicting who would choose and be chosen to participate in the regional integration of Europe. Switzerland, for example, should long have been a member of the EEC/EC/EU and Greece should not have joined. The former is functionally more a part of 'Europe' than most EU members; the latter is less an interdependent part of the region, both economically and politically, than many EU non-members.

Needless to say, once the EU went ahead and enlarged itself, neo-neofunctionalism might have incorporated this fact within its calculations, for example, with regard to the impact of greater interest diversity on transnational group formation or the likelihood that the sheer increase in numbers would have an effect upon the promotional role of the Commission. In both cases, as well as other possible examples, the prediction is seemingly straightforward: enlargement attenuates and delays the probability of spill-over—**unless** such a spill-over in task or authority is built into the negotiations surrounding the accession process as a means of compensating existing members or accommodating new ones. Whether these side-effects will be included is unpredictable from the strictly neo- or neo-neofunctionalist perspective, but if they are included (and, by-and-large this seems to have been the case with all of the three previous enlargements), the impact could be considerable. To use the (outmoded?) jargon of the EEC, territorial enlargement has been exploited as an excuse for 'accelerating through the curve', i.e. getting through an inevitably contentious political process by expanding the integration agenda to include some functional 'goodies' for everyone and/or to make sure that the Commission will have additional resources or clout to monitor the subsequent distribution of benefits and reward those who experience the greatest difficulty.

Neo-neofunctionalists would also pay a lot of attention to whether, as a result of the successful negotiations, the full *acquis communautaire* had been imposed upon new members, since this is the 'bedrock' upon which their theory rests. Not only did they presume the irreversibility of tasks already acquired, but they also tended to presume that new ones would be delegated to the same regional institution, i.e. to the Commission in the case of the EEC/EC/EU. And it was this process of incremental and voluntary accumulation (over an indeterminate length of time and across successive crises) that would eventually produce 'transcendence', i.e. a supranational state.

Neo-neofunctionalists with their greater sensitivity to a wider range of possible outcomes would certainly keep their eye on how enlargement treated the *acquis communautaire*, but they would be less alarmed by lengthy *dérogations* and occasional opt-outs and they would not be at all surprised to find that some of the newly acquired tasks would not be assigned to the Commission but to independent regional agencies.[20] This would be taken as important evidence that the EU was not heading towards 'stateness', but towards some novel arrangement of multi-lateral governance—a *consortio* or a *condominio* in my jargon.

Faced with the non-committal attitude of neo- and neo-neofunctionalists towards enlargement (and, as far as I can tell, the complete silence of federalists),[21] the field of speculation has been left to 'rationalists' and 'constructivists'. I am incapable of judging independently what (if anything) these approaches have to offer. I gather from José Ignacio Torreblanco that neither is conclusive and that it is somehow desirable to accommodate both 'interests' and 'principles' if one is to understand the pace and extent of Eastern enlargement.[22]

I would, however, like to conclude by reminding those who deal with this manifestly under-theorized aspect of regional integration that the issue is not resolved when a candidate country is admitted and this is ratified by itself and existing members. What is particularly significant from the perspective of the process as a whole is how the newcomer behaves once s/he has been admitted to the club. So far with the first three enlargements, this seems not to have been a controversial issue.[23] The conditions of entry have been regarded as sufficiently fair; the distribution of initial burdens and benefits reasonably equitable;[24] the assignment of voting weights and thresholds relatively proportionate; the side payments and exemptions generous enough; and the EU institutions flexible enough that no country seems to have joined and then seriously regretted doing so.

Eastern enlargement, however, may shake that comfortable assumption. The conditions demanded have been more onerous—and more ostensibly political as well as economic and social; the willingness to pay compensations and allow for exemptions for 'sensitive' products and issues much less forthcoming; the sheer numbers so large that delicate inter-institutional balances are bound to be upset. Under these conditions, the extension to cover a wider and more diverse territory may not ensure subsequent conformity to existing rules (and, remember that unanimity is still necessary for many decisions). Baring some miracle from the Convention that is currently meeting, it will almost certainly weaken rather than strengthen EU institutions (as it has in the past). Just as a proper and complete theory of integration must also be a potential theory of disintegration, so an adequate theory of enlargement should also be a theory of (potential) contraction.

# Notes

1. E.B. Haas (1975), (2001).

2. I am not alone in this suspicion. Even that 'theorist of obsolescence', Ernst Haas, has observed it—particularly with regard to the work of Andrew Moravcsik. Moravcsik's alleged 'liberal' theory of intergovernmentalism shares a number of core assumptions with neofunctionalism (while making 'extraordinary efforts to distinguish his work from these sources'). Haas, 'Does Constructivism . . .', n. 10, p. 30. I would go even further. If Moravscik were to concede that the calculation of member-state strategies was affected not only by 'domestic interests', but also (and even increasingly) by transnational firms, associations, and movements working through domestic channels, then, his approach would be virtually indistinguishable from neofunctionalism—just much less specific in its assumptions and hypotheses. His epistemology would have to admit that the gradual processes of 'low politics' could be unobtrusively encroaching upon 'high politics'; his ontology would have to include the prospect that transformation might be occurring, not just successive iterations of the same power game played by rational-unitary national states.

3. James Caporaso and Alec Stone Sweet are exceptions. In their concluding chapter to Stone Sweet, A., Sandholtz, W., and Fligstein, N. (eds.) (2001), p. 224, they acknowledge the intellectual debt they owe to neofunctionalism and admit that they, as well as 'some but not all members of (their) group, are quite comfortable being called (modified) neofunctionalists'.

4. An exception is Walter Mattli (1999) where a wide range of integration efforts inside and outside Europe and over a long period of time are compared. The approach, however, is 'parsimonious' and 'rational', i.e. diametrically opposite to the one taken here.

5. Unfortunately, no one seems to be following me in this usage. Either the concept of MLG and PCG is just too 'indigestible' or the user assumes that territory always trumps function and, hence, PCG is redundant.

6. 'A Revised Theory of Regional Integration' (1970), pp. 836–68. Also published in Lindberg, L. and Scheingold, S. (eds.) (1971), pp. 232–65. This was one of the first 'heavy' articles I published and it passed virtually ignored. I know of no one who has ever used it or even taken it seriously. Many statements by critics of neofunctionalism—that it is teleological, predicts automatic integration, has no testable hypotheses, lacks a rigorous theory—demonstrate (at least, to me) that they must never have read my piece. I admit that the complexity of its argument is formidable. Emergent properties, unintended consequences, strategies adopted under uncertainty, and successive decision-cycles interact with changes in prior structures and values to produce outcomes that could not possibly have been imagined otherwise. I liked to call it 'concatenation'; today, it might be called 'chaos'. That was its major theme, namely, that regional integration among consenting national states was bound to be complex and required a theory that was capable of transforming itself along with that process. Perhaps, its failure was due to my not being a specialist on the (then) European Economic Community, but on two very obscure (and later unsuccessful) regional arrangements in Latin America. Perhaps, it was because shortly thereafter I lost all interest in the topic (along with most of the others appearing in the volume). Perhaps, I would like to think, it was because the article was ahead of its time. The present article is my effort to prove the latter.

7. A.L. Stinchcombe (1968), p. 32.

8. *Ibid.*, pp. 28–9.

9. *Ibid.*, p. 80.

10. For example, K. Deutsch et al. (1957); A. Etzioni (1965) were two contemporaneous works that both had stressed the importance of violence or the threat of it in international integration movements.

11. 'Does Constructivism . . .' (see n. 1), p. 25 *et seq.*

12. For the argument that these legal developments could be incorporated into a

neofunctionalist approach, see Burley, A.-M. and Mattli, W. (1993). In my view, they do not fit so well. The ECJ's pro-integrative rulings based on vague clauses in the treaties and their effect in asserting the supremacy of 'Community Law' over national law, depended upon a quite different form of interdependence than envisaged by neofunctionalism, i.e. that embodied in a common legal profession, doctrine of jurisprudence, and respect for the rule of law which extended across intra-European borders into the very entrails of the national state.

13. This is not, however, the sort of 'obsolescence' that Ernst B. Haas had in mind in the articles cited in n. 1.

14. 'Three Neo-Functional Hypotheses about International Integration', *International Organization* (Winter 1969), vol. 23, no. O, pp. 562–4.

15. Lindberg, L. and Scheingold, S. (1970) had argued that by treating each decision as a distinct unit, 'within system' comparisons could draw upon a much larger case base. Of course, this may not expand the ranges of variation very much, since there is likely to be substantial autocorrelation in many variables.

16. Amitai Etzioni in his *Political Integration* (*op. cit.*) had speculated that it may be necessary to use coercion in such circumstances and he calls this moment, the integration 'showdown'.

17. And, of course, concern with trans- or supranational democracy poses no problem for reproductive theorists, since they see no need for it in either intergovernmental or regulatory integration arrangements. At best, the new level of coordination might impose some necessity to modify the practices of 'domestic democracy' at the national level.

18. Needless to say, space precludes any further discussion of these issues here. I have,

however, commented on them in my *How to Democratize the European Union . . . and Why Bother?* (2000a).

19. 'Imagining the Future of the Euro-Polity with the Help of New Concepts', in Marks, G., Scharpf, F., Schmitter, F.C., and Streeck, W. (1996), 121–50.

20. Which, of course, is precisely what the 'regulationists' in the upper-right hand corner of Figure 3.1 would expect and advocate.

21. I suppose that, for federalists, the answer to the question of 'who belongs' is simple: any country or sub-unit of a country that voluntarily chooses to accept the rights, obligations, and rules embedded in the federal constitution. In the case of 'asymmetric federalism' where these rights, obligations, and rules are not the same for all members the issue becomes more difficult to resolve—and EU institutions have definitely evolved in an asymmetric direction. Historically, federalists have implicitly assumed a quite high level of prior cultural similarity and normative consensus—which is one reason (among several) why de Tocqueville was so convinced that American federalism was not an appropriate state form for Europe. See my 'Federalism and the Euro-Polity' (2000b), pp. 40–7.

22. 'Accommodating interests and principles in the European Union: The Case of Eastern Enlargement', paper presented at the ARENA Conference on 'Democracy and European Governance', Oslo, 4–5 March 2002.

23. Greece may be an exception, but she too seems to have become less prone over time to violating the Club's implicit understandings, although her behaviour with regard to the admission of (Greek) Cyprus will test this in the near future.

24. Here, the British demand for a strict and costly *juste retour* is another exception.

# Guide to further reading

HAAS, E.B. (1976), 'Turbulent Fields and the Theory of Regional Integration', *International Organization* 30, 173–212. One of the classic early texts on theory building and analysis of regional integration based on a neofunctionalist approach.

—— (2001), 'Does Constructivism Subsume Neofunctionalism? A "Soft Rationalist" Solution', in *The Social Construction of Europe*, Christiansen, T., Jørgensen, K.E., and Wiener, A. (eds.) (London: Sage). A critical appreciation of more recent—constructivist—theorizing in European integration studies, assessed from a comparative, neofunctionalist perspective.

LINDBERG, L. and SCHEINGOLD, S. (eds.) (1970), *Europe's Would-Be Polity: Patterns of Change in the European Community* (Englewood Cliffs, NJ: Prentice Hall). The classic early edition representing the entire spectrum of the most distinguished neofunctionalist scholarship at the time.

PUCHALA, D. (1972), 'Of Blind Men, Elephants, and International Integration', *Journal of Common Market Studies* 10, 267–85. Again, a classical reading in European integration theories which brings the problem of grand theory in a field of multiple analytical puzzles to the fore.

SANDHOLTZ, W. and ZYSMAN, J. (1989), 'Recasting the European Bargain', *World Politics* 42, 95–128. A seminal reading which offers a new perspective on the relevance of neofunctionalist approaches for analyses of the relaunched integration process with a strong economic drive after the Single European Act (1987).

# 4

# Liberal Intergovernmentalism

## *Frank Schimmelfennig*

## Introduction

According to a *bonmot* among EU scholars, liberal intergovernmentalism (LI) is a theoretical 'school' with no 'disciples' and a single 'teacher': Andrew Moravcsik. It must be said in all fairness, however, that LI is an application of rationalist institutionalism, a larger class of International Relations theories (with numerous teachers as well as disciples) to the field of European integration. Moreover, LI has quickly acquired the status of a baseline theory against which new theoretical conjectures are tested and which is used as a 'first cut' to explain new developments in European integration.

A number of LI's salient characteristics have given it this status. First, it builds on 'intergovernmentalism', a traditional school of thought in European integration studies (see, e.g. Hoffmann 1995), but gives it a much more sophisticated and rigorous theoretical underpinning (in addition to substantive refinement). Second, it is 'grand theory' seeking to explain the 'major steps toward European integration' (Moravcsik 1998: 4) from 'Messina to Maastricht' (the subtitle of Moravcsik's *magnum opus*, 'The Choice for Europe') and on to 'Amsterdam' (Moravcsik and Nicolaïdis 1999) in a multi-causal framework. Third, by the standards of European integration theory, it is 'parsimonious theory', which can be summarized in a few general propositions that claim to explain the core of European integration. Last, but not least, there is widespread agreement that LI *does* explain much of state behaviour in the EU.

In this chapter, I will, first, give an overview of the main assumptions and propositions of LI ('The liberal intergovernmentalist theory of European integration'), and then turn to some of the criticism that has been raised against it ('Critique'). In 'A typical case: consolidation of the common market', I summarize Moravcsik's analysis of the establishment of the Common Agricultural Policy—an 'easy case' for LI but also one that is of central importance in European integration. By contrast, I will show that LI provides only a partial explanation of the Eastern enlargement of the EU and needs to be complemented with an analysis of community effects on intergovernmental bargaining ('Liberal intergovernmentalism and enlargement'). In the conclusion, I briefly discuss avenues for dialogue and synthesis.[1]

# The liberal intergovernmentalist theory of European integration

It is certainly a virtue of a 'single-author theory' such as LI that it is more likely to represent a coherent set of assumptions and propositions than theories and approaches to which multiple authors contribute. Still, Andrew Moravcsik deserves credit for explicitly stating the assumptions of LI, for developing a consistent and testable set of propositions based on them—and for making a summary of LI a relatively easy undertaking.[2] I propose to distinguish the assumptions and propositions of LI according to three levels of abstraction as illustrated in Table 4.1.[3]

## IR rationalist institutionalism

At the *highest level* of abstraction, LI is a variant of rationalist institutionalism in International Relations (IR) theory specifically tailored to explain European integration. These theoretical roots point to the fundamentals of LI.

First, European integration is similar enough to general international politics, and the European Union is sufficiently like other international institutions, that it can be profitably studied and explained in an *IR perspective*. Indeed, Moravcsik maintains that the 'EC is best seen as an international regime for policy co-ordination' (1993: 480) and that the 'revisionist quality' of LI consists in the 'effort to normalize the actions of European governments—to treat them as a subset of general tendencies among democratic states in modern world politics' (1998: 5). IR theories traditionally assume that states are the central actors in international politics and that they act in a context of anarchy, that is, in the absence of a centralized authority making and enforcing political decisions. Policy-making in international politics generally takes place in intergovernmental negotiations.

The second fundamental is a *rationalist framework*, which entails a general explanatory programme and basic action-theoretic assumptions. As for the explanatory programme, rationalism is an individualist or agency theory, which requires an

**Table 4.1** Overview of liberal intergovernmentalism

| Level of abstraction | Preferences | Cooperation | Institutions |
| --- | --- | --- | --- |
| High | IR rationalist institutionalism: state actors in international anarchy, rational choice of international institutions | | |
| Medium | Liberal theory of state preferences | Bargaining theory | Functional theory of institutional choice |
| Low | Domestic economic interests | Intergovernmental asymmetrical interdependence | Credible commitments |

explanation of, first, actor preferences and, second, collective outcomes as a result of aggregated individual actions based on these preferences. The core action-theoretic assumption is 'rational choice': actors calculate the utility of alternative courses of action and choose the one that maximizes their utility under the circumstances. Rationalist institutionalism in IR theory then seeks to explain the establishment and design of international institutions as a collective outcome of interdependent ('strategic') rational state choices and intergovernmental negotiations in an anarchical context.

Within this general rational-institutionalist IR framework, and at a *medium level* of abstraction, LI puts forward a liberal theory of national preference formation, a bargaining theory of international negotiations, and a functional theory of institutional choice. These theories are used to explain a sequence of negotiation outcomes: domestic negotiations on national preferences; then, international negotiations on substantive international cooperation; and, after agreement has been reached, international negotiations on the choice of institutions.

According to *liberal theories* of International Relations, 'the foreign policy goals of national governments are viewed as varying in response to shifting pressure from domestic social groups, whose preferences are aggregated through political institutions' (Moravcsik 1993: 481). As a consequence, state preferences are neither fixed nor uniform: they may vary within the same state across time and issues, and they may vary between states depending on different domestic constellations of preferences, institutions, and power. Nevertheless, LI continues to treat the state as a unitary actor according to the IR tradition because it assumes that national governments develop a consistent preference order as a result of domestic political bargaining and that domestic actors do not play a significant independent role in negotiations beyond the state.

To explain the substantive outcomes of international negotiations, Moravcsik follows rationalist institutionalism in IR in using a *bargaining theory of international cooperation*. Rationalist institutionalism distinguishes first- and second-order problems of international collective choice in problematic situations of international interdependence—that is, situations in which non-cooperative behaviour is the individually rational choice but in the end leaves all states worse off. The first-order problem consists in overcoming such collectively suboptimal outcomes and achieving coordination or cooperation for mutual benefit. The second-order problems arise once the suboptimal outcomes are overcome. First, how are the mutual gains of cooperation distributed among the states? Second, how are states prevented from defecting from an agreement in order to exploit the cooperation of others?

In this context, bargaining theory argues that the outcome of international negotiations, that is, whether and on which terms cooperation comes about depends on the relative bargaining power of the actors. Bargaining power is a result of the asymmetrical distribution of (i) information; and (ii) the benefits of a specific agreement (compared to those of alternative outcomes or 'outside options'). Generally, those actors that have more and better information are able to manipulate the outcome to their advantage, and those actors that are least in need of a specific agreement are best able to threaten the others with non-cooperation and thereby force them to make concessions.

Finally, to explain the establishment and design of international institutions, IR rationalist institutionalism relies mainly on a *functional account* (Keohane 1984): states establish international institutions to manage and overcome the first- and second-order problems of international cooperation. With regard to the first problem, rationalist institutionalists argue that international institutions may help states reach a collectively superior outcome, above all by reducing the transaction costs of further international negotiations on specific issues and by providing the necessary information to reduce the states' uncertainty about each other's preferences and behaviour. With regard to the second-order problems, they establish rules for the distribution of gains and reduce the costs of controlling the behaviour of states and sanctioning non-compliance. Different institutional designs then reflect the specific problems of cooperation caused by, above all, the severity of distributional conflict and enforcement problems and by uncertainty about the preferences of other actors and the state of the world (Koremenos, Lipson, and Snidal 2001).

## Propositions on European integration

The theoretical approaches of IR rationalist institutionalism still beg three questions: what kind of domestic preferences matter most for European integration, which actors and issues shape European bargains, and what explains the specific institutional design of the European Union. At the *lowest level* of abstraction, LI therefore puts forward *concrete propositions* on the determinants of preference formation, bargaining, and institutional choice *in European integration*. Moravcsik asks whether national preferences have been driven by general geopolitical ideas and interests or by issue-specific economic interest, whether substantive integration outcomes have been shaped by supranational entrepreneurship or intergovernmental bargaining, and whether EU institutions reflect federalist ideology, the need for technocratic management, or an interest in securing credible member state commitments. It is these issues that have driven the long-standing debate in European integration studies between neofunctionalists and supranationalists on the one hand, and intergovernmentalists, on the other. Moravcsik's analysis defends an intergovernmentalist account of European integration but adds new elements to it and does so at a considerably higher level of theoretical elaboration and sophistication than traditional, realist intergovernmentalism. In its most condensed form, it is the general argument of LI that

EU integration can best be understood as a series of rational choices made by national leaders. These choices responded to constraints and opportunities stemming from the economic interests of powerful domestic constituents, the relative power of each state in the international system, and the role of institutions in bolstering the credibility of interstate commitments (Moravcsik 1998: 18).

First, LI argues that the *preferences* of national governments in European integration are mainly issue-specific. Insofar as European integration has been predominantly *economic*, so have state preferences. While the general interest in European integration resulted from the pressure to cooperate for mutual benefit from economic gains in an expanding and 'globalizing' international economy, concrete preferences emerged 'from a process of domestic conflict in which specific sectoral interests, adjustment costs and, sometimes, geopolitical concerns played an important role', and reflected 'primarily the commercial interests of powerful economic producers' in market integration and 'secondarily the macro-economic preferences of ruling governmental coalitions'—as in monetary integration (Moravcsik 1998: 3). In other words, domestic interests, reflecting mainly the competitiveness of the national economy, acted as a filter between the structural incentives of the international economy and the national preferences in European integration. As a consequence, governments pursue integration as 'a means to secure commercial advantages for producer groups, subject to regulatory and budgetary constraints' (Moravcsik 1998: 38). This driving force of integration generates distributional conflict among the states.

Moravcsik does allow for some impact of ideological geopolitical preferences: 'naked economic preferences would probably have led to a highly institutionalized pan-European free trade area with flanking policies of regulatory harmonization and monetary stabilization' (Moravcsik 1998: 6). Ideological or geopolitical preferences are needed in addition to issue-specific economic preferences to explain the quasi-constitutional set-up of the EU, its limited membership, and the extensive scope of policies covered by EU integration. Moreover, all of the cases in which geopolitical interests did have a relevant influence involved Germany (Moravcsik 1998: 476–9).

Second, LI describes the most relevant bargaining processes in European integration as processes of *intergovernmental bargaining* concerning the *distribution* of gains from substantive cooperation. More concretely, they have in the past consisted of *hard* bargaining,

in which credible threats to veto proposals, to withhold financial side-payments, and to form alternative alliances excluding recalcitrant governments carried the day. The outcomes reflected the relative power of states—more precisely patterns of asymmetrical interdependence. Those who gained the most economically from integration compromised the most on the margin to realize it, whereas those who gained the least or for whom the costs of adaptation were highest imposed conditions (Moravcsik 1998: 3).

This account has two negative implications: First, Moravcsik argues that the first-order problem of international cooperation is *not* the main problem in European integration. Transaction costs are generally low, and information and ideas are plentiful and symmetrically distributed among states (Moravcsik 1998: 479–80) so that interstate negotiations alone reliably produce efficient outcomes. Instead, the second-order problem of distribution is paramount. Second, and as a corollary, the bargaining power of supranational actors is low because they are deprived of their main bargaining resource: scarce and asymmetrically distributed ideas and information. Supranational entrepreneurship is not necessary to reach efficient agreements, and supranational institutions lack the power to bargain successfully for concessions by the member states.

Third, *institutional choice* is again driven by governments—and by their concern about each other's future compliance with the substantive deals reached. In other words, whereas EU governments do not need or want supranational institutions to define their preferences, to provide them with the information necessary to reach efficient substantive agreements, or to devise rules of distribution, they rely on them to solve the second-order problems of control, sanctioning, and incomplete contracting—mainly through credible pre-commitments. By transferring sovereignty to international institutions, governments effectively remove issues from the influence of domestic politics, which might build up pressure for non-compliance if costs for powerful domestic actors are high. They also remove them from decentralized intergovernmental control, which may be too weak to secure compliance, in particular if powerful member states violate the rules (Moravcsik 1998: 9, 73). The degree to which governments favour the pooling of sovereignty (voting by other procedures than unanimity) and the delegation of sovereignty to supranational institutions, depends on the value they place on the issues and substantive outcomes in question: the higher the gains of a cooperative agreement for a government, and the higher the risk of non-compliance by other governments, the higher its readiness to cede competences to the EU to prevent potential losers from revising the policy (Moravcsik 1998: 9, 486–7).

Besides its more sophisticated theoretical apparatus, two features characteristic of liberal or pluralist IR theories distinguish LI from traditional, realist intergovernmentalism in integration theory (Hoffmann 1966, 1982): the relevance of domestic politics and international institutions. Most importantly, whereas realist intergovernmentalism takes nation states as the fundamental actors in European integration and starts from *state* preferences derived from its position in the international power structure and its interest in autonomy and security (*geopolitical* interests in Moravcsik's terminology), LI regards the *issue-specific* preferences of *domestic* interest groups as fundamental. Second, LI follows 'neoliberal institutionalism' (Keohane and Nye 1977; Keohane 1984) in using an economic theory of institutions and stipulating international interdependence as well as international institutions as necessary conditions of durable international cooperation.[4] By the same token, LI incorporates factors traditionally attributed to the neofunctionalist or supranationalist accounts of European integration: international interdependence as a catalyst of societal (albeit not transnational) demand for integration (Caporaso 1999: 163; Stone Sweet and Sandholtz 1998: 7) and delegation to supranational organizations capable of acting against the short-term preferences of governments (Stone Sweet 2003).

Despite these differences, the core of the traditional intergovernmentalist critique of functionalism and federalism is shared by LI. Just as his predecessors, Moravcsik holds that state governments call the tune in European integration. They pursue diverse interests generated at the national, domestic level; they engage in hard intergovernmental bargaining; and they are in control of the integration process. Rather than the gradual supranational integration and weakening of the nation state, intergovernmentalists emphasize its 'survival' and 'endurance' (Hoffmann 1995: 89, 102) or even 'regeneration' (Hoffmann 1982: 35) and 'strengthening' (Moravcsik 1994) in European integration. Moravcsik argues that European integration provides state executives with institutional and informational resources, which help them to weaken parliamentary control and to loosen the grip of powerful domestic interest groups such as trade unions. The more domestic issues become the subject of European politics, the more the state is able to use its traditionally strong autonomy in foreign policy to control the domestic agenda, to increase the costs of domestic opposition, to exploit information asymmetries, and to enhance its legitimacy (Moravcsik 1997).

At the same time, Moravcsik asserts that the EU does not suffer from a 'democratic deficit'—at least in comparison with the reality of existing nation state governments and taking into account that it specializes in regulatory activities, which are generally less in need of democratic legitimacy than, say, the redistributive policies of the welfare state. Checks and balances between EU institutions, 'indirect democratic control via national governments, and the increasing powers of the European Parliament are sufficient to ensure that EU policy-making is, in nearly all cases, clean, transparent, effective and politically responsive to the demands of European citizens' (Moravcsik 2002: 605).

## Critique

Liberal intergovernmentalism claims to explain the 'major steps toward European integration' (Moravcsik 1998: 4), that is, the intergovernmental conferences and treaty amendments that have changed the core policies and the institutional set-up of the EU. The criticisms I outline in this section dispute this claim and argue that the LI analysis of these big decisions is inadequate.

By contrast, I will not go into three other types of criticisms: first, I will not discuss criticisms of Moravcsik's interpretation and explanation of individual state preferences and policies as well as particular events in various stages of European integration.[5] Second, I will not address the meta-theoretical or methodological critique that rejects the 'positivist' methodology, the causal analysis and hypothesis-testing design, or the rationalist framework of LI as such.[6] Third, I will leave aside the obvious criticism that LI is not able to explain all of EU politics, in particular its day-to-day policy-making under the first (EC) 'pillar', because Moravcsik himself limits the scope of LI to treaty negotiations and other issues of unanimous decision-making.[7] I group the major points of criticism under three headings: biased case selection, internal theory problems, and neglect of integration dynamics.

*Biased case selection.* Even if one accepts that LI is a theory of constitutional change rather than day-to-day policy-making, the selection of cases may appear biased in favour of LI. For instance, Fritz Scharpf points out that a theory based on economic interests and intergovernmental bargaining was bound to have a high degree of *a priori* plausibility for the *intergovernmental* negotiations focusing on issues of *economic* integration and requiring unanimous agreement (Scharpf 1999: 165). By contrast, 'constitutional changes reached through Commission strategies and Court decisions (which have constitutional force when they interpret the Treaty) are completely excluded from consideration' (Scharpf 1999: 167; cf. Pierson 1998: 33). So are Council decisions (for instance, on the 'comitology'; see chapters by Peterson and Pollack in this volume) and inter-institutional agreements, which have changed the institutional set-up and distribution of competences independently of intergovernmental negotiations.

*Internal theory problems.* Even within a rationalist perspective, the tripartite framework of LI and its specific hypotheses about European integration may be disputed. For instance, the analytical separation of substantive bargaining and institutional choice is questionable. As Moravcsik's case studies amply demonstrate, member-state governments do not first settle substantive policy issues and then turn to the selection of institutional arrangements but have institutional preferences in addition to policy preferences, bargain on policies and institutions at the same time, and make linkages between the two. With regard to institutional choice, Scharpf argues that fear of defection is not generally the core reason for delegation but that many collective action problems in the EU are mere coordination problems (such as standard-setting). In these cases, governments delegate decisions to supranational organizations in order to reduce the transaction costs of determining a common solution rather than to ensure compliance (Scharpf 1999: 165–6).

*Neglect of integration dynamics.* The most fundamental attack on the LI analysis of major integration decisions has been staged by the proponents of supranational or historical institutionalism (SI or HI).[8] An SI/HI account of integration is compatible with rationalist institutionalism and may well equal an LI account—but only for the initial 'grand bargain' and the original choice of institutions. In subsequent rounds of intergovernmental negotiations, however, member-state governments may have changed their preferences (e.g. after a change in government) and will be constrained by unanticipated and/or undesired consequences of their previous decisions, which are difficult or costly to redress (Pierson 1998: 30–4). In particular, supranational organizations will 'work to enhance their own autonomy and influence within the European polity, so as to promote the interests of transnational society and the construction of supranational governance' (Stone Sweet and Sandholtz 1998: 26).

The most important institutionalist case against LI is the autonomy and power of the European Court of Justice and the legal integration it promoted. Institutionalists show how the European Court of Justice interpreted its competences in an integrationist way not anticipated and desired by the governments; how it strengthened national courts and private litigants, empowered the Commission, and influenced the distribution of gains from market integration; and finally propelled the states towards accepting the trading institutions and the enforcement regime it designed for the internal market (see, e.g. Burley and Mattli 1993; Stone Sweet 2003).

Andrew Moravcsik admits that the Court is an exception. In general, however, he claims—in his response to the HI critique and on the basis of the historical evidence presented in 'The Choice for Europe'—that state preferences were basically stable over time; the constraints they faced in the later phases of integration were anticipated and desired (e.g. in order to prevent defection from agreements); governments remained in firm control of supranational organizations; and change was driven by structural economic trends rather than supranational entrepreneurship and decisions (Moravcsik 1998: 490–4).

# A typical case: consolidation of the common market

## Scope conditions

Andrew Moravcsik states several scope or antecedent conditions for LI, that is, conditions under which the theory is assumed to have greatest explanatory power.

First, LI should work best with *intergovernmental decisions under unanimity*, which are typical of treaty-amending negotiations and decisions in the European Council but also generally pertain to the second and third pillars of the EU, the Common Foreign and Security Policy and cooperation in Justice and Home Affairs. Conversely, for day-to-day EU decisions following other decision-making rules and involving the Commission and the European Parliament, rational-choice institutionalism (see Pollack, this volume) is more pertinent. However, even for decisions made in these institutional settings, LI is useful in explaining preferences.

Second, *domestic economic interests* most clearly shape state preferences, the 'more intense, certain, and institutionally represented and organized' they are (Moravcsik 1998: 36) and the less 'uncertainty there is about cause-effect relations' (Moravcsik 1999a: 171). This is particularly true of EU policies in agriculture and trade. Conversely, 'the weaker and more diffuse the domestic constituency behind a policy' (*ibid.*) and the more uncertain or modest are 'the substantive implications of a choice', the less predictable are national preferences and the more likely ideological preferences will be influential (Moravcsik 1998: 486–9; Moravcsik and Nicolaïdis 1999: 61). According to Moravcsik, this condition applies partially to monetary policy as well as to institutional choices such as assigning powers to the European Parliament.

Third, *intergovernmental bargaining* is the dominant pattern when transaction costs are low and information is plenty and symmetrically distributed. Conversely, supranational influence is possible when 'national governments face high ex ante transaction costs and significant informational (or ideational) asymmetries favour supranational entrepreneurs'. These conditions typically arise, Moravcsik argues, not in situations where international bargaining is complex or difficult, but when domestic coordination problems are severe (1999a: 173). In Moravcsik's analysis, the Single European Act (SEA) is the only major case in which these conditions have applied. The failure of European multinational firms to discover their common interests and to organize for effective collective action and the failure of interest groups and domestic ministers to aggregate the numerous bureaucratically disparate proposals into an integrated internal market package gave supranational entrepreneurs in the Commission and the

Parliament a comparative advantage in initiating the SEA, mobilizing a latent trans-national constituency, and generating a more efficient outcome (Moravcsik 1999b: 292–8).

Given these scope conditions, of the five macro-case studies in 'The Choice for Europe', LI should be most suitable to explain the consolidation of the common market because tariffs and agriculture were the most relevant issues in this step toward integration. Apart from the case study on the initial negotiations on the Treaties of Rome, two other cases focus on monetary policy (more likely driven by economic ideas), and the SEA case study is an exception (because of domestic coordination problems).

## Consolidating the common market: establishing the Common Agricultural Policy

The consolidation of the common market roughly spanned the 1960s. It included the removal of internal, and harmonization of external, tariffs and the creation of the Common Agricultural Policy (CAP). Of these issues I focus on the CAP. To this day, it has remained a core element of the 'European bargain' and continues to consume the better part of the EU's budget expenditures. Indeed, it is arguably the most important single foreign economic policy pursued by any industrialized government today—fundamentally shaping the domestic and global political economy of developing nations and transatlantic relations. Farmers' associations have intense preferences, are highly organized, and exercise a strong influence on governments—the ideal conditions for LI's theory of preferences. In contrast with tariff reductions, agricultural policy had to be decided by unanimity vote without a right of proposal for the Commission—the textbook setting for hard intergovernmental bargaining. For Moravcsik, this institutional 'capture' is endogenous. It is precisely because agricultural interests are so strong, and because nearly all industrialized governments are committed to their subsidization where necessary, that they are privileged in EU-level negotiations. For any LI analysis of integration, the initial task is to explain state preferences by the structure of domestic economic interests, then to analyse the intergovernmental bargaining and its outcomes, and finally to account for the choice of institutional provisions.

Preferences on a common agricultural policy varied strongly among the major governments and were inversely related to preferences on agricultural trade beyond the EC: while France 'most intensely favoured liberalization of commodities trade within a preferential European zone with modest support prices', it 'strongly opposed agricultural trade liberalization in the GATT'. Germany opposed internal liberalization 'unless very high common support prices were paid' but 'was prepared to make GATT concessions . . . that preserved domestic arrangements'. Britain was 'sceptical of any agricultural policy' and favoured a liberalization of global agricultural trade instead (Moravcsik 1998: 161).

These preferences mirror the importance and competitiveness of the agricultural sector in the three countries: 'Farming employed 25 percent of Frenchmen, 15 percent of Germans, and only 5 percent of Britons. Germany and Britain were large net importers but only marginal exporters of agricultural goods', whereas France was a large surplus producer and exporter. Whereas Germany and Britain were uncompet- itive in agriculture, French exports were expected to benefit greatly from intra-EC liberalization as long as high prices relative to the world market were guaranteed. Britain as a net importer was interested in maintaining its preferential agreement with the Commonwealth in order to buy agricultural products at relatively low prices (Moravcsik 1998: 89–90). By contrast, Germany with its still sizeable and politically influential agricultural sector 'sought to maintain high support prices behind protect- ive barriers' (Moravcsik 1998: 98). In addition, these preferences mirror the power asymmetries between the highly organized farming sector, on one hand, and the much larger but diffuse and unorganized groups of taxpayers and consumers, which were forced to foot the bill.

The bargaining outcome demonstrates, first, the lack of Commission influence. The 'closed, high-priced, comprehensive, and administratively decentralized agricul- tural policy' was 'the precise opposite of what the Commission had sought': a liberal but centralized policy to further the structural adjustment of small, inefficient farms (Moravcsik 1998: 205–6, 161). Member states were better informed about each others' preferences than was the Commission and they easily defeated the proposals of Commissioner Mansholt (Moravcsik 1998: 230–2).

Second, because of its comparatively strong interest in the CAP, France was in an inferior bargaining position on this issue but was able to secure the agreement of the other member states through issue-linkage, that is, threats and concessions on issues it was less interested in. In the area of the common market, France was able to exploit the intense German preference for trade liberalization. The French government linked the acceleration of internal tariff removal to a schedule for the adoption of the CAP, threatened to block further tariff cuts if Germany did not give up its favoured bilateral agricultural trade agreements, and 'held up the EC's mandate for the Kennedy round of GATT negotiations to force German concessions on the CAP' (Moravcsik 1998: 206–8).

On the other hand, the existence of highly organized and politically influential agri- cultural interests in both France and Germany resulted in logrolling: Germany was able to secure long transition periods for its bilateral quotas and direct subsidies to placate German farmers in return for its consent to the CAP (Moravcsik 1998: 212–13). Similarly, Germany agreed to wheat prices that damaged its farmers—in return for the permission to subsidize them and for high prices for animal products, the mainstay of German agriculture.

With regard to institutional choice, preferences and behaviour reflected issue- specific concerns, too. Despite its allegedly federalist attitudes, the German government resisted qualified majority voting on the CAP because it feared being in the minority and being forced into lower levels of protection for its agricultural producers. And in spite of its purportedly ideological aversion to supranational institutions, France under De Gaulle insisted on a centralized CAP in order to assure German compliance and to lock in permanent financing at high price levels before Britain was admitted.

## Liberal intergovernmentalism and enlargement

### Overview of existing work

Given its focus on the major treaty-amending decisions of the European Union, LI should, in principle, be capable of explaining EU enlargement. Just as treaty amendments on the 'deepening' of the EU, 'widening' involves intergovernmental negotiations and unanimous decisions. Yet, enlargement has not been a major empirical subject of LI analysis. Two studies of enlargement close to LI, Mattli (1999) and Gstöhl (2002), focus on the interest of candidate states in membership but do not analyse the enlargement decisions of the EU. Mattli explains the interest in membership by the negative impact of integration on the economies of outsiders and a sustained 'performance gap' between insiders and outsiders. Outsider governments are willing to pay the price of integration, i.e. reduced autonomy, to the extent that membership will improve their economic performance and thus their chance of retaining power. By contrast, Gstöhl argues that, in addition to economic incentives, identity-related political impediments are necessary to explain the interest in EU membership of former EFTA members.

In 'The Choice for Europe', only the issue of British membership in the 1960s is analysed in some detail (Moravcsik 1998: 164–220). According to Moravcsik, both British interest in membership and De Gaulle's opposition to it were primarily motivated by economic concerns. Whereas Britain's commercial interests were harmed by exclusion from the customs union, France feared low-price commercial competition and, most of all, British opposition to the CAP (see above). Only the explanation of German support for the French opposition to British membership has to resort to geopolitical interests: its economic interests were closer to the British than to the French. France gave up its opposition only after the CAP was established. Even then the French government demanded a permanent financing arrangement for the CAP as a condition of UK entry. In the negotiations on British membership, the British bargaining position was weak because Britain 'was more commercially dependent on the Six than vice versa' (1998: 220). Britain preferred membership to exclusion and was therefore willing to make major concessions to France, which had little economic interest in British membership and could thus extract those concessions (mainly on the CAP) in exchange for giving up its veto.

In a recent paper, Andrew Moravcsik and Milada Vachudova apply the bargaining theory of LI to Eastern enlargement and argue similarly that 'applicant countries have consistently found themselves in a weak negotiating position vis-à-vis their EU partners, and accordingly have conceded much in exchange for membership' (Moravcsik and Vachudova 2002: 3. For a published shortened version of this paper, see Moravcsik and Vachudova 2003). As in the British case, whereas market expansion is usually profitable to members and non-members alike, non-members generally benefit more from being included in the Community's internal market than members benefit from expanding this market to a few additional and often small countries. This asymmetrical interdependence is most striking in the case of Eastern enlargement. The collective GNP of all ten Eastern candidates is approximately 5 per cent of that of the current members, and whereas the share of EU exports and imports of the total foreign trade of the candidates rose to between 50 and 70 per cent in the 1990s, their share of EU foreign trade remained below 5 per cent. The inflow of Western capital is critical for the Central and Eastern European (CEE) economies whereas Eastern capital in Western economies is a negligible quantity.

Given their inevitably strong dependency on the EU market and EU capital, the candidates preferred accepting the EU's conditions of accession to being excluded from EU membership. These include not only the adoption of the *acquis communautaire* but also initially lower subsidies from the EU budget than current members and transition periods on some rights such as the free movement of labour. These 'special provisions reflect the demands of narrow special interests or the concerns of voting publics in the existing members' (Moravcsik and Vachudova 2002: 10), which they could force upon the candidates thanks to their superior bargaining position. For the candidates, it was nonetheless rational to accept these conditions. If they chose to remain outside the EU, they would have to adopt EU rules to gain market access anyway but continue to suffer from EU anti-dumping measures and import restrictions (on the agricultural products, steel, and textiles where they are most competitive). Membership still gives them access to substantial EU funds, a firm end date for discrimination, and, most importantly, the decision-making rights that only members enjoy.

This, however, is only a partial analysis of Eastern enlargement. A complete LI analysis would again require an explanation of the enlargement preferences of EU members and the intra-organizational bargaining process.[9]

## Enlargement preferences

Liberal intergovernmentalism provides a plausible explanation of the member states' enlargement preferences. State preferences diverged both on the speed and the extension of (the first round of) EU enlargement. Whereas the 'drivers' advocated an early and firm commitment to Eastern enlargement, the 'brakemen' were reticent and tried to put off the decision, and whereas one group of member states pushed for a limited (first) round of enlargement focusing on the central European states, others favoured an inclusive approach for all ten candidates. Table 4.2 shows the distribution of these preferences among the member states.[10]

The distribution of enlargement preferences largely mirrors the geographical position of the member states. Except for Greece and Italy, the countries bordering on Central

**Table 4.2** Member state enlargement preferences

|  | Limited enlargement | Inclusive enlargement |
|---|---|---|
| **Drivers** | Austria, Finland, Germany | Britain, Denmark, Sweden |
| **Brakemen** | Belgium, Luxemburg, Netherlands | France, Greece, Ireland, Italy, Portugal, Spain |

and Eastern Europe were the 'drivers' of enlargement; except for Britain, the more remote countries were the 'brakemen'. The countries of the 'central region' of the EU preferred a limited (first round of) enlargement, whereas the Northern countries, with the exception of Finland, and the Southern countries favoured a more inclusive approach.

The member states' geographical position vis-à-vis Central and Eastern Europe can be understood as a proxy variable for 'the imperatives induced by interdependence and, in particular, the. . .exogenous increase in opportunities for cross-border trade and capital movements' that should determine national preferences according to Moravcsik (1998: 26). International interdependence increases with geographical proximity. Member states on the Eastern border of the EU are both more sensitive to developments in Central and Eastern Europe and more likely to benefit from trade with this region than the more remote member states.

Moreover, in light of this argument, member states should be most interested in the membership of those countries with which they share a border or are in close proximity. This explains why member states in the centre of the EU were content with the Commission's 1997 proposal to limit accession talks for the first round of Eastern enlargement to the central European candidates (plus Estonia). It also explains why France, Greece, and Italy, all southern states, gave their special support to Bulgaria and Romania, southeastern candidates, whereas Denmark and Sweden, northern states, most strongly advocated the cause of the Baltic states, the northernmost of the Central and Eastern European applicants. That Finland did not join Denmark and Sweden in pushing for extended enlargement on the eve of the Luxembourg European Council of December 1997 may be explained by the fact that Estonia, Finland's direct neighbour and most important economic partner among the Baltic countries, was on the Commission's shortlist for fast-track accession negotiations.

The divergent state preferences are not fully explained, however, by different levels of gains from the control of negative and the exploitation of positive interdependence with Central and Eastern Europe through enlargement. In this case, we would only see different degrees of enthusiasm for, but no opposition to Eastern enlargement. In order to explain why most member states, including the border countries of Italy and Greece, played the role of 'brakemen' in the enlargement process, potential losses from enlargement must be included in the analysis. The unequal distribution of these losses mainly results from differences in socio-economic structure among the EU member countries and the divergent preferences these structures produce.

Eastern enlargement was bound to create particularly high costs for the poorer, less highly developed, and more agricultural members. These costs result from trade and budgetary competition. First, the 'less developed' member states were likely to be more adversely affected by trade integration with the East because they specialize in the same traditional and resource-intensive industries (like agriculture, textile and leather as well as metalworking) as the CEE economies (Hagen 1996: 6–7).

Second, all CEE members will become structural net recipients. For the foreseeable future, EU transfers to these countries will outweigh their contributions to the Community budget. Moreover, because of the CEECs' high share of agricultural production and their low levels of wealth and income, Eastern enlargement seriously affects the CAP and the structural policies which together comprise around 80 per cent of the Community budget. If these policies had remained unchanged, the Community budget would have had to increase by 20 per cent to two-thirds of its current volume depending on the scenario and the calculation.[11] It was therefore clear early on that a reform of the CAP and the structural policies was an indispensable pre-condition of enlargement. Any reform, however, would inevitably lead to transfer reductions for EU farmers as well as to fewer regions eligible for financial support and would thus disproportionately affect the present main beneficiaries of the budget. Correspondingly, all of them (Spain, Greece, Portugal, and Ireland) were among the brakemen and later challenged the Commission's opinion that enlargement could be funded on the basis of the current budget limit (*Financial Times*, 15 September 1997, 2; IEP/TEPSA 1998).

In addition, geopolitical interests have influenced enlargement preferences. Proximity and (asymmetrical) interdependence not only give rise to economic gains but also to influence. The more remote member states therefore had reason to fear that future CEE members would side with Germany and other border states in EU decision-making and thereby cause a power shift in favour of Germany and the 'North-east' in general. This is the standard interpretation of French reticence towards enlargement (see, e.g. Grabbe and Hughes 1998: 5) but emphasis on the Mediterranean region appears to have affected the Greek and Italian positions, too.

British preferences obviously deviate from this structural pattern because Central and Eastern Europe is neither geographically close nor economically important to Britain. The early and strong British commitment to enlargement is generally attributed to the 'Europhobia' of the Conservative governments. It appears to have been based on the calculation that an extensive 'widening' of the Community would prevent its further 'deepening' and even dilute the achieved level of integration (see, e.g. Grabbe and Hughes 1998: 5).

In sum, economic interests go a long way in giving a plausible account of state preferences but in some important cases geopolitical or ideological interests seem to have been decisive. This finding is entirely consistent with LI expectations and the LI analysis of other treaty-amending negotiations.

## Bargaining outcomes

Given this constellation of preferences, the initial outcome of intergovernmental negotiations, the association of Eastern European countries to the EU without the promise of eventual membership, is also fully covered by LI expectations.[12]

When the EC proposed, in early 1990, to conclude association agreements, it did so without promising future membership. The Council also rejected later attempts by the CEE countries as well as Britain and Germany to include an explicit commitment to enlargement in the treaties. In the association agreements, the EC offered the CEE countries a fast and asymmetrical liberalization of trade in industrial products. However, it reserved protectionist 'anti-dumping' and 'safeguard' measures for itself and made an exception of exactly those sectors (agriculture, textiles, coal, iron, and steel) in which the CEE economies were competitive. The negotiations about substantive policies were dominated by sectoral interest groups and sectoral policy-makers in the Commission as well as in the member governments, and these actors were more concerned with the costs of trade liberalization in their domain of interest than with the general political goal of assisting the associated CEECs in their political and economic transformation (Sedelmeier and Wallace 2000: 439; Torreblanca 2001). By contrast, 'the advocacy alliance . . . has had little by way of outside support on which to draw, either from socio-economic groups that might stand to gain, or from broader political circles, or from public opinion' (Sedelmeier and Wallace 2000: 457).

The substantive outcome reflects the asymmetries in bargaining power. As Moravcsik and Vachudova argue, the CEE countries were not in the position to credibly threaten the reluctant member states with alternative unilateral or multilateral policy options. Neither were the 'drivers' within the Community, mainly Britain and Germany. For them, the economic and political stakes in the East were too small compared to those in the EU. In this situation, association was the highest level of cooperation with the CEE countries the member states could agree on. Through trade liberalization and regulatory adaptation, it enabled the potential winners of enlargement to intensify their economic involvement in CEE markets, while protecting the potential losers of enlargement against the costs of trade and budget competition. Despite constant complaints about the EC's failure to commit itself to the goal of enlargement and to provide a more generous market opening, the CEE countries accepted the Europe Agreements because association was still preferable to weaker trade agreements.

Under these conditions, however, it is puzzling for LI why the European Council decided at its June 1993 Copenhagen summit that the associated countries would become members and embarked upon a process of preparing them (and the EU) for accession. Neither structural economic facts or trends, nor domestic interests, member state preferences, and the asymmetries in bargaining power had changed in the meantime. Nor did the decision take place under conditions that would make a successful LI explanation less likely: it was a unanimous intergovernmental decision; it affected intense and well-organized interests in agriculture and trade; and studies on the effects of Eastern enlargement converged on the finding of (albeit moderate) net economic and financial costs for the member states.

## Community norms and rhetorical action

How can we then account for the decision to enlarge? In my own analysis of Eastern enlargement, I propose to conceptualize the EU as a 'community organization' and include the effects, which a community environment has on the bargaining power and strategies of the actors, in the explanation (Schimmelfennig 2001, 2003. See these articles for more detailed evidence and references). Most fundamentally, a community is characterized by a common ethos—the constitutive values and norms that define the collective identity of the community (who 'we' are, what we stand for, and how we differ from other communities). The community ethos of the EU is based on a liberal-democratic identity as stated in Article 6(1) of the Treaty on European Union: 'The Union is founded on the principles of liberty, democracy, respect for human rights and fundamental freedoms, and the rule of law . . .'. These principles also apply to enlargement: 'Any European state which respects the principles set out in Article 6(1) may apply to become a member of the Union' (Art. 46 TEU).

Community actors cannot just bargain, that is, exchange threats and promises, but need to argue, that is, legitimize their preferences on the basis of the community ethos, and to be concerned about their image and credibility as community members. For those actors that pursue ethos-conforming preferences, the ethos adds legitimacy to their goals and thus strengthens their bargaining power. Conversely, actors that pursue self-serving goals not in line with the ethos run into image and credibility problems, which compromise their future ability to argue and act successfully. As a consequence, community members whose preferences and actions violate the community ethos can be shamed and shunned into compliance.

Indeed, the CEE governments and the 'driver' governments among the member states used arguments based on these community principles to compensate for their inferior material bargaining power and shame the reticent majority into acquiescence with enlargement. First, the CEE countries portrayed themselves as part of the European, liberal international community. CEEC representatives have argued that they have traditionally shared the values and norms of European culture and civilization. Advocates then framed enlargement as an issue of the EU's identity, arguing that it ought not to be seen and decided from the vantage point of national interests and material cost-benefit calculations. They invoked the constitutive values and norms of the EU and the intentions of the founding fathers of the Community. Finally, advocates accused the reticent EU member states of acting inconsistently and betraying the fundamental values and norms of their own community if they failed to commit themselves to enlargement.

The most systematic and formal attempt to rhetorically commit the Community to Eastern enlargement can be found in the Commission's report to the Lisbon summit in June 1992, entitled *Europe and the Challenge of Enlargement*. The Commission referred to the Community's vision of a pan-European liberal order as creating specific obligations in the current situation: 'The Community has never been a closed club, and cannot now refuse the historic challenge to assume its continental responsibilities and contribute to the development of a political and economic order for the whole of Europe' (European Commission 1992).

As a result of this argumentative interaction, the enlargement skeptics were shamed into acquiescing to Eastern enlargement as the legitimate policy. The evidence suggests that the rhetorical action of the 'drivers' did not change the basic enlargement preferences of the 'brakemen' but effectively 'silenced' and prevented them from openly opposing the enlargement project and its gradual implementation. Moreover, the enlargement process gathered momentum and was kept on track although the internal reform of agricultural and structural policies as well as EU institutions and decision-making procedures was delayed and sharply contested and has not met the objective of preparing the EU for the accession of the CEE countries.

## Conclusion: avenues for dialogue and synthesis

Liberal intergovernmentalism is principally open to dialogue and synthesis with other theories of integration. This is, of course, easiest when contending theories share the rationalist foundation and the 'positivist' or analytical methodological commitment of LI. Not only is LI itself a synthesis of traditional, realist intergovernmentalism with a liberal theory of domestic preference formation and a functional theory of inter-national institutions—traditionally postulated by the neofunctionalist or supranation-alist contenders of intergovernmentalism. It can also be linked and synthesized with other theories through scope conditions specifying their respective 'domains of appli-cation' (Jupille, Caporaso, and Checkel 2003: 21–2). For instance, with its empirical domain in 'European integration', that is, institutional changes in the EU polity, LI co-exists well with rational-choice institutionalism, with which it shares basic theoret-ical and methodological assumptions and which has its empirical domain in European Union politics, the day-to-day policy-making within the institutions explained by LI (Pollack 2001, in this volume).

In a similar way, LI would in principle be amenable to dialogue with HI or supra-nationalism, its most relevant rival for a 'grand theory' of European integration—which, however, does not contest LI's rationalist foundations. For instance, Moravcsik concedes that the SEA and the launch of the internal market programme are not fully covered by LI and Geoffrey Garrett, otherwise also sceptical of ECJ autonomy, sees a major role of the Court in providing states with a 'focal point' for agreement on this programme (Garrett and Weingast 1993). Conversely, supranationalists like Stone Sweet (2003) use the internal market as the pivotal case to vindicate their own theory. In general, in addition to high transaction costs or informational asymmetries, it might be fruitful to theorize and test other conditions, which allow supranational organiza-tions to increase their autonomy beyond what governments intended and to influence subsequent intergovernmental negotiations and bargains.

Finally, the enlargement case demonstrates that LI can also be complemented and synthesized with ideational explanations borrowing from social constructivism (compare Checkel and Moravcsik 2001). Moravcsik states that ideology is likely to play a role when economic interests are weak and cause-effect relations are uncertain. Extrapolating from the enlargement case, one might add that identity- and norm-based community effects are more likely to exert an influence on substantive outcomes and institutions if an issue has a strong constitutive or identity dimension, the norms involved have high legitimacy in the EU and resonate strongly with domestic ideas of the actors (Schimmelfennig 2003). Thus, we should be able to observe such community effects not only in the case of Eastern enlargement but also in such constitutional politics issues as the parliamentarization of the EU or the institutionalization of human rights at the EU level, about which LI has little to say.

These avenues for dialogue and synthesis should not obscure, however, the centrality of LI for the theory and explanation of European integration. First, LI is parsimonious and general. It uses a limited number of parameters (in particular the domestic issue-specific preference structure of a few major member states) to explain the main substantive and institutional outcomes in the European integration process. Second, it sets high methodological standards. Moravcsik carefully specifies testable hypotheses including alternative explanations and uses primary, original sources to support his findings. Third, there is widespread agreement that it does explain fundamental sources, processes, and outcomes of European integration. The theoretical, methodological, and empirical achievements of LI justify its status as a baseline theory of European integration.

Finally, one should not forget the paradoxical effects of a baseline theory in a competitive academic market: new studies will be framed against it and seek to show that it does not explain all aspects of European integration, or that it does not do so sufficiently, thereby creating the appearance of general criticism while indirectly reproducing general acceptance of the theory's baseline status.

# Notes

1. For comments on a previous version of this chapter, I thank Thomas Diez and Berthold Rittberger. I am particularly grateful to Andrew Moravcsik for an extensive critique and many helpful clarifications and suggestions. The usual disclaimer applies.

2. For Moravcsik's own detailed exposition of LI, see Moravcsik (1993) and Moravcsik (1998: 3–77).

3. Note that these levels of abstraction should not be confused with levels of analysis (domestic and international negotiations).

4. With regard to interdependence and institutions, however, realist intergovernmentalism in integration theory has always been more 'liberal' than mainstream (neo)realism. See, e.g. the essays collected in Hoffman (1995).

5. 'The Choice for Europe' has been the subject of serious historiographical debate. See, e.g. the special issue of the *Journal of Cold War Studies* (2/3, 2000) on French policy under De Gaulle.

6. Such issues will be taken up in the contributions to the section on 'Constructing Europe'. See also the exchange between Diez (1999) and Moravcsik (1999c).

7. Moravcsik (1999a: 174–5). For such a critique, see, e.g. Garrett and Tsebelis (1996). See the section on 'Analysing Governance' for approaches that focus on this aspect of EU politics.

8. For a representative collection of texts, see, e.g. Sandholtz and Stone Sweet (1998).

9. This analysis is absent in Moravcsik and Vachudova (2002). For the following, I draw on my own work on Eastern enlargement, published in Schimmelfennig (2001, 2003).

10. For analyses of member state preferences, see, e.g. Grabbe and Hughes (1998: 4–6) and IEP/TEPSA (1998).

11. See, e.g. Baldwin, Francois, and Portes (1997: 152–66); Weise et al. (1997: 258).

12. For a detailed account of the association negotiations, see Torreblanca (2001).

# Guide to further reading

HOFFMANN, S. (1995), *The European Sisyphus. Essays on Europe, 1964–1994* (Boulder: Westview Press). This is a collection of important essays by the most prominent representative of traditional, realist intergovernmentalism.

MORAVCSIK, A. (1998), *The Choice for Europe: Social Purpose and State Power from Messina to Maastricht* (Ithaca: Cornell University Press). This book presents the most complete outline of liberal intergovernmentalist theory and a detailed analysis of five major cases of European integration from the Treaties of Rome to the Treaty of Maastricht.

—— (1993) 'Preferences and Power in the European Community. A Liberal Intergovernmentalist Approach', *Journal of Common Market Studies* 31(4), 473–524.

This is an earlier and shorter explication of the liberal intergovernmentalist approach, which includes an application of the theory of 'two-level games' to European integration.

—— and NICOLAÏDIS, K. (1999), 'Explaining the Treaty of Amsterdam: Interests, Influence, Institutions', *Journal of Common Market Studies* 37(1), 59–85. This article adds another case of treaty-amending negotiations to the cases assembled in 'The Choice for Europe'.

'Review section symposium: The choice for Europe: Social purpose and state power from Messina to Maastricht' (1999), *Journal of European Public Policy* 6(1), 155–79. This review section unites critiques by important EU scholars and a response by Andrew Moravcsik.

# PART II

# ANALYSING EUROPEAN GOVERNANCE

# 5

# Governance and Institutional Development

*Markus Jachtenfuchs and Beate Kohler-Koch*

## Introduction*

In recent years, the term 'governance' has become very popular in research on European integration (Armstrong and Bulmer 1998; Bulmer 1994; Hooghe and Marks 2001; Kohler-Koch and Eising 1999; Marks et al. 1996; Scharpf 2002). Governance concepts are also increasingly used in domestic politics (Campbell, Hollingsworth, and Lindberg 1993; Kooiman 1993; Rhodes 1997) and in international relations (Keohane 2001; Young 1999). Usually, a rapidly increasing usage of a concept goes hand in hand with a loss of precision of its meaning. The works quoted above are only the tip of an iceberg in an incredibly rich and varied field. In addition, even within the more narrow confines of European governance, there are distinct national academic traditions (Wallace 2003).

Given this complexity in a rapidly evolving field of research, this chapter does not attempt to explore the varieties of governance approaches (cf. Jachtenfuchs 2001 for an overview) but puts forward an argument about the contribution that a governance perspective can make towards a more comprehensive understanding of the development of the Euro-polity as compared to other approaches such as classical integration theory, policy analysis, or the constitutional debate. In our view, this contribution is threefold. First, a governance perspective is able to link policy-making and institution-building. Second, it re-introduces the competition for political power into the analysis. Third, it allows for discussion of normative issues of a good political order for the EU without losing contact with empirical research on how political life in the EU actually functions.

# Approaches to European integration

## Three separate discussions

To understand how and why the Euro-polity emerged and evolved and how it functions is the broad concern of much of the literature on European integration. Several of these approaches are dealt with in other chapters of this book. However, three distinct academic discussions are particularly relevant to an understanding of the contribution of a governance perspective on European integration as they are closely related to one another but at the same time have specific and sometimes complementary blind spots.

*Classical integration theory* is an analytical approach for explaining why states chose to empower the EU to perform certain tasks in specific areas. Since the 1960s, a society-centred version (neofunctionalism; cf. Haas 1964; Sandholtz and Stone Sweet 1998; Schmitter, in this volume) competed with a state-centred version (intergovernmentalism; cf. Hoffmann 1966; Schimmelfennig, in this volume). Contrary to the neofunctionalism of the 1960s, which had a strong normative orientation because it considered 'international organization' to be a promising political strategy in a volatile international environment and a means to overcome the self-fulfilling nature of realism as a theory of political action, recent scholarship adopts an almost exclusively analytical perspective. European integration seen as a subset of international relations theory asks about the conditions under which states create and reform international institutions.

*Policy analysis* has dealt with European integration from a totally different angle and developed in parallel with and independently from classical integration theory. The explanatory goal of policy analysis is to find out how public problems are solved in various institutional contexts and in different types of political processes. As a by-product, it has shown the enormous variety in institutional structures on the micro-level below the level of intergovernmental conferences. However, it proved difficult to generalize from these empirical findings because of the increasing complexity of context variables even among allegedly similar countries. Studies of EU policies suffer from the same problem. However, if the claim for universal theory is given up, partial theories offer a promising path (Scharpf 1997). Increasingly, studies of this type contribute to a better understanding of how the European multi-level system works. The perspective is mainly analytical, but normative issues loom strongly in the background as it is very difficult to analyse policy processes without having an idea about good or appropriate solutions to policy problems.

The *constitutional debate* is a third perspective that many scholars would not even consider as theory. Many contributions to it emerge from think tanks and constitute applied research that does not seek new knowledge but rather to apply existing theories. However, there has for a considerable time existed a strong explicit normative theory (Friedrich 1969) which is now culminating in an intense debate on what the Euro-polity should look like (Abromeit 1998; Schmalz-Bruns 1999; Schmitter 2000). The term 'constitutional debate' here refers to the body of literature dealing with the question of what a legitimate and effective polity for the particular social and political setting of the European Union should look like. It is not restricted to those writing about a possible EU constitution. This field of polity-making is not the exclusive domain of lawyers but a typical domain for political scientists. Constitution-making is the field where analytical and normative theories are most closely linked. Constitution-makers have to take into account driving social forces analysed by classical integration theory and the conditions for effective problem-solving identified by policy analysis. The focus on constitutional policy sheds light on issues of legitimacy, democracy, and community-building that are largely outside the explanatory scope of the first two approaches of integration theory. However, the constitutional debate far too often loses contact with empirical reality as it is analysed by classical integration theory and policy analysis. Both these approaches, in turn, risk omitting key issues of social science and legal analysis.

## Governance as an integrated approach

Each of the three approaches has distinct explanatory interests and blind spots. Policy analysis tends to take the polity as a stable background variable, theories of international institutions put issues of legitimacy at the margin, and normative theories of institutions would often profit from a better empirical grip on reality. We argue that a governance perspective is able to link these separate discussions and thus to improve our knowledge about the EU.

In academic as well as in public discourse the usage of the term 'governance' has seen a rapid increase. As a result, it is sometimes difficult to find areas where governance does *not* take place. In our view, governance should be narrowly defined in a way that does not include all kinds of goal-oriented action irrespective of its social context. This would exclude usages such as 'corporate governance' from our definition. Second, while openly admitting the unavoidable normative connotations of many key social science concepts, we do not think that the concept of governance should determine the substantive outcomes of governance. This would exclude overly prescriptive terms such as 'good governance' which are so prominent in the discussion of international organizations (e.g. OECD 2001; United Nations 2000). Finally, the concept should not be restricted to the acts and omissions of governments within territorial states. Thus, we define governance as the continuous political process of setting explicit goals for society and intervening in it in order to achieve these goals (cf. Kohler-Koch 1993, 2002; March and Olsen 1995; Zürn 1998).

This definition should constitute a viable compromise between an all-encompassing but vague notion of governance and a too narrowly defined one which is already conceptually linked to the existence of the territorial state. The threshold should be sufficiently high in order not to equate each action with an act of governance. Governance thus involves setting goals and making decisions for an entire collectivity, including individuals or groups who have not explicitly agreed to them. It also involves a rather high level of intervention which may stabilize or alter a given status quo.

How does such a conceptual lens help to better understand the European Union and to integrate the three theoretical approaches outlined above? The answer lies in two propositions that are neglected by these approaches taken in isolation. First, we argue that the way policy is made changes the institutional framework in a broader sense. The institutional structure of the EU in this view does not only comprise the text of the basic treaties but also informal components of institutions that are often neglected in analysing the European Union.

Over the years, this has been an incremental and cumulative process. Rules of behaviour are being defined and changed. Once agreed upon, these rules may acquire the same prescriptive force as formal rules. They emerge either in the normal policy process or as explicit 'inter-institutional agreements'. The prime example for the first type of rules is 'comitology'. Only after numerous committees, and practices and rules of behaviour within these committees, had emerged in highly specific policy fields did the Council adopt a formal regulation on comitology, which it later revised (see Christiansen and Kirchner 2000; Joerges and Vos 1999 for overviews). Comitology touches the core of the EU law-making process and the relationship between the Commission and the member states. It is now clearly a part of the EU's constitution (Joerges and Neyer 1997). Examples for the second type of rules are the budgetary agreements or those concerning the hearings of designated Commissioners before EP committees.

These rules change normative and cognitive expectations as well as the behaviour of actors in the EU system. They are part of the 'rules of the game' (North 1993: 12) comparable to the written Treaty rules. However, this constitutional dimension of policy-making is easily overlooked.

Second, changes in governance also change the course of integration. By integration, we understand not only the explicit constitutional decisions about the relationship between the EU and its member states but also incremental and informal changes in that relationship. Several factors work in this direction. The EU creates a 'communicative universe' (Bogdandy 2003): regular reporting in the most diverse forms about actual member state behaviour with respect to EU legislation or policies increases the level of information about other member states' policies. Member states may always choose to ignore a piece of legislation or a policy but the information about this behaviour spreads through the EU system. This may turn out to be disadvantageous in cases where the same member state has a strong interest in the observation of a certain regulation by all others. It also increases the need for justification of non-conforming behaviour. This again is not a heavy sanction but adds to the constraints of policy-making.

Governance approaches also build on regime theory and the compliance literature. The key difference is that international regimes are issue-specific whereas the EU is almost universal in scope. The EU thus acts as a comprehensive institution in which the individual member state is embedded in a system of information and assessment in virtually every field of politics. As a result, member states mutually observe each other and constantly remind one another of their duties and obligations as members of a larger community. This does not mean that those duties and obligations are always perfectly observed. But there is pressure for mutual information and empathy in a multi-level system of governance. Similar forces may apply to the Open Method of Co-ordination (Hodson and Maher 2000) and to integrating civil society into the EU policy process as this favours the emergence of a European political space.

These mechanisms and their effects have long been observed. We do not argue that they are new; they are not even restricted to the European Union although they find their most developed expression here. But we do argue that a governance perspective is better able to see their interrelationship.

# The shape of governance in the EU

## Characteristics of the multi-level system

The structure of the EU polity *ceteris paribus* is responsible for the way political processes take place and what policy outputs look like. Turning Lowi's argument (Lowi 1964) on its head, we argue that polity determines politics and policy. However, in order to establish precise cause-effect relationships, the particular characteristics of the EU polity which matter for political processes and political outcomes must be singled out. This endeavour has to proceed at a rather low level of abstraction if it is to yield specific results that go beyond sweeping generalizations. As the independent variable of this type of inquiry is not the EU (which is unique) but more concrete parts of its institutional setup (which may exist in other states or international organizations as well), this approach does not suffer from the eternal n=1 problem of EU studies but allows for comparative inquiries. In this section we discuss some examples of this type of non-concrete element of the Euro-polity.

One such non-concrete element for comparison is represented by policy areas in the EU—commonly referred to as pillars—which differ significantly from each other. Although comparative policy analysis usually reveals remarkable differences between policy fields even within one and the same territorial state, the differences in the EU are far more decisive. The Commission monopoly of initiative, the EP's increasingly asserting itself as a second law-making chamber, or judicial review by the ECJ may account for systematic characteristics of EU policy-making in that particular structure, such as a possible asymmetry between 'negative' and 'positive' integration (Scharpf 1996). However, the very institutional structure that is responsible for this asymmetry is not present in the second or third pillar. Hence, there are large differences in terms of political conflicts, policy outcomes, and problem-solving capacity between what is familiarly perceived as the supranational area, on the one hand, and these 'transgovernmental' (Wallace 2002: 265) areas of the EU, on the other.

The governance approach argues that in the entire system, member states are still very important. An overall assessment of the distribution of policy-making powers between the European and the member state levels suggests that the EU is stuck somewhere in the middle (Schmitter 1996), with large variations between policy fields. For over half a century, there has been no uniform development towards ever increasing powers for supranational institutions. The emerging picture is more one of power-sharing between different levels with the member states retaining a very substantial role in decision-making, including the exclusive power to extend or reduce EU policy-making competencies. Even more important is that whereas supranational institutions have a substantial share in policy-making, the competition for political power takes place almost exclusively at the member state level. Although the homogeneity of political groups within the European Parliament has steadily increased over the years (Hix 1999: ch. 6), there is no independent European arena for competition for political power. The members of key European institutions are chosen by the member states, and changes in the party balance in the EP have at best a small impact on the outcomes of the EU policy-making process. As a result, European elections are still 'second-order national elections' (Reif and Schmitt 1980). Major political debates usually take place within neatly separated national political spaces. The European public space is fragmented and ephemeral (Eder 2003).

In short, political competition at the EU level is weak compared to federal states. Compared with other international organizations, EU-level institutions are strong in terms of their ability to shape policy outcomes and in terms of the resources at their disposal. In some respects (e.g. in the case of the ECJ) they are as strong as their national counterparts. But the sometimes striking similarities between the EU and territorial states—which are often overlooked by classical integration theory—should not obscure the fact that the EU does not possess the two most important sources of power: the legitimate use of physical force and independent taxation (Genschel 2002; Weber 1978: 54).

A result of these characteristics and a further specific feature of the EU's institutional structure is the fact that EU politics is not characterized by hierarchical and majoritarian decision-making and implementation but by negotiations among independent actors and institutions. These negotiations have to cope with two conflicting goals (Scharpf 1994). The first is that decisions have to respect member state autonomy. The EU institutions or other member states cannot strictly speaking enforce the implementation of a decision upon an unwilling member state as they lack the means of force. Even if they were possessed of those means, the long shadow of future EU co-operation would suggest using them with great reluctance because each member state could find itself in a similar position in the future.

A one-sided emphasis on preservation of autonomy would prevent or at least hinder the resolution of collective action problems among EU member states. For this reason, member states have an interest in a general orientation of decision-making that is compatible with Union-wide policies. This is the second goal. Both goals are not merely general characteristics of decision-making but also normative principles. In the supranational structures, the special relationship between the Commission and the Council (Wallace 2000) is the institutionalization of those two principles. In the transgovernmental structure, the institutionalization of autonomy is much stronger.

The last example of an element of the Euro-polity that shapes politics and policy is the fact that it is a multi-level system. The literature on 'multi-level governance' (e.g. Hooghe and Marks 2001) regards this as the single most important characteristic of the EU. However, it is important to avoid interpreting this notion in terms of neatly separated layers in analogy to the ideal-typical model of US-federalism. The European multi-level system is much more similar to the German system where decisions taken at the higher level are dependent upon the consent of the lower level (Scharpf 1988). As a result, institutional self-interest often prevails over substantive interests. Both systems are also heavily biased towards the preservation of autonomy.

However, one should not fall into the other extreme and overstate the similarities between European and German federalism. Thus, in Germany, the upper (federal) level and the lower (*Länder*) level are linked by the ubiquitous presence of integrated political parties across governmental levels. In this setting, a conflict between the levels of government is often transformed into a conflict between government parties and opposition parties at the federal level (Lehmbruch 2000). Due to the weakness of political parties and political competition at the EU level, this unifying factor across levels is absent in EU politics. For this reason, negotiators at the EU level are less strongly bound to mandates and positions set at the lower level than is the case in German federalism. Because of the absence of this unifying factor, governments may even liberate themselves from the grip of their domestic constituencies by pointing to the necessities of compromising in a large negotiation system (Grande 1996). Actors in such a setting can resort to tactically motivated self-commitments (Schelling 1960: 22). On the whole, the relationship between the different levels in the EU is characterized by loose coupling. In Germany, levels are tightly coupled (Benz 2003). The absence of strong political parties at the European level, one of the structural sources of the EU's democratic deficit, presents a major factor for promoting agreement among governments. The different logic of party competition is not the only important factor that accounts for differences between European and German (and US) federalism. It has been used here merely as an illustration for the argument that referring to the EU as a multi-level system has no explanatory power unless research reveals the mechanisms by which the levels of such a system are linked.

## Sharing authority in a multi-level system of governance

The intellectual challenge of the multi-level governance model is that it does not just describe the dispersion of authoritative competence across territorial levels but draws attention to the interconnection of multiple political arenas in the process of governing (Hooghe and Marks 2001: 3–4). The Treaties provide mechanisms to reconcile the push for autonomy and member state control with the needs of efficient collective decision-making. But studying supranational procedures in the first pillar, or transgovernmental ones in the second and third pillars, just highlights to what extent both national governments and Community institutions, above all the Commission and the European Parliament, have become an integral part of joint decision-making. It does not inform us about the management of political responsibility and political influence. National governments are accountable to national parliaments and the electorate. In federal systems, in addition, they have to consider the positions of sub-national units. Furthermore, state agents have to cooperate with private interest groups in order to attune public policy-making to societal demands. Managing the public-private interface is a challenge for national actors and Community institutions, whereas adjusting national systems of democratic accountability to a multi-level polity is the main task of governments.

Member state governments are faced with a 'negotiation-accountability dilemma' (Benz 2003: 8). Negotiations in the Council are mixed-motive games in which each participant aims at a collective decision that, nevertheless, should pay tribute to partial interests. Flexibility in negotiating positions that allow for a give and take across issue areas or rely on future trade-offs facilitates agreements. The price for avoiding deadlock in negotiations is the degrading of national accountability. Flexibility demands a high degree of autonomy which even the governing majority in parliament will be hesitant to accept. Member states have resorted to different formal and informal strategies in order to reconcile parliamentary accountability—and also regional participation—with the imperatives of efficient European negotiations. Irrespective of the diverse kinds of solutions, the main difference is between strategies of 'tight' or 'loose' coupling'.

Although parliaments in only two member states have the formal right to issue binding propositions (Benz 2003), they can exert a *de facto veto* by threatening not to ratify treaty agreements or to oppose the transposition of directives. In daily practice, however, at least the majority party in parliaments seeks to avoid putting a government under narrow constraints. For the sake of decision-making efficiency some form of 'loose coupling' would be advisable, but most of the time actors resort to informal consultations. The 'critical dialogue between government and majority faction' (Benz 2003: 33) proved to be an efficient instrument of political concertation but it functions best when both sides avoid publicizing conflicting positions and in this way it is adverse to transparency and public accountability. An indication that de-coupling may be on the rise is the establishment of national parliamentary offices in Brussels, which enables them to become European actors in their own right.

The quest for influence in a system with dispersed allocation of governing authority has stimulated all kinds of actors to go transnational. National interest groups have adapted to the opportunities of multiple access and now pursue a dual strategy, lobbying both at home and in Brussels. Likewise, EU associations and transnational public-interest groups now target both EU institutions and member state governments. Their incorporation into the European policy-making process at national and Community level is determined by the value they can add to ebcient and appropriate problem-solving and the resources they command to make their voices heard. The Commission, in particular, has been eager to prop up its role as political entrepreneur by inviting external expert advice. In recent years the argument that interest-group and expert involvement are improving the quality of policy deliberations has been supported by the opinion that policy-making in the EU needs to increase its legitimacy. In order to win public acceptance for the EU, the Commission seeks to involve public interest groups in particular (European Commission 2000: 5). It has also made a plea for 'better involvement and more openness' (European Commission 2001: 4), that is, for opening up the policy process and for getting more individuals and organizations involved. Whether these pleas will achieve their stated goals remains to be seen (Scharpf 2002). They are, however, an indication of a strongly perceived need on the part of the Commission to increase the legitimacy of the policy process by involving more actors.

Networking is the most characteristic feature of EU governance (see Peterson in this volume) and a plethora of committees are nodal points of communication. A culture of consultation and dialogue is prevalent for two reasons. The first is, that in contrast to a parliamentary democracy, diverging interests cannot be framed in opposing ideological positions and decided by party competition. The Commission is supposed to be a non-political technocratic body, the Council is by nature an 'all-party government' and the European Parliament, because of the requirements of qualified majority vote, is most of the time forced to form a broad conservative-socialist coalition in order to gain influence. Hence, the logic of interest intermediation within each institution and, to an even larger extent, the logic of institutional interaction preclude a strong link between party politics and the substance of policy prevalent in the member states.

The second reason is that with new problems on the horizon and the complex context of fifteen national political systems, policy-making entails above all defining the problem and analysing the given situation. Therefore, it is plausible to assume that gathering expertise and argument will be the prevailing pattern of interaction. It is well accepted that the Commission takes the lead when negotiations concentrate on analysing the factual. Advisory committees assisting the Commission in drafting policy proposals and even comitology committees are geared to support the decision-making process by providing expert knowledge. The Commission even has a legal duty to take '... account ... of any new development based on scientific facts' (EC Treaty, Art. 95, 3) which is widely read as an obligation to consult scientific experts (Dehousse 2002: 14). As soon as negotiations turn to a discussion of what might be a fitting and appropriate solution, scientific deliberations become deficient. The mode of communication changes from arguing to bargaining, and government representatives take the lead because they, and not the Commission, are considered to be in a better position to make judgments on questions of social and political compatibility. But even then, the convincing argument in line with consensual knowledge is the common currency to trade negotiating positions.

## Governance, integration, and system transformation

After having discussed how the specific setup of the Euro-polity structures political processes and policy-making, we will now turn to the aspects of how the practice of governance shapes the EU's constitution and how these changes in governance lead to changes in the overall structure of the European multi-level system.

## Patterns of governance and constitutional reality

In the literature, there are two contrasting views about what the constitution of the EU actually is and what the major factors for change are. In the intergovernmentalist account, the EU constitution consists of the basic Treaties and major agreements (such as the one on the European Monetary System in the late 1970s). It is changed through agreements among the member states at intergovernmental conferences or European Council meetings (cf. Moravcsik 1998 and his contribution in this volume). The competing view argues that while this is true, it is not the entire picture. In this view the EU constitution has more fluid boundaries. Besides the Treaties and major agreements, it also consists of norms from other sources (Shaw 1999). These norms are easily overlooked because they do not result from highly publicized intergovernmental bargains but from small incremental steps that often have only a low visibility. Incrementalism makes it easy to obscure a hidden agenda: '. . . integrationists promote their ambitions by stealth' (*The Economist*, September 14, 2002: 33). It may, indeed, be called a 'brilliant, but also slightly sinister strategy' (*ibid.*) that constitutional moves are buried in a mass of technical detail, boring people into submission. In this section, we discuss a number of examples of how seemingly minor provisions acquire a constitutional dimension and contribute to a change in the overall structure of the system.

The first example is the 'notification obligation' (for more detail see Bogdandy 2000, 2003). There is no general act which regulates the Commission's right to ask member states to provide information. But individual directives, especially those relating to legal harmonization of the single market, include legal obligations to inform the Commission. In the field of technical standards and regulation the member states have to provide information at every step of their legislative process and they are prevented from adopting a new regulation before the Commission and other parties concerned have had an opportunity to react. Where the Commission regards an EU regulation as being more appropriate than a national one, the member government may not proceed with its own initiative. Interference with member state autonomy has expanded over the years by moving in three directions. The Commission gained a central position by defining the procedures to be applied, in particular by institutionalizing a special standing committee and involving private economic interests. Furthermore, the scope of application has been enlarged and, above all, compliance has become compulsory because the European Court of Justice affirmed direct applicability.

Thus a minor change in reporting obligations over the years led to a changed equilibrium between the national and the supranational level. It did so in two ways: first, by strengthening the institutional position of the Commission in the European policy-making process; and, second, by opening the national decision-making process to transborder interference. For the sake of building up the single market, the notifying obligation has led to a change in legislative culture. The better informed national administrators are likely to take into consideration policy initiatives by other member states and appraise the relative benefit of a common EU regulation.

Another case illustrating how procedural provisions and institutional reforms interact is provided by the area of social policy. For example, social policy regulations at EU level were until recently underdeveloped for economic and political reasons. The Community's preoccupation with market building, the uneven distribution of negotiating powers between the social partners, and the reluctance of member state governments to renounce social policy authority explain quite well this low standing. Institutional constraints made it easier to block social initiatives than to endorse them. After the introduction of majority voting in some areas of social policy, not only governments but also social partners, in particular the employer associations, changed their attitude. They agreed to a Commission initiative to launch a new and innovative corporatist procedure which was—with small corrections—inserted into the Treaty of Maastricht. Management and labour are now not only endowed with the power to conclude voluntary agreements but, within the social dialogue, they can reach binding agreements that may subsequently be turned into Community law (Arts. 138, 139 EC Treaty; see Falkner 2000 for more detail). The Treaty provisions privilege the social partners in relation to both the Commission and the Council. It furnishes them with a right of initiative, otherwise the prerogative of the Commission, and with the right of policy formulation, which under the Community method is the joint task of Commission, Council, and Parliament.

For the sake of our argument, it does not matter that they succeeded only twice in reaching an agreement (on parental leave and on atypical work) because this was due mainly to economic and political context conditions. The more important point is that small changes in governance procedures at the European level had a considerable impact throughout the system. In the shadow of a Council vote, the Commission found it easy to persuade management and labour to engage in Euro-corporatism and to form an advocacy coalition strong enough to make its point in the Treaty negotiations. A practice has now been established which opens new opportunity structures for social partners, who now are core actors under this new 'negotiated legislation' procedure (Falkner 2000: 719). It not only tips the balance between actors in policy-making at the European level, but quite obviously has implications for the national policy process. The corporatist EU policy community has gained influence on national patterns of interest intermediation. Including social actors in the implementation of policies is supported by law,[1] by a shared normative belief system endorsing 'social partnership' as an uncontested norm, and by institutionalized patterns of communication and interaction that reach across national borders (Falkner 2002).

In 1994, in view of the persistently high level of unemployment, the European Council took the first step by agreeing to an intergovernmental exchange of information. This approach was then given a legal base by incorporating a new title into the Treaty of Amsterdam providing for a more elaborate procedure and an institutional infrastructure. The constitutionalization did not confer any additional legislative or legal competence. It was merely an exercise in benchmarking, introducing reporting obligations, creating procedures for target setting, monitoring and evaluation, and assigning responsibilities (to the Commission and the Employment Committee) for managing the exchange of information, consultation, and review.

The new provisions have been rated by some as 'largely symbolic actions' (Leibfried and Pierson 2000: 273) whereas others see the new approach in employment policy as the beginning of a re-structuring of the state (Deppe, Felder, and Tidow 2003). In the perspective of normative democratic theory it is a concept that deviates from fundamental requirements of parliamentary democracy. The idea that only those who have to bear the cost of implementation have the right to participate in formulating and carrying out regulations runs counter to the fundamental right of equal democratic responsibility. An equally fundamental opposition has been voiced by proponents of European supranationality. A 'deliberative supranationalism' which leaves decisions on political targets and commitments to corresponding behaviour to voluntary agreements is accused of eroding the basis of the Community system (Weiler 1999; for a critical evaluation see Joerges 2002: 28–31). Such far-reaching conclusions seem, however, to be premature. Up to now the new modes of governance are of limited importance because they are applied in only a minority of cases and most of them are to be found in just two areas, environmental and social policy. Furthermore, when subjected to empirical scrutiny (Héritier 2002) it turns out that they do not live up to the high expectations in terms of improving policy-making efficiency and implementation effectiveness. As a consequence, any further expansion may be restricted and established procedures could be changed to fit the Community method. It is open to debate whether the kind of cooperation now institutionalized in employment and other aspects of social policy is a 'starting point' or a 'resting point' (Wallace 2002: 32). In the past the Commission often started to facilitate cooperation between the member states by conducting studies, delivering opinions, and arranging consultations. Accordingly, some scholars see it in the perspective of an evolutionary pattern (Maurer, Mittag, and Wessels 2003) which in a protracted trial and error process moves towards communitarization. Others may argue that the Open Method of Coordination fits very well in the present functioning of EU institutions, which in daily practice have supplemented or partly replaced legal hierarchy with deliberation and negotiated compliance. Arguments in favour of this position are that the effectiveness of the comitology procedures rests mainly on a communicative approach to problem-solving (Joerges and Neyer 1997), and that the willingness of member states to respect Community law is advanced by 'horizontal enforcement', that is, a network of discussions and negotiations which help to keep the constraints of implementation flexible (Snyder 1993; Neyer and Wolf 2003).

One outcome, though, is quite evident. The new modes of governance do not deprive the Commission of influence. It is the Commission that encourages the social partners to launch a policy initiative. The Commission provides the infrastructure for exchanging information and sharing knowledge, it builds and cultivates networks of experts, performs as process-manager and PR agent of shared conceptions. It looks as if the Commission has regained ground which it lost to the European Parliament and the

Council with the introduction of the co-decision procedure. The effect is twofold. First, it supports the trend towards informality and selective networking. Both decrease the transparency and hence the accountability of governance. Second, it pushes a transnationalization of the European system. Member state governments lose their gatekeeping power especially in relation to resourceful actors. This has an impact not just on governing procedures but on substance. Interest intermediation at the European level is biased in favour of those who have the capacity to get organized and raise their voice and it is framed by the dominant logic of market formation. In this way the new modes of governance probably contribute to the process of uneven Europeanization (Deppe, Felder, and Tidow 2003), that is to say, the evolution of a system of deterritorialized regulation and territorially segmented accountability and mediation of public interests.

## Europeanization, the forgotten dimension of integration

For decades integration studies focused on the building of a supranational system of European cooperation and rarely asked how this might affect the domestic social and political systems. With the increase of EU regulation in the mid-1980s and the ensuing interest in policy studies, research on Europeanization became a growth industry covering a broad research agenda. Because research interests extend to different dimensions and embrace divergent theoretical approaches it is not surprising that Europeanization remains a fuzzy concept (cf. Eising 2003 and Radaelli 2000 for overviews). The prevalent view defines Europeanization 'as the process of influence deriving from European decisions and impacting member states' policies and political and administrative structures' (Héritier 2001: 3). It avoids any teleological connotations and leaves it open to empirical verification whether a conversion in outcome occurs or an internalization of the organizational logic of the EU takes place. Supranational legislation is the starting point and research explores and explains in a comparative perspective the processing of EU input in individual political systems.

The bulk of the literature is confined to impact studies of the EU on member states in terms of changing policies and, less so, on administrative structures and patterns of interest intermediation. But even in this relatively narrow field, and in spite of a considerable number of empirical explorations, there is limited agreement on causes and effects. The reasons why it is so difficult to make compelling generalizations are not hard to understand in view of the complexities of the issues giving rise to competing interest constellations, and the long and varied institutional histories of European countries, which national actors often either fiercely defend or consider a 'burden of the past' (Olsen 2001). The attempt to design a parsimonious concept of 'fit or misfit' (Caporaso, Cowles, and Risse 2001) is problematic because '. . . it tends to miss the complex dynamics of political processes induced by European policy inputs at the national level' (Héritier 2001: 9; see also Knill 2002: 201–4 and Goetz 2001: 220).

The main conclusion to be drawn from this debate is that policy regulation and administrative politics change, though in particular 'national colours' (Kohler-Koch

2001: 88). Member states have responded quite differently to identical EU input even under similar external and internal context conditions (Héritier and Knill 2001: 257). The two most obvious reasons are that national and sub-national actors have consider-able latitude when implementing an EU policy and that costs of adaptation differ. It makes a difference whether alterations are restricted to modifications within a given pattern of sector regulation or whether they strike at the core of national administrative traditions (Knill 2002: 41–5). In addition, the specific problem-solving approach of a particular country and its capacity for administrative reform are important.

Though the record of empirical investigation is mixed, the over-all picture is quite conclusive: decades of EU attempts at harmonization and system competition have left a mark on national systems but they have had no unifying effect. This first of all applies to policy regulation and administrative structures. It also holds true when looking at national governance beyond the narrow confines of administrative politics. Again, policy-making at the European level has forced governments to adapt. Empirical studies document the intensity of participation of national institutions in the processes of preparing, negotiating, implementing, and controlling European level decisions (Wessels 2000). But the shift in attention and resources and the requirements of adaptation have not led to dramatic modifications in the overall system design of the member states. 'Traditional national patterns are resistant and apparently flexible enough to be sufficiently capable of coping with the challenges from the European level' (Maurer, Mittag, and Wessels 2003).

These findings relate to the organization within governments for managing Euro-pean policy-making and do not provide a complete picture. In order to make a general assessment of the Europeanization of national governance, further dimensions need to be studied. An inclusive approach has to explore the shifting boundaries between the public and the private sphere, changes in public accountability and in the equilibrium between the legislative and the executive, and the organization of interest mediation, in particular with respect to the role of political parties. This is difficult because the record is mixed and not all dimensions are equally well explored. What follows is a tentative move in this direction.

One could argue that the public-private balance has changed because the inbuilt preference for liberalization and de-regulation in the single market programme has a tendency to set limits for public intervention. In addition, monetary union and above all the commitment to economic and financial stability has put national governments under strict and heavy constraints. However, these two obvious trends have to be viewed in proper perspective: efforts at re-regulation at the European level have been notable and, furthermore, social distributive and re-distributive policies have remained a national prerogative. The requirements of economic and financial stability set strict limits for public spending, but it is left to national governments to chose the appropriate measures of compliance. Furthermore, it can be argued that the provisions written into the Treaty merely express in political terms the logic of sound economic policy which would otherwise be enforced by market forces in an internationalized economy.

Economic and Monetary Union has brought about the most spectacular change in national governance but it is a self-chosen external constraint that does not alter the functioning of the domestic governance system. It is rather the empowerment of economic actors by an integrated market and the lobby opportunities for trade associations in a multi-level system that distort the given equilibrium of social forces in the member states. Their gain in autonomy contributes to a transformation in the role of the state, from an integrative institution with superior power to a mediator between competing societal interests, and it favours the emergence of a system of network governance (Kohler-Koch and Eising 1999).

The process of integration also impinged on the balance between the executive and the legislative. The extraordinarily high regulative output of the EU is a good indicator of the extent to which national parliaments have been deprived of their policy setting power. In addition, the internal dynamics of Council negotiations and committee work make it easy for governments to escape their political accountability. National parliaments have made efforts to regain parliamentary scrutiny over governmental action but have not succeeded. They have not found adequate procedures to square the circle, namely to exert control without blocking the decision-making process and to maintain an influence compatible with public accountability (Benz 2003). This trend is not restricted to EU involvement but extends to many fields of international regulation. The highly technical mission of regulating complex subject matters like international financial markets favours the emergence of transnational expert groups. Though part of a national ministry, they control access to the international arena and share exclusive knowledge and contacts. They become socialized into an international club and gain autonomy from any kind of national control—be it by parliament or by their own ministry (Lütz 2002: 328–30).

The liberation of internationalized technocrats from public control may be the flip side of the coin of a still provincial world of political parties. Parties become organized where the power is and despite a deep entrenchment of national policy-making in the supranational system of the EU, government power is still gained and lost in national elections. The national party system in many European countries is in flux but there are no indications that change relates in any way to the existence of a European Union (Mair 2000). Parties may have the EU on their agenda but an inward-looking public audience makes it difficult to attract attention to political choices. To make matters worse, the public discourse does not reflect political responsibilities. When voting for the European Parliament, the electorate takes into consideration the pro- or anti-European preference of a party although the EP has very little say in constitutional politics. In national elections parties are more often than not held accountable for the substantive policy outputs which were decided beyond their reach in Brussels. What is missing is the 'enlightened understanding' among citizens that is considered to be a prerequisite for a democratic process (Dahl 1989: 112).

## A governance perspective on Eastern enlargement

A governance perspective does not seek to explain the basic intergovernmental decisions on the extent and timing of enlargement (Schimmelfennig 2001) but is interested
in the consequences of enlargement for EU governance, EU institutional development,
and governance in applicant countries. The most important background condition for
understanding the consequences of Eastern enlargement for European integration is
that it considerably increases heterogeneity within the EU—heterogeneity in terms of
the level of economic development, administrative structures and capacities, systems
of political ideas, party systems, and constitutionalism, to name but a few examples.
Both policy-making and the constitutional structure of the EU have to cope with this
heterogeneity. However, the easiest way for dealing with heterogeneity—independence
of sub-units (e.g. states) which are comparatively homogeneous—is not available in the
EU with its integrated market and its high degree of legalization (Wolf and Zürn 2000).
Hence, the EU system will have to cope with this heterogeneity. What consequences can
be expected from a governance perspective?

With respect to the overall pattern of EU governance, one could expect a further
increase in the importance of soft instruments. After enlargement, the increase in the
diversity of member state preferences will make decisions in the Council more difficult
to reach, and strict and uniform rules more difficult to adopt. More flexibility in terms
of the substance of the decisions may therefore be expected in order to avoid deadlock.
The EU already has a long-standing record of using suitable instruments. As the specific
conditions for policy-making in the new member countries are far less known to the
present EU members and the European Commission than is the case among the present
members, the need for information is going to increase.

This creates a demand for information obligations and related instruments as
described in the previous section. The intensity of communication about member
state policies in the EU is going to increase, and new member states will be intensely
observed by both the old member states and by the Commission. This is not a one-sided
process: the new member states are also likely to use information about policy-making
in the EU and in other member states for increasing their policy-making options. On
the whole, the EU may lean more towards the principle of autonomy than towards the
principle of community. As a result, instead of more or less uniform policies agreed
upon by common decisions, the role of regulatory competition among different systems of policy-making may increase. There is, however, an alternative course of events:
applicant countries are required to make a rapid transition from pre-modern, undifferentiated forms of socialist governance to the post-modern EU form of governance.
The capacity to make that transition depends largely on the policy infrastructure in
place but could be eased by the lack of rigid, long-standing systems of governance in
transition states.

Which of these two possibilities—increasing regulatory competition and informality, or comparatively easy adaptation of Eastern European countries to West European

models—prevails, depends not least upon the perceived effects of Europeanization among voters and political parties. The high fluidity of East European party systems as compared to their West European counterparts makes it very difficult to predict whether a durable pro-/anti-European division is likely to emerge as a result of EU membership. But such a division is more than a remote possibility, and even a reluctance towards supranational integration among the parties from Eastern Europe that make their way into the European Parliament could endanger the present centrist and pro-European majority within the EP. A more Euro-sceptic EP would seriously affect the power relationships among Commission, Council, and Parliament.

A further potential result of increased heterogeneity as a result of enlargement and the ensuing emphasis on autonomy instead of community as a basic principle of European constitutionalism is the relative increase of transgovernmentalism as compared to supranationalism. This would not only amount to a change in the overall systems structure but would have consequences for democracy and responsibility. From a governance perspective, it is more problematic because it leads to a further empowerment of the executive at the expense of parliaments. The information advantages of executives make *ex ante* parliamentary control very demanding and parliaments are in a weak position when they demand *ex post* changes to policy packages agreed upon in difficult negotiations. On the whole, the positive side of enlargement—the creation of a larger security community, welfare gains from a larger market, and a stabilization of new democracies—may be accompanied by a strengthening of the negative side of integration—political decisions may escape effective democratic control.

## Conclusion

In the study of European integration, we have identified three distinct theoretical viewpoints, classical integration theory, policy analysis, and the constitutional debate. We have also identified three issues which are important for understanding how the EU works and how it interferes with the political options of citizens, organized groups, and member states, but which are not adequately dealt with by the three approaches mentioned above. We argue that a governance perspective is able to put these issues in their appropriate place by drawing on insights from all three theoretical approaches.

The first issue concerns democracy, legitimacy, and the normative assessment of what an appropriate political order for the EU should look like. As classical integration theory is concerned with the problem of how peaceful international cooperation is possible, it remains largely indifferent to these issues. In its conceptualization of social reality, cooperation and peace are values in themselves which are difficult to put into existence. Hence, instruments for the normative assessment of different forms of cooperation are less developed than in other fields of political science where peaceful cooperation among actors is largely taken for granted, e.g. in the study of political systems of Western democracies. For classical integration theory, however, it is difficult to accept that it is precisely the extraordinarily high levels of cooperation and institution-alization in the European Union which is problematic for democracy. Policy analysis goes a step further than classical integration theory because it deals with the conditions for effective and efficient problem-solving, that is, with the output-side of democracy. In its conceptualization of social reality, the question of responsible and responsive problem-solving (i.e. the input-side of democracy), which is at the core of the consti-tutional debate, is largely absent. The constitutional debate, however, all too often excludes questions of power and of the social prerequisites of political institutions.

Second, a governance perspective is well equipped to treat the EU system as a whole instead of focusing on a single level of the European multi-level system or on a small number of policy areas. This allows one to recognize changes in the overall architecture of the system caused by daily incrementalism. It also avoids treating EU politics as a zero-sum game between actors at different levels. Third, it places the competition for political power at the core of integration research. In classical integration theory, this issue has often been reduced to a zero-sum conflict between member states on the one hand, and supranational institutions on the other, over control of the EU system. However, the competition for political power in the EU does not take place among states alone but also among political parties. The logic of party politics in the EU is not only an interesting subject in itself but has a major impact on substantive policies and on political responsibility.

Combining insights from these theories within a governance perspective does not create a comprehensive theory of European integration but a broader view of the integration process. This is a major advantage. As the object of study is not the EU as such but only parts of it, such as 'networks' or 'loosely coupled systems', a transfer of concepts, hypotheses, and results between research on European integration and research on other issues is easily possible. In such a governance perspective, the EU is not a single case but part of a larger research programme on the study of governance within and beyond the nation state which invites comparisons across institutional boundaries.

In a broader perspective, such a view may help to remind us that the EU is not only an emerging institution for the reduction of transaction costs between states or for efficient problem-solving and conflict management, but also a political order which has a massive influence upon the lives of individuals. This political order not only emerges through intergovernmental constitutional conventions with broad press coverage but also in small steps behind our backs. This is a silent revolution leading to the transfor-mation of the core institution of modern political science—the state—in the region where it originally emerged. The study of governance in the European Union and beyond should not only lead to a better understanding of these broader processes but also remind us that what is at stake is not only the technocratic optimization of policy processes but also an appropriate political order in Europe.

# Notes

* Comments by Thomas Diez, Knud Erik Jørgensen, and Antje Wiener are gratefully acknowledged.

1. The Treaty of Amsterdam (Art. 137(4) EC Treaty) stipulates that member states may entrust management and labour, at their joint request, with the implementation of adopted directives. In addition, several directives explicitly promote social partner involvement in national implementation on the assumption that they know best what is needed and appropriate.

# Guide to further reading

Héritier, A. (ed.) (2002), *Common Goods. Reinventing European and International Governance* (Boulder: Rowman and Littlefield). The book explores how collective action problems can be solved institutionally when countries are faced with cross-boundary problems and simultaneous lack of hierarchical guidance.

Hooghe, L. And Marks, G. (2001), *Multi-level Governance and European Integration* (Oxford: Rowman and Littlefield). The authors explain why multi-level governance has taken place and how it shapes conflict in national and European political arenas.

Jachtenfuchs, M. (2001), 'The Governance Approach to European Integration' *Journal of Common Market Studies* 39, 245–64. A review of literature dealing with the reasons for the emergence of the governance debate and its main propositions.

Kohler-Koch, B. (ed.) (forthcoming), *Linking EU and National Governance* (Oxford: Oxford University Press). An interdisciplinary approach exploring the links between the two major levels of governance in the EU.

Scharpf, F.W. (1999), *Governing in Europe. Effective and Democratic?* (Oxford: Oxford University Press). This text explores how European and national institutions and political strategies could be mutually supportive with respect to the welfare state and argues that under certain conditions, multi-level governance in Europe could indeed regain both effectiveness and legitimacy.

# 6

# Policy Networks

*John Peterson*

## Introduction[1]

Modern democratic governance—imposing overall direction or control on the allocation of valued resources—often bears little resemblance to traditional Weberian notions
of hierarchy or neoconservative ideas of delivering public services through private markets. Instead, public policies are made and delivered via some kind of hybrid arrangement involving a range of different actors, including some representing private or
non-governmental institutions. Public policies, by definition, are the responsibility
of *public* authorities and aim to satisfy some vision of the 'public good'. Yet, modern
governance, not least in the European Union (EU), reflects a shift 'towards a sharing of
tasks and responsibilities; towards doing things together instead of doing them alone'
(Kooiman 1993: 1; see also Thompson et al. 1991; Peters 1996; Rhodes 1997).

   The term 'network' is frequently used to describe clusters of different kinds of actor
who are linked together in political, social, or economic life. Networks may be loosely
structured but still capable of spreading information or engaging in collective action.
Academic work on networks is often vague or abstract, or both (see Peterson and
O'Toole Jr. 2001). But growing interest in network forms of governance reflects how
modern society, culture, and economy are all increasingly products of relations involving mutuality and interdependence, as opposed to hierarchy and independence.
Linkages between organizations, rather than organizations themselves, have become
the central analytical focus for many social scientists.

   The term *policy* network connotes 'a cluster of actors, each of which has an interest,
or "stake" in a given . . . policy sector and the capacity to help determine policy success
or failure' (Peterson and Bomberg 1999: 8). Analysts of modern governance frequently
seek to explain policy outcomes by investigating how networks, which facilitate bargaining between stakeholders over policy design and detail, are structured in a particular sector. Three features of European Union (EU) governance give sustenance to policy
network analysis.

   First, the EU is an extraordinarily 'differentiated polity' (Rhodes 1997). Decision
rules and dominant actors vary significantly between policy sectors, such as regional
development or external trade policy. Battles for policy turf are frequent and fierce, as

are attempts to build high firewalls around policies in a given sector so that they cannot be altered or undone by actors from other sectors. One consequence is that EU policy networks tend to be discrete, distinct, and largely disconnected from one another, even when they preside over policies that are clearly connected, such as agriculture and environmental protection. Most have diverse memberships, extending to public and private, political and administrative, and 'European' and national (and often international and sub-national) actors, and lack clear hierarchies. But the general picture is one of great diversity. The extension of the EU's competence to new areas, such as monetary and defence policy, has been accompanied by the creation of new, more diverse, and anomalous policy structures. Policy network analysis helps us to describe the EU despite its 'polycentricity', or tendency to generate ever more and more dissimilar centres of decision-making and control (Peterson and Bomberg 2000).

Second, EU policy-making resembles supranational policy-making in other international organizations (IOs), such as the World Trade Organization or International Monetary Fund, in that much of it is highly technical. In these and other IOs, experts who share specialized knowledge and causal understandings tend to identify and 'bond' with each other, and often seek to depoliticize the policy process. In the EU, as in other IOs, technical expertise 'can become an exclusionary device, a device that is more effective at the supranational level because representative institutions like parliaments, that can play a surveillance role by holding experts accountable, are weak' (Coleman 2001: 97; see also Radaelli 1999).

Third, EU policy-making is underpinned by an extraordinarily complex labyrinth of committees that shape policy options before policies are 'set' by overtly political decision-makers such as the college of Commissioners, Council of Ministers, or European Parliament (EP). The Union relies heavily on ostensibly apolitical committees of officials, experts, and other stakeholders to surmount dissent, broker agreement, and move the policy agenda forward. EU policy formulation and implementation are usually scrutinized closely and repeatedly by national officials, via Council working groups and the arcane 'comitology' system, with committees at different levels performing different functions and having different but overlapping memberships. Two inevitable questions arise: first, whether and how much agents representing the EU's supranational institutions are empowered by their roles as brokers of intergovernmental agreements; and, second, whether and how often 'representatives of civil society such as consumers' organizations or agricultural producers' interest groups who might have access to, or even participate in, domestic policy networks might be frozen out at the supranational [EU] level' (Coleman 2001: 97). In any event, it is clear that EU policies are significantly shaped and closely scrutinized by different kinds of officials and experts in the EU's committee system, both before and after ultimate policy decisions are taken by overtly political actors.

There exists no agreed 'theory' of policy networks that would lead us to predictive claims about European integration or EU policy-making. Yet, most analyses of the EU which employ the policy network as a metaphor seek to test the basic proposition that the way in which networks are structured in any EU policy sector will determine, and thus help explain and predict, policy outcomes. Nearly all contend that policy outcomes often cannot be explained by exclusive recourse to the mediation of national preferences. In order truly to *theorize* policy network analysis, more (and more thorough) case studies of the actual policy effects of governance by policy network are needed, along with a larger dose of normative thinking about how to design networks that are efficient and legitimate, particularly as the EU encroaches on progressively more and more diverse national policies (Scharpf 1999, 2002).

## Policy networks and EU governance

Policy network analysis starts with three basic assumptions. First (again), modern governance is frequently non-hierarchical. Few policy solutions are simply imposed by public authorities. Governance involves mutuality and interdependence between public and non-public actors, as well as between different kinds of public actor, not least in federal or quasi-federal polities such as the EU. Second, the policy process must be disaggregated to be understood because 'relationships between groups and government vary between policy areas' (Rhodes 1997: 32). In other words, it makes little sense to talk generally of a 'strong state' or 'corporatist state'—let alone a 'strong' or 'weak' international organization—because states and IOs are much stronger vis-à-vis affected interests in some policy sectors than in others.

Third and finally, governments remain ultimately responsible for governance, but that is not the whole story. Before policies are 'set' by elected political actors, policy choices are shaped and refined in bargaining between a diverse range of actors, including some who are non-governmental, all of whom have an interest in what policy is chosen. Policy networks can narrow options and shift the agenda by pursuing 'strategies that generate new political and economic forces' (Thatcher 1998: 406). Sometimes, they can go so far as to 'play a role in the determination of their own environment, with repercussions for the fit between political interests, organizational structures and economic objectives' (Thatcher 1998: 406; see also Dunn and Perl 1994; Peterson 1995). To cite a specific example, the materialization of an EU social policy regime can be explained in part as the product of collective action on the part of an emergent social policy network to create a more favourable environment for EU intervention (see Falkner 1999).

Arguably, policy network analysis is never more powerful an analytical tool than when it is deployed at the EU level. The Union is a unique polity, with no government or opposition, and powerful policy-makers who are non-elected, such as European Commissioners or members of COREPER. Its policy remit extends to highly technical matters of regulation, including new technologies, thus making the politics of expertise a crucial determinant of outcomes. With its own system of law and the capacity to impose its will on a polity of around 370 million citizens (soon to be 470 million), the EU may seem enormously powerful. Yet, it is extraordinarily weak in terms of resources, and relies heavily on assets and expertise located in national capitals or the private sector. One effect is to blur the distinction between public and private that is at the heart of traditional notions of 'public policy'. To try to describe how the EU works *without* the metaphor of a network is a challenge on a par with seeking to explain, under the same injunction, how international terrorists operate (see Biersteker 2002).[2]

That said, the policy networks literature can be hard going. It features a variety of models and, confusingly, sometimes employs the same term to mean different things. For example, the so-called Rhodes model of policy networks (see below) employs the term 'policy community' to mean a particularly tightly integrated and single-minded policy network (see Rhodes 1990; Marsh and Rhodes 1992; Rhodes 1997; Marsh 1998). Yet, elsewhere policy community is used to refer to the broader universe of 'actors and potential actors who share a common identity or interest' in a certain policy sector (Wright 1988: 606). Sometimes, works from different sub-disciplines seem like islands in a stream. Keck and Sikkink's (1998) masterful study of 'advocacy networks' of activists in international politics sometimes uses terminology that is incongruous with the 'advocacy coalition' framework developed in the public policy literature primarily by Sabatier (Sabatier and Jenkins-Smith 1993, 1998). Legal theorizing about network forms of governance can seem impenetrable (see Ladeur 1997).

The Rhodes model of policy networks has probably been employed more often than any other in the study of EU governance (see Peterson 1995; Bomberg 1998; Daugbjerg 1999; Falkner 1999; Peterson and Bomberg 1999; Falkner 2000). Simply put, the model assumes that three key variables determine what type of policy network exists in a specific sector:

(1) the relative *stability* of a network's membership: do the same actors tend to dominate decision-making over time or is membership fluid and dependent on the specific policy issue under discussion?

(2) the network's relative *insularity*: is it a cabal which excludes outsiders or is it highly permeable by a variety of actors with different objectives?

(3) the strength of *resource dependencies*: do network members depend heavily on each other for valued resources such as money, expertise, and legitimacy or are most actors self-sufficient and thus relatively independent of one another?

A continuum emerges with tightly integrated *policy communities* on one end, which are capable of single-minded collective action, and loosely affiliated *issue networks* on the other, which find it far more difficult to mobilize collectively. The internal structure of policy networks is usually considered an independent variable, in that the structure of a policy network will help determine policy outcomes. For example, policy communities have more capacity than issue networks to steer or control the policy agenda.

Policy network analysis is increasingly used to make sense of internationalized policy-making environments such as the EU. A primary aim is often to determine what interests—national or supranational—dominate bargaining within transnational networks (see Coleman and Perl 1999). The answer is usually revealed by considering two questions. First, does the policy sector in question give rise to much public sector activism? In other words, to what extent are politicians and senior public officials directly active and involved, and determined to impose their wills? Second, how much autonomy do supranational institutions have in any given sector? In the EU's case, are the Commission, EP, and Court endowed with their 'own resources' in terms of Treaty powers or funding, or are they largely dependent on national and private actors?

One of the strengths of the Rhodes model is that, despite occasional discrepancies in terminology, most other models of governance by network are compatible with it. Take, for example, the concept of 'epistemic communities' developed by Peter Haas (1992: 3) as a way to describe how policy-making can become dominated by 'network[s] of professionals with recognized expertise and competence in a particular domain', particularly those subject to internationalized policy-making. Or, consider Sabatier's (1993: 25) advocacy coalition framework, which holds that policy shifts usually occur when the sectoral agenda is seized by overtly political networks consisting of various kinds of policy activist, including public officials representing multiple levels of government, who 'share a particular belief system' and work together over relatively long periods of time (ten years or more) to force policy change. If EU governance is conceived as occurring within a multi-level system in which policies emerge after a fairly standard sequence of different types of decision, it is plausible to see EU governance at the sub-systemic level (in space) and policy-shaping stage (in time) as largely a competition between epistemic communities and/or advocacy coalitions (sometimes by competing versions of them) to steer or control policy networks, with which their own memberships overlap, in specific sectors. Sometimes, epistemic communities and advocacy coalitions may form alliances, particularly to shift the policy agenda in the direction of radical policy change as occurred, for example, when the EU embraced quite radical liberalization of its agricultural sector during the Uruguay Round which gave birth to the WTO in the early 1990s (see Ullrich 2002).

More generally, policy network analysis can help us explain why EU policy outcomes in a particular sector reflect purely technocratic rationality or, alternatively, the overtly political agenda of key actors (Peterson 1995: 79–80; see also Peters 1998: 29–30). For example, the Framework programme for funding collaborative research has quietly expanded to become the third largest item of expenditure in the Community's budget, not least because much decision-making about precisely who gets what from the programme has been delegated to epistemic communities of researchers and scientists (Peterson and Sharp 1998: 163–87). Alternatively, highly politicized environmental policy debates over auto emissions, packaging waste, or biotechnology can be viewed as battles between competing advocacy coalitions—broadly advocating environmental protection vs. industrial interests—for influence within EU environmental policy networks.[3]

Policy network analysis often works 'best' when deployed together with other theoretical accounts of EU politics or policy-making, for two reasons. First, its explicit task of explaining sub-systemic policy-shaping means that it is compatible with intergovernmentalist or neofunctionalist accounts of decision-making at the highest political levels, where 'history-making' decisions are taken which determine how the EU changes or evolves as a polity. Moreover, policy network analysis often can explain actual policy outcomes that are hard to explain using either of these theoretical accounts (which, after all, are not really theories of *policy-making*). Policy network analysis is also congruent with most institutionalist treatments of the EU,[4] particularly ones which focus on ultimate policy choices, for which authority is very much shared by the EU's institutions (Peterson and Shackleton 2002: 361–3).

Second, policy network analysis adds value to alternative, meta-theoretical conceptions of EU governance. For example, the idea that informal, sector-dedicated, mostly self-organized policy networks are responsible for a large portion of EU governance is obviously amenable to the broader notion that the Union produces a kind of 'network governance', in which 'political actors consider problem-solving the essence of politics and . . . the setting of policy-making is defined by the existence of highly organised social sub-systems' (Eising and Kohler-Koch 1999: 5). Its compatibility with a theoretical portrait of the EU as a system in which actors must constantly seek to 'escape from gridlock' is no less obvious:

> . . . the decisional processes are obstacle-ridden, cumbersome and, to say the least prone to stalemate. This in turn gives rise to attempts to use escape routes by those actors who constitute nodes in the multiplicity of criss-crossing interactions, with subterfuge being the only way to keep policy-making going (Heritier 1999: 97).

Policy network analysis also has affinities with constructivist accounts that highlight the ability of international organizations such as the EU to generate new categories of actor and norms. Increasingly, IOs have rational and legal authority to make rules; none more so than the EU. As they make rules, IOs define international tasks (preventing the spread of AIDS in Africa), create new categories of actor ('political refugees'), and generate new norms (minority rights). They thus generate new social knowledge that can alter the interests of actors in policy-making that occurs at a level beyond the state (see Barnett and Finnemore 1999; Christiansen et al. 2001). For instance, EU governments have gradually come to identify their own self-interest in the prevention of 'social exclusion', with the EU hastening a shift in policy priorities in this direction and, particularly, the Commission 'sponsoring' a new social exclusion lobby (see Atkinson 2002; Bauer 2002). This example seems to vindicate assumptions that are central to the portrayal of the EU as a system of 'multi-level governance' (see 'Evaluating policy network analysis' below): that is, the Commission retains 'virtually a free hand in creating new networks' (Marks et al. 1996: 359) and is often empowered by its position at the 'hub of numerous highly specialized policy networks' (Marks et al. 1996: 355).

## The origins of policy network analysis

In broad terms, the application of policy network analysis to the EU is a product of the widely shared view that the European Union is *not* an ordinary, 'garden variety' IO, but rather a system of governance in its own right. As such, leading theories of European *integration* can tell us little about the EU's processes for making *policy* (see 'The importance of policy networks for integration' below). Having emerged as the source of a large slice of the total universe of all public policies in Europe, it is natural that tools developed by analysts of public policy at the national level are increasingly deployed at the EU level.

The precise origins of policy network analysis in the public policy literature are a matter of dispute. Richardson (2000: 1006) claims 'British origins of what is now termed the network approach'. Rhodes (1990: 32) concurs that 'American political science was not the major formative influence' on early work which sought to make sense of the British 'post-parliamentary' state using network analysis in the late 1970s. Yet, an eclectic range of early work in the UK, US, *and* Europe on interest intermediation—via both corporatist and pluralist structures and focused on intergovernmental (that is, local-national) and government-industry relations—attempted to develop the idea of networks as an analytical concept. An important example is Heclo's (1978) spirited critique of the idea that the American policy process was subject to dynastic rule by 'iron triangles' of mutually supportive legislators, bureaucrats, and private actors. On the contrary, Heclo (1978: 102) argued, the policy process was influenced by a diverse collection of stakeholders grouped into 'issue networks'—that is, complex networks focused on specific issues—which extended far beyond those actors with the formal power to set policy: 'Looking for the few who are powerful, we tend to overlook the many whose webs of influence provoke and guide the exercise of power'. Jordan (1981; Jordan and Schubert 1992) can claim credit for developing the idea that issue networks were one variant of network—and a rather extreme one—which existed on a continuum ranging from very loose to very tightly integrated. The common denominator of early work on networks, which pre-dated the EU's emergence as a true polity, was an ambition to explain how and why interests were mediated in settings that resembled neither open 'markets' of transactions between independent entities nor hierarchies in which governments—or any other actor—imposed control.

To make a long story short, international political developments in the decade or more after 1990—globalization, devolution (in Europe and elsewhere), and economic liberalization—gave rise to new and different forms of governance, in which power was increasingly shared horizontally. Policy network approaches became both more common in the policy literature and progressively more ambitious. No longer were its advocates content to present policy networks as mere metaphors. New attempts were made to try to theorize about them, and describe, explain, and predict policy outcomes by examining exchanges within policy networks (Peterson 1995; Bomberg 1998; Daugbjerg 1999; Nunan 1999; Falkner 2000; Andersen and Eliassen 2001). The results were decidedly mixed, with some observers finding a widening gap between aims and achievements (see Le Galès and Thatcher 1995; Thatcher 1998).[5]

## The importance of policy networks for integration

To understand the basic hypotheses and arguments endemic to this approach, it must be acknowledged that policy network analysis does *not* constitute a theory of political or economic integration, in Europe or anywhere else. In fact, scholars began to investigate the EU using policy network analysis in the early 1990s precisely because the time-honoured debate between intergovernmentalism and neofunctionalism, although revived in interesting new permutations (see Moravcsik 1991; Tranholm-Mikkelsen 1991; Burley and Mattli 1993), shed relatively little light on actual EU *policy*, and the complex systems that emerged for making it (Rosamond 2000: 105–13). Both inter-governmentalism and neofunctionalism were and remain macro-level theories of international relations, which are designed to describe, explain, and predict the broad thrust and path of European integration as a process. Neither are intended to describe, explain, or predict the policy outcomes that arise from this process, as policy network analysis seeks to do.

Even proponents of policy network analysis would be hard-pressed to identify the central features—main assumptions, causal propositions, core predictions—of a 'network theory' of policy-making. Nonetheless, network analyses usually focus on one or more of three basic arguments:

*How policy networks are structured in discrete EU policy sectors has tangible, measurable effects on policy outcomes.*

Put another way, EU policy outcomes are determined by how integrated and exclusive policy-specific networks are, and how mutually dependent are actors within them. We should expect different kinds of outcome in sectors, such as pharmaceuticals or agriculture, where tightly integrated, cabalistic policy communities are guardians of the agenda, than in sectors populated by loosely bound issue networks, such as environmental policy. One testable (although still to be proven) hypothesis is that more integrated networks will tend to block radical change in EU policies, while outcomes are far harder to predict when pre-legislative bargaining occurs within issue networks. More generally, policy networks are an independent or 'intervening' variable: 'analyses look at the ways in which network structures affect the selected aspects of the behaviour of actors and their interactions—for instance in the spread of information, strategies of actors, exchanges amongst them and policy outcomes' (Thatcher 1998: 410).

*Quasi-federal polities such as the EU naturally give rise to governance by policy network.*

Federalism is, by nature, a method for reconciling competing values: strong yet small government, minimum 'federal' standards alongside local discretion, and private sector autonomy with the provision of public goods. These values cannot be reconciled either through strict hierarchies or pure market structures. Rather, they must be reconciled through negotiation and the exchange of resources and ideas. Logically, structured but informal policy networks arise to facilitate this kind of negotiation, particularly in today's federal systems (including the EU), most of which have moved away from 'dual federalism', with ostensibly separate jurisdictions between levels of government, and towards 'cooperative federalism', in which interdependence between levels of government is accepted and even welcomed (see Peterson and O'Toole Jr. 2001).

*Governance by policy network gives rise to management and legitimacy concerns, particularly in the EU.*

Despite claims to the contrary (see Moravcsik 2002), it is commonly held that the EU suffers from both management and legitimacy deficits. The management deficit arises from the lack of incentives for any actor in non-hierarchical networks to invest in management capacities (Metcalfe 2000). The legitimacy deficit results from a lack of clear rules of process, transparency, or judicial review to govern informal bargaining within EU networks (see Dehousse 2002). Moreover, the technical discourse of supranational policy-making is an important reason why networks of government officials and experts are usually subject to less scrutiny than is the case at the national level. In fact, the empowerment of national actors by virtue of their participation in EU policy-making, which is generally not subject to close political control, may well enhance their authority at the national level and empower them in bargaining that takes place within domestic networks (Ansell and Weber 1999; Coleman 2001).

The 'news' that the EU governs largely by policy network is not, by any means, all bad. Informal bargaining within networks can help build consensus in a system which strives to avoid creating clear losers. Policy networks can diffuse norms of good governance, particularly to states—such as those in Central and Eastern Europe—whose civil services are still maturing. They can also help to ensure that private actors have a sense of ownership of EU policies. Nevertheless, the salience of the EU's management and legitimacy deficits points to the need for normative thinking about how EU policy networks should be structured, managed, and subjected to oversight and control. Complex interdependence between national and EU policy-making means that a lot of EU governance is always going to rely on exchanges within policy networks. Thus, it makes sense to design networks that can manage effectively and are part of the solution to the EU's legitimacy problem.

## Evaluating policy network analysis

While the EU's future, especially in advance of radical enlargement, is very much unwritten (see Weiler 2002), there is no denying that it is a uniquely successful experiment in transnational governance. Eventually, it could emerge as:

a source of institutional innovation that may yield some answers to the crisis of the nation state. This is because, around the process of the formation of the European Union, new forms of governance, and new institutions of government, are being created, at the European, national, regional and local levels, inducing a new form of state that I propose to call *the network state*[6] (Castells 1998: 311; see also Howse and Nicolaïdis 2002).

Upon close examination, the 'network state' turns out to be a rather frustrating concept. Its 'actual content . . . and the actors involved in it, are still unclear, and will be so for some time' (Castells 1998: 311). What *is* clear is that EU governance occurs simultaneously at multiple levels of government, thus giving rise to 'multi-level governance' (MLG) as a descriptive term for what the EU offers. In theory, and at least sometimes in practice, power is distributed between the EU, national, regional, and local levels according to the principle of subsidiarity: that is, the Union as a whole legislates only in areas (such as air pollution or external trade policy) where policy problems cannot be solved at lower levels of government. To portray the EU as a multi-level system of governance is to assume that actors representing different levels of government are interdependent. They thus 'network' with each other to design, implement, and enforce EU rules.

Yet, MLG is clearly far more prominent in some policy sectors—above all, cohesion policy—than others, such as competition policy (although even here it could be argued that the EU is shifting towards more network-type governance). MLG was probably less of a general model of EU governance at the end of the 1990s than many would have predicted at the beginning of the decade, when a 'Europe of the Regions' seemed within reach as European integration and regional devolution accelerated simultaneously (Marks 1992; Marks et al. 1996). Indicative, perhaps, is Castells' (1998: 331) emphasis on the importance of the EU's Committee of the Regions (CoR) as the 'most direct institutional expression' of subsidiarity, despite general consensus ten years after the CoR's creation that it had 'earned itself an unenviable reputation for being possibly the Union's most pointless institution' (Coss 2002).

Actual theory-building about governance via 'vertical networks' which link actors representing different levels of government has been rare. In fact, it might be argued that very little progress has been made since Keohane and Hoffmann (1991: 13) observed that the EU was evolving into a polity in its own right, 'organised as a network that involves the pooling and sharing of sovereignty rather than a transfer of sovereignty to a higher level'. About all we can safely conclude from existing research is that most EU policy networks seem to be more *horizontal* than vertical in structure: most are linked to national networks of policy stakeholders (which are considerably embedded in them), but are mainly Brussels-centred and dominated by actors representing national governments and the EU's institutions (see 'Challenges and prospects of policy network analysis' below), with sub-national actors rarely in positions of much power. EU policy networks are an important purveyor of multi-level governance, but it is difficult to view them as facilitating the dawn of a 'Europe of the Regions'.

## Critique

Policy network analysis has not been short of critics (Kassim 1993; Dowding 1995; Le Galès and Thatcher 1995; Peters 1998; Thatcher 1998; Dowding 2001). It tends to be criticized on four specific grounds:

> *'Policy network' may be a useful metaphor, but it does not constitute a model or theory.*

König's (1998: 387) complaint is illustrative:

a growing number of studies use the network concept as a metaphor describing the complexity of social and political life, but they have neither explained why private and public actors are mutually dependent, whether their dependency is restricted to the boundaries of specific subsystems and how this dependency affects public decision-making, nor generated testable hypotheses regarding the causal importance of policy networks for public decision-making.

Many proponents of policy network analysis would accept these criticisms. Most would concede that theorizing about policy networks remains at an early stage. Nevertheless, theory-building must always start by building on metaphors which abstract from reality, and then point the analyst towards variables that may determine outcomes. Ultimately, policy network analysis may not *answer* many important questions about EU governance. However, it often points the analyst to where the answers may be found: the subterranean netherworld of officials, lobbyists, and experts, a world often quite distant from the political world of ministers and parliamentarians.

> *Policy-making in Brussels is too fluid, uncertain, and over-populated with an enormously diverse collection of interests for stable networks to exist or persist.*

According to this view, 'EU governance is . . . best described as uncertain agendas, shifting networks and complex coalitions' (Richardson 2000: 1021). This set of circumstances is considered to be bad news for proponents of policy network analysis because:

the utility of network typologies is open to question in situations in which there is rapid change (both of institutions and actors), a lack of clear sectoral/subsectoral boundaries, complexity of decision-making and a potentially large number of actors drawn from different levels of policy formation, as are claimed, for instance, to exist in European policy-making (Thatcher 1998: 398).

Proponents of this view sometimes go as far as to question whether stable networks exist at all in Brussels. Actors may form alliances and work together on specific issues— thus the term 'issue network'—but most actors are promiscuous. Thus, once formed, networks quickly disintegrate. It is not surprising, given such fluidity, that 'case studies of EU policy-making tend to examine individual decisions rather than whole sectors or sub-sectors' (Kassim 1993: 21). This criticism lacks credibility, for at least three reasons. First, stability of membership is a variable, not an assumption, of the policy network approach. The EU, more than most systems of governance, may give rise to loosely integrated and fluid issue networks more often than stable policy communities. But the matter is one for empirical investigation. Moreover, it is possible to find policy episodes—such as the 1989 directive on automobile emissions (Peterson and Bomberg 1999: 190–1)—when an insecurely structured issue network managed to overcome its own fluidity and capture the policy agenda long enough to produce an outcome that would not have been predicted by pluralist or incrementalist theories. In any event, as the EU matures it is possible—perhaps likely—that 'more stable and manageable networks of policy-makers are likely to emerge' (Mazey and Richardson 1993: 4).

The maze of EU committees, whose members outnumber the total number of officials in the Council and Commission combined by about three to one (Van Schendelen 1998: 6), is meant—perhaps above all—to provide stability to policy-making.

Second, the claim that the EU's fluidity cannot be 'captured' by policy network analysis is usually made on the basis of very little evidence. Kassim's (1993) 'sceptical view' of policy networks is based almost exclusively on evidence from the air transport sector, which is far more nationalized *and* 'globalized' than most other European industries (and thus not very 'Europeanized'). Richardson's (2000) dismissal of policy network analysis as overused and inappropriate at the EU level relies mainly on secondary sources on national lobbying strategies and EU external trade policy.

Third and finally, relatively loosely constituted networks are, somewhat ironically, often more effective channels of communication than tightly integrated policy communities. The so-called 'strength of weak ties' argument (Granovetter 1973) holds that:

In a world of cliques of tightly knit social circles, individuals are better off investing time in acquaintances (or 'weak ties') because it is through acquaintances that cliques are bridged and that information diffuses through a policy network . . . information communicated by strong ties—within-clique communication—will tend to be redundant, and will tend to travel short distances relative to the size of the network as a whole (Carpenter et al. 1998: 418–19; see also Granovetter 1973).

It may be that communication is more important as a lubricant to the policy process in the EU than in most other systems of governance. Consensus is ingrained as a norm and a vast number and diversity of policy stakeholders must typically agree before an EU policy may be 'set'. Timing is particularly crucial in EU policy-making: the losers in policy debates (despite attempts to avoid creating any) are frequently those who are unaware of when a dossier is 'ripe' and ready for a decision, and are caught out because they lack adequate communication channels.

*Policy network analysis lacks a theory of 'power'.*

This criticism is a serious one, but it neglects the *interstitial* nature of policy network analysis: that is, the power of classical EU actors—particularly member governments— is not denied but it is not viewed as wholly determinant of EU outcomes.[7] Network analysis looks for explanations in exchanges that cover over the cracks or crevices that separate different levels in a system of MLG, or different sets of institutional actors in systems where multiple institutions wield a slice of power. It assumes that the EU system produces outcomes that cannot be explained exclusively by recourse to the mediation of national preferences, as is sometimes claimed (see Bueno de Mesquita and Stokman 1994). Policy network analysis is 'pitched' at a meso- or sub-systemic level of decision-making, and thus is entirely compatible with macro-theories of politics, such as pluralism, élitism, and Marxism (see Daugbjerg and Marsh 1998). In the EU's case, more or less power is concentrated at the sub-systemic level depending on which EU policy sector is under scrutiny: for example, a considerable amount of power for determining the Common Agricultural Policy (CAP) is delegated to the sub-systemic level, while relatively little power resides at this level in relation to the Common Foreign and Security Policy (CFSP). Thus, policy network analysis is likely to tell us more about how the CAP is determined than how the CFSP is made (see 'Application: policy network analysis and the CAP' below).

Consensus has become widespread that policy network analysis should be deployed within a portfolio of theories pitched at explaining outcomes at different levels of governance (see Peterson and Bomberg 1999; Wallace 2000; Andersen and Eliassen 2001; Peterson 2001; Bomberg and Stubb 2003). Interestingly, the plausibility of *intergovernmentalist* theories of power in EU governance is frequently conceded in such schema, as only one kind of actor—national actors—are powerful at *every* level in what has clearly evolved into a multi-level system of governance. However, most proponents of policy network analysis reject as artificial and false the dichotomy between 'intergovernmental' and 'supranational governance', since virtually 'no administrative [EU] action can be developed without national administrative authorities being associated with it' (Azoulay 2002: 128).

*The literature on policy networks is often vague and caught up with insular, and purely academic debates about terminology.*

Sometimes, debates in the public policy literature between advocates of competing models—and especially between network 'theorists' and their detractors—seem increasingly unproductive. They often focus on rather trivial questions of terminology, and can be embarrassingly self-absorbed (Marsh and Rhodes 1992; Rhodes 1997; Marsh and Smith 2000; Richardson 2000; Dowding 2001; Marsh and Smith 2001).[8] Still, few serious students of European integration would deny that governance by networks is an essential feature of the EU. In fact, governance by network may be becoming a steadily *more* important feature of the EU, as evidenced by recent initiatives including (inter alia) the use of interest groups or NGOs in the implementation of environmental or development policies, the Commission's (2001) emphasis on dialogue with civil society in its White Paper on Governance, and the increasing ubiquity of the so-called 'Open Method of Coordination' of national policies through exchanges between purpose-built EU level networks of national officials (see Hodson and Maher 2001; Mosher and Trubek 2003).

## Application: policy network analysis and the CAP

Any survey of recent literature on EU governance will uncover a variety of analyses using policy network analysis as an investigative lens. Cohesion policy (Ansell 1997; Ward and Williams 1997; Bache 1998; Bomberg and Peterson 1998, 1999) and research policy (Peterson 1991; Peterson and Sharp 1998) are two of the most frequent targets of investigation via this method, not least because they are bastions, respectively, of policy-making by linked clusters of national, sub-national, and supranational actors and unusually technocratic procedures. However, the Common Agricultural Policy

(CAP) has probably been the focus of policy network analysis as much as any other EU policy sector (see Smith 1990; Daugbjerg 1999; Coleman 2001; Ullrich 2002), for at least three reasons.

First, CAP decision-making is shared between networks of product-specialized officials ('the beef people', 'the cereals people', etc.) responsible for managing specific markets on a day-to-day basis, and the Agriculture Council, which is one of the busiest and most insular of all versions of the Council of Ministers. The Commission and Council Secretariat together act as institutional nodes that facilitate communication and exchange within a broader CAP policy network. This network's autonomy and guardianship of the policy agenda—within the broad political framework set by the European Council and multi-year EU budget—are jealously guarded. The EU's agricultural policy network is a true policy *community*. Second, although the CAP is one of the EU's only truly common policies, in the sense that it effectively replaces national policies, it is in fact highly decentralized with considerable discretion held by national agricultural ministries and ministers (see Grant 1997). Arguably, the CAP is considerably less 'common' today than it was when the problem of surplus production reached outright crisis proportions in the early 1980s, and powerful networks of experts were given autonomy to manage the crisis. More generally, as a case, the CAP seems to lend credence to the general hypothesis that as the focus of policy activity becomes more international, a supranational network dominated by experts can be expected, in most cases, to emerge. Over time, however, most policy networks become more subject to domination by *national* actors and intergovernmental bargaining, even if they are configured *horizontally* and sometimes enjoy considerable autonomy from their national political masters (Coleman 2001).

Third, the CAP is a favourite whipping boy of Eurosceptics, who cite its wastefulness, regressiveness, and easy exploitation by transnational networks of criminals, including the Italian mafia and Irish Republican Army (Galeotti 2001: 213). In reality, of course, the main problem is a classic 'pooled sovereignty, divided accountability' problem (Peterson 1997): national administrations, not EU institutions, are mainly responsible for spending controls and the policing of fraud. A well-publicized CAP scam in the UK in summer 2002 saw Edward Leigh, the fiercely Eurosceptic chair of the relevant parliamentary committee, slam the British *national* system for spending CAP funding, and its responsible ministry, as 'appallingly lax'.[9] The wider point is that regardless of the reputed virtues of governance by policy network, the CAP is emblematic of the management and legitimacy deficits to which this form of governance can give rise.

## Policy network analysis and enlargement

The uncertainty facing a radically enlarged EU of twenty-five or more member states is vast. The immediate future of European integration is perhaps hazier now than it ever has been before. As such, it suffices to make just three points about how policy network analysis might help us to shed light on the EU after its next enlargement, and the ones subsequent to it. First, the EU–25 that should arrive by 2004 is likely to be fundamentally different from the old EU–15. But a number of patterns are so well-established that they will persist far into the future. One is that all new member states take time to adjust to the EU's unique brand of deciding by subterfuge, or 'escaping from deadlock' (see Heritier 1999); that is, essentially ignoring or subverting the formal rules and advancing the policy agenda through bargaining within informal policy networks. As such, formal accession to the EU does *not* make new member states full, 'equal' members of the European Union (see Peterson and Jones 1999). Rather, new officials, and private and non-governmental actors from new member states must learn the rules of the game that apply to policy-specific networks, and get used to bargaining within them.

Second, there is no question that the states lined up to join in 2004 or afterwards have far less mature, proficient, or professional civil services compared to the EU norm. Most are relatively inexperienced participants in international organizations, and many have never encountered a Western-style lobbying system. A central issue is thus whether policy networks within an enlarged EU will be able to perform the function of disseminating norms of compliance with EU rules, despite vast disparities in levels of economic modernization (and thus economic interests) and public sector leverage in the face of private sector power.

Third and finally, it is going to become far more difficult to reform the EU of the future. The 2004 intergovernmental conference (IGC) was considered by many member governments as Europe's last shot at embracing truly meaningful reform of the Union's institutions, before an EU–25 emerged with far too many veto players to make it possible to change anything very important.[10] Olsen (2002: 593–4), one of the most clever of all students of institutional change, offers a final word on networks and enlargement:

In the European Union governance takes place in polycentric, multilevel policy networks of public and private actors . . . Reformers are not omnipotent. There is no single sovereign centre with the authority and power to change fundamentally the policy order while many factors other than reformers' choices influence change. Furthermore, reform capabilities often have to be developed as an inherent part of the reform process, a key issue in many applicant countries . . . Comprehensive reforms tend to be highly divisive and European reformers face enduring differences that cannot be hidden behind apolitical rhetoric.

# Challenges and prospects of policy network analysis

## The contribution of policy network analysis

The impact of policy network analysis on European integration theory has been significant. Yet, for the most part its significance arises from the way in which it has given theorists a language to describe and perhaps sometimes to explain—more rarely to predict—what European integration has wrought in terms of a governance system. The EU has, over time, become more eclectic as a polity as its policy competence has expanded, and more polycentric (Peterson and Bomberg 2000). For example, contrast the new, highly centralized system for monetary policy with the new, highly decentralized system of regulating food safety or medicinal products via new European agencies (Majone 2002; McNamara 2002). Then, consider the notion that states may develop a distinct 'policy style' (Richardson 1982), depending on how proactive or reactive, and how consensual or autocratic policy-making is. One important rationale for studying the EU using policy network analysis is that it is futile to try to characterize its policy-making process as reflecting one policy style when it incorporates so many different ones across its full range of policies. The policy network perspective reveals a repertoire of adaptable network systems at the EU level rather than a single pattern.

To take the point further, it might be argued that there is great variety between EU policy networks for good reason: because a very diverse set of arrangements are needed for the EU to surmount different obstacles to cooperation in different areas of policy. Of course, governance by policy network is not without its pathologies, particularly the problem of networks being 'captured' and transformed into insular policy communities, dominated by vested interests and lacking transparency. But policy network analysis can help us explain both continuity in EU policy outcomes, *and* the Union's (occasional, at least) capacity for policy innovation.

It also can be argued that policy network analysis of the EU has 'grown up' considerably in recent years. Gradually, in the wake of the earliest applications of the policy network concept to EU governance (most of which were concerned with MLG), it has become clear that the policy networks that matter most in EU decision-making are more *horizontal* in structure—that is, dominated by actors representing the core EU institutions, representatives of EU member states, and powerful, Brussels-based lobbyists—as much or more than they are 'vertical', or knitting together mutually dependent actors representing multiple levels of governance. To be clear, EU policy networks are invariably linked to national networks in the same sectors. But the extent to which the former stand apart from control by national capitals may be taken as another sign of the coming of age of the European Union as a polity in its own right.

The main contribution of EU policy network analysis to theorizing about European integration is its emphasis on the Union's inescapable diversity and complexity. A dizzying array of different kinds of actor can claim to be a policy stakeholder in a continent-sized polity of 370 million people, which incorporates a rich variety of national systems of interest representation. Transnational networks of the kind that preside over the policy agenda in the EU and other international organizations are usually seen to be looser and less tightly integrated than their counterparts at the national level. But the more single-minded amongst them clearly can exploit the space between the EU and its member states in pursuit of their own interests (see Josselin and Wallace 2001).

## The future development of policy network analysis

The future of policy network analysis is dependent to a considerable extent on its relative success in performing three functions.

*Can it effectively describe, explain, and even predict outcomes arising from the use of new EU policy methods and modes?*

In recent years, a number of new alternatives to the traditional Community method of legislating have emerged, including the Open Method (Hodson and Maher 2001; Atkinson 2002), 'co-regulation' by private actors acting voluntarily with public regulators, and rule-making by new European regulatory agencies (see Dehousse 1997; Majone 2002). Most involve less EU legislation *per se* or less stringent or detailed legislation, and depend more on coordination between national officials and ministries. A crucial question for future researchers is precisely what sort of interaction and overlap, with what effects, occur between domestic policy networks at the national level and Brussels-based EU networks (for an exception, see Nunan 1999).

*Can policy network analysis generate clearer and more rigorous hypotheses about what constitutes 'success' for different kinds of network?*

Long-established policy communities for whom EU policy brings benefits, and traditionally has done, might be considered successful when they are able to veto policy change. Alternatively, more recently established or emerging networks might measure their success by the extent to which they are able to force new issues onto the EU policy agenda. In any event, we need clearer theoretical propositions about what sort of interests are empowered by which type of policy network structures, and which find themselves disadvantaged by certain types of network, and why.

*Is it possible to develop normative propositions about how EU policy networks can be structured and managed in order to serve the greater European good?*

Thus far, most policy network analyses have generated thick description of the EU policy process, while eschewing normative propositions or prescriptions. Especially in a radically enlarged EU, future research could usefully develop overtly normative analyses of how policy networks can be constructed to help solve problems of compliance (Haas 1999), management (Metcalfe 2000), and legitimacy (Peterson and O'Toole Jr. 2001).

## Conclusion

We have reviewed the (disputed) origins of policy network analysis as a tool for study-ing the policy consequences of European integration. The most basic assumptions of policy network analysis—including *the* basic assumption that network structure par-tially determines outcomes—have been examined critically, along with its main argu-ments. More generally, we have reviewed the main criticisms of a model that has never been short of critics, and found much to criticize. In particular, far more work needs to be done before policy network analysis can be considered truly to be a theory, as opposed to a mere metaphor.

It may seem somewhat facile and predictable to conclude by calling for more the-oretical development and empirical research. Yet, it is worth reminding ourselves of something quite remarkable about the study of the EU: how little we know about the internal workings of the EU (as well as most other IOs), as opposed to European integration as a broad political process. As Barnett and Finnemore (1999) argue, the theoretical lenses used to understand international cooperation between states tend to be rigidly economistic, and focused on assessing supply and demand for cooperation. Cooperation is, of course, an anomaly in an international world that is still viewed as anarchic by most international relations scholars. 'Consequently, our research tends to focus on the bargains states strike to make or reshape IOs. Scholars pay very little attention to what goes on subsequently in their day-to-day operations or even the larger effects they have on the world' (Barnett and Finnemore 1999: 726). If nothing else, the rise of policy network analysis represents a sincere effort to understand how the EU works, day-by-day, and with what effects on the wider world. Arguably, policy network analysts are the least preachy of all types of scholar concerned with European integra-tion because they are most willing to admit that there is much about the EU that we still do not understand very well.

## Notes

1. I am grateful to the editors, Elizabeth Bomberg, Renaud Dehousse, Grant Jordan, and Laurence J. O'Toole Jr. for useful com-ments on earlier drafts.

2. The latter task seems impossible. Take, for example, the following policy prescription: 'Among the most effective strategies of defence against a global terrorist network is the develop-ment of a networked response. Transnational networks need to be mobilized, global civil society needs to be engaged and private sector financial institutions need to be employed to suppress or freeze the financial assets of terrorist networks' (Biersteker 2002: 83). Or, consider an expert's view of progress in the 'war on terrorism': 'Now you're into a situation where there is a network of networks . . . With al-Qaeda, if you take out nodal points in the network, they will regrow' (quoted in *Financial Times*, 9–10 November 2002: 8).

3. Thatcher's (1998) contrast between policy network analysis and what he calls 'policy learning models', such as epistemic commun-ities and advocacy coalitions, and his claim that

'policy network frameworks cannot simply be mixed with other approaches' are two of the less convincing points made in his otherwise thoughtful critique of policy network analysis. If we compare different approaches and concepts such as policy network, issue network, policy domaine, etc. we find that 'the fundamental principle underlying all these approaches is that relations between actors, rather than the actors' individual attributes, hold the key to explaining public policy decisions' (Knoke 1998: 508).

4. By some accounts, policy network analysis is actually a variant of institutionalism (see Hall and Taylor 1996; Lowndes 1996; Peters 1999).

5. Dissent about the utility or analytical power of policy network analysis is summarized and evaluated at 'Critique' below.

6. Emphasis in original. The astounding breadth of Castells' scholarship sometimes exposes a lack of depth of knowledge about the EU (a frequent problem for those who study the subject 'part time'). For example,

Castells (1998: 314, 317) repeatedly claims that qualified majority voting was extended in the late 1980s in the 'European Council', rather than in the Council of Ministers.

7. I thank Renaud Dehousse for making this point to me.

8. As much as the authors cited here may be diligently seeking to advance or critique policy network analysis, their frequent resort to self-citation and tendencies to try to rewrite their and other authors' places in the literature mean that a diligent postgraduate student could be forgiven for concluding that recent debates seem to have become so petty and personal that the approach itself is best avoided.

9. Quoted in *Financial Times*, 22 August 2002, p. 4.

10. Arguably, the decision in 2002 to give the (then) ten applicant states closest to membership full right of participation in the 2004 IGC meant that there were already too many veto players to make meaningful reform likely.

## Guide to further reading

BOERZEL, T.A. (1998), 'Organizing Babylon —on the different conceptions of policy networks', *Public Administration*, vol. 76, no. 2, 253–73 is a thoughtful (and critical) summary review of the literature on policy networks.

KECK, M.E. and SIKKINK, K. (1998), *Activists Beyond Borders: Advocacy Networks in International Politics* (Ithaca, NY and London: Cornell University Press) is one of the most impressive studies of how international politics has been transformed by the rise of transnational networks generally.

MARSH, D. (ed.) (1998), *Comparing Policy Networks* (Buckingham: Open University Press) is a recent edited collection of essays

using policy network analysis, including several that are preoccupied with the EU.

PETERSON, J. and BOMBERG, E. (1999), *Decision-Making in the European Union* (Basingstoke and New York: Palgrave) uses policy network analysis to probe decision-making in a diverse range of EU policy sectors.

SKOGSTAND, G. (2003), 'Legitimacy and/or policy effectiveness?: network governance and GMO regulation in the EU', *Journal of European Public Policy*, vol. 10, no. 3, 321–38 focuses on questions of legitimation surrounding policy networks, with a case study of the EU's internal debate on GMOs.

# 7

# The New Institutionalisms and European Integration

*Mark A. Pollack*

## Introduction

The European Union is without question the most densely institutionalized international organization in the world, with a welter of intergovernmental and supranational institutions and a rapidly growing body of primary and secondary legislation, the so-called *acquis communautaire*. Small wonder, then, that the body of literature known under the rubric of 'the new institutionalism' has been applied with increasing frequency and with increasing success to the study of the Union as a polity and to European integration as a process. In fact, however, the 'new institutionalism' in social theory has evolved into plural institutionalisms, with rational-choice, sociological and historical variants, each with a distinctive set of hypotheses and insights about the EU. This chapter examines the new institutionalisms in rational choice and historical analysis and their contributions to EU studies, briefly summarizing the core assumptions of each approach before discussing specific applications to the study of the European Union and the question of EU enlargement, and concluding with an analysis of the strengths and weaknesses of institutional approaches to the study of European integration.

## The origins of rational-choice and historical institutionalism

The new institutionalism(s) in political science did not, of course, originate in the field of EU studies, but reflected a gradual and diverse re-introduction of institutions into a large body of theories (such as behaviourism, pluralism, Marxism, and neorealism) in which institutions had been either absent or epiphenomenal, i.e. reflections of deeper factors or processes such as capitalism or the distribution of political power in a given domestic society or international system. By contrast with these institution-free accounts of politics, which dominated American political science between the 1950s and the 1970s, three primary 'institutionalisms' developed during the course of the 1980s and early 1990s, each with a distinct definition of institutions and a distinct account of how they 'matter' in the study of politics (March and Olsen 1984, 1989; Hall and Taylor 1996).

The first of these institutionalisms arose within the rational-choice approach to the study of politics, as pioneered by students of American politics. To simplify only slightly, the contemporary rational-choice institutionalist literature began with the effort by American political scientists to understand the origins and effects of US Congressional institutions. During the late 1970s, rational-choice scholars like Richard McKelvey (1976), William Riker (1980), and others noted that, in formal models of majoritarian decision-making, policy choices are inherently unstable, 'cycling' among multiple possible equilibria, with no single policy able to command a lasting majority among legislators. Yet substantive scholars of the US Congress noted that the House and Senate were indeed able to agree on stable policies, raising the question of how and why such stability was achieved. In this context, Kenneth Shepsle (1979, 1986) argued that Congressional institutions, and in particular the committee system, could produce 'structure-induced equilibrium' by ruling some alternatives as permissible or impermissible and by structuring the voting and veto power of various actors in the decision-making process. In more recent work, Shepsle and others have turned their attention to the problem of 'equilibrium institutions', namely, how actors choose or design institutions to secure mutual gains, and how those institutions change or persist over time.

Shepsle's innovation and the subsequent development of the rational-choice approach to Congressional institutions have produced a number of theoretical off-shoots with potential applications in comparative as well as international politics. For example, Shepsle and others have examined in some detail the 'agenda-setting' power of the Congressional committees that are the linchpin of his structure-induced equilibrium, specifying the conditions under which agenda-setting committees could influence the outcomes of certain Congressional votes (Shepsle and Weingast 1984; Ordeshook and Schwartz 1987). Shepsle's 'distributive' model of Congressional committees has, however, been challenged by Keith Krehbiel (1991) and other scholars, who agree that committees possess agenda-setting power but argue that the committee system serves an 'informational' rather than distributive function by providing members with an incentive to acquire and share policy-relevant information with other members of Congress.

In another offshoot, students of the Congress have developed principal-agent models of Congressional delegation of authority to regulatory bureaucracies (and later to courts) and the efforts of Congress to control those bureaucracies (Moe 1984; McCubbins and Schwartz 1987; Cooter and Ginsburg 1996). More recently, Epstein and O'Halloran (1999) and others (Huber and Shipan 2000) have pioneered a 'transaction cost approach' to the design of political institutions, arguing that legislators deliberately and systematically design political institutions to minimize the transaction costs associated with making public policy. Although originally formulated and applied in the context of American political institutions, these approaches are applicable in other comparative and international political contexts, including that of the European Union.

By contrast with the formal definition of institutions in rational-choice approaches, sociological institutionalism and constructivist approaches in international relations (examined in detail by Thomas Risse in his chapter in this volume) define institutions much more broadly to include informal norms and conventions as well as formal rules, and they argue that such institutions 'constitute' actors, shaping the way in which actors view the world. Moreover, by contrast with rational-choice models, in which actors are regarded as strategic utility-maximizers whose preferences are taken as given, sociological institutionalist accounts often begin with the assumption that people act according to a 'logic of appropriateness', taking cues from their institutional environment as they construct their preferences and select the appropriate behaviour for a given institutional environment. In the case of the EU, sociological institutionalist and constructivist scholars such as Risse (1996), Jeffrey Lewis (1998), and Jeffrey Checkel (2001) have examined the process by which EU and other institutional norms are diffused and shape the preferences and behaviour of actors in both domestic and international politics.

Historical institutionalists, finally, took up a position in between the two camps, focusing on the effects of institutions *over time*, in particular the ways in which a given set of institutions, once established, can influence or constrain the behaviour of the actors who established them (Hall and Taylor 1996). In an early formulation by Peter Hall (1986), and later cited with approval in a seminal article by Kathleen Thelen and Sven Steinmo (1992), Hall argued that:

Institutional actors play two fundamental roles in this model. On the one hand, the organization of policy-making affects the degree of power that any one set of actors has over the policy outcomes . . . On the other hand, organizational position also influences an actor's perception of his own interests, by establishing his institutional responsibilities and relationship to other actors. In this way, organizational factors affect both the degree of pressure an actor can bring to bear on policy and the likely direction of that pressure (Hall 1986: 19).

So defined, historical institutionalism can be interpreted as a theoretical 'big tent', capable of accommodating the insights of the rival rationalist and sociological institutionalist research programmes.

Historical institutionalism is, however, more than just a half-way house between its fellow institutionalisms (Thelen 1999; Pierson 2000). What makes historical institutionalism distinctive, rather, is its emphasis on the effects of institutions on politics *over time*, and in particular its rejection of the usual *functionalist* explanation for institutional design. In such functionalist approaches, political institutions are assumed to have been deliberately designed by contemporary actors for the efficient performance of specific functions, such as the provision of policy-relevant information or the adoption of expert and credible policies, and little or no attention is paid to historical legacies. In contrast with this view, historical institutionalists argue that institutional choices taken in the past can persist, or become 'locked in', thereby shaping and constraining actors later in time. Institutions, it is argued, are more or less 'sticky', or resistant to change, both because of the uncertainty associated with institutional design, and because national constitutions and international treaties can create significant transaction costs and set high institutional thresholds (such as a supermajority or unanimous agreement) to later reforms (Pollack 1996: 437–8).

In perhaps the most sophisticated presentation of this strand of historical-institutionalist thinking, Paul Pierson (2000) has suggested that political institutions and public policies are frequently characterized by what economists call 'increasing returns', insofar as those institutions and policies generate incentives for actors to stick with and not abandon existing institutions, adapting them only incrementally to changing political environments. Insofar as political institutions and public policies are in fact characterized by increasing returns, Pierson argues, politics will be characterized by certain interrelated phenomena, including: *inertia*, or *lock-ins*, whereby existing institutions may remain in equilibrium for extended periods despite considerable political change; *a critical role for timing and sequencing*, in which relatively small and contingent events that occur at *critical junctures* early in a sequence shape (that is, provide the institutional context for) events that occur later; and *path-dependence*, in which early decisions provide incentives for actors to perpetuate institutional and policy choices inherited from the past, even when the resulting outcomes are manifestly inefficient. With regard to the last concept of path dependence, perhaps the most influential notion in recent historical-institutionalist work, Pierson cites with approval Margaret Levi's definition:

Path dependence has to mean, if it is to mean anything, that once a country or region has started down a path, the costs of reversal are very high. There will be other choice points, but the entrenchments of certain institutional arrangements obstruct easy reversal of the initial choice. Perhaps the better metaphor is a tree, rather than a path. From the same trunk, there are many different branches and smaller branches. Although it is possible to turn around or to clamber from one to the other—and essential if the chosen branch dies—the branch on which a climber begins is the one she tends to follow (Levi 1997: 28, quoted in Pierson 2000: 252).

Perhaps most importantly, Pierson points out that the presence of increasing returns to institutions—and therefore the occurrence and importance of phenomena such as inertia, sequencing, and path-dependence—is not a constant, but a *variable*, which can be expected to vary systematically across different types of political institutions and policies. For example, some institutions, such as national constitutions, involve considerable start-up costs, generate adaptive effects among large numbers of people, and can be changed only by a large majority of parliamentarians and the electorate, and should therefore generate increasing returns, inertia, and path-dependent behaviour. By contrast, however, other institutions or public policies may involve lower fixed costs, fewer adaptive effects, and lower institutional barriers to wholesale reform, and in these cases the effects of historical events and path-dependence will be significantly reduced. In theory, therefore, historical institutionalism and its component concepts such as increasing returns and path-dependence offer the prospect, not just of claiming that 'history matters', but of explaining *how* and *under what conditions* historical events do—or do not—shape contemporary and future political choices and outcomes.

Defined in this way, historical institutionalism constitutes an implicit or explicit rejection of ahistorical or functional rational-choice theories of institutions, in which institutions are assumed to be established and maintained because those institutions efficiently perform certain institutional functions for their creators *in the present*. In fact, historical institutionalists point out, political institutions are frequently subject to increasing returns, and their effects therefore outlive the constellation of interests that adopted them, making historical analysis—and not just a functional analysis of present-day actors and institutions—a necessary part of any explanation of contemporary political outcomes. *'Rather than assume relative efficiency as an explanation'*, Pierson argues, *'we have to go back and look'* (Pierson 2000: 264, emphasis in original).

Nevertheless, while historical institutionalist accounts do constitute a rejection of ahistorical and functionalist accounts of institutionalism by some rational-choice scholars, the most influential historical institutionalists applying path-dependent accounts of economics and politics generally adopt assumptions about actor preferences and behaviour that are fully consistent with rational-choice approaches (David 1985; North 1990; Arthur 1994; Krugman 1996; Pierson 2000). For this reason, the discussion that follows does not consider historical institutionalism as a distinct and competing school of thought, but rather as a particular variant of rational-choice theory emphasizing the importance of inertia, sequencing, and path-dependence in the process of European integration.

## Applications to the study of the European Union

Within the past decade, all three of Hall and Taylor's new institutionalisms have been adopted by students of European integration, with results that have been reviewed extensively elsewhere (Pollack 1996; Jupille and Caporaso 1999; Aspinwall and Schneider 1999, 2001; and Dowding 2000). Rational-choice institutionalist analyses of the EU arguably date back to the late 1980s, with Fritz Scharpf's (1988) pioneering work on 'joint-decision traps' in the EU and other federal systems, and continued into the 1990s and 2000s with work by George Tsebelis, Geoffrey Garrett, and others who sought to model in rational-choice terms the selection and above all the workings of EU institutions. Simplifying considerably, we can say that rational choice analyses have examined all three of the major functions of government at the Union level: (1) executive politics, i.e. the delegation of executive powers to the European Commission and other agencies, and their exercise of those powers; (2) judicial politics, specifically the European Court of Justice's role vis-à-vis EU member governments and national courts; and (3) legislative politics, including decision-making within the Council of Ministers as well as the ever-changing legislative role of the European Parliament. The remainder of this section briefly discusses each of these bodies of literature, with special attention to the first question of executive politics, followed by (4) a brief discussion of historical institutionalist approaches emphasizing joint-decision traps, lock-ins, and European integration as a path-dependent process.

## Executive politics and the question of comitology

Throughout the history of the European Community, and now Union, scholars have debated the causal role of supranational actors, and in particular the role of the executive Commission in the processes of European integration and policy-making, with neofunctionalists generally asserting, and intergovernmentalists generally denying, any important causal role for supranational organizations in the integration process. By and large, however, neither neofunctionalism nor intergovernmentalism has generated testable hypotheses regarding the conditions under which, and the ways in which, supranational institutions exert an independent causal influence on the process of European integration. In that context, rational-choice institutionalists have devoted increasing attention over the past decade to the question of delegation to, and agency and agenda-setting by, supranational organizations such as the Commission. These studies generally address two specific sets of questions. First, they ask why and under what conditions a group of (member-state) *principals* might delegate powers to (supranational) *agents*, such as the Commission, the European Central Bank, or the Court of Justice. With regard to this first question, rationalists like Moravcsik (1998), Majone (2000), and Pollack (2003) have drawn from the theoretical literature on delegation in American, comparative, and international politics in order to devise and test hypotheses about the motives of EU member governments in delegating specific powers and functions to the Commission and other supranational actors.

Simplifying considerably, such *transaction-cost* accounts of delegation argue that member-state principals, as rational actors, delegate powers to supranational organizations primarily to lower the transaction costs of policy-making, in particular by allowing member governments to credibly commit themselves to international agreements and to benefit from the policy-relevant expertise provided by supranational actors. Despite differences in emphasis, the empirical work of these scholars has collectively demonstrated that EU member governments do indeed delegate powers to the Commission, the European Central Bank, and the Court of Justice largely to reduce the transaction costs of policy-making, in particular through the monitoring of member-state compliance, the filling-in of framework treaties ('incomplete contracts'), and the speedy and efficient adoption of implementing regulations that would otherwise have to be adopted in a time-consuming legislative process by the member governments themselves. By the same token, however, the same studies generally concede that transaction-cost models do a poor job of predicting patterns of delegation to the European Parliament, which appears to have been delegated powers primarily in response to concerns about democratic legitimacy rather than in order to reduce the transaction costs of policy-making.

In addition to the question of delegation, rational-choice institutionalists have devoted greater attention to a second question posed by principal-agent models: what if an agent—such as the European Commission, the Court of Justice, or the European Central Bank—behaves in ways that diverge from the preferences of the principals? The answer to this question in P-A analysis lies primarily in the administrative procedures that the principals may establish to define *ex ante* the scope of agency activities, as well as the oversight procedures that allow for *ex post* oversight and sanctioning of errant agents. Applied to the European Union, principal-agent analysis therefore leads to the hypothesis that agency autonomy is likely to vary across issue-areas and over time, as a function of the preferences of the member states, the distribution of information between principals and agents, and the decision rules governing the application of sanctions or the adoption of new legislation (Pollack 1997, 2003; Tallberg 1999, 2000; Tsebelis and Garrett 2000b).

Much of this literature on delegation and agency focuses on the rather arcane question of *comitology*, the committees of member-state representatives established to supervise the Commission in its implementation of EU law. For rational-choice theorists, comitology committees are *control mechanisms* designed by member-state principals to supervise their supranational agent (the Commission) in its executive duties. In this approach, member-government preferences are assumed to be fixed, the aim of comitology is control rather than deliberation, and the rules governing a committee *matter* in determining the discretion of the Commission in a given issue-area. More specifically, rational-choice analysts have analysed the differences among the three primary types of comitology committees—namely, advisory committees, management committees, and regulatory committees—noting that, in formal models of executive decision-making, the Commission is least constrained under the advisory committee procedure, and most constrained under the regulatory committee procedure, with the management committee procedure occupying a middle ground (Steunenberg et al. 1996, 1997). Under these circumstances, rationalists predict, EU member governments will prefer and select comitology committees designed to maximize their expected utility by producing favourable 'policy streams' in a given issue-area; and they will carefully calibrate the autonomy or responsiveness of the Commission through the selection of specific comitology procedures (Pollack 2003; Franchino 2000). These same authors also predict that the European Parliament (EP), as a co-legislator with the Council of Ministers, will have a strong institutional preference for inclusion in the comitology process (from which it has been traditionally excluded); and they suggest further that, insofar as the Commission is answerable to the Parliament and tends to share its policy preferences, the EP should be in favour of non-restrictive comitology that leaves the Commission relatively unfettered by the preferences of the member governments.

By contrast with this rationalist view of comitology as a control mechanism, Christian Joerges and Jürgen Neyer (1997a, 1997b) draw on Habermasian accounts of deliberative democracy as well as constructivist analysis in political science to argue that EU comitology committees provide a forum in which national and supranational experts meet and *deliberate* in a search for the best or most efficient solutions to common policy problems. In this view, comitology is not an arena for hardball intergovernmental bargaining, as rationalists assume, but rather for a technocratic version of deliberative democracy in which informal norms, deliberation, good arguments, and consensus matter more than formal voting rules, which are rarely invoked. In support of their view, Joerges and Neyer (1997a) evidence their study of EU foodstuffs regulation, where they find that the importance of scientific discourse limits the ability of delegates to discuss distributional issues, particularly in scientific advisory committees, which in turn focuses debate and deliberation onto scientific questions. In addition, the authors point out, delegates not only meet regularly in comitology committees but often have also met as part of advisory committees and working groups involved in the adoption of the legislation in question—an ideal setting for long-term socialization into common European norms. In this way, the authors argue, comitology committees pass from being institutions for the strategic control of the Commission to being forums for deliberative interaction among experts for whom issues of control and distribution, as well as the carefully contrived institutional rules of their respective committees, recede into the background in favour of a collective search for the technically best solution to a given policy problem.

Comitology, then, emerges as a key area in which rationalist and constructivist theorists provide competing accounts and hypotheses on a common empirical terrain, which offers the unusual prospect of direct, competitive empirical testing. Unfortunately, as I have argued elsewhere (Pollack 2003: ch. 2), testing such hypotheses requires researchers to deal with serious methodological challenges, including the measurement of elusive concepts such as 'deliberation' (for constructivists and sociological institutionalists) and 'autonomy' and 'control' (for rationalists). Faced with these difficulties, students of comitology have pursued two distinct research strategies to test hypotheses about the significance of EU committees. The first and best established is the use of case studies and process-tracing, which would allow us to understand the respective preferences of actors such the Commission and of the member governments, and examine the process of committee decision-making in practice. Among rational-choice analysts, Schmidt (1997) and Pollack (2003) have engaged in such case-study analysis, in areas such as the liberalization of telecommunications and electricity, merger control, the management of the Structural Funds, and the negotiation of the Uruguay Round. Their findings, although tentative, suggest that member governments do indeed use comitology committees as instruments of control, and that Commission autonomy and influence vary as a function of the administrative and oversight procedures adopted by the Council. By contrast, however, Joerges and Neyer's empirical research in the foodstuffs sector, although not reported in the form of a case study, de-emphasizes the control functions of comitology in favour of the emergence of deliberative interaction among delegates in scientific advisory committees. These disparate results suggest the need for further empirical work, and careful case selection, to determine the extent of, and the conditions for, the use of comitology committees as a means of control or a forum for deliberation, respectively.

Given these difficulties of a case-study approach, scholars are increasingly turning to a second research strategy, examining delegation as a *dependent variable* that can be expected to vary with variables such as uncertainty, political conflict, and other aspects of the political environment (Huber and Shipan 2000: 41). Applying such an approach to the rationalist/constructivist debate outlined above, we can derive two distinct and testable sets of hypotheses about the preferences of EU member governments and supranational organizations with regard to the choice of comitology committees. Rational-choice approaches suggest that the choice of comitology procedures *matters* in shaping policy outcomes, and that the Commission, Parliament, and member governments should have systematic preferences over the choice of committee type and be willing to accept both search costs and costs of negotiation in order to secure their preferred institutional outcome. Specifically, rational-choice analysts predict that the Commission should systematically prefer the 'lighter' advisory procedure to the man-agement procedure, and the latter to the most stringent regulatory procedure. The Parliament, by contrast, should have a strong preference for being formally included in the comitology procedure; the EP should also prefer less constraining regulatory pro-cedures for the Commission, if and insofar as its preferences are systematically closer to the Commission's than to the pivotal voter in the Council. The Council, finally, should generally prefer more restrictive comitology than the Commission or the Parliament, but preferences within the Council should vary across member governments and issue-areas, as governments attempt to tailor comitology types so as to maximize their expected utility from the delegation decision. By contrast, constructivist and sociolog-ical institutionalist accounts would predict that, insofar as deliberation characterizes the workings of comitology committees, formal voting rules should not be significant determinants of policy outcomes, and hence EU member governments and institutions are unlikely to engage in the sort of detailed, issue-specific calculations of expected utility predicted by rationalists in the choice of comitology committees. Rather, and in keeping with the general assumptions of sociological institutionalism, we should expect to see EU member governments and supranational actors behaving according to a 'logic of appropriateness', eschewing detailed calculations of utility in each and every Regulation or Directive in favour of consensual norms or institutional templates which define the 'legitimate' institutional form (e.g. the type of comitology committee) appropriate to a given issue-area.

At the time of writing, empirical study of the choice of comitology procedures remains in its infancy (see Franchino 2000; Dogan 2000; Pollack 2003); nevertheless, most of the available quantitative, qualitative, and case-study evidence supports the rationalist hypothesis that EU member governments, as well as the Commission and the Parliament, are aware of the implications of different committee procedures for member-state control and Commission autonomy, and all three sets of actors display procedural preferences consistent with the predictions of the principal-agent approach. These findings do not, of course, demonstrate conclusively that deliberation does *not* take place in comitology committees, or that those committees are used exclusively by member governments with fixed preferences as a means of constraining the Commission. Deliberation, argumentation, persuasion, and collective preference forma-tion may take place in at least some comitology committees, as Joerges and Neyer

(1997a, 1997b) argue. Establishing the presence of, and conditions for, such deliberation, however, will require an extensive and carefully designed research programme, including intensive, long-term studies of the actual workings of comitology committees, with observations cutting across different types of committees and different issue-areas. In the absence of such ambitious studies, the available evidence suggests that the key institutional actors representing the Commission, Parliament, and member governments, choose and calibrate comitology rules *as if* they matter; and that these same rules are employed, albeit infrequently, as explicit mechanisms of control when the Commission, as an agent, strays too far from the preferences of the member governments, its collective principals.

## Judicial politics and legal integration

In addition to the lively debate about the nature of EU executive politics, rational-choice institutionalists have also engaged in an increasingly sophisticated research programme into the nature of EU judicial politics and the role of the European Court of Justice in the integration process. Writing in the early 1990s, for example, Geoffrey Garrett first drew on principal-agent analysis to argue that the Court, as an agent of the EU's member governments, was bound to follow the wishes of the most powerful member states. These member states, Garrett argued, had established the ECJ as a means to solve problems of incomplete contracting and monitoring compliance with EU obligations, and they rationally accepted ECJ jurisprudence, even when rulings went against them, because of their longer-term interest in the enforcement of EU law (Garrett 1992). In such a setting, Garrett and Weingast (1993: 189) argued, the ECJ might identify 'constructed focal points' among multiple equilibrium outcomes, but the Court was unlikely to rule against the preferences of powerful EU member states, as Burley and Mattli (1993) had suggested in a famous article drawing on neofunctionalist theory.

Responding to Garrett's work, other scholars have argued forcefully that Garrett's model overestimated the control mechanisms available to powerful member states and the ease of sanctioning an activist Court, which has been far more autonomous than Garrett suggests. To simplify considerably, such accounts suggest that the Court has been able to pursue the process of legal integration far beyond the collective preferences of the member governments, in part because of the high costs to member states in overruling or failing to comply with ECJ decisions, and in part because the ECJ enjoys powerful allies in the form of national courts and individual litigants, the ECJ's 'other interlocutors' which refer hundreds of cases per year to the ECJ via the 'preliminary reference' procedure of Article 234 (Weiler 1994; Mattli and Slaughter 1995, 1998; Stone Sweet and Caporaso 1998; Stone Sweet and Brunell 1998; Alter 2001). In this view, best summarized by Stone Sweet and Caporaso (1998: 129), 'the move to supremacy and direct effect must be understood as audacious acts of agency' by the Court. At the same time, however, they argue that:

. . . judicial politics in the EC is not easily captured by [principal-agent] imagery. The Court's constitutionalization of the treaty system produced profound structural changes. Among other things, it reconstituted relationships among the ECJ, national judges, and private and public actors at the national and transnational levels. Often enough, the impact of the Court's rule-making is to effectively constrain member-state governments, both individually and collectively. The P-A framework is ill-equipped to capture these dynamics.

Stone Sweet and his collaborators are undoubtedly correct in their assertion that a simple principal-agent model of member government-ECJ relations cannot constitute a satisfactory theory of EU legal integration, since the ECJ must necessarily address other actors, including the individual litigants who bring cases as well as the national courts that are responsible for submitting and applying the bulk of all contemporary ECJ decisions. By the same token, however, no satisfactory theory of EU legal integration can *omit* the principal-agent relationship between the member governments and the ECJ, since it is this relationship that sets the bounds of ECJ discretion through the adoption and amendment of the treaties and through the threat or use of control mechanisms such as legislative overruling and non-compliance; and indeed, rational-choice approaches to the ECJ have gradually become more complex, and have been subjected to greater empirical testing, in response to critics (Garrett 1995; Garrett, Kelemen, and Schulz 1998; Kilroy 1999).

## Legislative politics and the role of the European Parliament

A third strand within the rational-choice literature on the EU has attempted to model the EU legislative process, including both the relative voting power of member states in the Council of Ministers, as well as the variable agenda-setting powers of the Commission and the European Parliament under different legislative procedures. As Dowding (2000) points out, this literature has thus far focused on three primary questions: (1) the utility of power-index analyses for the understanding of member governments' influence in the Council of Ministers (see, e.g. Garrett and Tsebelis 1996, and the special issue of the *Journal of Theoretical Politics*, vol. 11, no. 3); (2) the conditions for the EP's agenda-setting powers under the cooperation procedure (see, e.g. Tsebelis 1994; Moser 1996a, 1996b; Tsebelis 1996); and (3) Tsebelis' controversial claim, based on a formal model, that the European Parliament has *lost* agenda-setting power in the transition from the cooperation procedure to the Maastricht version of co-decision (Tsebelis 1997; Tsebelis and Garrett 1997a, 1997b; Crombez 1997; Moser 1997; Scully 1997a, 1997b, 1997c, 1997d). By and large, each of these debates has focused on the proper specification of the formal models in question, rather than on the empirical support for these models, with the result that these debates have been effectively 'tuned out' or disregarded by the majority of qualitatively oriented non-modellers in EU studies. In recent years, however, several studies have appeared using both qualitative and quantitative methods to test these various models (Kreppel 1999; Tsebelis and Kalandrakis 1999; Tsebelis et al. 1999), and the recent creation of two major databases of EP votes[1] should increase the quality and quantity of empirical tests in the years to come.

Overlapping with these studies of the EU legislative procedure, finally, are the growing number of rational-choice analyses of decision-making *inside* the European Parliament, whose party system, committee procedures, and voting behaviour have been studied by scholars in legislative studies. Among other findings, these studies have demonstrated the growing cohesiveness of pan-European party groupings, whose membership is now a better predictor of voting patterns among MEPs than nationality; the importance of cross-party coalitions among the major party groups in the legislative process; and the emergence of a two-dimensional political space, in which MEPs contest policies across the salient issues of both integration and left-right questions (Tsebelis 1995; Hix and Lord 1997; Raunio 1997; Scully 1997a; Hix 2001; Kreppel and Tsebelis 1999).

## Unintended consequences, joint-decision traps, and path-dependence

Thus far, we have looked at the executive, judicial, and legislative politics of the European Union through the standard lenses of rational-choice theory, in which institutions are either: (1) independent (or intervening) variables that explain how and why individuals, organizations, and states are driven towards what Shepsle (1986) calls 'structure-induced equilibria' by EU institutions; or (2) dependent variables created and maintained by rational actors to perform certain functions for the actors that created them—what Shepsle (1986) calls 'equilibrium institutions'. Implicit or explicit in such accounts is the notion that institutions, once created, are indeed 'sticky' and persist over time; yet the functionalist assumption that institutions are indeed *chosen* to perform certain functions is seldom tested empirically, and little attention is usually given to the specific question of how institutions evolve and shape political outcomes *over time*. Thus, despite the substantial contributions of rationalist approaches to our understanding of the EU, much of the rational-choice literature on the EU arguably under-emphasizes the central point of the early neofunctionalist literature, namely the concept of European integration as a *process* which does indeed unfold over time, often as a result of the unintended consequences of early integration decisions that become difficult for the EU's constitutive member states to control or overturn.

For these reasons, the past decade has witnessed the widespread adoption of historical institutionalism by scholars such as Bulmer (1994), Pierson (1996), Armstrong and Bulmer (1998), Wiener (2000), and the authors in Cowles, Risse, and Caporaso (2001), each of whom emphasizes to a greater or lesser degree the temporal dimension of European integration as an historical process. In doing so, however, these authors generally adopt the earlier and more broad definition of historical institutionalism discussed above, at the expense of formulating specific and testable hypotheses about the *conditions* under which institutions do—or do not—become locked-in and/or produce path-dependent processes of political development (e.g. European integration). For example, Armstrong and Bulmer's (1998) excellent analysis of the origins and implementation of the single European market programme explicitly adopts historical institutionalism as the theoretical framework for the study, deriving four sets of insights about the effects of institutions on policy outcomes, and contrasting their approach against rational-choice analyses; but the authors explicitly eschew hypothesis-testing, and they make no effort to formulate or test hypotheses about the conditions under which institutions will be more or less constraining, more or less productive of increasing returns, and hence more or less likely to produce a path-dependent process of European integration. Yet it is precisely such hypotheses, I would argue, that set historical institutionalism apart from rationalist (and sociological institutionalist) accounts, and that promise to create real value-added in the study of European integration. Indeed, without specific hypotheses about the conditions for lock-ins and increasing returns, historical institutionalists lack the conceptual tools for explaining *which* institutions are subject to lock-ins, *how* those institutions shape historical trajectories over time, and *under what conditions* the unintended consequences of early institutional choices will be either constraining to, or easily reversed by, the EU's constitutive member states.

Despite these challenges, a number of scholars have begun to put forward more discriminating and testable hypotheses about the differential impact of EU (and other) institutions over time. In a pioneering article, for example, Fritz Scharpf (1988) argued that the institutional rules of certain joint decision-making systems, such as German federalism or the European Union, lead to what he called 'the joint decision-trap', in which a given institution or policy, once instituted, tends to remain in place, rigid and inflexible, even in the face of a changing policy environment. Such joint-decision traps, Scharpf specified, were particularly likely in institutions characterized by three inter-related rules: intergovernmentalism (as opposed to federalism or supranational decision-making); a voting rule of unanimity (as opposed to majority); and a default condition in which a policy or institution would persist (as opposed to being terminated) in the event of no agreement. Under these specific conditions, Scharpf argued, policies such as the EU's Common Agricultural Policy could become entrenched or locked-in, even in the face of ever-growing agricultural surpluses or other pressures, as long as a single member state remained able to block policy or institutional reforms. On the other hand, Scharpf implied (albeit without elaboration) that a change in any of these three rules—for example, a move to supranational or majoritarian decision-making, or a change in the default rule providing that policies be terminated unless periodically reauthorized—could alleviate the joint-decision trap and allow for ready adaptation of existing institutions to changing circumstances.

Similarly, Pierson's (1996) study of path-dependence in the EU seeks to understand European integration as a process that unfolds over time, and the conditions under which path-dependent processes are most likely to occur. Working from essentially rationalist assumptions, Pierson argues that, despite the initial primacy of member governments in the design of EU institutions and policies, 'gaps' may occur in the ability of member governments to control the subsequent institutions and policies, for four reasons. First, member governments in democratic societies may, because of electoral considerations, apply a high 'discount rate' to the future, agreeing to EU policies that lead to a long-term loss of national control in return for short-term electoral returns.

Second, even when governments do not heavily discount the future, unintended consequences of institutional choices may create additional gaps, which member governments may or may not be able to close through subsequent action. Third, Pierson
argues, the preferences of member governments may change over time, most obviously
because of electoral turnover, leaving new member governments with new preferences
to inherit an *acquis communautaire* negotiated by, and according to the preferences
of, a different government. Given the decision rules of intergovernmentalism and
unanimity emphasized by Scharpf, however, individual member governments are likely
to find themselves 'immobilized by the dead weight of past initiatives' (Pierson 1996:
137). Fourth and finally, Pierson argues, EU institutions and policies may become
locked-in not only as the result of change-resistant institutional rules from above, but
also through the incremental growth in political support for existing, entrenched institutions *from below*, as societal actors adapt to and develop a vested interest in the con-
tinuation of specific EU policies. In the area of social policy, for example, the European
Court of Justice has developed a significant jurisprudence on gender equality which
certainly exceeds the original expectations of the member governments. Rolling back
these unexpected consequences, however, has proven difficult, both because of the need
for a unanimous agreement to overturn an ECJ decision in this area, and because of the
domestic constituencies (e.g. working women) with a vested interest in the maintenance of the *acquis*.

   While both Scharpf and Pierson offer us important insights, their most important
contribution is not the idea that institutions are 'sticky' and subject to lock-ins—which
is a generic and rather banal institutionalist claim—but rather their statements about
the *conditions* under which we should expect lock-ins and path-dependent behaviour.
In Scharpf's analysis, for example, lock-ins occur only under a specific set of decision
rules; in other areas, joint-decision traps may be avoided insofar as existing institutions
and policies either expire (hence their default condition is *not* the status quo) or can be
amended by supranational decision or by qualified majority (breaking the logjam of
unanimous intergovernmental decision-making). Similarly, while Pierson calls our
attention to the prospects of micro-level adaptations to EU policies and institutions,
and hence increasing returns, not all EU policies create such effects, and we should
therefore expect variation in the stability and path-dependent character of different EU
policies and institutions. To take only one example, the EU's Structural Funds might at
first glance seem to be a classic candidate for a joint-decision trap and path-dependent
behaviour, like the Common Agricultural Policy. By contrast with the CAP, however,
the Structural Funds must be reauthorized at periodic intervals by a unanimous agreement among the member states, and this 'default condition' of expiration, together
with the uneven pattern of reliance on the Structural Funds across member states and
their citizens, allows EU member states to reform the funds more readily, and with less
incidence of path-dependence, than we observe in Treaty reform or in the Common
Agricultural Policy.

   By employing such a conceptual tool-box, historical institutionalists promise to
go beyond the neofunctionalist observation that European integration generates

unintended consequences, and specify under what conditions member states cannot
—or, in some cases, can—reverse and contain the effects of those unintended consequences on the subsequent 'path' to European integration. The challenge for future
historical institutionalist analysis of the EU therefore lies in moving beyond the use of
historical institutionalism as a metaphor for history, or as a 'big tent' reconciling rationalist and sociological approaches, and applying historical institutionalist concepts
with precision to predict and explain *variation* in the stability and path-dependence of
EU institutions and policies over time.

## The new institutionalisms and EU enlargement

The enlargement of the European Union poses multiple challenges to EU policy-makers,
and multiple research questions to students of European integration (Wallace 2000;
Schimmelfennig and Sedelmeier 2002). Simplifying slightly, we can say that the bulk of
the recent scholarship focuses on four primary questions raised by the current enlargement of the EU:

(1) Why did the European Union decide, during the course of the 1990s, to enter
    into enlargement negotiations with as many as twelve new members, despite the
    obvious budgetary and institutional challenges this would pose for the members
    of the EU?

(2) How can we account for the subsequent negotiations between the European
    Union and the individual candidate countries, including the preponderant
    bargaining power of the Union but also its occasional willingness to enter into
    compromises with the candidate countries?

(3) What effects, if any, have the European Union and its promise of eventual mem-
    bership had on the process of political and economic reform in the candidate
    countries, particularly the former communist countries of Central and Eastern
    Europe?

(4) What effects is the projected enlargement of the Union from fifteen to as many
    as twenty-seven members likely to have on the institutions and policies of an
    enlarged EU?

Simplifying once again, it seems fair to say that sociological institutionalist and constructivist scholars have devoted greater attention than either rational-choice or historical institutionalist scholars to the first two questions, while historical institutionalists
have devoted somewhat greater attention to the process of reform in Central and
Eastern Europe, and rational-choice institutionalists have applied their familiar tools to
projecting the impact of enlargement on the institutions of an EU of twenty-seven or
more members.

With regard to the first and second questions, regarding the EU's decision to accept membership applications from and negotiate membership agreements with the new democracies of Central and Eastern Europe, a number of sociological institutionalist and constructivist scholars argue that the conduct of the EU's member governments at the very least presents a puzzle for rationalist accounts of European integration. In this view, rational-choice theory cannot explain why and how EU member governments have, gradually and somewhat grudgingly, embraced the goal of EU enlargement despite the substantial financial costs of enlargement (particularly for countries like Spain which fear the diversion of EU structural and agricultural aid to the less developed CEE states). Such decisions, it is argued, cannot be explained except with reference to the acceptance of common norms and common standards of legitimacy, according to which the Union cannot reject pleas for membership from neighbouring countries that credibly invoke 'European' values such as democracy and free markets (Sedelmeier 2000; Fierke and Wiener 1999). In an interesting twist on this essentially constructivist argument, Schimmelfennig (2001a) argues that while rational-choice calculations of material interests can explain member-state preferences on enlargement, their reluctant decision to enlarge represents a case of rhetorical entrapment in which governments, having professed allegiance to a set of common Community norms, were then constrained to live up to those norms in their public behaviour. Indeed, Schimmelfennig's argument occupies an intermediate space between rationalist and constructivist (or sociological institutionalist) analyses, since the informal norms of democracy and free markets do not appear to 'constitute' the EU's member governments, but rather to act as external constraints for governments concerned about their reputation on the international scene. Finally, it is worth pointing out that the sociological institutionalist account is not uncontested; indeed, as Andrew Moravcsik and Milada Vachudova (2002) have pointed out, the issue-specific material interests of EU member governments provide at the very least a good first-cut set of predictions about their behaviour in the enlargement negotiations, and the relative success of rationalist and constructivist accounts of those negotiations remains a matter for further empirical research.

Turning to the third major question posed by enlargement—namely, the effects of the EU on the policies and institutions of the applicant countries—we find arguments associated with all three variants of the new institutionalism. A number of scholars, drawing on the influential 'Europeanization' literature within the EU (Cowles, Risse, and Caporaso 2001) and on the early literature on post-Communist transitions (Stark 1992), adopt an historical-institutionalist perspective, noting the path-dependent nature of national institutions and national policies, and underlining the variation in the acceptance and transposition of EU norms by candidate countries, each of which has integrated new elements of the *acquis communautaire* in line with its own distinct national traditions (Vachudova 2002; Scherpereel 2002). Other scholars, writing in a constructivist or sociological institutionalist vein, acknowledge the importance of historical legacies but emphasize the constitutive power of EU and international norms for the élites of the newly democratizing countries of Central and Eastern Europe, arguing that international social learning and the diffusion of legitimate norms have played a central role in the transition from communist to 'European' politics and policies in each of these countries (Checkel 2001; Epstein 2001; Gheciu 2002). Once again, however, Schimmelfennig (2001b) has raised doubts about some of the more far-reaching claims of international socialization in the CEE countries, arguing that Western material incentives (e.g. the EU's policy of 'conditionality' in its relations with candidate countries), rather than international or transnational social influence, appear to have been the primary inducement for the adoption of EU norms in the countries of the former Soviet bloc. Here again, further work is needed both to map the considerable diversity in CEEC responses to EU demands, and to understand the causal mechanisms (material incentives or socialization) underlying this diversity.

Fourth and finally, the imminent enlargement of the EU to as many as twenty-seven member states raises significant questions about the operation of EU institutions and policies with a substantially enlarged membership, and it is perhaps here where rational-choice institutionalist analysts have been most active, modelling the effects of enlargement and of the Treaty of Nice (designed in large part to prepare for enlargement) on the distribution of voting power among member states, as well as the member states' collective ability to reach agreement on new policies. Specifically, a number of rational-choice models based on the provisions of the Treaty of Nice have demonstrated that, contrary to some of the claims put forward by member-state representatives after the Nice European Council, the likelihood of reaching agreement will actually *decrease* in an enlarged, post-Nice EU (largely because of the raising of the QMV threshold from 71.2 per cent of all weighted votes to 73.9 per cent), while the relative voting weight of each of the individual members will also decrease as their numbers increase; larger member states, however, will benefit disproportionately from the Nice reforms in an enlarged EU (Baldwin et al. 2001; Bräuninger and König 2001; Felsenthal and Machover 2001). More generally, one of the most striking features of the Treaty of Nice was the extent to which the methods of rational-choice scholars were in fact replicated by the delegations to the Nice European Council, where negotiators reportedly brought calculators to assess (albeit not always accurately!) the impact of proposed institutional changes on their respective voting weights. In this case, more than any other, rational-choice analysts can reasonably claim not only to have accurately depicted, but also to have influenced, the decision-making characteristics of EU member governments in the process of European integration.

## Challenges and prospects of rational choice and historical institutionalism

Over the course of the past decade, the new institutionalisms—including sociological institutionalism or constructivism as well as the rational-choice and historical variants analysed in this chapter—have arguably become the dominant approaches to the study of European integration. Moreover, despite the differences among them, all three institutionalisms offer substantial advantages over the traditional neofunctionalist and intergovernmentalist theories of European integration, in three ways. First, whereas the old neofunctionalist/intergovernmentalist debate was limited almost exclusively to EU studies, new institutionalist analyses draw explicitly from and can in turn contribute to the development of general theories of politics. Indeed, the rational-choice and historical institutionalist theories reviewed in this chapter share basic assumptions and approaches not only with each other, as I have argued, but also with a wide variety of rationalist theories of EU politics (e.g. liberal intergovernmentalism), comparative domestic politics (e.g. Thatcher and Stone Sweet 2002), and international politics (Milner 1998), and the theoretical compatibility of these studies in turn allows for comparison with relevant domestic and international cases outside the EU.

This observation points to a second advantage, namely that institutional analyses generally challenge the traditional distinction between international relations and comparative politics, and indeed we have seen that the basic concepts of institutionalist analysis are applicable both at the 'international' level of the EU and at the level of member states, where the mediating impact of domestic institutions can help explain patterns of Europeanization among current member states and applicant countries.

Third and finally, all three institutionalisms have advanced considerably over the past decade, in terms of both theoretical elaboration and empirical testing. At the start of the 1990s, for example, the rational-choice institutionalist literature on the European Union was in its infancy, concerned primarily with the elaboration of formal models in the absence of empirical testing. Since then, however, rational-choice scholars have made real progress in both the specification of formal models and the gathering of new data to test them. Historical institutionalist accounts, by contrast, have been slower to move beyond the concepts of lock-in and path-dependence as broad metaphors for the integration process, but here too recent work has begun to refine the theory into distinct, testable hypotheses. In that context, the primary challenge for rational-choice institutionalists consists in the specification of new and more accurate models of EU institutions, and the testing of those models through a range of empirical approaches including qualitative as well as quantitative analysis; while for historical institutionalists, the primary challenge is to specify and test more precise hypotheses about the mechanisms of path-dependence, the conditions under which it does or does not take place, and the impact of temporal factors on the path of European integration.

Despite their multiple strengths and promise, finally, a careful balance sheet reveals two potential weaknesses of rational-choice and historical institutionalism as those approaches have been defined in this chapter. First, both varieties of institutionalism are essentially mid-level theories, concerned largely with the effects of institutions as intervening variables in EU politics. As such, neither theory constitutes in and of itself an adequate theory of European *integration*, the ultimate causes of which typically remain exogenous to the theory. Historical institutionalism has begun to address some of these questions, examining the ways in which initial integrative acts *may* create unintended consequences and lead to an endogenous, path-dependent process of integration, but even in such accounts the root causes of integration may be external to the theory itself. Here again, however, the compatibility of rational-choice and historical institutionalism with other rationalist theories of politics offers the prospect of linking mid-level analysis of EU institutions with broader theories that might explain the integration process more fully. Second, the rational-choice approach to the EU is based on a highly restrictive set of assumptions about the nature of actors and institutions—assumptions that have been fundamentally questioned by sociological institutionalists and constructivists, who believe that rational-choice theory is blind to the most important constitutive and transformative effects of EU institutions on the preferences and identities of the people who interact with them. To the extent that EU institutions do indeed have such effects—an empirical question which begs continuing research—rational-choice institutionalists may be systematically underestimating the importance and impact of the European institutions that are their primary object of study.

## Note

1. The first of these databases, collected by George Tsebelis with a grant from the National Science Foundation, is publicly available on Tsebelis' website at www.sscnet.ucla.edu/ polisci/faculty/tsebelis/eudata.html. The second is being compiled by the European Parliament Research Group, whose web page can be found at: www.lse.ac.uk/Depts/eprg/Default.htm.

## Guide to further reading

ASPINWALL, M., and SCHNEIDER, M. (eds.) (2001), *The Rules of Integration: Institutionalist Approaches to the Study of Europe* (New York: Manchester University Press). Edited volume featuring a number of institutionalist analyses of the European Union, with critical comments on each paper and an excellent introduction by Aspinwall and Schneider.

DOWDING, K. (2000), 'Institutionalist Research on the European Union: A Critical Review', *European Union Politics* 1(1), 125–44. Review article on institutionalist applications to the European Union, with a strong focus on the recent advances, and the remaining challenges, in rational-choice theory.

HALL, P.A. and TAYLOR, R.C.R. (1996), 'Political Science and the Three New Institutionalisms', *Political Studies* 44(5), 936–57. An excellent review article, summarizing the basic assumptions and arguments of what the authors call the 'three new institutionalisms' in political science: rational-choice, historical, and sociological.

JOERGES, C. and NEYER, J. (1997), 'From Intergovernmental Bargaining to Deliberative Political Process: The Constitutionalization of Comitology', *European Law Journal* 3(3), 273–99. A sociological institutionalist criticism of the rational-choice approach to supranational delegation, emphasizing the possibilities for deliberative decision-making in 'comitology' committees.

JUPILLE, J. and CAPORASO, J.A. (1999), 'Institutionalism and the European Union: Beyond International Relations and Comparative Politics', *Annual Review of Political Science* 2, 429–44. Another excellent review of institutionalist approachs to the European Union, emphasizing the promise of institutionalism as an approach capable of overcoming the gap between comparative politics and international relations.

PIERSON, P. (2000), 'Increasing Returns, Path Dependence, and the Study of Politics', *American Political Science Review* 94(2), 251–67. A cutting-edge discussion of historical institutionalism, emphasizing the importance of increasing returns and path-dependence in political life.

POLLACK, M.A. (2003), *The Engines of European Integration: Delegation, Agency and Agenda-Setting in the EU* (New York: Oxford University Press). An extended rational-choice institutionalist discussion of delegation to, and agency and agenda-setting by, supranational organizations, with particular attention to the Commission and the European Court of Justice.

SCHIMMELFENNIG, F. and SEDELMEIER, U. (2002), 'Theorizing EU Enlargement: Research Focus, Hypotheses, and the State of Research', *Journal of European Public Policy* 9(4), 500–28. An excellent theoretically informed review of the literature on enlargement, which focuses specific attention on the differing theoretical assumptions and empirical emphases of the various approaches.

TSEBELIS, G. and GARRETT, G. (2001), 'Legislative Politics in the European Union', *European Union Politics* 1(1), 9–36. Theoretically informed overview of legislative procedures in the European Union by two of the leading scholars in rational-choice institutionalism.

# PART III

# CONSTRUCTING
# THE EUROPEAN UNION

# 8

# Social Constructivism and European Integration

*Thomas Risse*

## Introduction

Social constructivism has reached the study of the European Union (EU) only recently, at least as compared with International Relations or Comparative Politics in general.[1] The publication of a *Journal of European Public Policy* special issue in 1999 marks a turning point in this regard (Christiansen, Jørgensen, and Wiener 1999; but see Jørgensen 1997). Social constructivism entered the field of EU studies mainly as a 'spill-over' from the International Relations discipline, but also because of profound misgivings among scholars about the rather narrow focus and sterility of the debates between neofunctionalism and (liberal) intergovernmentalism. Research inspired by social constructivism promises to contribute substantially to European integration studies, both theoretically and substantially, as I argue in the following. This chapter proceeds in the following steps. First, I will introduce social constructivism as an approach to the study of European integration and a challenge to more rationalist approaches such as liberal intergovernmentalism, but also a version of neofunctionalism. Second, I take a closer look at the question of European identity as a particular subject area to which research inspired by social constructivism can contribute. Third, the chapter discusses some constructivist contributions to the study of EU enlargement. I conclude with remarks on the future of European integration research inspired by social constructivism.

## Social constructivism as an approach to European integration

There is considerable confusion in the field of European studies on what precisely constitutes social constructivism and what distinguishes it from other approaches to European integration. As a result, it has become fairly common to introduce constructivism as yet another substantive theory of regional integration, such as liberal intergovernmentalism (Moravcsik 1993) or neofunctionalism (Haas 1958; see Schmitter's contribution to this volume). Yet, it should be emphasized at the outset that social constructivism as such does not make any substantive claims about European integration. Constructivists may join an intergovernmentalist reading of interstate negotiations as the central way to understand the EU. They may equally join the neofunctionalist crowd emphasizing spill-over effects and the role of supranational institutions (see, e.g. Haas 2001). And constructivists could certainly contribute to the study of the EU as a multi-level governance system and to an institutionalist interpretation of its functioning (see Jachtenfuchs and Kohler-Koch's as well as Pollack's contribution to this volume).

It is equally misleading to claim, as some have argued, that social constructivism subscribes to a 'post-positivist' epistemology (how can we know something?), while conventional approaches are wedded to positivism and the search for law-like features in social and political life. Unfortunately, terms such as 'positivism' are often used as demarcation devices to distinguish the 'good self' from the 'bad other' in some sort of disciplinary tribal warfare (for an excellent discussion of this tendency in International Relations theory see Wight 2002). However, if 'post-positivism' means, first, a healthy scepticism toward a 'covering law' approach to social science irrespective of time and space and instead striving toward middle-range theorizing; second, an emphasis on interpretive understanding as an intrinsic, albeit not exclusive, part of any causal explanation; and, third, the recognition that social scientists are part of the social world which they try to analyse ('double hermeneutics' see Giddens 1982), then—is anybody still a 'positivist' (to paraphrase an article by Legro and Moravcsik 1999)? In sum, while there are some radical constructivist positions denying the possibility of intersubjectively valid knowledge claims in the social sciences, this view is by no means a defining and unifying characteristic of social constructivism as a meta-theoretical approach to the study of social phenomena (on this point see also Ruggie 1998).

## Defining social constructivism

So, what then is 'social constructivism' (for the following see, e.g. Adler 1997, 2002; Fearon and Wendt 2002; Wendt 1999; Christiansen, Jorgensen, and Wiener 2001)? It is a truism that social reality does not fall from heaven, but that human agents construct and reproduce it through their daily practices. Berger and Luckmann (1966) called this 'the social construction of reality'. Yet while this is a core argument of social constructivism, as a truism it does not provide us with a clear enough definition. Therefore, it is probably most useful to describe constructivism as based on a social ontology which insists that human agents do not exist independently from their social environment and its collectively shared systems of meanings ('culture' in a broad sense). This is in contrast to the methodological individualism of rational choice according to which '[t]he elementary unit of social life is the individual human action' (Elster 1989: 13). The fundamental insight of the structure-agency debate, which lies at the heart of many social constructivist works, is not only that social structures and agents are mutually co-determined. The crucial point is that constructivists insist on the mutual *constitut-iveness* of (social) structures and agents (Adler 1997: 324–5; Wendt 1999: ch. 4). The social environment in which we find ourselves, defines ('constitutes') who we are, our identities as social beings. 'We' are social beings, embedded in various relevant social communities. At the same time, human agency creates, reproduces, and changes culture through our daily practices. Thus, social constructivism occupies a—sometimes uneasy—ontological middleground between individualism and structuralism by claiming that there are properties of structures and of agents that cannot be collapsed into each other.

This claim has important, if often overlooked, repercussions for the study of the European Union. The prevailing theories of European integration—whether neo-functionalism, liberal intergovernmentalism, or 'multi-level governance'[2]—are firmly committed to a rationalist ontology which is agency-centred by definition (see Haas's recent interpretation of neofunctionalism in Haas 2001). This might be helpful for substantive empirical research, as long as we are primarily in the business of explaining the evolvement of European institutions. If institution-building and, thus, the emergence of new social structures are to be explained, agency-centred approaches are doing just fine. Here, a constructivist perspective will complement rather than substitute these approaches by emphasizing that the interests of actors cannot be treated as exogenously given or inferred from a given material structure. Rather, political culture, discourse, and the 'social construction' of interests and preferences matter.

Take the debate on the future of the European Union as it has evolved from the 1990s onwards. Do the German and French contrasting visions of a future European political order reflect some underlying economic or geopolitical interests? If this were the case, we would expect most French politicians to plead for a federalist vision of the EU, since France should be obviously interested in binding a powerful Germany as firmly as possible to Europe. In contrast, most German contributors should embrace a 'Europe of nation states', as a means of gaining independence from the constraining effects of European integration. Thus, an emphasis on material power as well as economic or security interests would mis-predict the positions in the current debate. Those positions, however, can be explained as reflecting competing visions of a good political and socio-economic order which are deeply embedded in the two countries' contrasting domestic structures and political cultures.

Yet, such an emphasis on ideational, cultural, and discursive origins of national preferences complements rather than substitutes an agency-based rationalist account. 'Soft rationalism', which takes ideas seriously, should be able to accommodate some of these concerns. The more we insist that institutions including the EU are never created from scratch, but reflect and build upon previous institutional designs and structures, the further we move away from rational-choice approaches, even of the 'soft' variety. The issue is not so much about path-dependent processes and 'sunk costs' as emphasized by historical institutionalism (Pierson 1996), but about institutional effects on social identities and fundamental interests of actors. Thus, a constructivist history of the EU would insist against liberal intergovernmentalism in particular, that we cannot even start explaining the coming about of the major constitutional treaties of the Union without taking the feedback effects of previous institutional decisions on the identities and interests of the member states' governments and societies into account. Finally, such a re-written history of the EU would focus on the ongoing struggles, contestations, and discourses on how 'to build Europe' over the years and, thus, reject an imagery of actors including governments as calculating machines who always know what they want and are never uncertain about the future and even their own stakes and interests.

The differences between constructivism and a liberal intergovernmentalist approach to European integration are, thus, pretty clear as the latter is firmly based on a rationalist ontology that takes actors' preferences as given. It is less clear, though, how constructivism differs from neofunctionalism. On the one hand, neofunctionalism constitutes an actor-centred approach to European integration (see Haas 1958, 2001). It starts with egoistic utility-maximizing actors who cooperate to solve some collective action problems. At some point, the functional logic takes over ('spill-over') leading to further integration. On the other hand, neofunctionalism also talks about normative integration, the 'upgrading of common interests', and the shift of loyalties (identities) from the national to the supranational levels. This latter language implies some constitutive effects of European integration on the various societal and political actors. If European integration is supposed to transform collective identities, we have moved beyond a narrow rational-choice approach and toward a much 'thicker' understanding of institutions. In sum, there are aspects to neofunctionalist accounts that resonate pretty well with a constructivist focus on the constitutive rather than the purely regulative impact of norms.

## Agency, structure, and the constitutive effect of norms

The constructivist emphasis on the mutual constitutiveness of agency and structure becomes even more relevant for the study of European integration, the more we focus on the *impact* of Europeanization on the member states and their domestic policies, politics, and polities. Recent work on European integration has started to look at the various ways in which the integration process itself feeds back into the domestic fabric of the nation states (e.g. Cowles, Caporaso, and Risse 2001; Goetz and Hix 2000; Börzel 2002; Knill 2001; Kohler-Koch and Eising 1999; Héritier et al. 2001). Thus, European integration studies increasingly analyse the EU as a two-way process of policy-making and institution-building at the European level which then feed back into the member states and their political processes and structures. It is here where the difference between the methodological individualism emphasized by rational choice, on the one hand, and the constructivist focus on the mutual constitutiveness of agency and structures matters a lot.

The reason for this can be found in the way in which social constructivists conceptualize how institutions as social structures impact on agents and their behaviour. Rationalist (or 'neo-liberal' in International Relations jargon, see Keohane 1989) institutionalism views social institutions including the EU as primarily constraining the behaviour of actors with given identities and preferences. These actors follow a 'logic of consequentialism' (March and Olsen 1989, 1998) enacting given identities and interests and trying to realize their preferences through strategic behaviour. The goal of action is to maximize or to optimize one's interests and preferences. Institutions constrain or widen the range of choices available to actors to realize their interests. The EU's liberalization of telecommunications markets, for example, broke up state monopolies while empowering foreign companies to penetrate the markets of their competitors (Schneider 2001).

In contrast, social constructivism and sociological institutionalism emphasize a different logic of action, which March and Olsen have called the 'logic of appropriateness': 'Human actors are imagined to follow rules that associate particular identities to particular situations, approaching individual opportunities for action by assessing similarities between current identities and choice dilemmas and more general concepts of self and situations' (March and Olsen 1998: 951). Rule-guided behaviour differs from strategic and instrumental behaviour in that actors try to 'do the right thing' rather than maximizing or optimizing their given preferences. The logic of appropriateness entails that actors try to figure out the appropriate rule in a given social situation. It follows that social institutions including the EU can no longer be viewed as 'external' to actors. Rather, actors including corporate actors such as national governments, firms, or interest groups are deeply embedded in and affected by the social institutions in which they act.

This relates to what constructivists call the *constitutive* effects of social norms and institutions (Onuf 1989; Kratochwil 1989). Many social norms not only regulate behaviour, they also constitute the identity of actors in the sense of defining who 'we' are as members of a social community. The norm of sovereignty, for example, not only regulates the interactions of states in international affairs, it also defines what a state *is* in the first place. Constructivists concentrate on the social identities of actors in order to account for their interests (e.g. Wendt 1999: ch. 7; also Checkel 2001a). Constructivism maintains that collective norms and understandings define the basic 'rules of the game' in which they find themselves in their interactions. This does not mean that constitutive norms cannot be violated or never change. But the argument implies that we cannot even describe the properties of social agents without reference to the social structure in which they are embedded.

Consequently, the EU as an emerging polity is expected not just to constrain the range of choices available to, say, nation states, but the way in which they define their interests and even their identities. EU 'membership matters' (Sandholtz 1996) in that it influences the very way in which actors see themselves and are seen by others as social beings. Germany, France, Italy, or the Netherlands are no longer simply European states. They are EU states in the sense that their statehood is increasingly defined by their EU membership. The EU constitutes states in Europe insofar as it maps the political, social, and economic space enabling private and public actors to define their interests and go about their business (Laffan, O'Donnell, and Smith 2000; Jönsson, Tägil, and Törnqvist 2000). EU membership implies the voluntary acceptance of a particular political order as legitimate and entails the recognition of a set of rules and obligations as binding. This includes that European law is the 'law of the land', and, thus, a constitutional order 'without constitution' (at least for the time being, see Weiler 1995; Shaw 2001). Thus, constructivists emphasize that the EU deeply affects discursive and behavioural practices, that it has become part of the 'social furniture' with which social and political actors have to deal on a daily basis. Such a view implies that EU membership entails socialization effects (Checkel 2000, 2001b). At least, actors need to know the rules of appropriate behaviour in the Union and to take them for granted in the sense that 'norms become normal'.

Constructivist emphasis on norm-guided behaviour and constitutive rules does not imply, however, that norms are never violated. Any study of the implementation of the *acquis communautaire* shows that compliance rates vary significantly among member states and across issue-areas (Börzel 2001). Acceptance of a social and political order as legitimate might increase compliance rates with the law. However, we all occasionally run a red light. Does this mean that we do not accept the rule as binding and valid? Of course not. We can infer from the communicative practices of actors whether or not they consider a norm as legitimate. Do they try to justify their behaviour in cases of rule violation? Do they recognize misbehaviour and offer compensation?

## Communication and discourse

The emphasis on communicative and discursive practices constitutes a final characteristic feature of social constructivist approaches. If we want to understand and explain social behaviour, we need to take words, language, and communicative utterances seriously. It is through discursive practices that agents make sense of the world and attribute meaning to their activities. Moreover, as Foucault reminds us, discursive practices establish power relationships in the sense that they make us 'understand certain problems in certain ways, and pose questions accordingly' (Diez 2001: 90). And further, '[a]lthough it is "we" who impose meaning, "we" do not act as autonomous subjects but from a "subject position" made available by the discursive context in which we are situated' (*ibid.*, referring to Foucault 1991: 58).

There are at least two ways in which the study of communicative practices has recently contributed to our understanding of the European Union. First, some scholars have started applying the Habermasian theory of communicative action to international relations (Habermas 1981, 1992; Müller 1994; Risse 2000). They focus on arguing and reason-giving as an agency-centred mode of interaction which enables actors to challenge the validity claims inherent in any causal or normative statement and to seek a communicative consensus about their understanding of a situation as well as justifications for the principles and norms guiding their action, rather than acting purely on the basis of strategic calculations. Argumentative rationality means that the participants in a discourse are open to be persuaded by the better argument and that relationships of power and social hierarchies recede into the background. Argumentative and deliberative behaviour is as goal-oriented as strategic interactions, but the goal is not to attain one's fixed preferences, but to seek a reasoned consensus. As Keohane put it, persuasion 'involves changing people's choices of alternatives independently of their calculations about the strategies of other players' (Keohane 2001: 10). Actors' interests, preferences, and the perceptions of the situation are no longer fixed, but subject to discursive challenges. Where argumentative rationality prevails, actors do not seek to maximize or to satisfy their given interests and preferences, but to challenge and to justify the validity claims inherent in them—*and* are prepared to change their views of the world or even their interests in light of the better argument.

Applied to the European Union, this emphasis on communicative action allows us to study European institutions as discourse rather than merely bargaining arenas allowing for deliberative processes to establish a reasoned consensus in order to solve common problems. Joerges and Neyer in particular have used this concept to study the EU comitology (Joerges and Neyer 1997b; Neyer 2002), while Checkel has emphasized persuasion and social learning in various settings of the EU and other European institutions (Checkel 2000, 2001a, 2001b).

The second way in which discursive practices have been studied in the EU, does not so much focus on arguing and reason-giving, but on discourse as a process of construction of meaning allowing for certain interpretations while excluding others (see also Wæver's contribution to this volume). In other words, this work focuses on discursive practices as means by which power relationships are established and maintained. Who is allowed to speak in a discursive arena, what counts as a sensible proposition, and which constructions of meaning become so dominant that they are being taken for granted? Rosamond's work on European discourses on globalization has to be mentioned here as well as Diez's study of the British discourse on European integration (Rosamond 2001; Diez 1999, 2001; see also Larsen 1999).

The latter work is related to a somewhat more radical version of social constructivism than those contributions mentioned so far. To the extent that these more radical positions deny the possibility of truth claims in social sciences, they take a different epistemological stance than the moderate constructivists discussed here. However, these distinctions should not be exaggerated. When it comes to actual empirical research, most scholars of 'discourse analysis' still use rather conventional methods of qualitative content analysis to make their points (compare Larsen 1999; Marcussen 2000; Jachtenfuchs, Diez, and Jung 1998; Marcussen et al. 1999).

## The three contributions of social constructivism

In sum, there are at least three ways in which social constructivism contributes to a better understanding of the European Union. First, accepting the mutual constitutiveness of agency and structure allows for a much deeper understanding of Europeanization including its impact on statehood in Europe. Second and related, emphasizing the constitutive effects of European law, rules, and policies enables us to study how European integration shapes social identities and interests of actors. Third, focusing on communicative practices permits us to examine more closely how Europe and the EU are constructed discursively and how actors try to come to grips with the meaning of European integration.

In the following, I apply these abstract arguments to the question of European identity, which is highly relevant for the construction of Europe in both political and analytical terms.

# The social construction of European identity

## The contested nature of European identity

Most people agree that a viable and legitimate European polity requires some degree of identification in order to be sustainable. But European identity is a contested idea.[3] Many people discuss the relationship between European and national identities in zero-sum terms. They follow *essentialist* concepts of collective identities taking cultural variables such as membership in ethnic groups as a given which then develop into national identities during the process of nation-building. If the causal connection between 'culture' and 'identity' is seen as a one-way street, there is not much one can do about this and supranational or post-nationalist identities are impossible. Collective identities will rest firmly with the nation state as the historically most successful connection between territory and people. French will remain French, while British remain British, and Germans remain Germans. 'Euro-pessimists' challenge the prospects for further European integration on precisely these grounds. They argue that a European polity is impossible, because there is no European people, no common European history or common myths on which collective European identity could be built (see Kielmansegg 1996).

Yet, we know from survey data and other empirical material that individuals hold multiple social identities. As a result, people can feel a sense of belonging to Europe, their nation state, their gender, and so forth. It is wrong to conceptualize European identity in zero-sum terms, as if an increase in European identity necessarily decreases one's loyalty to national or other communities. Europe and the nation are both 'imagined communities' (Anderson 1991) and people can feel a part of both communities without having to choose some primary identification. Analyses from survey data suggest and social psychological experiments confirm that many people who strongly identify with their nation state, also feel a sense of belonging to Europe (Duchesne and Frognier 1995; Martinotti and Steffanizzi 1995; Herrmann, Brewer, and Risse forthcoming).

This finding is trivial for scholars studying collective identities, but nevertheless it has important implications for the political debates about Europe and the nation state. Take the contemporary debate about the future of the European Union and about a European constitution. Many people still hold that Europe lacks a *demos*, one indicator being the lack of strong identification with Europe in mass public opinion. Yet, 'country first, but Europe, too' is the dominant outlook in most EU member states, and people do not perceive this as contradictory. Moreover and more important, the real division in mass opinion is between those who identify exclusively with their nation, on the one hand, and those perceiving themselves as attached to both their nation and Europe, on the other. Citrin and Sides show that the individual willingness to support further European integration increases quite dramatically from the former to the latter group. They argue, therefore, 'that willingness to grant the EU authority does not require an identification that actually prioritises Europe over the nation' (Citrin and Sides forth-coming). In other words, the European polity does not require a 'demos' that replaces a national with a European identity, but one in which national and European identities co-exist and complement each other. This is a significant empirical finding that speaks directly to the current debate on the future of the Union.

Most scholars working on collective identities today have abandoned essentialist conceptualizations of social identities, but embrace versions of *social constructivist* reasoning (see, e.g. Cederman 2001; Giesen 1993, 1999; Eder and Giesen 1999). From this perspective, the connection between cultural variables such as ethnic belongings or religious or ideological affiliations, on the one hand, and collective identities, on the other, is more historically contingent, tenuous, and subject to constructions and re-constructions. Accordingly, social identities contain, first, ideas describing and categorizing an individual's membership in a social group or community including emotional, affective, and evaluative components. Common Europeanness, for example, could constitute such a community. Second, this commonness is accentuated by a sense of difference with regard to other communities. Individuals frequently tend to view the group with which they identify in a more positive way than the 'out-group'. But a sense of collective European identity is always accompanied by the need to differentiate 'Europeans' from 'others', be it Soviet Communism during the Cold War, Islamic fundamentalism, or Anglo-American laissez-faire capitalism.

## 'Europeanness' and national identities

Two conclusions follow. First, there might be much more Europeanness enshrined in national cultures and, hence, a much stronger collective European identity than is usually assumed. This identification process might encompass a much longer—and probably also more contested—history than the forty years of European integration. Second, however, it becomes very unclear whether Italians, French, or Germans mean the same when they talk about their 'Europeanness'. The French notion of 'mission civilisatrice', for example, might translate into a European civilizing mission these days. But Germans would probably not feel very comfortable when confronted with such an interpretation of Europeanness. Insights from social psychological research suggest that increasing European identities among Italians, Germans, and the French might actually lead to less positive evaluations of Italians, Germans, and the French vis-à-vis each other. If people simply transfer the positive values and identity components of their in-group to a larger collectivity, they might distance themselves more strongly from out-groups belonging to the lower-level category (Mummendey and Wenzel 1999). If Germans strongly identify with Europe, but 'Europe' is simply Germany writ large, the social distance they feel to Italy might actually increase.

But we need to go beyond the rather simple insight that European and national identities can go together. The question is how multiple identities relate to each other. First, identities can be *nested*, conceived of as concentric circles or Russian Matruska dolls, one inside the next. My identity as a Rhinelander is nested in my German identity, which is again nested in my Europeanness. Second, identities can be *cross-cutting*. In this configuration, some, but not all, members of one identity group are also members of another identity group. Some women might feel a strong gender identity, but only a subgroup of them might also identify with Europe, while the latter group also encompasses women without a strong sense of gender identity.

There is a great deal of evidence that we can think of the relationship between European and other identities as nested and/or cross-cutting. We find the 'Russian Matruska doll' model of nested European and other identities on both the level of élites and of ordinary people. This concept suggests some hierarchy between people's sense of belonging and loyalties. European and other identities pertaining to territorially defined entities can be nested into each other so that 'Europe' forms the outer boundary, while one's region or nation state constitutes the core. The survey data mentioned above that mass publics in most countries hold national and regional identities as their primary sense of belonging, while Europe runs a distinct second, are consistent with such a concept of how multiple identities relate to each other. Reports about Commission officials also suggest a nestedness of European identity, but here 'Europe' forms the core, while national identification recedes into the background (Laffan forthcoming). Social context and the different salience of European affairs could explain the difference between the social identities of Commission officials and those of citizens in most EU member states. For the latter, Europe and the EU are distant realities at best and probably more remote than their imagined national communities. Hence the ordering whereby national identities form the core and European identity the outer boundary of the Russian doll. For Commission officials, the social context works the other way round and pushes toward stronger identification with Europe. This account is broadly consistent with a sociological institutionalist account according to which the institutional setting in which people act and are embedded, exerts strong effects on their social identities.

There is a third way of conceptualizing the relationship between European and other identities that people might hold. We could call it the 'marble cake' model of multiple identities. Accordingly, the various components of an individual's identity cannot be neatly separated on different levels as both concepts of nestedness and of cross-cutting identities imply. What if identity components influence each other, mesh and blend into each other? What if my self-understanding as a German inherently contains aspects of Europeanness? Can we really separate out a Catalan from a European identity? Or take the major European party families. From the 1950s on, Christian Democratic parties in Continental Europe were at the forefront of European integration. Europeanness has always been a constitutive component of post-World War II Christian Democratic ideology originating from the inter-war period. The same holds true for modern Social Democrats in Europe. It is interesting to note that the turn toward accepting capitalism and the social market economy which the German Social Democrats experienced in the late 1950s, the French Socialists in the early 1980s, and British Labour in the 1990s, went hand in hand with a strong identification with European integration (although conceptualized in different ways) in each of these cases. Today, Europeanness forms a constitutive part of modern Social Democratic ideology (for details see Marcussen et al. 1999; Risse 2001).

A most important corollary of the 'marble cake' concept concerns the content and substance of what it means to identify with Europe. Different groups might fill it with very different content. Indeed, a longitudinal study of political discourses about Europe among the major parties in France, Germany, and Great Britain revealed that the meaning of Europe varied considerably (Marcussen et al. 1999). For the German political élites, 'Europe' and the European integration meant overcoming one's own nationalist and militarist past. The French élites, in contrast, constructed Europe as the externalization of distinct French values of Republicanism, enlightenment, and the *mission civilisatrice*. While French and German political élites managed to embed Europe into their understandings of national identity, the British élites constructed Europe in contrast to their understandings of the nation, particularly the English nation.

## EU and European identity

Yet, we need to distinguish European and EU identity. This is particularly important if we want to find out which effects, if at all, Europeanization and European integration have had on identity change. People might feel a sense of belonging to Europe in general, while feeling no attachment to the EU at all—and vice versa. Yet, as Laffan suggests, the EU as an active identity builder has successfully achieved identity hegemony in terms of increasingly defining what it means to belong to 'Europe' (Laffan forthcoming). As argued above, EU membership has significant constitutive effects on European state identities. States in Europe are increasingly defined as EU members, non-members, or would-be members. Their status in Europe and to some degree also worldwide depends on these categories. There is no way that European states can ignore the EU, even such devoted non-members as Switzerland.

Moreover, the EU has achieved identity hegemony in the sense that 'Europe' increasingly denotes the political and social space occupied by the EU. In the context of Eastern enlargement, Central and Eastern European (CEE) states want to 'return to Europe', as if they were currently outside the continent. When Italy prepared itself for entering the Euro zone, the main slogan was 'entrare l'Europa' (entering Europe!) as if Italy—one of the six founding members of the European Community—had ever left it (Sbragia 2001). In these contexts, Europe is used synonymously with the EU. To the extent that people identify Europe with the EU, this would be a remarkable achievement of forty years of European integration. If Europe and the EU are used interchangeably, it means that the latter has successfully occupied the social space of what it means to be European. One could then not be a 'real' European without being an EU member. The EU increasingly fills the meaning space of Europe with a specific content.

Bruter points out in this context that it makes a difference whether Europe is defined in civic or cultural terms (Bruter forthcoming). 'Culture' in this understanding encompasses everything from history, ethnicity, civilisation, and heritage to other social similarities. 'Civic identity' instead is much more circumscribed and refers to identification of citizens with a particular political structure such as the EU or the political institutions of the nation state (see also Eisenstadt and Giesen 1995). Bruter argues that the distinction allows differentiation between identification with the EU as a distinct civic and political entity, on the one hand, and a larger Europe as a cultural and historically defined social space, on the other. 'Europe' as a civic and political space is largely defined by the EU. European institutions—both the EU and the Council of Europe—deliberately try to construct a post-national civic identity in the Habermasian sense (Habermas 1994, 1996; Dewandre and Lenoble 1992) emphasizing democracy, human rights, market economy, the welfare state, and cultural diversity. These values have become constitutive for the EU, since you cannot become a member without subscribing to them. As the enlargement debates show, the self-description of the EU and the dominant discourses surrounding it have moved quite a long way toward building a polity and going beyond simple market integration (see also Laffan, O'Donnell, and Smith 2000).

But does this civic understanding of European identity resonate with European citizens? Current Eurobarometer data unfortunately do not allow for distinguishing between cultural and civic understandings of European identity. But there is some evidence that is at least consistent with such a view. Education, income, and ideology all have a positive impact on levels of attachment to Europe. Moreover, attachment to 'Europe' is strongly correlated with support for the EU and willingness to cede authority and sovereignty to EU institutions in various policy domains. Finally, the more people identify with Europe, the less xenophobic and the more positive they are toward Eastern enlargement. Hostility toward immigrants, in contrast, correlates strongly with exclusively national identifications (Citrin and Sides forthcoming).

Social identities not only describe the content and the substance of what it means to be a member of a group. They also describe the boundaries of the group, i.e. who is 'in' and who is 'out' (Neumann 1996). As a result, we can infer quite a bit about the substance of European identity, if we know more about the European 'others'. The first problem we encounter in this context concerns Europe's 'fuzzy boundaries'. Where does Europe end? A quick look at those international organizations that carry 'Europe' in their name shows that there is no uniform answer to the question. Europe is characterized by overlapping and unclear boundaries. The EU itself currently ends at the former East-West border of the Cold War, but will expand considerably toward the east and south-east during the next ten years. The European Economic and Monetary Union with the single currency encompasses twelve of the fifteen EU member states. The European Single Market, which includes the European Economic Area (EEA), encompasses some non-EU members such as Norway. 'Schengenland' with its absence of internal border controls, has even more complicated borders, since it includes the non-member Norway, but not the EU member Great Britain.

In sum, 'Europe' as a space of political organization and institutionalization has no clear boundaries. Moreover, 'othering' is context-dependent. As much as there is no fixed meaning what Europe constitutes positively, there are no fixed European 'others'. In the discourse centring around the European welfare state and the European social model, we find repeated references to the US and to Japan as European 'others' (see also Rosamond 2001). In the German discourse on the future of European integration, Germany's own past of militarism and nationalism constituted the European 'other' against which the European integration project was to be built (Risse 2001; Risse and Engelmann-Martin 2002). In a similar way, the recent European-wide controversy about the ascent to power of a right-wing party in Austria constructed the 'out-group' as some sort of enemy within, since nobody denied that Austria was a legitimate member of the EU. The issue was whether European values of democracy and human rights were consistent with the rise to power of a xenophobic party, which did not distance itself sufficiently from the European Nazi past. In sum, Europe has many 'others' that are referred to and represented in a context-dependent way. This does not mean at all that anything goes, but it warns us not to reify the concept of European identity and to fix its meaning once and for all.

This short survey of current research on European identity demonstrates how one would approach a crucial issue for the future of Europe from a social constructivist perspective. Three points need to be reiterated here. First, questions such as European identity, which are usually bracketed by conventional approaches to European integration, assume centre-stage in a constructivist account. This shows how a particular perspective serves as a theoretical lens with which to look at questions which are normally overlooked or under-theorized by other theoretical perspectives. Second, the sociological institutionalist account adopted here allows for highlighting the constitutive effects of Europeanization on people's social identities. The EU not only increasingly regulates the daily lives of individuals in various respects; it also constitutes 'Europe' as a political and social space in people's beliefs and collective understandings. Third, studying questions of European identity highlights the importance of analyzing the discursive construction of meanings mentioned above. European identity is not a given or falls from heaven; it is a specific construct in time and space whose content actually changes depending on the social and political context in which it is enacted.

# The enlargement puzzle from a social constructivist perspective

One criticism of research on European identity concerns the 'so what?' question. The discussion above explored European identity as the 'dependent variable' (to use conventional social science jargon). But does it actually matter in terms of explaining observable outcomes in European integration? At the end of the day, political scientists want to account for political processes and outcomes and a constructivist focus on collective meaning constructions makes sense only if it helps us to understand these processes. Thus, I now use European identity as an explanatory factor to account for a crucial issue in European integration, namely Eastern enlargement.

The Eastern enlargement of the European Union not only represents a major challenge for the EU itself, but also a puzzle for conventional theories of European integration. As Schimmelfennig has convincingly demonstrated (Schimmelfennig 2000, 2001, forthcoming; Sedelmeier 1998), liberal intergovernmentalism offers a plausible first-cut explanation for the association agreements of the Central Eastern European (CEE) countries with the EU. However, EU *membership* for the CEE countries is an entirely different story. The membership preferences of CEE countries are pretty clear, since representation in EU policy-making processes is to be preferred over simple association agreements. Moreover, CEE countries might expect some security benefits from EU membership (in addition to their NATO membership). Yet, all of this does not explain why EU member states—including Germany—should decide in favour of EU enlargement. As Schimmelfennig shows, a majority of EU member states should actually be opposed to enlargement (including France and all southern European states; Schimmelfennig 2001: 50). Yet, the 1993 Copenhagen European Council agreed 'that the associated countries . . . shall become members of the European Union' and formulated conditions of admission. As Sedelmeier shows in detail (Sedelmeier 1998), members of the European Commission in particular served as norm entrepreneurs pushing and cajoling EU members into a commitment in favour of enlargement. How can this decision be explained?

Schimmelfennig uses a sociological institutionalist account to argue that the EU constitutes a liberal community of states committed to the rule of law, human rights, democracy, and to a social market economy. His argument resonates with the concept of security communities based on a collective identity of its members (see, e.g. Adler and Barnett 1998; for the original argument see Deutsch et al. 1957). Since the values of the community constitute its members, the members undertake a normative obligation toward 'states that share the collective identity of an international community and adhere to its constitutive values and norms' (Schimmelfennig 2001: 58–9). Therefore, these states are entitled to join the community.

In other words, the collective identity of the EU as a liberal community explains the enlargement puzzle to a large degree. Rhetorical commitment to community values entrapped EU member states to offer accession negotiations to the CEE and other Eastern European countries despite the initial preferences against enlargement. These initial and materially derived preferences also explain why the enlargement negotiations are such a cumbersome process and why the necessary policy and institutional reforms of the EU to prepare the community for twenty-five or more members are still lacking (see Sedelmeier 1998 for details). Schimmelfennig's analysis represents a clever attempt to combine a constructivist account emphasizing constitutive norms and collective identities with a rationalist explanation focusing on narrowly defined egoistic interests. Fierke and Wiener push this analysis one step further by using speech act theory to show how Western states including EU members had committed themselves during the Cold War to welcome a free and democratic Eastern Europe into the Western Community. Their work on EU and NATO enlargement shows how normative commitments acquire their own dynamics as social rather than material capabilities (Fierke and Wiener 2001).

Yet, two theoretical puzzles remain, one for rationalism, the other for constructivism. The rationalist puzzle concerns the problem of how one can assume rational actors with pre-social (egoistic) preferences, on the one hand, who are—at the same time—embedded in the social structure of a community affecting their collective identities via constitutive norms, on the other. A rationalist ontology has a hard time accounting for constitutive norms presupposing a social structure in which actors are embedded. The constructivist puzzle concerns the fact that constitutive norms might affect the actual behaviour of actors only to a limited degree. The EU's collective identity might explain the enlargement decision as such, but not the bickering of the member states during the actual negotiations with Eastern European countries. In other words, when it comes to paying a price for one's collective identity in terms of offering beneficial conditions to new members, the EU looks more like an exclusive club dictating the terms of accession to new members. A rationalist account such as liberal intergovernmentalism seems sufficient to account for the EU's behaviour during and in the outcome of the actual enlargement negotiations, as Schimmelfennig argues (Schimmelfennig 2000, 2001).

## Conclusions

This chapter has tried to make three points. First, I presented a short overview on social constructivism as a distinct research programme and tried to show what it contributes to the study of European integration. Second, I used the question of European identity to illustrate empirically social constructivism 'at work'. Third, I presented a constructivist account of the EU's Eastern enlargement in order to demonstrate that an identity-based explanation is better able to account for the enlargement decision itself than conventional theories of integration such as liberal intergovernmentalism.

My overall conclusion is that the introduction of a social constructivist research programme to the study of the EU was long overdue. It is all the more remarkable that this research has quickly left the stage of meta-theorizing and concern for ontology and epistemology behind and has now entered the realm of concrete empirical work dealing with real puzzles of European political life. Thus, social constructivist research on the EU has quickly entered the realm of 'normal social science'. Still, some see a 'characteristic unwillingness of constructivists to place their claims at any real risk of empirical disconfirmation' (Moravcsik 2001b: 177). It is, of course, ultimately up to the readers of constructivist work to decide whether their claims contribute to the accumulation of our knowledge about the EU. Most empirical work from a construct-ivist perspective does engage alternative explanations and demonstrates its claims against competing hypotheses. More important, it is not clear whether scientific progress is to be achieved through rather sterile debates between competing 'isms' (see below). And it is even less clear why European integration theories grounded in rational choice approaches should always serve as the 'baseline' against which the value added of constructivist contributions has to be judged.

So, what remains to be done? My concluding remarks centre around the lack of a social constructivist theory of European integration on a par with, say, liberal inter-governmentalism, as Moravcsik has called for (Moravcsik 2001a). It is true that social constructivism has not (yet?) generated a set of mid-range propositions that could compete with conventional integration theories such as neofunctionalism or liberal intergovernmentalism. Checkel's attempts at developing a constructivist theory of socialization processes in Europe probably comes closest to such an attempt (see, e.g. Checkel 2000, 2001a, 2001b).

But should we strive for yet another stylised theory of integration offering a compre-hensive account of European integration, this time from a constructivist perspective? And can we reasonably expect one to emerge from constructivism? As argued above, social constructivism does not represent a substantive theory of integration, but an ontological perspective or meta-theory. Constructivist insights might be used to generate theoretical propositions, e.g. on collective identity constructions, their causes and their effects on the integration process. Sociological institutionalism as the constructivist-inspired version of institutionalist research can be used to generate hypotheses about the impact of Europeanization on domestic change which can then be tested against or supplemented with more rationalist accounts of institutional effects (Börzel and Risse 2000, 2002). And so on. But to expect a full-fledged constructivist theory of regional integration is probably not on the cards.

Moreover, we probably do not need another stylised theory of integration resting on a single logic of social action and interaction. Do we really need to establish another attempt at theoretical hegemony in EU studies, this time from a constructivist per-spective? It seems to me that the theoretical fistfights in the study of European integration are over—they have never interested scholars of comparative politics or public policy as much as students of international relations. The latter seem to have internalized the realist worldview of an eternal struggle over power and hegemony as a fruitful way of scholarly theory-building. If it is indeed true that there is more than one social logic of action and social rationality, our theories need to take this insight into account. I have argued above that we need to distinguish the rational choice logic of consequentialism from the sociological institutionalist logic of appropriateness and that both are different from the logic of arguing. Yet, real actors in the real world of the EU tend to combine various logics of action in their behaviour. They pursue egoistic interests—embedded in a society constituting their collective identities. They argue about the right thing to do—in order to pursue some goals and to solve collective action problems.

As a result, future theories of European integration should strive to integrate the various logics of social action and resulting propositions about human behaviour in order to figure out in which ways they complement each other and where they offer competing accounts. Constructivist reasoning contributes to this endeavour by emphasizing processes of social action such as rule-following and meaning construction through reason-giving which is a practice that rational choice accounts normally do not address.

## Notes

1. For comments on the draft manuscript I thank Tanja Börzel and the two editors of this volume.

2. Whether 'multi-level governance' represents a full-fledged theory of integration or rather an analytical framework to study it, remains unclear (see the contribution by Jachtenfuchs and Kohler-Koch in this volume; also Hooghe and Marks 2001).

3. The following discussion is partly based on Risse (forthcoming).

## Guide to further reading

ADLER, E. (1997), 'Seizing the Middle Ground. Constructivism in World Politics', *European Journal of International Relations* 3(3), 319–63; (2002) 'Constructivism and International Relations', in *Handbook of International Relations*, Carlsnaes, W. et al. (eds.) (London: Sage), 95–118. These two articles by a leading scholar of international relations introduce students to the core arguments and debates of social constructivism.

CHRISTIANSEN, T. et al. (eds.) (2001), *The Social Construction of Europe* (London: Sage). Published originally as a special issue of the *Journal of European Public Policy*, this volume shows in an exemplary fashion what social constructivism can contribute to the study of the European Union.

HERRMANN, R.K. et al. (eds.) (forthcoming), *Identities in Europe and the Institutions of the European Union* (Lanham, MD: Rowman and Littlefield). This volume represents the state of the art on the study of European identity comprising approaches from social psychology, sociology, political science, and linguistics.

JØRGENSEN, K.E. (ed.) (1997), *Reflective Approaches to European Governance* (London: Macmillan). This is one of the first social constructivist volumes focusing on the European Union.

RISSE, T. (2001), 'A European Identity? Europeanization and the Evolution of Nation State Identities' in *Transforming Europe. Europeanization and Domestic Change*, Cowles, M.G. et al. (eds.) (Ithaca, NY: Cornell University Press), 198–216; Risse, T. et al. (1999), 'To Euro or Not to Euro. The EMU and Identity Politics in the European Union'. *European Journal of International Relations* 5(2), 147–87. These two articles discuss the evolution of élite identities pertaining to the European

Union and present an account of how these identities influence crucial EU decisions such as the introduction of the single currency.

SCHIMMELFENNIG, F. (forthcoming), *Rules and Rhetoric. The Eastern Enlargement of NATO and the European Union* (Cambridge: Cambridge University Press). This book represents an excellent and theoretically informed account of the NATO and EU decisions to enlarge at the intersection of rationalist and sociological institutionalism.

WENDT, A. (1999), *Social Theory of International Politics* (Cambridge: Cambridge University Press). Wendt's book has already become a 'classic' text on the fundamentals of social constructivism in international relations.

# 9

# Integration Through Law

## *Ulrich Haltern**

## Introduction

The overarching interest of 'Integration Through Law' (ITL) is to examine the *role of law* in the process of European integration. It must seem puzzling at first blush that there exists a movement at all setting out to examine the role of law in the process of European integration. Is it not obvious, after all, that no serious study of, say, a federal system can disregard the various landmark decisions of that system's constitutional or supreme court? And yet, during the 1970s and 80s, it seemed that the dialogue between lawyers and political scientists had become difficult, with both disciplines abandoning their mutual interest. The division between legal and political analysis, though explicable in many ways, led to neglect, or misconceptions, of the role of law in the construction of the Communities (Weiler 1982; Caporaso 1998: 338). Equally, with few exceptions, political scientists had paid little attention to the role that legal institutions might play in fostering integration, especially the European Court of Justice (ECJ) and member states' courts (Burley and Mattli 1993: 42).

The early and mid-80s saw calls for an interdisciplinary approach to 'law in context', led by legal scholars such as Stein (1981), Snyder (1990), Rasmussen (1986), and Weiler (1981, 1982, 1987a, 1987b). The most detailed exposition of the ITL movement's work was Cappelletti, Seccombe, and Weiler (1986a–c). Today, the ECJ is all the rage, hailed as the creator of the Community legal system and the constitutionalizer of the Treaties. With political scientists no longer ignoring the Court, the literature has expanded dramatically. However, an exclusive focus on the ECJ gives an incomplete, and at times erroneous, picture of judicial integration. The rule-of-law Community has been, in Stone Sweet's words, a 'participatory process, a set of constitutional dialogues between supranational and national judges' (Stone Sweet 1998: 305). This has spawned detailed country studies and a number of works focusing on the relationship between the ECJ and national courts (e.g. Slaughter, Stone Sweet, and Weiler 1998; Stone Sweet 2000; Alter 2001). In the face of such revived interest in interdisciplinary approaches to EU law, with lawyers examining the law in a political, social, and economic context, and political scientists developing impact analyses of judicial politics, ITL has evolved into something less teleological and coherent, and rather more fragmented and 'contested' (e.g. Bańkowski and Christodoulidis 1998).

# Law and integration

## Studying European law

The very study of law in the process of European integration poses difficult problems. EC law 'represents, more evidentially perhaps than most other academic law subjects, an intricate web of politics, economics and law' which virtually cries out to be understood by means of an interdisciplinary, contextual approach to law (Snyder 1990: 9). Yet, it has all too often been taught as a highly technical set of rules, a dense doctrinal thicket hardly extending beyond 'black-letter law' (Snyder 1990: 9–31; Shaw 1996b), which is clearly inadequate. Recent years, however, have seen an abundance of analyses of EC law 'in context' and a mainstreaming of interdisciplinary and contextual thinking. Scholarship has moved away from de-contextualized analysis of judicial doctrine and instead turned to insights from other bodies of scholarship and disciplines, including legal-philosophical accounts, sociological analyses, and studies of the impact the Court's work has had on social and political change (de Búrca 2001: 2).

## ITL and integration theory

It is not easy to locate ITL in the wider field of European integration theory. It appears there are both linkages and divisions (Burley and Mattli 1993; Joerges 1996). Liberal intergovernmentalism seems to be furthest from the ITL rationale. While it rationalizes the ECJ's power (efficiency, avoidance of prisoner dilemma and free-rider problems, capacity to overcome domestic opposition) (Moravcsik 1993, 1998), liberal intergovernmentalism seems like a Newtonian model of the EU (big things moving at low speed) compared to the Einsteinian ITL movement (small things moving at high speed) (Weiler 1998c: 56). In Wincott's words (1995a), Moravcsik focuses on nodal 'history-making moments' such as treaty revisions. Models of multi-level governance, in contrast, appear to parallel many of the debates ITL has taken up (Marks et al. 1996; Pernice 1999). Both share the ability to depict complexity as the principal feature of the EU's policy system. Neofunctionalism has always entertained close ties to legal integration theories, notably through the early Ipsen and Burley and Mattli's renewal (Ipsen 1972; Burley and Mattli 1993). Their message is that law's integrative force rests not on law in itself, but on actor interests (Joerges 1996).

## The place of law

The place of law in European integration is obvious but should, as Shaw reminds us (1996a: 370–3), never be taken for granted. The Union may have entered a period in which it searches for its distinctly European political imagination (Ward 2001). Should the search prove fruitful, the place of law in Europe's imagination will be open to negotiation and change. Should it prove fruitless, it is doubtful whether falling back onto legal integration is a viable option. We do not know if Europe will in the future be a 'Community of law'. We do know, however, that law has been a major *leitmotiv* in the history of European integration. Law has brought an order with a very specific and clear purpose (Shaw 1996a: 3). That purpose is the promotion of a process of integration on a number of levels, including the economic, the monetary, and the political. The Court has rarely lost sight of the aim of integration. It is generally perceived to have pursued a vigorous policy of integration over the years, to have taken on the task of giving flesh to the bare bones of the Treaty, and to have given special weight to the enhancement of EC law's effectiveness and integration into member state legal systems. Many portray the Court as 'a hero who has greatly advanced the cause of integration' (Alter and Meunier-Aitsahalia 1994: 536). While this is not an undeserved profile (for caveats see Craig and de Búrca 1998: 78–81; de Búrca and Weiler 2001), the question is whether we will see different roles for law, and the Court.

## Two periods

During the Community's formative period, the Court lifted the EC legal order from the classical international into a supranational (and arguably, constitutional) sphere. It established the principles of direct effect, supremacy, and pre-emption, and made the member states fully responsible for reversing the effects of violations of EC law which affect individuals, for example through ordering governments to pay damages. It is this period that ITL has succeeded in theorizing thoroughly with admirable insight. I will explain some of them in the section on 'The role of law in European integration: examples'.

There is now, however, a vigorous new emphasis on constitutionalism. It is above all this last move away from formal law to theories of good governance and constitutional values (among many others) that seems indicative of a re-assessment, and heavy quali-fication, of the original ITL movement (Everson 1998). It may be that there is a new convergence of political science and legal research, the reasons being, on the one hand, the normative turn of political science studies and, on the other hand, the renewed interest in non-functional, non-outcome-driven concepts of the 'new constitution-alism' in legal studies (Wincott 1998; Lehning and Weale 1997; Weiler 1999; Shaw 2001). Joerges locates the beginning of this shift towards conceptions of Europe as a regulatory polity in the early 1980s. We are witnessing a transformation 'from integration research to a theory of governance for the EU' (Joerges 2002: 26). I believe that the debate over good governance is part of a struggle over the development and nature of a European political imagination (Haltern 2003). According to some, Europe must be 'something that Europeans believe in, not something the legitimacy of which is assigned merely by treaties and courts of law' (Ward 2001: 25). Awakening a European political imagina-tion—the very contents of which is, to date, highly contested—would lead Europe out of the current malaise of mounting economic problems and declining social legitimacy with its citizens. Recent developments—the Charter of Fundamental Rights, the Laeken Declaration, the debate on the future of Europe, the Convention drafting a

European Constitution—all point in this direction. I will deal with this aspect of the role of law in European integration in the section on 'A cultural study of law: the European imagination of the political'.

# The role of law in European integration: examples

ITL does not advance one single argument ready for summary. This is therefore the place to sketch some of its main claims. I will start with some of the more famous analyses of important legal doctrines, like pre-emption, supremacy, and direct effect. To add an institutional focus, I will continue with the role of the ECJ and of national courts. Finally, I will present Weiler's celebrated distinction between political and legal supranationalism.

## Doctrines: pre-emption, supremacy, direct effect

The role of law in European integration and in the Union's process of constitutional-ization is best reflected in its base doctrines of direct effect and supremacy. They are the core of a legal architecture construed gradually and oft-described (Weiler 1991; Ipsen 1972; Bogdandy 2000a; de Witte 1999). The European Court established the doctrine of *direct effect* in 1963[1] and has subsequently developed it in a series of important deci-sions. The doctrine provides that Community norms that are clear, precise, and self-sufficient (that is, not requiring further legislative measures) must be regarded as the law of the land in the sphere of application of Community law. Direct effect applies not only to the EC Treaty itself, but also to secondary legislation. With few exceptions, EC law creates enforceable legal obligations not only in vertical relations between public authority and individuals, but also in horizontal relations between individuals *inter se*. Community norms with direct effect may be invoked by individuals before state courts, which must provide adequate legal remedies (Weiler 1999: 19).

The implications are far-reaching, because the Court, by introducing the doctrine of direct effect, inverses the public international law assumption that legal obligations are addressed to states only, and do not create direct effect for nationals of that state. It is, typically, up to the state itself to determine the scope and reach to which, if at all, international obligations may produce direct effect for individuals. Under the doctrine of direct effect of EC law, however, states are faced with legal actions before their own courts at the suit of individuals. As a practical implication, individuals became the principal 'guardians' of the integrity of the Community legal order.

The full effect of the doctrine of direct effect is realized only in combination with the doctrine of EC law *supremacy*. Unlike federal constitutions, the EC Treaty does not con-tain a supremacy clause. However, starting in 1964,[2] the European Court developed a rigid, or 'absolute' (de Witte 1999: 190–1) version of supremacy. EC norms trump pro-visions of national law independent of their respective hierarchy of norms or the time of their enactment. This means that in the sphere of application of Community law, *any* Community norm (be it an Article of the EC Treaty or an administrative regulation) trumps *any* national norm (be it a provision from the member state constitution or an administrative regulation) whether enacted before or after the Community norm (so the general legal rule *lex posterior derogat legi priori*[3] does not apply in this respect). Community law is not merely the law of the land then—it is the higher law of the land (Weiler 1999: 22).

In addition, the Court declared Community law to have the effect of pre-empting member states from taking legislative action (doctrines of *pre-emption* and of *exclusivity*). Also, it held that the grant of internal competence has to be read as implying an external treaty-making power. Competence would have to be implied in favour of the Community if it were necessary to serve legitimate ends—which is nothing less than the reversal of another international law doctrine, according to which treaties have to be interpreted in a manner that minimizes encroachments on state sovereignty (Weiler 1999: 23). The Court has moved the EU legal order firmly out of the classical international law ballpark into something more akin to constitutionalism. This move was accompanied by sweeping statements about the nature of the Community legal order. As early as 1964, the Court referred to the EEC Treaty as being 'in contrast with international treaties'; later it unabashedly called the Treaty 'the basic constitutional charter'.

Of course, 'the ECJ can say whatever it wants, the real question is why anyone should heed it' (Alter 1996: 459). Why, for example, would member states agree to, or at least acquiesce in, a profound transformation of the Community system—something that many called a judicial rewriting of the Treaties (e.g. Hartley 1999: 131, '*de facto* amendment')? Why would the member state courts willingly go along in the face of the radicalism of the ECJ's doctrinal construct? Most of these riddles have largely been solved (e.g. Weiler 1993, 1994; Alter 1996, 1998; Burley and Mattli 1993; Slaughter and Mattli 1995; Garrett 1992, 1995; de Búrca and Weiler 2001; Stone Sweet 1998). Member state executive and legislative branches remain relatively deferential. There can only be speculation about the reasons. I find most convincing the idea that structural jurisprudence, in the eyes of the national branches, ensured that bargains struck in the decisional process will stick, thereby creating a common interest in upholding the judicial doctrinal moves and an expectation of support for the Court (Weiler 1993: 428–9; 1994: 526–7; similarly Moravcsik 1998 who suggests that member states decide in favour of supporting supranational institutions in order to lock future governments in, and that by the same token, future governments will not dispute ECJ decisions as they know this will bring down the consensus[4]). Another intriguing thought is that the Community strengthens, rather than weakens and constrains, the state, and thus creates incentives for national political players to support (and then exploit) integration (Moravcsik 1994). Finally, governments perhaps did not understand what was going on until it was too late because legal discourse was distinct from the normal power and interest-based language of politics (Burley and Mattli 1993).

Interestingly, member state courts have accepted ECJ jurisprudence (Mattli and Slaughter 1998), and have turned out to be the real linchpins of the Community legal system (Alter 1998: 227). The reasons for this national judicial behaviour, which I will explain in the next section, are complicated and cast light on institutional aspects of European legal integration.

## Judicial review—ECJ and national courts in a constitutional dialogue

Judicial review in the Community is a tandem system of justice, one leg being located at the Community level, the other at member state level. Review of member state actions at the Community level starts, according to Articles 226–9 of the EC Treaty, when either the Commission or an individual member state brings an action. This procedure, despite the remarkable fact that it is a compulsory jurisdiction and that the Commission —a body of civil servants—can bring an action, borders on the intergovernmental, with predictable defects for efficiency. It is political in nature; there is a monitoring problem and work overload for the Commission; and it lacks teeth because no real enforcement mechanism exists (Weiler 1991: 2420). These weaknesses are remedied to a large extent through the Article 234 procedure, a review mechanism of member state actions on the member state level. The largest number of cases reaches the ECJ by way of preliminary references through national courts according to Article 234. The importance of this procedure cannot be overestimated: it has become, writes Weiler (1993: 421), 'the principal vehicle for imposition of judicially driven Community discipline'. When a question concerning the interpretation of the Treaty is raised before a national court, the court may suspend the proceedings, and request a preliminary ruling from the ECJ. Once the ruling is made, it is sent back to the national court which decides the case on the basis of that ruling. This system is not political in nature because it bypasses political actors. The monitoring problem is solved because it is now private individuals who happen to be harmed acting as some sort of private attorney-general. Most importantly, since EC law is now spoken through the mouth of the national judiciary, it sports national enforcement mechanisms and national habits of obedience (Weiler 1991: 2420–2). Clearly, for this system to work it is vital that national courts go along and make preliminary references to the ECJ. They have, and the Article 234 procedure has been a spectacular success.[5] Now why is it that national courts went along willingly? Alter (1998) distinguishes between four explanations of legal integration: legalist, neo-realist, neofunctionalist, and inter-court competition.

The neo-realist argument claims that legal decisions at the EC level and at the national court level are shaped by national interest calculations. Garrett (1992, 1995) and others (e.g. Golub 1996) argue that the ECJ has had little independent or unforeseen impact on integration: that although straying a little, it has acted largely as a faithful agent of member states' interests. Member state courts, being subject to political pressure and influences from their own governments and thus eager to remain in the arena of acceptable latitude, would therefore cooperate willingly. However, there is no consistent evidence for the realist assertion that national interests or political concerns are directly shaping judicial behaviour (actually, there may be emerging evidence to the contrary: Stone Sweet and Brunell 2000: 125).

Neofunctionalist explanations focus rather on the incentives created by the EU legal system to motivate actors within EC institutions and within national legal systems to promote integration. The Court's incentive structure gives national actors a direct stake in continued legal integration. Most importantly, lower courts and their judges were given the power of judicial review even in those jurisdictions where such power was weak or non-existent (e.g. France) or reserved to the highest court in the land (e.g. Germany) (Weiler 1994: 523). Further examples of the financial prestige or political power of national actors advanced through legal integration include individual citizens obtaining new rights and tools to promote their interests, and lawyers specializing in EC law getting more business (Alter 1998: 238–9; Burley and Mattli 1993).

Legalist approaches explain judicial behaviour based on legal logic and legal reasoning. While some see national courts convinced by the ECJ's legal argument, others believe that formalism—the compliance pull of a judicial dialogue between the ECJ and its national counterparts in 'Legalese'—is a major reason for member state courts to accept Luxembourg doctrines (Weiler 1993: 423–4). Furthermore, national courts watch their brethren in other member states. Sensitive to transnational trends, their own acceptance is facilitated (Weiler 1994: 521–3).

Finally, there are inter-court explanations of different kinds. Stone Sweet focuses on 'constitutional dialogues' between the ECJ and national judges (and, sometimes, also national legislators) (Stone Sweet 1998). Alter (1998: 241–6) favours the inter-court competition thesis, according to which different courts have different interests vis-à-vis EC law. National courts use EC law in bureaucratic struggles between levels of the judiciary and between the judiciary and political bodies, thereby (inadvertently) facilitating legal integration. In contrast to Weiler, Burley, and Mattli, Alter identifies competing interests for lower and higher courts; indeed, 'it is the difference in lower and higher court interests which provides a motor for legal integration to proceed' (Alter 1998: 242). Higher courts, for instance, have a relatively static interest in thwarting the expansion and penetration of EC law into the national legal order. Lower courts, on the other hand, were part of a dynamic which, in the end, allowed them to cajole higher courts to accept EC law supremacy.

## Political and legal supranationalism

Weiler (1981) famously detected a relationship between the Court's activism and inactivism in the political institutions. He was struck by the remarkable fact that the Court developed its most important doctrines—direct effect, supremacy, pre-emption —between the mid-1960s and the mid-1980s. That was precisely the period during which the Community legislative process was conducted under the shadow of the Luxembourg Compromise and the lurking threat of the national veto. The Community had largely retreated to something just short of consensus-based intergovernmentalism, seemingly losing much of its momentum and its ambitious institutional and constitutional features. The development of new areas of activity was largely stifled. The erosion of what Weiler called 'decisional supranationalism' was, however, countered by a deepening of 'normative supranationalism', Weiler's term for the legal development sketched above. Rather than a parallel evolution one could find, in the Community, diverging trends. The reason may have been an equilibrium: 'a large ... and effective measure of transnational integration coupled at the same time with the preservation of strong, unthreatened, national member states' (Weiler 1981: 292). The member states, in other words, viewed with equanimity the Court's construction of supremacy and direct effect doctrines precisely *because* each state retained a veto over the acts that would attract these constitutional characteristics. Even more so, states had an incentive to encourage the attachment of such characteristics to the legal rules in order to secure the enforceability of hard-fought compromise agreements in the Council. '"Normative supranationalism" held together "decisional intergovernmentalism" in a dynamic balance' (Weatherill 1995: 65).

All this has changed, of course, with the (re)turn to majority voting after the Single European Act and the 1992 programme resulting in the Maastricht Treaty. The rise of qualified majority voting has stripped individual states of their veto power. The 'foundational equilibrium', then, is shattered (Weiler 1991: 2462). Member states now face not only the constitutional normativity of measures often adopted against their will, but also the operation of this normativity in a vast area of public policy. This may have a number of destabilizing effects. One is the challenge of compliance: loyalty becomes precarious. There is ample evidence of challenges to the constitutional architecture, from the member states (acting individually or as a collectivity), from national actors (mostly constitutional courts), and from public opinion (Weiler 1999: 99–101). These trends also call into question the capacity and legitimacy of the constitutionalizing preferences of the Court. Another effect, of course, is the democracy and legitimacy problem. Majority voting exacerbates the democratic deficit by weakening member state parliamentary control of the Council, and brings to the fore the problem of redefined political boundaries (Weiler et al. 1995). It is this last problem—what is the acceptable radius of the principle of majority? what makes us feel we 'belong' to a polity?—that ITL cannot solve. Europe today contends with questions of identity, political imaginations, belonging, loyalty and responsibility, all of them beyond the reach of a legal approach. I shall come back to these in the section on 'A cultural study of law: the European imagination of the political'. The ECJ's human rights jurisprudence—considered in the following section—can be understood as the bridge between the ITL conception of law and questions of European identity.

## Integration through law and human rights

Human rights mark the boundary between 'us' and 'them'. Rights are distributed as a token of membership; little wonder, then, that it is here where ITL and identity interlock. Human rights seem ideal to verify ITL's claim that common rights, via common values, are linked to a culture of rights giving birth to a common sense of belonging.[6]

The Treaties did not contain any express provisions concerning the protection of human rights (for the reasons see Weiler 1986). The Court initially resisted attempts by litigants to invoke unwritten principles of law, including the protection of human rights, as part of the Community legal order.[7] In the 1969 *Stauder* case, however, a change of heart took place.[8] From this time onwards, the Court has developed a rich and nuanced human rights jurisprudence, and has been ready to invalidate Community legislation that violates EC fundamental rights. The rights 'text' that underlies this jurisprudence is not a written document. Rather, as the Court has repeatedly stated, fundamental rights form an integral part of the general principles of EC law. In finding those rights, the Court draws inspiration from constitutional traditions common to the member states and from international conventions, particularly the European Convention for the Protection of Human Rights and Fundamental Freedoms (ECHR) of 1950.

## ITL insights and deficits

ITL deserves unconditional praise for illuminating accounts of why the Court invented, out of thin air, unwritten European human rights. ITL detected the connection between the Court's human rights jurisprudence and its fashioning of a constitutional order through the doctrines of direct effect and supremacy. Importantly, the Court had reserved for itself the right to declare Community law invalid.[9] It anticipated the challenges from member states' courts, which little later would indeed be posed in the form of threats from the German and the Italian Constitutional Courts to invalidate Community measures that they perceived as violating their national bills of rights. In 1974, fearing that the ECJ would provide insufficient protection to individuals against fundamental rights infringement by the Community, the German Court reserved for itself the authority to reverse Community measures conflicting with national fundamental rights guarantees.[10] The same year, the Italian Court declared that Italy might withdraw from the Community were such conflicts to arise.[11] The European Court could not let those challenges pass and risk losing its position as ultimate umpire of the judicial architecture of the Community because that would have ended the uniformity of Community law. The European Court had to make it possible for *it* to review Community legislation against human rights protections, in a fashion similar to review by the highest courts of member states. It had to persuade its counterparts at the national level that it would be a strong guarantor of fundamental rights, through decisions which suggested, for example, that it would provide a greater level of protection to individuals than guaranteed by the ECHR. While the 'surface language' of the Court's human rights jurisprudence, as it first emerged in *Stauder*, is about human rights, its 'deep structure' is *not* about protecting individual rights but rather about supremacy (Weiler 1986: 1119). *Stauder* and numerous decisions that followed become, in this light, inevitable sequels to the Court's direct effect and supremacy jurisprudence.

ITL has been less successful, though, in its grasp of the identity side of rights. It conceived of rights as an integrating force (Frowein, Schulhofer, and Shapiro 1986: 231) and relied on them as a logic for creating group identity that transcends national barriers. It is here that the rhetoric of rights and the rhetoric of citizenship interlock (Soysal 1994; Shaw 1997). The Advocate General's opinion in the case I will discuss below—the little known *Konstantinidis* case of 1993[12]—is a prime example of the way ITL conceptualizes rights. However, rights protection and the Maastricht citizenship clauses make dubious candidates for championing European identity and alleviating the Union's gaping deficit in social legitimacy. The ECJ's opinion in the *Konstantinidis* case will testify to that. *Konstantinidis* has all the right ingredients for a paradigmatic case. First, it is about human rights, which, due to the new Charter of Fundamental Rights of the EU,[13] are not merely a new flash-in-the-pan, but which represent the intersection of law and identity—the very intersection ITL fails to understand. Second, the Advocate General presents the essence of ITL's argument about law's role in integration, which is, basically, a modernist narrative of progress. In looking closely at the Advocate General's opinion, we will understand the allure, and failure, of ITL's ambitions. Third, the Court ultimately rejects the Advocate General's basic notions of human rights, law, and progress, and ultimately deflates ITL's most deeply held aspirations.

## Case study: facts and holding

The case begins simply, but ultimately implicates no less than the warring visions of the identity of Europe. It starts with a Greek national living in Germany, Χρήστος Κωνσταντινίδης, transliterated in his passport as Christos Konstantinidis, who became engaged in a Kafkaesque dispute with the German authorities over nothing less than his right to his name. In 1990 Mr Konstantinidis applied to the German Registry Office to correct a misspelling of his name in the marriage register. Upon examining his application, however, the German authorities determined that his name had, from the first, been improperly transliterated under German law. The spelling, they found, did not comply with the system of transliteration established by the International Organization for Standardization (ISO), the use of which is mandated by a 1973 treaty to which both Germany and Greece are parties. They ordered that pursuant to the ISO he must henceforth be known as Hréstos Kónstantinidés.

The poor man was horrified. The new spelling disguised his ethnic origin (Hréstos, as the Advocate General observed to the ECJ, does not look or sound like a Greek name and has a vaguely Slavonic flavour) and offended his religious sentiments by destroying the Christian character of the name. Mr Konstantinidis was also a self-employed masseur and hydrotherapist, and wished to avoid the inconvenience and loss of business from having to change the name by which he was known to his clientele.

The newly christened Hréstos sought protection from the German courts, which referred the matter to the European Court of Justice for a preliminary ruling under the Article 234 EC Treaty procedure. In his Opinion of 9 December 1992, Advocate General Jacobs reached the logical conclusion that Mr Konstantinidis must be protected by human rights. He suggested that Mr Konstantinidis should be able to invoke European Community human rights against Germany. Wherever a Community national goes to earn his living in the European Community, he argued, 'he will be treated in accordance with a common code of fundamental values'. Then AG Jacobs said: 'In other words, he is entitled to say *"civis europeus sum"*', I am a European citizen, 'and to invoke that status in order to oppose any violation of his fundamental rights'. The ECJ was not so sure. It chose to stay out of the human rights/citizenship arena. While the Luxembourg judges saw fit to afford some protection to Mr Konstantinidis, they did not buy into, or even refer to, AG Jacobs' sweeping concept. Rather, they decided the case exclusively on the basis of Article 52 (now Art. 43) of the Treaty of Rome (embodying the economic freedom of establishment) and the principle of non-discrimination on the basis of nationality. The German authorities, concluded the Court, were not entitled to insist on spelling the applicant's name in such a way as to misrepresent its pronunciation since such 'distortion exposes him to the risk that potential clients confuse him with other persons'.

## Advocate General Jacobs

The doctrinal implication of the case is a simple one. It was generally accepted that with the exception of two small, narrowly circumscribed exceptions, the Court lacked competence to review member state actions for fundamental rights violations. That was the task of member states' courts; the Luxembourg Court would review only Community actions.[14] In contrast, AG Jacobs suggests that whenever an EC national goes to another member state in reliance on the rights of free movement in the Treaty, any failure to respect a fundamental human right of that national, whether or not it is connected with his or her work, should constitute an infringement of EC law. Clearly, AG Jacobs' view would significantly expand human rights review through the ECJ.

On a deeper level, the case is about the depth and foundations of European integration. The language of rights introduces a range of values into the Community's legal and policy-making processes. These values differ sharply and obviously from the Community's legacy of economic focus. Rights-talk, in this reading, denotes a certain moral content to Community law and policies, and thus offers a means of developing a moral and ethical foundation for the Community (de Búrca 1995: 52). Human rights protection seems to be able to fill the cold modernist void, the spiritual absence that lies at the heart of the European integration project (Allott 1991: 2499).

Citizenship, as a membership right, connects the polity and the rights-bearer. '*Civis europeus sum*', Jacobs has the European consumer say, and attempts to trade in the market-citizen (or *homo economicus*, or *Marktbürger*: Everson 1995; Ipsen 1972: 102) for citizenship cast in terms of human rights, and in modernist, cosmopolitan terms at that. His mind-set is best illustrated by an example he gives. Immediately before he suggests that any individual should be able to claim '*civis europeus sum*' and rely on the 'common code of fundamental values', he hypothesizes about the ECJ's right to intervene if a member state institutes a Draconian penal code under which theft is punishable by amputation of the right hand. Identifying a form of oppression which horrifies us and which we have reason to expect would horrify anyone from our cultural or social background is a great strategy for arguing for a universal claim (Waldron 1999). AG

Jacobs makes a strong appeal to what he, and surely we, his Western readers, associate with the *humanity* of the individual. Viewed in this way, AG Jacobs is a cosmopolitan. He identifies a core of what makes us human—in his penal code hypothetical bodily integrity; in his argument in the case itself, identity conferred through a name—and entrusts a supranational court with upholding it across all boundaries.

Ironically, in a cultural reading, these cosmopolitan and universalist arguments are put to work for a very situated, bounded, geographically and historically sharply defined communal self. Consider, first, that the Draconian penal code hypothetical conjures up the stereotyped epitome of Europe's Other. Iran, Afghanistan—backward countries under Koran law, in far-away corners of the world, rejecting the enlightened wall between the church and the state as well as the essentialist notion that common human rights standards can be arrived at and ought to be upheld everywhere in the world. Invoking the Other, and provoking the foreseeable response, reifies a distinctly Western liberal democratic identity. Inventing Europe in the mirror of the Orient, by inventing the Orient, has a long tradition in Europe (Delanty 1995: 84–99). Hence, at the heart of the human rights argument lies the image of the bedeviled Orient. Remember, second, that AG Jacobs uses Latin (*'civis europeus sum'*) to voice his citizenship concept. Latin was the European *lingua franca*, the language of diplomacy and polite society, far into the sixteenth century. Latin still conjures up a common Europeanness, much more so than French does. It is considered the root of European civilization.

Consider, third, that it was Paul who repeatedly said to the Romans, '*Civis Romanus sum*', to keep the Roman soldiers from physically abusing him and his followers. AG Jacobs, in using the parallel phrase, appeals to the deep strata of Latin Christendom, which, as a cultural framework, has become interchangeable with the idea of Europe. Christianity, moreover, is not only the undercurrent of contemporary European culture. It also carries with it a siege-mentality. Islamic invasions along with the Barbarian and Persian gave a European identity to Christendom as the bulwark against the non-Christian world. Note that it also provided Western monarchies with a powerful myth of legitimation. The Advocate General, in surprisingly few words, summons up the rich texture that is part of the idea of Europe.

Thus, there are two layers in the Advocate General's argument. On the one hand, he claims that names are cultural universals, and that to tamper with them is to deprive individuals of their identity. In a way, he protests against Germany's distorting Christos' *first name*, which signifies his uniqueness and individuality as a human being. This is a violation sufficiently egregious to evoke our universalist, abhorred response, which is why Christos Konstantinidis needs the Court's protection under the blanket of human rights. On the other hand, he argues that Germany has violated the rights of 'one of us', a *European* citizen who can claim membership in the same polity as the rest of us. Here, AG Jacobs protests against Germany's distorting of Mr Konstantinidis' *last name*, which provides the bearer with family and extended kinship ties. It identifies Konstantinidis as a Greek national, and hence as part of the Community family. The violation should be made good not because it is so egregious, but because this is no way to treat a member of your extended family.

These two layers do not necessarily contradict each other. In fact, they work well together in that they provide the notion of citizenship with a core of organic essentialism. This core—in the first version of the argument, Aristotelian; in the second, European-centred—undermines competing claims to identity and loyalty. If the organic-cultural core of what defines membership in a community is as AG Jacobs claims it is, how can there be a different one when it comes to a different polity? Is it possible, after all this, that there *is* a different polity that can lay claim to loyalty?

The problem with this vision is its displacement of nationality (O'Leary 1995: 542–3), and thus the finality of just another super-state. The distribution of human rights in the European Union becomes, in other words, the thick wall separating Us from Them, those who belong from those who don't, and Europe from the Other (see Weiler 1992 with respect to non-Community nationals). This flies in the face of the third sentence of Article 17(1) of the EC Treaty, which reads: 'Citizenship of the Union shall complement and not replace national citizenship'. Moreover, it is out of touch with reality. Citizens do not identify with the Union; rather, they feel alienated, and do not trust Brussels (OPTEM 2000). The reason may be that the nation, through its myths, provides a social home, a shared history, and a common destination. It is the emotional, romantic side of belonging. Weiler (1999: 324–57) calls it the Eros, while the supranational is Civilization. If this is true, the Advocate General's effort to wave yet another catalogue of rights before the public will be meaningless in the attempt to create an effective attachment of the European citizens to their new polity, and bring them to accept the redrawn functional boundaries. It would also fail to reflect the complicated multi-layered structure of European integration, citizenship, or individual identity (MacCormick 1999; Schepel 1998). It is impossible to funnel polycentricity, legal and cultural pluralism, and plurality into the old vessels of unity and exclusivity. It is political imagination, not law, not human rights, that the integration project needs now (for further elaboration see 'A cultural study of law: the European imagination of the political' below).

## The Court

Far from taking up AG Jacobs' proposals, the Court in its brief decision does not even mention human rights. While it is legitimate to interpret this silence as a fabulous example of judicial minimalism, there is, I believe, a more interesting reading of it. The Court does have a theory on citizenship and identity. That theory emerges from the Court's elaborate silence[15] and its use of *economic* law to protect Mr Konstantinidis.

The context of the Court's theory is that of economic existence. In the process of globalization, locality becomes devalued, and geographical space is cancelled out. What counts is playing the mobility game as part of the factors of production. Rather than being degraded, one feels in control. In spite of the disempowering, often disheartening, and paralyzing environment of uncertainty, man is, all of a sudden, in command again. The price, however, is that personal identity is fluid. Markets require a fluidity of capital, human and fixed. Identities, in other words, can be adopted and discarded like a change of costume. Bauman (1995: 88) has likened modern life to a pilgrimage into the desert where one is in constant danger of losing one's identity. That is exactly what happens to Konstantinidis: he loses his name, unquestionably the main bearer of identity. Konstantinidis learns, through painful experience, that mobility means to subject oneself to forces that will change identity in unknown ways, and that he is not the sole master of his identity.

The Court, then, essentially negates what the Advocate General believes. AG Jacobs is a modernist: identity is in the hands of the individual, and the goal is not to impinge upon it. He believes in a manageable world and in rationality. History, to the Advocate General, is progress. The task is an impossible one: humanity as such, order, harmony, certainty. While the horizon can never be reached, it is precisely the *foci imaginarii* that makes the path inescapable. If humanity is essentialist, human rights protect at least an essentialist core. The more human rights the better, and the more encompassing their scope the better, too. It is a matter of logic, therefore, to apply human rights judicial review to the member states. It protects Christos Konstantinidis in his being a human (or at least, in his being one of us). His humanity is, *inter alia*, his autonomy, and as an autonomous, sovereign agent, he has the capacity to choose to travel beyond the boundaries of his known world. Protecting that autonomy means absorbing the risk involved in his endeavour. Choice, and morality, is private; risk is public. Christos Konstantinidis' freedom must be unharmed—it is the job of the government to protect it. The tools of protection are, of course, human rights, as the ultimate weapon at the disposal of the enlightened agent.

The Court, it seems, is skeptical. It appears comfortable with the notion of citizenship as consumer identity. Commentators are uniformly and customarily critical of such suggestions. Weiler (1998b), for example, speaks of 'bread-and-circus democracy' and a 'Saatchi & Saatchi Europe'. However, there is strong evidence that today 'we can learn more about the operations and values of social communication from Saatchi & Saatchi than from [Justices in the US Supreme Court] Holmes and Brandeis' (Collins and Skover 1996: 70). Individuals use consumption to say something about themselves. The kinds of statements they make reflect the kind of universe surrounding them. The meanings and rituals of consumption mark out the categories and classifications which constitute social order. We might want to imagine the post-modern consumer as ironic and knowing, reflexive and aware of the games being played, with considerable cultural capital. There is even a communal side to consumption, which takes on more and more social functions as a form of sociality, even solidarity (Shields 1992: 110).

The Court, it seems, understands this. It has refused to pretend that Europe is composed of individuals carrying their immutable identities around with them, and has recognized instead the risk that identities will be changed, perhaps erased, by forces beyond individual control. Identities are not pre-social, monolithic, or unchanging. They are multi-layered, complex, and impacted in unpredictable ways by disordered cultural spaces. The Court recognizes that Konstantinidis, like all of us, is not just a self-defined independent agent. Power is exercised not primarily by him, but by the changing social environment around him. The Court displays a post-modern sensibility by limiting that power as is appropriate to Konstantinidis' endeavour as an economic pilgrim.

## Conclusion and critique

In a way, the Court takes up AG Jacobs' suggestion of linking the Konstantinidis case to the notion of citizenship. European citizenship, however, will not be defined through essentialist human rights, or exclusive demands on loyalty. According to the Court, a theory of European citizenship has to take into account the existing practice of citizenship in Europe (for theoretical elaboration of the concept of citizenship practice as the politics and policy that contribute to establishing the terms of citizenship in a particular context, see Wiener 1998). That practice does not support liberal, communitarian, or republican theories of citizenship. The European experience of citizenship is framed by economic ratio. There is a gap, then, between the projected nature of the European polity on the one hand, which has appropriated cherished symbols of statehood and which lays claim to its citizens' political loyalty, and the nature of the European citizens' experience of citizenship on the other hand, which is dominated by rituals of trade, travel, and consumption. The Advocate General models his vision of citizenship according to the projected nature of the polity. Applying human rights against member state actions would accomplish the project of rights-based citizenship, and at the same time the project of an ever-more federal Europe. The Court, in contrast, models its vision of citizenship on the practice, and experience, of citizenship. It refuses to bridge the gap between Europe's reach and citizenship's practice by projecting onto the individual attributes that have long dissolved, and hopes that have proved illusory. To the theorist, the Court's decision is therefore an appeal to align theory and practice by looking to experience rather than Utopia.

The case confirms earlier critical assessments of ITL, such as the movement's teleological bias, which saw the development of law as self-consciously tracking substantive integrationist outcomes (Shaw 2001: 79). Also, we see there is little room for ITL's 'over-eager, and sometimes arrogant, substitution of juridification for politicisation' (Everson 1998: 389). The critique of outcome-driven legitimacy chimes in with the evolving debate on EU constitutional legitimacy, which has moved from issues of formal validity via the democratic deficit to issues of identity (Weiler 1998a). This is my main point of criticism in the following section.

# A cultural study of law: the European imagination of the political

## The meaning of law

While ITL views law primarily as a tool for integration, as an 'instrument' and as an 'object' (Cappelletti et al. 1986d: 4, 15, 36), a cultural study understands it as a social practice. Through law, we understand self and others, and make actions meaningful.

Law's rule is a system of beliefs—a structure of meaning within which we experience public order (Kahn 1997, 1999; for philosophical foundations see Cassirer 1953; Geertz 1973). As such, law's value lies not in objective facts (as ITL has it) but in the deployment of power to sustain these beliefs. What needs investigation, then, is the structure of meaning within our experience of public order as the rule of law occurs. That is a dimension wholly untapped by ITL. Functional analysis cannot grasp the meaning of law. It is the imagination that constructs the past and the future of the polity, just as the political identity of the citizen.

A cultural study of law reveals differences in the reach of national law and of EU law on our identity and imagination. While these two are practically the same with respect to their normativity, there is a world of difference as to their success in structuring our political perception. National law differs in its meaning, texture, and constitutive reach on our imagination of the political from EU law. Being the source and product of the imagination of political existence, law serves as memory and storage of political meaning. National legal meaning is in a different ballpark from European legal meaning. National law usually has a richly textured cushion of cultural resources that it can rely on. It is a symbolic form which establishes a world of pre-existing rules to which individuals appeal in order to make sense of their lives. It serves as a community's memory in that it preserves existing meanings. There is a deep structure underneath the liberal surface of national law that establishes the legal text as 'ours' (Kahn 1997; 1999).

EU legal texts, however, are not 'ours'. They are just texts with no roots. Union texts do not constitute a collective self but a Common Market. Markets cannot tell us who we are: they operate through desires, which are mere placeholders (Kahn 1997: 86). Money, the universal means of exchange on the market, is the perfect example. There is nothing with less memory than money. There is an old saying that you shouldn't conduct money business with friends or foes. The perfect business partner is thus someone completely indifferent, gauged neither for nor against us. The category of price makes history and individuality disappear. It is precisely at the point of this total indifference where the European rationality of the market and the European social contract—concluded by unencumbered selves behind the veil of ignorance—converge (Haltern 2001).

With no history, identity, or individuality there can be no social and political meaning. We cannot reason about, or trade in, the symbolic dimension of meaning. The Union's legal texts are unable to stabilize anything deeper than the ever-changing fluid surface of trade, travel, and consumption. That is the reason why the EU, in the eye of the beholder, appears so breathless. As there is no memory to store meaning, meaning needs to be generated through political action, again and again. Meaning, in the Union, exists only within transitory and forgetful moments. Political action can never be allowed to come to an end, which is why citizens see Europe as politicians negotiating and re-negotiating. In this sense, Europe is revolutionary: history is being rewritten and re-rewritten. It is in the nature of revolutions to break with the past—and here is the reason why references to occidental culture, Christendom, and Latin as the one-time *lingua franca* seem so unpersuasive. Cut off from the past, Europe seeks cultural artifacts (like the flag, the anthem, or the Charter) in order to invent traditions and obtain some patina for its glossy new surface. ITL cannot see this because it contents itself with a contractarian justification. It has no words for the domain of symbolic forms and meanings. European legal discourse, however, has reached a stage where such shortcomings must turn fatal.

## The meaning of the political

The debate on EU constitutional legitimacy has moved from formal validity (the legitimacy of the Court's constitutionalizing legal discourse) via deontological concerns (the democratic deficit) to foundational myths (issues of European identity and demos) (Weiler 1998a: 372–8). We have thus arrived, as Ward (2001) notes, at the search for a European political imagination. The political, of course, is a contested domain. Its imagination is contingent upon the reality that surrounds it. Living in a world of economic transactions, consumption, and markets, the political is widely replaced by the market. Identity is as fluid as money-flows, citizenship becomes more a matter of consumption than of political rights and duties (Urry 1995: 165), and as Shore writes, 'The citizen-hero of the new Europe thus appears to be the Euro-consumer' (Shore 2000: 84).

That, however, may quickly change. As soon as the political enters the domain of ultimate values and meanings, it becomes incommensurable with the values of the market. We need no reminder of this after September 11. At the centre of such imagination stands the nation state. It exists as a meaning borne by citizens willing to invest their bodies in its continued existence as an order of law. Its power rests on the willingness of individuals to take up, as their own self-identity, the identity of the state. The modern nation state has been extremely successful in mobilizing its population to make sacrifices in order to help sustain the state's continued historical existence (Kahn 2003).

We stand dismayed and helpless before the tenacity of the nation state's political imagination. Living in Europe, we like to think we have outgrown the autonomy of the political and have entered the age of post-politics (Žižek 1999). We describe politics as a site of competition between interest groups. Ultimate political meanings have given way to a multiplicity of particular interests. Many of those interests are just the same as those advanced through the market. Politics, therefore, appears as an alternative means of accomplishing market-ends. Indeed, there are signs that the political and the market are in fact increasingly being conflated, with 'citizens' and 'consumers' becoming essentially one and the same thing. Values have first materialized, and then dematerialized and now exist purely as signs circulating within a political economy of signs. It often seems there is little credible beneath or beyond the flat landscape of endless signification (Slater 1997). Perhaps, in Europe, the outlines of a liberal order—a post-political order stripped of its attachment to a popular sovereign—is emerging.

A slight change of perspective, though, may yank us back onto a terrain where we distinguish between friends and enemies, believe in ultimate values, crave for meaning that we derive from standing for some larger community which will outlive ourselves, and are ready to invest our bodies into the continued existence of the polity we live in. Do we want such a political imagination for Europe? If so, how do we get there? If not, can we prevent it? These are, I believe, the troubling, and pressing, questions that vex Europe today. ITL, however, cannot tell us anything useful in response.

## Prospects of integration through law: enlargement and conclusion

The coming enlargement round in 2004 will bring ten new member states to the Union. Membership perspective has been extended to the western Balkans. The sheer number of accession candidates leads to difficulties, such as institutional adaptation (efficiency of decision-making, institutional representation, transparency, accountability), policy adaptation (especially CAP and regional spending) as well as mounting financial burdens. Moreover, it is less the uniqueness of adding new members than the changing context in which it takes place—the absence of the Cold War—that leads to the insecurity and the repeated postponements in the handling of the enlargement process (Fierke and Wiener 2001). Previous enlargement rounds have shown that law, above all the rules, norms, and values associated with the governance of the Single European Market, have been able to integrate new economies into the Community. The same norms, one might think, should form the basis of a transformation of the political economy of CEECs and their membership in the EU. However, it may be different this time. The Union has imposed conditions for enlargement that involve, but exceed the Single Market, for example the respect of minorities. It becomes apparent that 'an important factor shaping EU policy is its identity towards the CEECs' (Sedelmeier 2000). In other words, the enlargement process is but a mirror of the general move towards issues of European identity and demos. Law will play an important role, of course, and it will be rewarding to examine its impact on identity constructions (Wiener 2001) and its uneven effect across different groups of actors inside the EU and among CEECs (Schimmelfennig and Sedelmeier 2002). The questions that I pointed out in the preceding section, however, cannot be addressed through the legal lens. Under such circumstances it is more than doubtful that law will be able to perform the tasks associated with it in the long-time member states ('deepening'). We may be witnessing a differentiation, even fragmentation of the EU body of law, one part overtaxed with exporting the Single European Market *acquis* to EU entrants, the other part fleeing into pathos.

A more optimistic reading of my critique of ITL would stress the fact that law, not political imagination, might be the way into the future. If we cannot think of awakening a European political imagination in the near future, with ten new member states joining in 2004, and at least two more a few years later, staying close to the tried and true, which is the law, will perhaps hold off an existential identity crisis for a few years to come. It is hard to say whether that is in any way realistic. What we can say, though, is that human rights will not be at the core of the coming, enlarged European Union (Bogdandy 2000b). Being the liberal project that it is, the Union is stuck between a 'politics of reason'—justice and rights—and a 'politics of interest'—the market. The value of a community cannot be explained either by appeal to abstract norms (justice) or to desire (the market). The Union lacks a 'politics of will'—a world where polities call upon citizens for sacrifice, where the popular sovereign shows itself by displacing interest, and where the most basic imaginative structure of political reality is the transtemporal community. None of this can be achieved through law, only through political imagination. Europe is at a crossroads, and caught, it seems, in a veritable dilemma.

It will become more and more difficult to say what we actually mean when we speak of 'European law'. What was thought of as a single body of rules has developed into a rich and inter-related patchwork of legal regimes, orders, and spaces. The emergence of cross-referenced legal fields (Harding 2000; Bańkowski and Christodoulidis 1998; Shaw 2001) makes it pretty much impossible to maintain ITL as a single movement. It will doubtless break up into diverse disciplines: material and institutional, grand theory and micro theory (Shaw 1995: 8), subject areas (equal treatment, environmental law, remedies, etc.). Much of EU legal studies has already moved in this direction (e.g. Craig and de Búrca 1999). Integrating political and legal analysis (Wincott 1995b) does not seem sufficient to hold all those diverse strands together. That, however, is not a sign of ITL's demise, but of its maturity. Still, if we are looking for a political imagination, we will have to turn elsewhere.

# Notes

* My thanks to Professors Bethany Berger, Thomas Diez, Dieter Grimm, Paul Kahn, Joseph Weiler, and Antje Wiener.

1. Case 26/62, *NV Algemene Transport- en Expeditie Onderneming Van Gend en Loos* v. *Nederlandse Administratie der Belastingen* [1963] ECR 1, [1963] CMLR 105.

2. Case 6/64, *Costa* v. *ENEL* [1964] ECR 585, [1964] CMLR 425.

3. A later statute takes away the effect of a prior one.

4. I owe this reading of Moravcsik 1998 to Thomas Diez.

5. Some fear the procedure may have been too successful: Weiler 2001.

6. Human rights protection has been one of the preferred topics of many proponents of the ITL movement, as well as one of the flagships of ITL (Frowein, Schulhofer, and Shapiro 1986). Considering that what is at stake is modernity's obsession with determining identities, it is not surprising that much of the battle over the New Europe takes place on the field of human rights protection (e.g. Coppel and O'Neill 1992, Weiler and Lockhart 1995, Bogdandy 2000b).

7. Case 1/58, *Stork* v. *High Authority* [1959] ECR 17; Cases 36, 37, 38, and 40/59, *Comptoirs de Vente du Charbon de la Ruhr 'Präsident', 'Geitling', 'Mausegatt' Enterprise I. Nold KG* v. *High Authority* [1960] ECR 423.

8. Case 29/69, *Stauder* v. *City of Ulm* [1969] ECR 419, then Case 4/73, *Nold* v. *Commission* [1974] ECR 491 (establishing the twofold legal foundation).

9. E.g. Case 314/85, *Firma Foto Frost* v. *Hauptzollamt Lübeck-Ost* [1987] ECR 4199.

10. German Federal Constitutional Court, *Internationale Handelsgesellschaft mbH* v. *Einfuhr- und Vorratsstelle für Getreide und Futtermittel [Solange I]*, 37 BVerfGE 271, (1974) 2 CMLR 540.

11. Italian Constitutional Court, *Frontini* v. *Ministero delle Finanze* (1974) 2 CMLR 372.

12. Case C–168/91, *Konstantinidis* v. *Stadt Altensteig, Standesamt und Landratsamt Calw, Ordnungsamt* [1993] ECR I–1191.

13. Solemnly proclaimed during the IGC in Nice on 7 December 2000 [2000] OJ C–364/1.

14. The two exceptions are as follows. First, member state actions implementing Community measures will be reviewed according to human rights ('agency' situation). The hallmark case is Case 5/88, *Wachauf* [1989] ECR 2609. Second, member states' measures adopted in derogation from the prohibition on restricting the free movement of the four factors of production will also be scrutinized according to human rights. The hallmark case here is Case C–260/89, *ERT* [1991] ECR I–2925.

15. While it may seem strange, at first glance, to distill a theory from silence, it is not so far-fetched for those who are familiar with the Court's jurisprudential culture. The Court and the Advocate General often seem to engage in a peculiar form of division of labour. The Advocate General eloquently summarizes arguments and precedents, and does not shy away from openly pointing to considerations that go well beyond narrow legal reasoning. The Court, in contrast, more often than not hides the ball. While it is far from being positivist it is not exactly outspoken with regard to the 'true' rationales that drive it. The result is that in order to obtain a complete picture one has to look not only to the decision, but also to the Advocate General's opinion. Only in superimposing one on the other, like two transparencies layered together against the light, can one see the meaning shining through the silence.

## Guide to further reading

Further overviews are provided by Wincott 1995b and Joerges 2002. Early analyses are Stein 1981 and Weiler 1982. Groundbreaking was Snyder 1990. A classic, of course, is Weiler 1991, which firmly established the author as Europe's towering figure. Weiler brings together law, political science, and political theory for the first time, establishing a whole new standard of EU scholarship and breaking the path for a new generation of scholars in his wake. (Weiler amended his 1991 analysis in Weiler 1999, 96–101.)

# 10

# Discursive Approaches

## Ole Wæver

## Introduction

Within the study of European integration, discourse analysis has begun to make its presence felt, although it has hardly gained a clear profile as either a contender for the position as one of the 'leading schools' or as a distinct interpretation of 'the nature of the beast' (Risse 1996). It should initially be observed that the editors have been perceptive in designating this branch 'discursive approaches'. Within International Relations (IR) in general, the heading would almost certainly be 'post-modernism' or 'post-structuralism', with discourse analysis seen as one of the (non-)methods used by 'post-ies'. Possibly, it is an indication of the position of European integration studies (EIS) in-between IR and Political Science, that the higher independent profile of 'discourse analysis' within political science influences the study of European integration. Or it is because EIS, compared to IR, has a more European profile. It is characteristic of the American intellectual scene that post-modernism has become established as a 'school' with extreme views and with a role as combatant within IR, whereas European IR has been more pragmatic about including post-modernism and discourse analysis as an approach to the study of international politics (Wæver 1998a). This chapter will not use 'discourse analysis' as a pretext for a general rehearsal of post-modern attacks on the mainstream. The chapter will report on work done by way of discursive approaches and discuss their value and limitations.

Two different categories of work fit the heading 'discursive approaches'. One consists of the relatively limited number of works that try to develop discourse analysis as '*a theory of European integration*'. The other is the vast field of studies *based on discourse analysis* that takes up key questions in the field of European integration, but is not conceived of as 'general integration theory'. The latter show up within sub-fields and policy areas (such as economic necessity, the commission, or defence; see, e.g. Rosamond 1999; Burgess 2000; Hay and Rosamond 2002; Wodak and Weiss 2000; McDonald 2000; Wind 1992; Wæver 1996c), but they are too diverse to be covered systematically in this chapter, and examples will be presented in the context of the general theories, where they fit. Thus the attempts to develop discourse analysis as a general theory are used as a structuring device for the chapter. It should be noted that this presents a picture that

is much more logically structured than the experience 'on the ground' where practitioners of discourse analysis will often feel that they simply analyse some European
subject of interest. I will focus (in the section on 'Separate "approaches" or "programmes" in European integration discourse theory') in particular on three distinct
'schools' or 'programmes'.

The concept of 'discourse analysis' is used in linguistics and in various parts of the
humanities for a great variety of things (e.g. for studies specifically aimed at analysing
oral communication), but in Political Science, IR, and EIS, it most often has connotations of mostly 'French' conceptions of discourse (Foucault and all that). When
developed as a general theory of politics and society, the main signpost is the theory of
Ernesto Laclau and Chantal Mouffe (1985). Most of the studies covered in this chapter
are situated explicitly within this family, and the general presentation of 'what is discourse analysis' will concentrate on this type. Nonetheless, the three research programmes
or approaches to be discussed will often do very different things and reach possibly
quite opposite conclusions. This is because in contrast to at least the general view of post-
modern approaches as 'less scientific', discourse analysis has entered EIS less committed
to a particular substantive position towards European integration than many of the
approaches covered in the other chapters of this book. Instead, discursive approaches
can be seen as either a methodology ('discourse analysis') and therefore compatible
with quite different theoretical approaches, or as a theoretical approach that had been
developed in other disciplines and has then been applied to EIS in different ways.

# Discourse analysis in the study of European integration

## The basic idea(s)

What does it mean to focus on 'discourse'? Why would one do that? What difference
does it make vis-à-vis other approaches? What are the implications for the kind of questions one can and cannot ask? What is 'discourse'? How is it studied?

Discourse analysis looks for structures of meaning. 'Things' do not have meaning in
and of themselves, they only become meaningful in discourse. As a consequence, it is
problematic to ground one's analysis in 'given' subjects or objects because both are constituted discursively, and one should therefore study this process of constitution first.
*Objects* of knowledge might be said to exist independently of language, but when they
enter in any meaningful way into human, social life, they enter not as name- and shape-
less objectivity, but 'as something': they are necessarily categorized and conceptualized.
The *subjects* of knowledge and action, similarly, are constituted in many different
ways—and have been so throughout history—for example, as 'man', 'reason', 'civilization', 'the nation', or 'the word of God'. Neither 'things', nor subjects and their intentions
are given by themselves. We therefore have to cut into these webs of meaning. Discourse
analysis does this.

One of the central concepts of this approach is obviously 'discourse'. Discourse can be defined as *a system that regulates the formation of statements* (cf. Foucault 1972; Dreyfus and Rabinow 1982; Bartelson 1995: 70; Torfing 1997; Wæver 1996a). In the context of EIS, it is usually assumed that the most important discourses are *political* discourses. Consequently, many studies focus on the delineation of what can meaningfully be said in a given political arena. This might very well be different from private views, and thus discourse analysis should be clearly distinguished from cognitive approaches, which analyse what people perceive and think. If cognitive approaches sometimes use public texts these serve as *indicators* for perceptions, thoughts, and beliefs, raising all kinds of problems regarding the validity of discourse as a source of knowledge about people's minds. Discourse analysis focuses attention on discourse as interesting in itself. It is not an indicator for something else and thus questions about whether 'they really mean what they say' are irrelevant. A discourse analysis tries to find the structures and patterns in public statements that regulate political debate so that certain things can be said while other things will be meaningless or less powerful or reasonable.

The relationship between discourses and actors is complicated. On the one hand, discourse is 'prior' in the sense that subjects are not given outside discourse and it is only from within discourse that certain subject positions are opened up from which one can speak. On the other hand, discourses only exist and are reproduced and transformed through practice. This amounts to what Thomas Diez (1999a: 603) has called 'linguistic structurationism' with reference to Anthony Giddens' view of the mutual dependence between structure and agency (see Giddens 1984). Another aspect of the relationship between actors and discourses is whether actors are fully in the grip of discourses. Many discourse analyses give this impression, when explaining a particular political position directly by discursive structures. This is problematic, because such analyses slide into the cognitivist position where discourse regulates the *consciousness* of actors, whereas the study of political discourse should focus on discourse as placed *in-between* actors. Thus actors need to be conceptualized as having at least the possibility of acting strategically in relation to discourse—both in relation to how they shape a political position in relation to a given discursive position and in how they try to transform the discursive structure itself (Wæver 1996a, 1998b; Hansen forthcoming).

Discourse analysis does not claim that discourse is all there is to the world, only that since discourse is the layer of reality where meaning is produced and distributed, it seems promising for an analysis to focus on it. Discourse does not stand apart from 'reality'. On the one hand, it is hard to conceive of any meaningful concept of a reality of which we can talk when excluding discourse and thereby meaning. On the other hand, where would discourse exist if not embedded in reality in the sense of actions, materiality, and institutions?

Especially if one wants to predict policy it is necessary to make two more specific assumptions about discourse: a certain inertia, and constraining effects on political options. A popular view of politicians is that they say anything that suits their immediate interest, pay no attention to what they said the day before, and feel free to change it tomorrow. However, most people who have studied political discourses have been surprised how coherent and systematic political language is. Political speech is not only a short-term justification of this or that decision but also a struggle over the resources for future battles that reside in the structuring of public discourse. Therefore, discourse analysts are often more interested in *how* a politician argues than *what* he says. Whether he argues for or against a specific decision is less interesting than what he does to the general political language and therefore to long-term possibilities.

## Philosophical roots

What traditions does discourse analysis draw on philosophically and how does this matter? Does it mean that one has to take courses in Heidegger, Nietzsche, and Derrida and then try to catch up with European integration a few years later?

Discourse analysis of the kind we discuss here has post-structuralist roots. This does mean influence from, e.g. Heidegger's analysis of how the 'Western metaphysics' is deeply imbedded in our whole vocabulary. There are Anglo-American ways to get to post-structuralism too, notably radical pragmatism such as Richard Rorty, but the most influential route goes from figures like Martin Heidegger and Friedrich Nietzsche via amongst others Michel Foucault, Jacques Derrida, Jacques Lacan, and Gilles Deleuze to formulations by Laclau and Mouffe, William Connolly, and Judith Butler, who locate themselves more explicitly in the field of Political Theory.

This pedigree means that if one is interested in engaging in meta-theoretical discussions *pro-et-contre* discourse analysis, or if one wants to address the deeper questions of methodology within discourse analysis, it is helpful to study these sources in order to get a sense of the mode of thinking within post-structuralism. (For instance, the Heideggerian inspiration actually implies that structures of meaning are abundantly stable and hard to escape—quite contrary to the popular image of post-structuralism as 'scepticism' regarding 'secure knowledge'.) However, the field of discursive approaches has matured sufficiently to make it possible to take the analytical frameworks provided by discursive approaches and apply them—just as many researchers doing neo-realist, rational choice or Marxist analysis read only the relevant IR theorists, while the leading theorists—and their critics—have (hopefully) based their work on more extensive studies of the original texts.

Inspired by structuralist linguistics, discursive approaches generally assume that meaning rests within systems of differences. But where structuralism ends in a static system of 'codes' that explain how meaning *works*, post-structuralism—most clearly articulated by Derrida—points out how ultimately the closure of meaning is impossible. No system of meaning can fall fully into place—it will always be unfinished and unstable—one sign refers to another. Discourses try to establish something as a 'transcendental signified', as that which we can point to as the ultimate ground (e.g. God, reason, the nation, or evolution), but nothing *is* just itself—it too makes sense only by reference to something else, and on we go in the eternal play of signs (Derrida 1978 [1967]). It should be noted that Derrida points to both the impossibility of closure and the constant longing for the fixity and security of any such ultimate basis. This is what Laclau and Mouffe (1985) build on in their influential theory of discourse. Partial fixations of political meaning are constantly attempted and make up much of the dynamics of politics, but any such attempt always has a loose end, an opening for a possible re-articulation. When the concept of 'democracy' is articulated to give it one particular meaning within a social-democratic discourse, for instance, the concept includes a surplus of meaning that enables a competing articulation of democracy through a neo-liberal discourse.

This 'French' side of discourse analysis inevitably includes an element of 'structural-ism', because the analysis will try to discern patterns or structures in discourse that are the precondition for specific political statements. It thus needs to have some conception of the whole, of what characterizes a particular epoch or a particular setting in order to analyse the 'condition of possibility' for a particular statement. While such an analysis might very well show how different discourses compete in a particular setting, it will need to have some idea of the overall conceptual landscape.

In contrast, there are also forms of discourse analysis that typically draw more directly on operational ideas from linguistics—e.g. metaphors or euphemisms—and show how particular tropes are used in discourse (e.g. Chilton 1996; Straehle et al. 1999). Journals such as *Discourse and Society* and *Discourse Studies* typically publish this kind of work. It will often be more attentive to the micro-features of texts than the more 'French' type, and it can show how, e.g. Jacques Delors used one family of metaphors while Jacques Santer and Romano Prodi have used metaphors drawn from other contexts, or it can trace particular, powerful metaphors such as 'the European common house' (Chilton and Illyin 1993). But what does this mean? Such analysis typically has less of a picture of the whole, and therefore, it is often, on the one hand, convincing—because it is well documented—and, on the other, not very good at leaving a major imprint on more general debates. In the future it would probably be advisable for discourse analysis to try to integrate these two sides, i.e. use more disciplined and precise ways of analysing texts while contextualizing these in more general, 'structuralist' interpretations that offer tools for interpreting the findings. One school within discourse analysis that tries to bridge this gap is the so-called 'critical discourse analysis' spearheaded by Norman Fairclough (1992, 1995; Chouliaraki and Fairclough 1999; cf. Titscher et al. 2000). It stretches from the micro to the macro level in texts. A weakness of this approach is the limited integration of the different elements and the tendency to resort to intuitive laundry lists of important questions to ask of a text—and it has been little used in IR and EIS so far.

## When and how discourse analysis entered political science, IR, and European integration studies

Discourse analysis has had strikingly different fates in Political Science and IR. In Polit-ical Science, in particular, the discourse theory of Laclau and Mouffe gained a certain niche prominence. Most political scientists have never heard of it and feel no need to relate to it—but it has gained enough of a foothold in certain departments to establish its own sub-culture within the field. In IR, in contrast, post-structuralism has gained a surprising prominence—and paid a price. During the 1980s, the two main rivals within

IR, realism and liberalism, transformed themselves into neo-realism and neo-liberalism respectively. In doing so, the gap between them was narrowed significantly. In particular, both approaches subscribed to the same rationalist ideal of science. The resulting 'narrow' debate between the two theories about how rational egoists act, including the debate over relative and absolute gains, left space for the next 'grand debate' to emerge between this almost consensual, rationalist 'neo-neo' position and a radical challenger of this position—which became post-structuralism (see Wæver 1996b). During the 1990s, a more moderate 'constructivism' then began to occupy the 'middle ground' between rationalism and post-structuralism (see Adler 1997). Among the costs for post-structuralism of this unlikely prominence was a radicalization and turn towards the meta-level where it became absorbed by debates about the discipline as such, while more operational elements like discourse analysis were downplayed.

The debate between rationalism and post-structuralism was not directly transferred into EIS, where the main debate took place between liberal intergovernmentalism and multi-level governance. Post-structuralist interpretations of the EU were rare—at least within EIS. While discourse analysis was applied here and there, only gradually did it coalesce into a candidate for independent treatment (cf. Diez 1999a; Walters 2002).

Although 'discursive approaches' in EIS have not been developed around a specific core argument on Europe, there are some recurrent themes. One is: *there is not one Europe but many*. Those who study Europe as a 'fact', naturally assume there is one Europe, but analysing discourse points to the role of competing 'Europes' (Wæver 1990; Stråth 2000b). A second argument, often indirect or implicit, is *against interpreting the EU in state terms*—be it in terms of intergovernmentalism or as a new and bigger state. Instead, it is proposed, the EU resembles a network or post-modern empire. This argument follows from a deconstruction of existing discourses and thus it is based on discourse analysis, but it stems at least as much from general arguments in post-modern IR and therefore it will not be dealt with in this chapter (but see Diez 1996, 1997, 1998; Börzel 1997). A third core argument is that *European questions are tied in with other issues*—not primarily due to cause-effect connections or strict logical implication, but because of *the relational nature of language, which means that concepts are valorized in relation to each other*. This, however, begs the question of what other issues to emphasize: gender, socio-economic divisions, national traditions, social cosmologies, or yet other possibilities. This is exactly one of the main issues on which the different 'schools' within Euro-discourse analysis differ.

## Separate 'approaches' or 'programmes' in European integration discourse theory

This section covers three examples of bodies of work that have each operationalized discourse analysis in a particular way in order to make it speak to European integration. Even if one is totally clear on what one takes to be 'discourse analysis', it is not clear how to take the step to 'Europe', and especially at what level it should be applied: specifically on 'European' discourses, or on national discourses on Europe, or with a particular conceptual focus. Three programmes are selected, primarily because they have been among the most prominent and influential, and secondarily because they are complementary in terms of the choices they make on basic questions.

## Governance and political struggle

A notable body of work has grown around the concept of (multi-level) governance and organized around the different ideas of legitimizing European governance, inspired by Beate Kohler-Koch and developed by Markus Jachtenfuchs, Sabine Jung, and Thomas Diez (see Jachtenfuchs et al. 1998; Jachtenfuchs 1995, 2001, 2002; Diez 1999a, 1999b, 2001; Jung 1999). To label this a programme or approach does not imply a fixed and unison subscription to one set of assumptions. It is rather a school in the sense of being an inter-connected stream of works stretching from Kohler-Koch's role in triggering this kind of work without herself doing discourse analysis as such (cf. Jachtenfuchs and Kohler-Koch 1996; Kohler-Koch 2000) over the individual and joint work by Jachtenfuchs, Jung, and Diez in the mid-1990s to their separate directions of development. In the work of this group of authors, the political battle lines are not located primarily between nation states or for and against integration as such but between different socio-economic models, which again rest on a number of wider suppositions of almost cosmological nature. This approach thereby places the main research issues squarely within politics in every sense of the term.

The most programmatic article from the research group (Jachtenfuchs et al. 1998) makes the case for 'polity-ideas' as a particularly important category of ideas to be emphasized within the general battle for supplementing rational choice studies of interests with a thorough study of ideas. Polity-ideas are *normative ideas about a legitimate political order*. In practice, the authors study political party documents in Germany, France, and the UK to reconstruct 'elements of polity-ideas', based on 180 different sub-categories within a general analytical scheme built around participation, output, and identity as possible dimensions of legitimacy. Another element in the approach is to establish four ideal-typical polity-ideas, two based on the modern state (one where it is carried through the nation states, i.e. intergovernmentalism, and one where the state is the EU, the federal state), and two beyond statehood (output-legitimized 'economic community', and 'network' legitimized by participation and identity). When tracking the debates in the three countries, one major finding is the relative continuity over time, another is the consistency within parties united by the same ideology, while national context accounts for the remainder of the variation.

Diez later (1999b, 2001) elaborated this analytical scheme in ways that made it more fully live up to the standards of discourse analysis. His key concept is 'discursive nodal points'—inspired by Laclau and Mouffe (1985), but defined somewhat differently. European governance is one such nodal point, and the four-pronged typology from the collective work is still used. However, the different polity-ideas are now linked to various meta-narratives that capture developments within 'deeper' concepts like politics, progress, and economy.

One of the strengths of this approach is that it offers a way to handle a problem characteristic of much discourse analysis: change. Diez's elaborate scheme offers a way to conceptualized degrees of 'translatability' between discourses, and this explains how easily one discourse can change or not change into another.

Another advantage is that this approach with its pre-defined list of elements offers instructions for how to read and what to look for. This part of the analysis therefore comes close to living up to the methodological standards pronounced by more traditional corners. It is not an impressionistic interpretation of a limited number of texts, but a quasi-automated cataloguing of a large number of texts. Thus, the actual 'coding' of the material might be reproducable by others and there is a quite systematic empirical data-set against which to assess the macro-interpretations. Methods for computer-supported, quantitative text analysis exist and have been used in IR (e.g. Alker 1996), and it is not impossible to imagine something similar being used for parts of an analysis like the search in this school for 'elements'.

Among the problems that mar the general 'governance' approach, and also, although to a lesser degree, Diez's later work are:

- The use of ideal types is 'un-discursive'. It goes against the basic idea of discourse analysis where no categories are universally valid: different discourses construct concepts and ideas differently, and therefore, it is surprising to see ideal types derived from general overarching considerations and then used as boxes into which discourses fit.

- The approach downplays national context. At first, this may sound like a good move, because it transcends traditional limitations from state-centric approaches, but thereby it also downplays the inter-connectedness of different discourses that are mutually defined in relation to each other, e.g. British Conservatives are very likely to develop their position in relation to Labour and this is usually more important to them than family connections to other Conservative parties. Rivals share traits either directly or in inverted form. However, as we will see in the following section, to take the opposite approach creates the opposite problem and points back to the value of Diez's approach.

If the story about Europe of this first group of authors is to be summed up, it must be: Europe is politics. The main battle lines are drawn between different general political orientations and relate to choices about other issues that are generally seen as political (e.g. socio-economic models). And the form of this struggle is about *legitimacy*, also a classical political category. As we will soon see, the two other approaches take us gradually into 'battles' further removed from the openly political, even if they surely want to argue that this is politics, too: firstly a theory that links Europe primarily to concepts of nation and state; secondly an approach that brings out hidden political investments in concepts like 'heading', 'crisis', and 'concept'.

## Foreign policy explained from concepts of state, nation, and Europe

A relatively distinct approach posits the configuration of concepts of nation, state, and Europe as the basis for building a quasi-structuralist theory of discourse as layered structures able to explain foreign policy options for a given state. This approach is more traditional than many other discursive approaches in its focus on *national* spaces of political debate and in its explicit ambition to *explain* (about which some post-structuralist discourse analysts remain sceptical). It has been marketed less as a theory of European integration than as a general bid for a theory of 'foreign policy', but all its main contributions have been on European states and often on EU member states' European policy, and the theory includes an explicit suggestion for how to analyse the interplay between, on the one hand, national discursive struggles among competing articulations of national traditions and, on the other, the process (or not) of European integration. Authors in this group include Ulla Holm (1992, 1997), Henrik Larsen (1997a, 1997b, 1999, 2000), Iver B. Neumann (1996, 2001, 2002), Lene Hansen (1997, 2001), Işıl Kazan (1994), and Ole Wæver (1990, 1991, 1995, 1996a, 1998b; see also Wæver et al. 1991)—but see closely related works by Haahr (2003), Merlingen (2000), Parsons (2000), Banerjee (1997), Kadayifei (1996), and Ruggie (1997).

The central idea of this approach is to see how the general lines of foreign policy, and thereby European policy, are based on different concepts of Europe and how these in turn are made possible by articulating differently concepts of state and nation. It is assumed that each country has a particular basic problematique of state and nation such as the French state-nation and the German concept of the romantic nation and the power state. The main positions can then be characterized by the way they choose among the relatively few available ways of relating to this concept. This is depicted in a model of layered structures inspired by Kenneth Waltz's concept of international structure (Waltz 1979). At the deepest level is the basic national concept of state-nation, at the second a purely relational conception of where the state/nation is in relation to Europe (internal, external, doubled, etc.), and at the third level are different concepts of Europe. The layered conception defines a way of studying stability and change because from any specific point, one can see possible changes as being more or less radical, and therefore more or less likely, depending on whether they happen at the third, the second, or the first layer. Similarly, it is important to a political situation whether the main rivals are within the same box or represent the different main options at, for instance, the second layer.

State, nation, and Europe are chosen because they are we-concepts, identities we hold simultaneously and which therefore have to be articulated with each other. European identity is not studied as a potential replacement for national identity, but because each nation's 'vision of itself' today includes a concept of Europe.

Thus this approach is not only a method for studying discourse, it is a theory of foreign policy. It is necessary for any political leader to be able to make sense of the big question of 'where are we heading', that is to be able to construct narratives of the nation/state, where it is coming from and where it is going. These increasingly include concepts of Europe as a way to project, for example, 'Germany' or 'France' into the future. European integration is only stable to the extent that the key countries can make sense out of their own future within a discourse that includes the current European project (see Wæver 1994, 1995, 1996a, 1998b, 2000). These discourses do not at all have to be identical between countries, they only have to be compatible. Thus, French policy has to be discursively compatible with the basic French concept of state-nation while it has to be politically compatible with German policy in particular. While this approach allows for interesting links to classical realism, the study of diplomacy, and the question of translations and mediation among countries (Kissinger 1957; Wæver 1995), it is weak on the possibility of an emerging European public sphere where discourses leave their national confines and meet directly in a European arena.

In contrast to the first set of authors, this approach therefore emphasizes the mutual dependence of (very different) internal national struggles. The German political debate, for instance, may be stable in itself because the leading political rivals share a commitment to deepen European integration because their state-nation concepts would become 'homeless' without such deepening. Yet, radical change is possible in Germany because this German constellation is dependent on a certain momentum at the European level and thus on the internal stability of French policy, which is much more doubtful. This school has mainly been carried forward by pro-European researchers in Euro-sceptical countries like Norway and especially Denmark, and can be seen as a warning about the fragility of European integration and the need for taking seriously the national peculiarities of debates on Europe.

The theory can be usefully compared to social constructivist theories of foreign policy that describe how a certain policy and self-conception is institutionalized—as typically in a number of studies on German foreign policy (e.g. Banchoff 1999; Berger 1996) that explain why German foreign policy remained relatively stable after the end of the Cold War and did not become more aggressive, as predicted by structural realism (Mearsheimer 1990). These studies put forward arguments why a given policy has been sedimented, but they have no 'deep structure' to explain why *both* this *and* some radically different positions are available. Consequently, this kind of social constructivist analysis has difficulty understanding change and is often forced to fall back on material structure. Identities and other social constructions explain inertia, not change. In contrast, the theory of layered discursive structure can account for even abrupt change because it follows from a change one level down the trunk of the tree-structure.

Because there are no ideal types, this approach faces a question about how to *find* discourse! How do you know a discourse when you meet one? And how do you avoid a circular argument where you first find a discourse in the texts and then you prove its importance and explanatory relevance—because it is (still) in the texts? Usually, the way out is sought in some form of combination of diachronic and synchronic analysis. In a first (synchronic) step, a wide selection of texts are read, not only of politicians but also of influential intellectuals. The aim is to get as clear an understanding as possible of the inner logic of a particular discourse which is ultimately an analytical construct but justified empirically by a first reading of texts. This establishes the structure that is to be used in a second (diachronic) step, studying political processes in more detail, focusing on the moves made by leading politicians, which are interpreted on the basis of the discourses as conceptualized in the first phase.

Again, some sociological/constructivist work, especially by Thomas Risse's research team at the European University Institute (Risse et al. 1999; Marcussen 1999; Marcussen et al. 1999) seems closely related because it includes a very similar reading of concepts of Europe in different national contexts as shaped by the different traditions of state and nation. While this work as such is presented in chapter 8 of this volume, it is possible to point out mutual advantages and disadvantages:

- The discourse analysis school is vulnerable to the criticism that 'discourse' floats freely, that it is 'all discourse', lacking an explanation of where discourses come from. Thus it will generally be seen as progress when Risse and other construc- tivists include a sociological explanation for the institutionalization and de- institutionalization of ideas. In particular the 'ideational life-cycle' is an interesting explanatory model in this respect.

- The sociological school in turn is very limited in its analysis of national traditions. These works do not get to the inner properties of ideas because they do not include a structural-linguistic component. Like the above-mentioned social constructivist work on foreign policy it focuses on the social explanations for the sedimentation of a particular idea, and can (externally to itself) explain its stability and change, but not how it relates internally to rival concepts in the national debate.

Other problems with the state-nation discourse theory are:

- The central place of national settings. The theory does allow for a European ('Brussels') scene as an overlapping layer (Wæver 1994), but this is secondary to the basic construction in terms of national spaces. In this sense, it turns the problem of the governance school upside down. While the latter emphasizes ideological orientations first and underplays national connections, the state-nation approach privileges national context over socio-economic orientation.

- It is quite traditional in its causal conception of discourse as an explanation for policy. It is structuralist more than post-structuralist and therefore misses the inner dynamics of language, the paradoxes and tensions within language as emphasized by, e.g. Derrida and Lacan. The discourses become too static, stable, and coherent, whereas a more fully post-structuralist analysis would emphasize the inherent tensions within any move towards coherence and thus their ironies and strange effects.

## The European project as productive paradox

A third—and in this case more loosely connected—body of work analyses the project of European integration itself, often using texts from the EU system and/or more general developments in the public debate related to Europe such as history books or the interventions of intellectuals. Here focus is on the way the integration project as such is conceptualized, what kind of identity it projects, how this interacts with more general changes in the European polity regarding legitimacy, history, the increasing importance of the media, concepts of citizenship, and politics (examples include Burgess 1997a, 2001; Delanty 1995a, 1995b; Derrida 1992; Johansen 1997; Pocock 1991; Rytkønen 2002; Schlesinger 1991; Stavrakakis forthcoming; Stråth 2000a, 2000b).

One advantage of this school is that it is often more strongly linked to general philosophical points especially from Derrida's deconstruction, because it focuses on the inner dynamics of *one* attempt to structure discourse. A danger of the two first schools is to depict language as too controllable, as a tool used in power games. Rationalist scholars underestimate language by treating it as a transparent media of representation and communication; but many social science post-structuralists might underestimate the particular features of language by treating it as a transparent media of power, purely a tool for politics. A more radical deconstructivist would instead want to emphasize how language plays games with actors. As mentioned, systems of signification never fully close up and fall into place—they always retain paradoxes, open ends, and impossibilities. The more insistently an actor tries to repress unpleasant elements, the more likely this is to show up in peculiar forms elsewhere in the text (Derrida 1974 [1967]; Wæver 1989). If one wants to depict, for example, a policy as 'un-political' and technical, this demands a grounding in some transcendent reference. Otherwise, it remains based on signs referring to signs referring to signs and thus openly a political choice. A transcendental grounding, in contrast, produces a forceful justification outside the text—but it has to be secured by operations internal to the text, and this will haunt the text through the effects of the moves necessary to do this grounding.

Interestingly, there seems to be a contrast between work on the US which tends to develop into rather monolithic, Foucault-inspired stories of how the identity needs of the US state have demanded continued production of self/other images and foreign threats (Campbell 1992), whereas the EU invites deconstruction, Derrida-inspired stories about ambiguity and ironies. In Derrida's own book on Europe (1992 [1991]), for instance, he underlines the simultaneous necessity to be responsive to the call for Europe and at the same time opening up Europe to its Other, to avoid closing it down as being identical to itself. Exactly because we (in the early 1990s Europhoria) move under the banner of a 'Europe' we don't really know the meaning of, it becomes a politics of anticipation rather than precedent. Thus, the analysis can critically investigate attempts to define European identity through cultural essentialism (cf. the critique in Delanty 1995b) while it also shows how another kind of paradoxical political identity is created that avoids classical pitfalls.

It is only possible to develop Europe if one remains attentive to rather philosophical questions. Derrida develops his conception of European culture by way of the general argument that '*what is proper to a culture is to not be identical to itself,* . . . *to be able to take the form of a subject . . . only in the difference with itself*' (1992: 9; emphasis in original). And when drawing on the *concept of Europe*, one has also to take on the *Europeanness of the concept of concept* (Burgess 2001). This shows how philosophical this can become, and sometimes, therefore, it almost stops being discourse analysis—because it is unclear what is actually read and the analysis turns into philosophical argument as such.

A specific advantage of this school is the possibility to link form and content, to study the position of media and culture and thus identity not only as object but also as practice (Schlesinger 1991; Burgess 1997b; Johansen 1997; Delanty 1998). The electronic media especially are changing both in their expression and in their organization in relation to states, and the nature of identities produced and reproduced in the dominant media are likely to change as well. It is common to note how national identity is about a glorious past and a heroic future, but the present is also conceived in a specific way. According to Benedict Anderson (1983), the modern nation is structured around an understanding of compatriots living *simultaneously* even if distant from oneself. Therefore its emergence depended on both epistemic innovations like 'homogenous empty time' and the single-point perspective and on technologies of communication with print and the novel later reinforced by newspapers, telephone, and radio. What kinds of political communities are likely to thrive in a media world fragmented into multiple TV-channels filled with hyper-reality and constant live-ness?

Many other contributions can be presented as reflections on what kind of identity Europe might be constructing. Traditional approaches typically ask what European identity *is* and thus they end up talking identity talk themselves (Europeans are united by their commitment to the enlightenment, but divided by confessions, etc.). Discourse analysis helps us to understand *how* identity is constructed, and quite different mechanisms have to be investigated. Most of the existing work on this issue connects identity to the question of legitimacy: does the European project necessitate a form of legitimacy which in turn demands a political identity (Smith 1992; García 1993; Howe 1995; Laffan 1996; Kostakopoulou 1997; Beetham and Lord 1998; Banchoff and Smith 1999; Hansen and Williams 1999)? If yes, how much can this be a *political* identity in contrast to more ethnic identities in the nation states (Habermas 1992; Kelstrup and Wæver 1993; Hassner 1997)?

Deconstruction here shows its value and discourse analysts question the questions traditionally asked and expose the terms of debate. Hansen and Williams (1999) have shown how this debate assumes a contrast between technical rationality and myth, whereas instrumental rationality has actually been the key myth in the self-understanding of the EU. Another typical deconstructive move is to show how the debate takes for granted a connection between identity, legitimacy, and polity that is transferred from the nation state and its heyday. A critical analysis of the debate itself opens a space for admitting the possibility of a different kind of legitimacy, one that is not a question of identity (cf. the first school discussed above, particularly Jachtenfuchs 1995). Thirdly, the impasse reached by much of the traditional debate, that cultural identity is both impossible and necessary, can be taken beyond logical contradiction to a dynamic understanding of the paradoxical nature of identity (Burgess 1997a; Stavrakakis forthcoming): Identity is not being but always longing and desire, and thus European identity politics can be grasped through an analysis of passions of politics and identification.

# Enlargement

When addressing enlargement with discursive approaches, two large fields of research immediately open up. The first one that follows from previous work is self/other constructs either between a Western (current EU) self and Eastern (new members) other or between the enlarged EU and non-Europe. To the extent that Eastern Europe figured in the set of differences that defined EU-Europe, redefinition of identity has to take place. This challenge might be aggravated by the way the *process* of enlargement negotiations have offered West Europeans many chances to define themselves vis-à-vis the 'not yet fully' European East. When the new members join, such mutual castigations will be very dangerous to the EU. The challenge is whether the next layer of potential candidates will occupy the position left vacant by the new members, which will reproduce the current discourse, or whether new discursive figures will take over, such as a more radical Othering of Russia, which some of the new members might favour (Neumann 1998a, 1998b).

The second option answers one of the questions that non-discursive approaches find most interesting: the rationale or justification for enlargement—why did the EU decide to do something as costly and cumbersome? Here, the best answer from within or close to discourse analysis comes from *speech act theory*, which is currently emerging within IR as a middle ground between constructivism and post-structuralism (cf. Fierke and Wiener 1999; Williams and Neumann 2000; Buzan et al. 1998: ch. 2). In relation to enlargement both Fierke and Wiener (1999) and Schimmelfennig (1997, 2000; see also Schimmelfennig's discussion of intergovernmentalism in this volume) show how speech acts (or 'rhetorical action' in Schimmelfennig's terminology) can explain the paradox of an enlargement process that does not seem to be in the self-interest of member states. Just as other acts, those done with words create unintended effects including commitments and moral obligations that are hard to get out of. More generally since they are *acts* they *change* reality (not only comment on it). Thus, words are not only derivatories in relation to politics, they often *are* politics.

Discourse analysis ought to be applied also to the *nature* of the enlargement process, especially its relative technochratization. A whole machinery is constructed to handle the negotiations and this rests on a specific construction of 'enlargement' as an issue and problem—an attempt to depoliticize the decisions about whom to accept through an 'objective' evaluation. Where much literature simply ridicules the thousands of pages produced on each country and the naivety of the non-political assumption, discourse analysis could handle the more interesting question how (and why) 'objective' and 'un-political' interpretations are produced politically.

The three approaches presented above each lead to specific research agendas:

• Governance studies will look at the competition between different models of legitimation in the 'old' and the 'new' EU, and in the relations between them, and thus especially at their changing balance and possible internal redefinition due to enlargement. Legitimacy by efficiency may become more difficult with enlargement, but the grand historical rationale is given new life by the role of the EU in healing Europe's division, and by allegedly extending the zone of peace (Friis and Murphy 2000).

• The state-nation approach can study the new member states according to its standard procedure, but will probably focus on how the main powers re-define their concept of Europe so that it encompasses enlargement, i.e. how is enlargement tied into their state-nation-Europe constellations? It is widely assumed that Germany has a special stake in Eastern enlargement, but should that be understood primarily in terms of material interests or a particular form of Europe? Will enlargement put increasing pressure on the French debate because state, nation, and Europe fit better together with a more tight and action-oriented EU?

• The third, 'depth-discursive' approach will surely engage in the already mentioned rethinking of external and internal differentiations and 'others'. Enlargement also recasts questions of responsibility and ethics.

## The future

Three final questions should be addressed:

First, what is the relevance of discursive approaches to other approaches? The most immediate overlap is with social constructivism where several studies demonstrate that there is a broad contact zone, and with governance approaches, where some of the literature, for instance on multi-level governance, is discursive in form. Other connections might be cultivated as well. The state-nation approach could make links to liberal intergovernmentalism because they share the tendency to channel politics through states, not directly as transnational processes, while they give competing explanations of 'preference formation'. The legal and constitutional debates (e.g. Weiler 1999; Wind 2001; see Haltern, in this volume) could also team up with discourse studies because legal analysis is often language oriented, but its in-depth study of one type of discourse could be more systematically imbedded in a more systematic understanding of the more general discourses.

What is the status and standing of discursive approaches? Much has been done within this approach, but it is often quite dispersed and often not seen as part of EIS. However, a few efforts are relatively concerted (those discussed as 'schools' here), and it is for discourse analysts to push these forward.

Finally, what are the challenges for the immediate future? Much internal debate is needed, not least on methodology (cf. Milliken 1999; Walters 2002; Malmvig 2002; Hansen forthcoming). The debates on methodology promise to become a dynamic field (which is probably surprising to most critics who see this as anti-method). There is a widespread sense that it is time to be more 'disciplined' and self-reflective about how discourse analysis is carried out. (Simulteneously, e.g. neo-realism, constructivism, and rational choice also turn towards intra-paradigm debates.) The meta-theoretical debates may be influenced by general developments within IR Theory, but it is probably more likely that the relative autonomy of EIS means a continued *Sonderweg* for discourse analysis within this field. Finally, it may be necessary to address some of the tensions that have run through this chapter stemming from the duality of discourse analysis as theory and as methodology.

Thus, discourse analysts within EIS face the dual challenge of simultaneously getting better at speaking to the other theories within the field and explaining what discursive approaches can contribute while engaging in complex internal debates on methodology and analytical strategy that necessarily demand specialized terminology and attention to the more exotic philosophical roots of these approaches. Discourse analysts will need to pay a great deal of attention to language—not least their own language.

# Guide to further reading

DERRIDA, J. (1992 [1991]), *The Other Heading: Reflections on Today's Europe* (Indiana: Indiana University Press). Probably the key instance of a deconstructivist reading of the concept and project of Europe. It transcends simplistic notions of self-other construction to investigate the intricate play of otherness within the European venture. And it provides a challenging reflection on the ethical requirement raised by 'Europe'.

DIEZ, T. (1999), 'Speaking "Europe": the politics of integration discourse', *Journal of European Public Policy* 6(4), 598–613. Diez makes a general case for the value of discourse analysis in European studies. This is done by way of three 'moves' of increasing radicality: J. L. Austin's theory of speech acts introduces a performative view of language. Michel Foucault's concept of discourse as the locus of power moves politics as well as the constitution of subjects more fully into language. Jacques Derrida's deconstruction builds on a concept of language even further removed from the ideal of communication and more in terms of technique which allows for, e.g. analyses of nodal points, meta-narratives, and translatability. Throughout the article uses examples from European studies to show the relevance of the different aproaches.

JACHTENFUCHS, M., DIEZ, T., and JUNG, S. (1998), 'Which Europe? Conflicting Models of a Legitimate European Political Order', *European Journal of International Relations* 4(4), 409–46. A wide-ranging article that is simultaneously programmatic and based on large empirical material. In a study mostly of political party documents in Germany, France, and the UK, the authors show the importance of 'polity-ideas', i.e. normative ideas about a legitimate political order. Four basic ideal types are derived logically, and the article shows how large data work can be synthesized in a discourse-based approach.

MALMBERG, M. and STRÅTH, B. (eds.) (2002), *The Meaning of Europe* (Oxford: Berg). This book contains a number of perceptive analyses of different concepts of Europe in different countries. It is not based on a shared form of discourse analysis, and lacks an explicit engagement with methodological questions, but it contains studies on many of the themes that future discourse analysts are likely to continue working on.

WÆVER, O. (1998), 'Explaining Europe by Decoding Discourses' in Wivel, A. (ed.), *Explaining European Integration* (Copenhagen: Copenhagen Political Studies Press), 100–46. This is a theory and methodology centred presentation of the 'concepts of state-nation-Europe' type of discourse analysis in European studies. France and Germany are the main empirical illustrations. The article is relatively detailed on practical questions such as 'what to read', 'how much is enough?' and the relationship between diachronic and synchronic analysis, and it presents the tree-shaped structure of depth-levels used in this approach.

# 11

# Gender Perspectives

## Catherine Hoskyns

## Introduction

Gender refers to the socio-cultural meanings given to masculinity and femininity and to the complex and varying relations between the two.[1] Applying gender perspectives, therefore, both to the rich patterns of history and to the theories constructed to order and explain them, means identifying these changing meanings and examining their causes and effects. Gender relations are rooted in perceptions of difference and structured inequality and have over long periods of time led to many women being disadvantaged. As a result most of the texts cited in this chapter take a concern with the situation of women as their starting point.

Increasingly, however, it has become clear that the particular forms of disadvantage that women face cannot be adequately examined without taking account of the complexity of gender relations and the varied positions of men. Use of the term gender also makes it possible to take a broader view of differences and identities and to ask 'not only the woman question'. Thus there has been a gradual move across a range of disciplines from women's studies to gender studies.

The term 'gender perspectives' is intended to include a spectrum of approaches and interventions. As Cynthia Weber implies, gender is not a variable that can be included or excluded at whim in theoretical constructs. Rather, it is a viewpoint that can alter not just the scope of theory but the concepts upon which it is based (Weber 2001: 89). The overall argument of this chapter, therefore, is that gender perspectives create a viewpoint rather than a theory (in the narrow scientific sense of that term) and that without sensitivity to this viewpoint any general theory attempting to explain European integration will be partial and misleading. The aim of taking such a stand is to give visibility to values and situations normally ignored or marginalized, thus helping to create more inclusive and better grounded histories and theories.

The relation between gender perspectives (a framework for analysis) and feminism (a politics of women's emancipation) requires explanation. Feminist approaches and interventions provide a large part of the history and substance upon which gender perspectives build; they also make explicit the focus upon women and change. Sandra Whitworth in her 1994 study of feminism and international relations discusses three varieties of feminism: liberal feminism (concerned with equality and the equal representation of women), radical feminism (foregrounding violence against women and sexual politics), and post-modern feminism (deconstructing the category 'woman' and emphasizing diversity). Gender perspectives, by twisting the lens a bit, blur these distinctions while opening the way to examine gender relations more broadly and engage with work on men and masculinity. Whitworth suggests a fourth version of feminism that she herself prefers. This might be called 'critical theory feminism' combining the insights of Critical Theory (discussed in more detail later in this chapter) with a gendered feminist politics. I am not keen on labels, but if I had to choose one, this would be my preference also.

This chapter falls into four parts. The first surveys empirical and theoretical work on women and gender as this has developed within or been applied to European integration studies; the second assesses why most theorizing on European integration is resistant to this material and what the possibilities are for change. These accounts are followed by two case studies demonstrating the significance of gender analysis in the EU context. The final section assesses these trends and considers options for the future.

## Developing perspectives

Gender perspectives in the field of European integration studies have developed out of a complex intermingling of activism among women, policy development, and scholarly analysis, mediated by different time frames and changing material conditions. Characteristic of these perspectives are scepticism about appearances and surface reality, a concern with power relations, and the pursuit of transformation.

There are in general three overlapping stages through which greater awareness among women about their situations enters into academic discourse. These are: identifying sex discrimination, generating material and research, and challenging fundamental concepts (Lovenduski 1981). There is no inevitability about reaching the third stage. The sequence for gendered accounts of and perspectives on European integration follows this pattern.

### Identifying sex discrimination

The set of events which sparked off the sequence, and which remains emblematic of feminist campaigning, began in the late 60s in Belgium. In this period, campaigns for equal pay by women in the arms factories near Brussels, the determination of women lawyers to use European law for the benefit of women, and unrest among Belgian airhostesses came together to bring pressure on the European institutions. The result was the famous *Defrenne* cases in the European Court of Justice, which in 1976 led to the activation of Article 119 of the Treaty of Rome on equal pay (now Art. 141) and the adoption of a series of implementing Directives.[2]

What these cases made clear was that Article 119 had the same legal effects as other Treaty articles. However, where other articles (even if contentious) were implemented through negotiation between existing political élites, Article 119 had been ignored until it was invoked by women who at that time were either outside the formal political system or marginalized within it. The overlapping interests of women with very different situations and class positions helped to make this breakthrough possible. The sequence of legislation that followed illustrated many of the key characteristics of European law and policy. Based on the notion of 'equal treatment', a concept already in use to remove barriers to trade, its main purpose was to reduce discrimination in the labour market, which was holding back the entry of women. While this was clearly an advance, the effect was to separate off and treat differently the economic role of women, while leaving their domestic role, and gender relations more broadly, unexamined. This was an early indication of the way in which social and political issues were neglected as a result of the EU's formation as primarily an economic community and single market. The (constructed) distinction between the economic and the social, and the different treatment given to each, has remained at the core of EU policy-making. It continues to affect the EU's women's rights/gender equality policy, despite important modifications.

The substance of the women's rights policy, and the case law it produced, began to take effect towards the end of the 70s. This was just at a time when the experiences of second wave feminism were producing insights and forms of analysis which began to problematize the whole question of what came to be called gender relations. This caused vivid debate particularly among women across the US and Western Europe. The identification and critique of sex discrimination was at its height.

## Generating material

For a while little attention was paid to this new European policy on women's rights, either by women generally or by EC analysts for whom it fitted no known parameters. Women lawyers were the first to take it seriously, in particular Eliane Vogel-Polsky in Belgium and Rights of Women (ROW), a collective of feminist lawyers based in London. The initial objective was to inform women about the new rights they were acquiring. But the material collected sparked off debate and analysis from a feminist perspective on the meaning of equality, and on the implications for women of distinctions between the public and the private.[3]

During the 1980s feminist theorizing began in a more sustained way to expose gender relations and investigate how assumptions, norms, and hidden structures created and perpetuated women's disadvantage. One example is Carole Pateman's classic study *The Sexual Contract* (1988). In this, she takes apart the idea of the social contract, which in modern society is seen as governing relations between the individual and the state, to reveal the unequal and unmentioned sexual contract embedded within it. This can be seen as an important step in revealing gender relations (although this term is not used) in order to explain and ultimately transform women's subordination.

Meanwhile, the publication of material on women in politics was increasing across Europe (Randall 1987). This highlighted the activities of women politicians, documented the overall absence of women in formal politics, and expanded the definition of politics to include the more grassroots-type involvements of women. Soon after, this analysis was projected to the European level providing useful comparative material and a study of how women's exclusion from public policy diminished debate and reduced the likelihood of effective implementation (Lovenduski 1986). Despite the lack of polemics and the scholarly nature of this work, it remained for the time being on the sidelines as far as both political science as a discipline and politics as a profession were concerned.

In the early 80s I was teaching courses on European integration at Coventry University after a considerable period of involvement in the women's movement. I had read about the *Defrenne* cases in the women's press and wondered how they came about. When this was neither elucidated nor referred to in the work then current on European integration, I had to research it for myself. What I discovered was of interest to women but (as I realized later) also revealing about EC political processes and relevant to theorizing about European integration (Hoskyns 1985). However, the publication of such material in feminist or activist journals meant that it was highly unlikely to influence mainstream thinking about the EC.

Gradually, work developed which involved examining in detail the women's rights policy and legal infrastructure emerging at EC level and analysing the involvement of women and women's political behaviour in this context. The main focus was on the public sphere. Doing this detailed work began to expose some of the socio-cultural and institutional forms that entrenched women's disadvantage but also provided opportunities for change. Studies in a comparative vein, which focused on the work experiences of women and their daily lives across Europe, were also under way. The statistical base and the extent of comparative material, in certain policy areas, were strengthened by the activities of the European Commission's Equal Opportunities Unit, which funded research and set up expert networks.

Parallel to this, campaigning and research was taking place on a much broader range of issues concerning women in Europe, which one might sum up under the term 'sexual politics' (Elman 1996). Part of this concerned issues such as abortion, sexual harassment, and domestic violence—all matters urgently in need of regulation. The other part concerned the more hidden side—pornography, prostitution, trafficking, violence against women, and labour exploitation. The aim here was to expose corruption and connivance and give some dignity and protection to the women involved. As Cynthia Enloe has shown in her classic studies of international relations and gender, such phenomena and the connections they have to mainstream society are generally ignored both by practitioners and theorists (Enloe 1989).

Highlighting these issues made clear the diversity of women's situations in Europe. This coincided with the critique by black women of the false universalism and ethnocentric nature of much of white feminism. The attempt by various women's organizations at European level to publish a study giving space to the critical voices of black and ethnic minority women showed how controversial a project this was, and how little political space there was in the European system for debate on these issues (Williams 2003). There is now much more material available on race relations and migration in Europe, a significant part of it dealing with or incorporating the experiences of women (Kofman et al. 2000).

The emphasis on diversity and identity is one of the reasons for the use of the plural in the title of this chapter. There is no longer, if there ever was, a single gender perspective that can be applied to the EU. By the early 90s, these multiple disruptions had created a much more fragmented setting for gender politics and campaigning, at EU level as elsewhere.

## Challenging concepts

As can be seen from the above (which even so mentions only a small selection of what is available) a broad range of material now exists documenting the situations of women in the EU and establishing different points of view. The move from documenting women to studying gender relations is an organic and gradual one and in the process more complex analyses have been developing which both *deepen* and *broaden* the gender debate. While these are not co-ordinated (and not necessarily coherent), they create a level of knowledge and understanding that can challenge the concepts and assumptions underpinning academic analysis, and through this influence policy. The dangers of co-option, of being accepted without inducing change, remain strong.

As far as *deepening* goes, one of the main contributions has been the increasingly detailed discussion of the relation between employment and caring. This has been conducted primarily by sociologists and lawyers and provides a telling critique of EU measures and the continued emphasis on the employment situations of women. Such analyses make clear that until the issue of 'who does the caring' is moved centre stage in policy debate, and deeply rooted assumptions about paid and unpaid work are reconsidered, talk of gender equality remains grounded in an imbalance that is reproduced in legal texts and welfare regimes (Luckhaus 1990). In respect of the EU, much of this debate has centred on analysis of the equal treatment rulings of the European Court of Justice (ECJ). Where once the Court was praised for its protection of the pregnant worker, its application of the 'dominant ideology of motherhood', which still sees caring as the main responsibility of women, has come under increasing attack (McGlynn 2000). The Court on many occasions has shown itself reluctant to use the equal treatment provisions to encourage or legitimize the role of men in caring. However, a small breakthrough occurred in 2001 when in *Griesmar* the Court for the first time ruled that a French provision which gave pension credits for caring only to mothers, should be extended to fathers also.[4] Whether the Court will continue in this direction is by no means clear, but the context in which it takes these decisions is being subtly altered.

Another example of *deepening* concerns the analysis of migration policy. Louise Ackers, working from the situation of internal women migrants in the EU (that is female EU citizens moving from one member state to another), shows how both the assumptions in the EU's free movement of labour policy and the lack of convergence in EU welfare systems affect women migrants severely and diminish their rights as citizens. The policies are thus innately gendered without this fact being recognized or remedied (Ackers 1998). Annie Phizacklea, dealing with general theories of migration, shows that neither orthodox theories assuming push/pull factors and rational choice, nor structural theories based on models of dependency and capital logic, can deal adequately with the situation of third world women on the move. A more sensitive theoretical stance is needed to understand what happens to migrant women's diverse motives and identities as these meet up with host country assumptions and changing regulations. She suggests (and this has relevance for the EU, see 'Constructing theories' below) that host country assumptions about women's place in the private sphere and in service, help to explain why many women migrants to the EU end up in marginal jobs, as servants and sex workers (Phizacklea 1998).

The above examples tackle theory and policy directly, using approaches that are critical both of concepts and of the policies deriving from them. Another strand of work, and this seems more common within political science, uses existing theories and methods but pushes them to include material of direct relevance to women and gender. One example of this is Sonia Mazey's account of the development of the EU women's rights policy, using a model of policy framing and advocacy drawn from policy studies. The fact that she finds a different trajectory here than in other policy areas (the European level having a strong influence on national agendas rather than the reverse) adds a new element (Mazey 1998). Bretherton and Sperling attempt something similar in their study of women's networks and the EU using a framework drawn from policy network analysis. They state clearly that they find the framework inadequate and suggest ways in which it could be broadened to provide a more inclusive model (1996). Perhaps the strongest example of this trend is in comparative politics where, using and expanding conventional methodologies, Stetson and Mazur have collected a wide range of comparative material on women and the state, much of it concerning the EU (1995). These examples seem likely to proliferate. Their impact on the mainstream of political studies is still limited.

*Broadening* is suggested by moves from more narrow sectoral studies and from issues dealing specifically with women towards consideration of the EU as a totality, and of the gendered structures and practices embedded in it. Jo Shaw has attempted this in EU legal studies, arguing that not only the women's rights policy but also the constitutionalizing and constitutive aspects of EU law need to be brought into gender analysis (2000). Similarly, Lena Hansen sees the EU as a functioning polity and examines the restraints on 'gendered subjectivities' that its totality sustains (2000). Studies of this kind begin to tackle or at least question the underlying assumptions, structures, and flows upon which the EU is based and which are often disguised in public discourse. What seems to be lacking so far is a 'gendered political economy' approach to the EU. Diane Elson's study of gender and macroeconomics gives some indication of how this might proceed. She sees as crucial the revaluing of the social in relation to the economic, and the recognition that economies cannot function without the social assets that are for the most part produced outside both the private and public spheres, namely in the household. Such a revaluing has implications for theories about the individual and the market and presents a challenge to embedded assumptions about the roles of men and women (Elson 2000). Gender analysis along these lines has started in the development field (Bakker 1994; Rai 2001). Elements for such an approach to the EU already exist (Conroy 1997; Rees 1998; Rubery 1998; Wiener 1998) but have not yet been drawn into a coherent whole. Were this to be done, it is likely that resistance would be considerable.[5]

## The policy context

Over the years the scope of the EU's women's rights/gender equality policy has increased, partly at least as a result of some of the activities and analyses discussed above. This has not gone as far as some would like, but it has been in the direction of giving more consideration to diversity and to the non-market role of women. There are directives on pregnancy, part-time work, and parental leave and soft law measures on sexual harassment, childcare, trafficking, and violence against women. Article 141 (ex 119) now incorporates a legal entitlement to positive action. All of these measures have been watered down in negotiation and are applied patchily at national level (EUSA Review Forum, 2002). Also significant has been the adoption in 1997 of what is now Article 13 of the EC Treaty extending the scope of the EU's anti-discrimination remit to include a wide range of criteria, in particular race and ethnicity.

The main change in recent years has, however, been the adoption of 'mainstreaming' as the organizing principle for the gender equality policy at EU level. This promises that a gender dimension will be incorporated into all policies of the EU. Furthermore, the commitment is 'constitutionalized' by being included in Articles 2 and 3(2) of the Treaty, which set the main objectives of the Union. Neither the reasons for nor the implications of this shift in approach are yet clear. In some ways it can be seen as a diversionary tactic, giving the Commission 'a good story to tell', without much need to implement. On the other hand, where women are ready to act, or protest, they have a greater legitimacy. In reality, rather than offering solutions, mainstreaming provides multiple new sites on which gender battles can be fought (Pollack and Hafner-Burton 2000; Mazey 2001).

Despite mainstreaming, high profile acts of the EU still tend to be taken without much regard for gender or the appropriate representation of women. This is true of the Commission's 2001 Governance White Paper, which makes no mention of gender, and the composition of the important Convention for the Future of Europe with only a tiny proportion of women members (Shaw 2001; European Women's Lobby 2002).

Much change has taken place in the gender debate in the EU over the past thirty years. However, actions like these betray the fact that core concerns and many of the core policy-makers remain largely untouched. In these areas gender is a marginal issue and women still relative outsiders in the public sphere. Can integration theories help to explain this situation or are they themselves compromised?

## Constructing theories

Thirty years of study of women and gender have provided a wealth of empirical material and analysis that can help to explain and illuminate the various processes at work within the EU. Strongly formulated gender perspectives have been developed. These can be applied to the EU but they do not, I would argue, constitute a gender theory of the process of European integration. A challenge is thus presented to the more general theories of European integration to make use of this material, and to be open and sensitive to a wider range of viewpoints. This means not ghettoizing or ignoring gender and other critical perspectives but seeing them as contributing continuously to the debate. Since theory constitutes as well as explains the questions it asks (and those it does not ask) such openness is important.

What would a gender-sensitive theory be like? In the first place it would have to be one that started with social relations rather than with reified and abstract concepts like state and nation. This would be a way of filling in 'the black box' between the individual and the state, which is present in many existing theories. Openness about norms and values would also be important and recognition that however objective and neutral scholars try to be, certain assumptions (and not least those about gender) influence the way they think and write. It would also need to be one that sought to theorize change, transformation, and power, and had a broad definition of the political. As Steve Smith makes clear, one of the main reasons why rationalist international relations theory cannot deal adequately with the EU is its restricted notion of politics (2000: 33). One test of this broader definition would be the extent to which the criminality, violence, and sexual exploitation which underpin much of European prosperity come within the scope of analysis (Locher and Prügl 2001). Phizacklea's reworking of migration theory from a gender perspective, discussed above, gives some indications of how this might be done (1998).

All this presents a challenge to existing theories though change is taking place. Much of the early debate about integration was more to do with closing off than opening up and it is discouraging to find that Ben Rosamond's otherwise excellent book on theories of European integration makes no mention of the extent to which existing theories are gendered (2000). Nevertheless, an approach from gender has a great deal to say about the role of theory in the European integration process, and by switching the focus suggests new lines of inquiry. In particular, it brings the imbalance between the social and the economic in EU policy-making into focus, puts the emphasis on democratic legitimacy and forms of participation, and prioritizes the analysis of power relations. These concerns raise a number of questions about the part that integration theories have played not only in explaining but also legitimizing certain key aspects of the EU's development and history. Bearing these questions in mind I shall now briefly examine the way theorizing about European integration has developed and what changes are taking place. This process starts right at the beginning when Ernst Haas 'invented' neofunctionalism to explain and interpret the workings of the European Coal and Steel Community (ECSC) and the ideas of Jean Monnet.

## Interpreting neofunctionalism

The details of neofunctionalist theory are set out elsewhere in this volume. What is of interest here is its ethos and influence. Neofunctionalism has a social dimension and sees policy-making as a process—it should therefore be possible to include gender thinking within its frame. Despite these positive aspects, however, neofunctionalism has ended up explaining and thus implicitly often promoting a bureaucratic, technocratic model of policy-making in the EU, which from the beginning separated the social from the economic. This not only excludes gender but also any concern with democracy. There are a number of reasons for this trajectory, at least in the early stages, most notably the fact that what Altiero Spinelli called 'the substance of politics' was lacking in relations between the six founder member states (1966: 4–7). One could argue convincingly (and many have) that in post-war Europe the only way integration could be initiated was through élite contact on low-key economic issues relying on 'a vague but permissive public opinion' (Haas 1968: xii). However, what neofunctionalism failed to do was problematize this situation or consider its implications.

As it is now clear, no real attempt was made after this to construct 'the substance of politics' although at the time Spinelli, Monnet, and Haas anticipated that this would happen. When I had the opportunity to interview Haas in 1996, I asked him about this, my concern as a feminist being to discover how characteristics so inimical to a gender sensitive EU had come to be embedded. In response, he made a number of illuminating comments. In particular, he made clear that in the 1950s public pressure was 'off' the ECSC because the acute welfare needs of people were being dealt with at national level. 'This was the necessary response', he said, 'concern for integration was not populist and there was no pressure for it to be so'. He also commented that although Monnet's initial idea was to involve trade unions and other social groups in the ECSC process, it became clear that trade unions (and presumably even more so other social groups) could not take advantage of the opportunities being offered. Thus European integration, by the time he came to study the process, 'was a very elitist enterprise'.[6]

These comments make clear that even in the 50s the separation of the economic from the social in EC policy-making was well underway. This was consolidated as governments began to appreciate the convenience of taking transnational economic decisions by bureaucratic means, while meeting social need at national level. At the same time, the imbalance in the capacity to respond to the new process was also evident. Economic interests were far more able to organize and respond than were popular forces. Thus ideology and politics were embedded in the process, even this early on.

Here then are some of the phenomena which taken together started to construct the EU in certain ways. They are still highly relevant today. Gender perspectives help to reveal and highlight these phenomena, if only because women are particularly disadvantaged by the distancing of the social from the economic, and at the same time likely to be among those who find transnational participation difficult due to lack of resources, and exclusionary practices.

## From intergovernmentalism to critical theory

One of the assumptions of neofunctionalism was that given the right circumstances, bureaucratic co-operation in economic and technical matters could bring about profound political change discreetly and without any widespread political mobilization or ideological debate. Such an analysis was challenged very quickly by those who thought it underestimated the resilience of the nation state, and its complexities. Stanley Hoffmann was one of the first to argue in this way, spawning a long line of intergovernmentalists giving centrality to the 'high politics' role of the state (1966).

Thus was born in theory terms a long lasting conflict between neofunctionalists and intergovernmentalists, pitting supranational institutions and processes against national entities and governments. In the 1980s, this supposed dichotomy exerted a hegemonic influence over explanations of European integration, squeezing out other possible questions and paradigms. Despite the seeming conflict, both theories were (and are) fundamentally uncritical of the process of integration in the sense that they do not acknowledge its endemic contradictions.

During the same period more political-economy approaches to European integration could be found in the work of neo-Marxists like Ernest Mandel and Stuart Holland but these were ignored in mainstream theorizing (Mandel 1967; Holland 1980). Also ignored was the growing impact of Critical Theory in the field of international relations. Critical Theory meets at least some of the criteria which gender analysis requires and has great relevance for the study of the EU. That it is not one of the theories included in this book is symptomatic of the neglect with which it has been treated in European integration studies.

Critical Theory springs from the Frankfurt School and was pioneered in the 1930s by among others Theodor Adorno and Max Horkheimer. Its best-known contemporary exponents are Jürgen Habermas and, within international relations, Robert Cox. Critical Theory takes issue with what are termed 'traditional theories' both for their assumption that theorists can be neutral observers and for their empiricism and concentration on knowledge that can be 'proved'. For Critical Theory, all facts and those uncovering them are historically and socially produced and no situation or aspect of society is immutable. Most importantly, Critical Theory looks to improve the human condition and seeks out the possibilities for transformation in existing situations and processes (Hoffmann 1987). The work of Habermas is particularly relevant to this book since he is concerned with political theory and communication and has sought to address the complexities of the EU.

Here then is a set of characteristics that comes near to those listed at the beginning of this section. However, there is little in Critical Theory that shows a sensitivity to gender and Nancy Fraser, among others, has taken Habermas to task for his gender blindness and failure to incorporate into his work a sufficiently subtle view of gender relations. This means that his model is 'bound to miss important features of the arrangements he wants to understand' (Fraser 1995: 35/36). Despite this, the concern of Habermas with public space, participation, and communication and his clear-sighted dissection of the EU as a polity, make him a theorist worth engaging with. Noting that in the EU there is 'an ever greater gap between being affected by something and participating in changing it', he attributes this to the separation of the economic from the social and to the way people are being turned into clients (1992: 9–11). These are perceptions that resonate sharply with the direct experience of women engaging with EU processes.

The generally subversive approach of Critical Theory and its commitment to change are characteristics both feminism and gender analysis can make use of. Whitworth uses 'critical theory feminism' to good effect in her studies of international institutions and gender (1994). Critical Theory (though in a more neo-Gramscian form) continues to challenge thinking about the EU with its analysis of disciplinary neo-liberalism, transnational class formation, and hegemonic forms of control. Current theories of European integration are taken to task for their bland acceptance 'that market forces are the expression of an inner rationality of universal human nature, that is held to be the essence of "the realm of freedom" in political affairs' (van Apeldoorn et al. 2003). The absence of attention to gender in this new wave of theorizing has been highlighted by a collection of essays drawn together under the title *Towards a Gendered Political Economy* (Cook et al. 2000). This is an important book with much in it of relevance to EU gender studies.

## The governance turn and social constructivism

The last decade has seen great change in theorizing about the EU. Critical Theory, post-modernism, globalization, and developments in the EU itself, have all had their effect. The most important of these changes has been the switch to analysing governance rather than explaining integration and the application of techniques and methods from comparative politics and policy analysis as well as from the discipline of international relations. Considering the EU as a complex policy arena has finally decentred neo-functionalism and intergovernmentalism and added more nuances to the supranational/national dispute. It also for the first time allows issues to do with legitimacy and democracy to be set centre stage.

Within this more open context, partial theories like policy network analysis, new institutionalism, and multi-level governance (all of which are discussed elsewhere in this volume) jostle and interact. This creates a situation where there is more possibility of making connections between, for example, the economic and the social in EU decision-making, or between the life experiences of different groups within European society. In this situation, gender perspectives and feminist interventions are more likely to have space and resonance.

Against this trend, there are still serious attempts in theorizing as well as in practical politics to preserve the separation between the economic and the social and to hide the implications of this from political scrutiny. In theoretical terms this trend is represented by the idea of the 'two-level game'. This terminology, while apparently addressing the relationship of international and national policy-making, in fact reifies the separation of the two, and furthermore expects that different criteria (especially as concern democratic accountability) will be applied to each. Andrew Moravcsik, whose liberal intergovernmentalism is discussed elsewhere in this volume, is a prime exponent of this view (1993, 2002) as is, from a different perspective, Giandomenico Majone (1998).

Such accounts are more than descriptive and explanatory, they are also constitutive. Moravcsik's assertion that lobbying should be taken account of at national level and included in the 'preferences' of individual states denies the fragmented nature of state interests and the transnational identity of many social groups. By failing to identify the imbalances in the existing system, such theories continue to support the élite nature of European economic decision-making, conveniently ignoring the fact that those furthering particular economic interests will always have the capacity to act internationally. Such theories pay no attention to the gendered consequences of these arrangements.

Social constructivism is the latest theoretical approach to be applied to European integration. This approach, although it comes in many versions, works across disciplines and brings a far wider range of phenomena into consideration than is customary in international relations (Christiansen et al. 1999). Social constructivist accounts deal particularly with identity formation, the process of socialization, and the importance of discourse in shaping and setting limits to what is achievable. Like Critical Theory, these accounts are not limited to 'facts which can be proved' and recognize that theories are affected by time and place and that scholars contribute to what they are explaining. Perhaps most important they link the social, political, and international and see international processes as embodying and being formed out of social relations.

The extent to which these theories embody gender perspectives is as yet by no means clear. However, what is clear is that by endorsing the link between the social and the international they lift the lid on a whole range of materials and approaches previously discarded and deemed irrelevant. This undoubtedly makes it more possible for gender perspectives to enter the mainstream (Locher and Prügl 2001). Women academics who have been writing on gender issues in the EU context for many years are now beginning to identify themselves as social constructivists (Mazey 2000).

However, what seems at the moment to be lacking in the social constructivist armoury is a sustained theory of power or even a concern with its distribution. Since gender is an important signifier of power and powerlessness, this is a crucial omission for gender analysis. Feminists in the past have sought to theorize power as having a constructive as well as a competitive side and to consider 'power to' (enabling) as well as 'power over' (coercive) (Squires 1999: 39–45). Many would also be nearer to Foucault in seeing power everywhere, and capable of access and use in all kinds of diverse situations. The level of macro and systemic power, however, remains a crucial element and gender perspectives have an important role to play in revealing these dimensions (Allen 1996). Such depictions, rather than power expressed only as an aggregate of capabilities, need to be theorized with regard to the EU.

This overview of theories suggests that although theories of European integration have shown little awareness of gender, they have in fact been highly gendered. The EU they have helped to construct is one which, despite the policy initiatives, in its overall shape has disadvantaged many women and partially at least deprived them of a voice. This is as a result of the continuing separation of the economic from the social and the absence of effective democratic control and popular participation. Features which were expected to be temporary were allowed to become formative. Theories which could have highlighted this situation and considered its implications were by and large silent on these issues.

What effect might it have if both theory and practice at the European level were more sensitive to gender perspectives and the experience of women? The next two sections examine first the current EU debate over legitimacy and then the enlargement process from this point of view.

## Case study 1—the legitimacy debate

The EU legitimacy debate really only took a public form in 1992 when the Danish population rejected the Maastricht Treaty by a vote of 50.7 to 49.3 per cent. Before 1992 Haas's 'permissive public opinion' was assumed to be still in existence with popular loyalty primarily satisfied at the national level. Since then, there has been continuing concern about how a more favourable view of the EU can be created and if possible the permissive consensus re-established. The dilemma is that the European Parliament, which is supposed to represent the democratic element, is neither well known nor trusted by the bulk of the populations. What people do trust (or are at least familiar with) are the national political systems. Thus popular dissent tends to manifest itself in votes (in member states' referenda where these are required) against extending the powers of the EU. The problem for those in power is how to satisfy a larger proportion of the population while not disrupting too far the current forms of decision-making or preventing further development. In these referenda and elsewhere there is a distinct and continuing gender gap, with fewer women than men willing to support extensions to the EU's competence.

These are problems which could have been identified earlier had more attention been paid to the attitudes of women and to the experience of EU policy-making on gen-der issues. For this was a policy which unusually for the EU addressed a mobilized con-stituency. And although those women involved in and knowledgeable about the EU policy were small in number, the women's networks did at their most complete stretch from decision-makers and experts through to trade unions and grassroots organiza-tions. There was also shown what one might call 'a capacity for participation'. Despite this, the gender policy never aroused great enthusiasm among women in a broad sense and was never able to 'deliver' women for the EU enterprise. If this is taken as a test case of the way EU as an institution affects broader publics, then there would seem to be three main reasons why the expected consolidation of support failed to take place. These are: the limitations of the policy itself, the blockages put in the way of genuine participation, and the failure of EU leaders to provide a compelling 'vision' of the EU's purpose and ethos.

The limitations of the policy have already been discussed. Suffice to say here that despite certain achievements, the policy in legislative terms has only in the most grudging way moved beyond equality in the labour market. Indeed, Brigitte Young argues that it has never moved beyond what 'disciplinary neo-liberalism' demands of women (2000). It is also the case that important elements in the Commission have not been consistently proud of this policy or used it as an example to be followed. This kind of ambiguity (now repeated in attitudes to mainstreaming) means that the EU as an entity has never in a high profile way been able to reach out to women on the basis of the gender policy.

## Participation

On the issue of participation, Sue Cohen, an activist with the UK Single Parents' Action Network has made a telling critique. Involved from 1985 to 1994 with the EU's Poverty Programme and a member of European Anti Poverty Network she describes the mixture of excitement, privilege, and frustration that she and other grassroots women felt with their participation in EU projects. The Commission consulted widely and numerous workshops were held on the subject of 'social solidarity' but it was only gradually that they became aware of the limits to the dialogue, the exclusions that were taking place, and the lack of political outcomes. 'If the Union is to become more participatory and democratic', she writes, 'then political knowledge and action will need to be informed by grassroots activists as well as corporatised agencies, by work in the home as well as paid employment, by the private as well as the public' (Cohen 2000: 13). Marks and McAdam show that while many social movements have adjusted their activities to the EU level 'no uniform structure of political opportunities has developed, or even shown signs of developing' (1996: 103).

These situations lead to what has been called 'the return to the national'. The norm in the gender policy field is for the Commission to supply materials, organize studies and workshops, and then when people become enthusiastic to direct them back to the national level to lobby and bring pressure. This may be realistic in tactical terms, but it is an admission that there is no open political system that can accept a popular transnational input.

Does this matter? In a sense it is all part of the 'two-level game' and the argument would be that such enthusiasms should be part of national politics and if cogent will be taken on board in state preferences. Inevitably, however, such treatment discourages popular involvement in the EU and unbalances decision-making. It also puts off key activists and in the long run encourages people to feel attachment only to the nation state. In a globalized world this may in the end prove counter-productive.

## The image of the EU

The Danish referendum in 1992 and subsequent referenda have highlighted the gender gap in support for the EU. These together with evidence from *Eurobarometer* surveys have been carefully analysed by Ulrike Liebert. Though the situation varies from country to country, the evidence shows that gender gaps over support for the EU have existed in all member states at least since 1983. Her conclusion is that for the most part women are wary of the EU, not because they are apolitical or lack information, but because they have different political interests. She also points out how little attention has so far been paid to this gender gap in mainstream public opinion or policy analysis. She feels her job is to 'illuminate the neglected part of the story' (Liebert 1999: 231).[7]

Liebert argues that the move to a greater emphasis on gender equality in the Amsterdam Treaty (1997) was an attempt to meet this dissatisfaction among women as well as a response to pressure from the Scandinavian governments. However, she expresses strong doubt as to whether this can now have the desired effect. Hansen sees it as a difficult problem for women activists at this stage to make up their minds whether they want a more participatory and open EU or on the contrary whether they should endorse the return to the national and try to keep what they can within the system they understand (2000).

Some would argue that both of these alternatives ascribe too much power to the EU and that what feminist thinkers and activists should be doing is devising alternative visions and opening up new political opportunities. One such attempt is the feminist notion of a 'transversal politics' which links people in diverse situations and attempts to establish a common space between them. Developed by Cynthia Cockburn and Nira Yuval-Davis in their work on women in conflict situations, these ideas are now encapsulated in the phrase 'rooting and shifting'. This conceptualization of politics envisages people who are 'rooted' in particular memberships and identities, 'shifting' to a situation of exchange with those in different circumstances (Yuval-Davis 1997; Cockburn 1998).

'Rooting and shifting' can be seen as a political response to current trends. These are particularly evident in the EU where people are sceptical of the EU's capacity to protect them in the face of global insecurities. 'Rooting and shifting' acknowledges that people wish to keep their local identities but tries to construct an affective politics beyond this. Though developed as a way of conceptualizing women's campaigning in a globalized world, it could equally well serve as a guiding principal on which to build EU citizenship.

## Case study 2—enlargement

Enlargement provides a striking case study for the salience of gender perspectives. Not only is it proving to be a traumatic and often painful process for women in the applicant countries, but it raises many questions for women in the existing EU. It is also an important test bed for the validity of mainstreaming as a method of policy delivery. Self awareness is required to do research in these circumstances and relations between western feminist academics and colleagues in Central and Eastern Europe (CEE) has often been fraught. Some better connections are now being made and studies are emerging which both give space to the views of CEE women and also reveal much about the nature of the enlargement exercise and how this shapes and is shaped by gender relations.

Gender studies of the enlargement process take many forms and reveal different layers of meaning. Four examples of recent work illustrate the complexity.

The first is a piece by Dubravka Ugrešić, which appeared in the *European Journal of Women's Studies* (1998). This describes in vivid terms the emotion invested in the new relationship between East and West in Europe and in the process of enlargement. The breaking of the old stereotypes and established roles appears as highly destabilizing as is the new emphasis on ethnic identity and border controls. Ugrešić points out that the exclusions in place, now that entry to Western Europe is a possibility, are greater and more demeaning than in the Cold War period. Then, when populations were firmly corralled behind walls and curtains, East Europeans could be seen as victims of the European 'other' and made welcome. Now in many ways they constitute a threat. Though Ugrešić does not refer to gender in her account, this is the kind of telling, personal analysis to which gender research gives prominence—and takes seriously.

The mood of mixed emotions, irony, and threat in Ugrešić's piece needs to be borne in mind when reading the study by Charlotte Bretherton of mainstreaming gender equality in the enlargement process (2001). She uses Simon Bulmer's distinction between ideas and interests, to show how in the enlargement negotiations ideas (supportive of gender equality) come up against interests (reflected in already institutionalized male dominance). Thus there is already a conflict at EU level over mainstreaming which resonates and can intensify gender conflict in the CEE.

In the European Commission, DG Enlargement has been one of the most reluctant of all the DGs to take on board the requirements of mainstreaming. Social policy in general has been downplayed in the enlargement negotiations and gender equality forms only a small part of this remit. Bretherton attributes this disregard to the fact that enlargement is seen as 'high politics' and thus assumed to be beyond any concern with gender disparities or social relations. It is also the case as we saw earlier that mainstreaming tends to be ignored in the core areas of EU activity.

As Bretherton points out, mainstreaming could have been of great help to CEE women faced with bewildering turns and unpredictable governments. In particular, it would have been useful to have gender monitoring in the allocation of money and useful also if issues relating to gender discrimination had been raised in the detailed meetings between EU and CEE officials which were part of the pre-accession screening. On the contrary, the message was given time and again that these issues were not important.

Without this broad commitment to mainstreaming, what was left was the need for CEE countries to comply with the EU's gender equality legislation, which formed part of the *acquis communautaire*. Most of this legislation, as we have seen, concerns equality in the workplace. However, Peggy Watson's careful examination of the situation of women in the CEE countries before and after 1989 suggests that generalizing equal opportunity policies from West to East and assuming that the underlying problems of women are the same is a strategy with many dangers. Sexual difference was not experienced as a source of political inequality under communism, and even now, when unemployment, criminality, masculinism, and class differences are on the rise, it is still not seen as the main determinant. Many men also suffer from frustration and unemployment and women are now more likely to identify with class positions than gender (Watson 2000). This suggests that a much more nuanced and targeted gender policy was required from the EU for the CEE countries—something that could have been forthcoming through mainstreaming had it been sensitively applied.

Susan Gal and Gail Kligman make similar points in their book *The Politics of Gender After Socialism* (2000). This study is the result of intense collaborative work and examines in detail the post socialist situation from the perspective of gender using insights from discourse and cultural theory as well as more traditional social science approaches. The results demonstrate how continuity and change interact and people reposition themselves and reinterpret phenomena in new situations. This is a study that probes the interstices and argues convincingly that without an adequate theorization and understanding of gender, the overall situation in the CEE countries will be misrepresented and misunderstood.

All of these studies contribute important findings to the study of enlargement. Many of them may be unpalatable to those in authority on both sides. Nevertheless, paying attention to these nuances can reveal pressure points and give early warning of changes taking place.

## Outlook

It is hard to evaluate exactly where we are in terms of the success or otherwise of gender perspectives in influencing study of the EU and the development of theories. Certainly progress has been made and far more material is now available. The arena for theorizing has opened up and significant gender material is beginning to be used in the European politics mainstream (Pierson 1998; Cram 2001). On the other hand, both the core of EU policy-making and many of the key concepts in theorizing European integration remain virtually untouched.

One sign of progress is that gender research has now moved out from a prime concern with the EU's gender policy and legal instruments towards a broader consideration of the gendered nature of the EU as a polity and the ramifications of this. I would argue, however, that this has not gone far enough and that more of an engagement with the EU's fundamental economic structure and ethos—a political economy approach in other words—is required. Neither core values nor the essence of policy-making are likely to change without this. To mount this challenge would mean gender theorists in areas such as international political economy and gender and development taking the EU seriously, and Critical Theorists including more centrally the gender viewpoint.

As far as theory is concerned, it is interesting that there has been far less engagement by feminists with integration theory than with the 'parent' discipline of international relations. In that field, feminist interventions were regarded as so disruptive that a defence had to be mounted, by Robert Keohane, among others (1989). This involved a paternalist attempt to tell feminists what kind of theorizing was and was not acceptable. Things have not yet reached that level on the European front and indifference is still the main weapon used against any likely incursions. There are a number of possible reasons for this: first, the EU is an 'uncertain entity' and therefore its politics and how to address them are unclear, secondly, there is a less obvious North/South dimension in its operations, and thirdly, gender interventions in respect of the EU came when European integration theories were already opening up towards governance and constructivism. As a result, a smoother engagement was possible. However, it should be remembered that feminists in international relations were beginning to attack the rationalist/market forces assumptions in the discipline and therefore threatening its foundations. Were this to happen in respect of integration theory then a much stronger response could be expected.

The use of the term gender is now well established in the field of European integration studies. It is also the accepted term for EU policy. While the academic justifications for its use are strong the implications for policy are still uncertain. The use of the term 'gender equality' suggests a broader remit for EU policy and the possibility of action in some key areas of gender relations. On the other hand, it is also strangely depoliticizing and obscures what was the cutting edge of the women's rights policy—its commitment to a better deal for women. This illustrates the dilemmas inherent in politics and theorizing around gender: advances towards the mainstream can easily lead to dilution. In the present climate, however, there seem to be possibilities for a constructive engagement between gender perspectives, Critical Theory and some aspects of social constructivism. These theories taken together have the potential to challenge the basic premises of the integration process and expose its inherent contradictions in a way that other theories do not.

# Notes

I should like to thank the following for help with this chapter: Christine Battersby, Alexander Kazamias, Linda Luckhaus, Heather MacRae, Sol Picciotto, Shirin Rai, Jill Steans and the editors of this volume. None of them are responsible for the opinions expressed, or any errors.

1. The meaning of gender and its relation to biological sex has been much debated. In general, insights from biology and psychoanalysis, as well as the social sciences, would suggest that sexual identities are more ambiguous and less 'given' than was previously assumed. For a full account of these debates and others around gender see Alsop, Fitzsimons, and Lennon *Theorising Gender* (2002).

2. Gabrielle Defrenne was an airhostess with the Belgian airline Sabena. She was forced to retire at 40 with minimal severance pay and loss of pension entitlements. For an account of why Article 119 was included in the Treaty see Hoskyns (1996) 52–7.

3. The binary divide between the public and the private has served many purposes most of them to the disadvantage of women. Many would now argue for a tripartite division: the public, comprising state activity including economic regulation and a public sphere for debate and action; the private, including economic exchange in the market and the actions and activities of civil society; and the domestic or familial, comprising the household in both its economic and social functions. See Squires (1999) 24–32.

4. ECJ Case C–366/99, *Griesmar*, judgment 29 November 2001. See also ECJ Case C–476/99, *Lommers* v. *Minister van Landbouw*, judgment 18 March 2002. Here the Court acknowledges that a measure (in this case places in a nursery reserved for women members of staff) 'whose purported aim is to abolish a *de facto* inequality, might nevertheless also help to perpetuate a traditional division of roles between men and women'.

5. As part of a gender mainstreaming initiative, a seminar was held in October 2001 on Gender and the EU's Broad Economic Policy Guidelines. Cogent papers by women economists apparently received a rather negative response from Commission officials.

6. Interview, San Francisco, 3 September 1996.

7. More detail on the Danish referendum from a gender perspective is given by Heather MacRae (2001). She uses this material to argue that integration cannot proceed effectively unless more attention is paid to gender and to national and cultural difference in the member states. For Macrae, a feminist approach to integration deconstructs boundaries and conceptual categories and broadens debate.

# Guide to further reading

*Primary work*

ELMAN, A. (ed.) (1996), *Sexual Politics and the European Union* (Oxford: Berghahn Books). Brings issues such as pornography, abortion politics, and sexual trafficking within the scope of European studies.

HOSKYNS, C. (1996), *Integrating Gender Women, Law and Politics in the European Union* (London: Verso) A detailed history of the EU's gender policy paying special attention to the agency of women.

LIEBERT, U. (1999), 'Gender Politics in the EU—the Return of the Public', *European Societies* 1(2), 197–239. Uses public opinion and policy analysis methods to dissect the reasons for the gender gap in support for the EU.

MAZEY, S. (ed.) (2000), 'Special Issue: Women, Power and Public Policy in Europe', *Journal of European Public Policy* 7(3). Collection of articles demonstrating new links between gender analysis and social constructivism.

*Other primary works*

BRETHERTON, C. (2001), 'Gender Mainstreaming and EU Enlargement: Swimming Against the Tide?', *Journal of European Public Policy* 8(1), 60–81. Useful analysis of mainstreaming in a contested area.

COHEN, S. (2000), 'Social Solidarity in the Delors Period', in Hoskyns, C. and Newman, M. (eds.), *Democratising the European Union—Issues for the Twenty First Century* (Manchester: Manchester University Press). Thoughtful discussion of why effective participation in EU processes is hard to achieve for grassroots movements.

EUSA Review Forum (2002), 'Progressive Europe? Gender and Non-Discrimination in the EU', *EUSA Review* 15(3). Nicely contrasting views from Mazey, Shaw, Elman, and Mark Bell on the current state of EU policy in these areas.

HANSEN, L. (2000), 'Gendered Communities: the ambiguous attraction of Europe', in Kelstrup, M. and Williams, M.C. (eds.), *International Relations Theory and the Politics of European Integration* (London: Routledge). Brings a consideration of gender into the EU legitimacy debate.

LOCHER, B. and PRÜGL, E. (2001), 'Feminism and Constructivism: World's Apart or Sharing the Middle Ground?', *International Studies Quarterly* 45, 111–29. Comes down on sharing the middle ground though with some reservations.

MAZEY, S. (1998), 'The European Union and Women's Rights—From the Europeanization of National Agendas to the Nationalization of a European Agenda', *Journal of European Public Policy* 5(1), 131–52. Theorizes the EU women's policy and sets it within the policy analysis frame.

—— (2001), *Gender Mainstreaming in the EU—Principles and Practice* (London: Kogan Page, European Dossier Series). Brief and succinct overview of and introduction to the policy and its implications.

PHIZACKLEA, A. (1998), 'Migration and Globalisation: a Feminist Perspective', in Koser, K. and Lutz, H. (eds.), *The New Migration in Europe* (London: Macmillan). Important article demonstrating a feminist reworking of mainstream theory.

YOUNG, B. (2000), 'Disciplinary Neoliberalism in the European Union and Gender Politics', *New Political Economy* 5(7), 77–98. A critical theory approach to gender politics in the EU.

*Main critiques*

JONES, A. (1996), 'Does "Gender" Make the World Go Round? Feminist Critiques of International Relations', *Review of International Studies* 22(4), 405–29. Argues that gender is a variable which must include concern with the interests of men as well as women.

KEOHANE, R. (1989), 'International Relations Theory: Contributions of a Feminist Standpoint', *Millennium* 18(2), 245–53. Classic lecture from IR scholar on how feminists should 'do feminism' in IR.

*Additional works*

ALSOP, A., FITZSIMONS, A., and LENNON, K. (2002), *Theorizing Gender* (Cambridge: Polity Press).

COOK, J., ROBERTS, J., and WAYLEN, G. (2000), *Towards a Gendered Political Economy* (London: Macmillan).

RAI, SHIRIN M. (2002), *Gender and the Political Economy of Development* (Cambridge: Polity Press).

REES, T. (1998), *Mainstreaming Equality in the European Union: Education, Training and Labour Market Policies* (London: Routledge).

SQUIRES, J. (1999), *Gender in Political Theory* (London: Polity Press).

WHITWORTH, S. (1994), *Feminism and International Relations* (London: Macmillan).

WEBER, C. (2001), *International Relations Theory: a critical introduction* (London: Routledge), ch. 5 on gender.

# 12

# Taking Stock of Integration Theory

## *Antje Wiener and Thomas Diez*

## Introduction

This volume sought to achieve two goals. First, it was compiled to assess the state of the art in European integration theorizing. To that end, we brought together a group of scholars who are able to present and reflect upon the core theoretical contributions that have been developed since the early stages of analysing European integration and governance. The second goal of the book was the generation of a critical discussion about the object and process of theorizing European integration as such. To that end, the choice of contributions reflects the variation in disciplinary context, historical stage of theorizing, and the comparative dimension of approaches. This analytical dimension of the book is sustained by the 'best' and 'test' case scenarios, which have been included in each chapter to test the robustness of each approach.

This concluding chapter brings the past-present-future theme running through the book as well as through each contribution, to a close. In the remaining sections we offer *first* a historical overview over the type and focus of each theoretical approach to European integration developed by the contributors ('past'); *second*, we develop a comparative assessment of the respective strengths and weaknesses of each approach according to the definitions of 'theorizing' and 'integration' developed in the introductory chapter ('present'); and *third*, we elaborate on the emergent and most challenging issues that stand to be addressed by forthcoming adaptations and scrutinizations of European integration theories ('future').

We argue that the different theoretical perspectives developed in the ten contributions to this volume demonstrate an emerging robustness of European integration theories. The variation in approaching the respective 'test case' of European enlargement reveals the need for both rigorously prescriptive and normative approaches to European integration. As the social constructivist, the critical legal approach, the gender perspectives, and the discursive approaches presented in chapters 8–11 demonstrate in particular, core constitutional issues that determine the quality of emergent transnational political orders (March and Olsen 1998; Olsen 2002) such as values and norms, identity, and equality have been receiving relatively less analytical attention than approaches that seek to explain institutional and regulatory processes. Yet, the two-tiered development of massive enlargement and constitutional revision which the process of European integration has come to face in post-Cold War times require a more robust theoretical and analytical understanding of the interplay between process and substance. While a decade ago the constitutional topic 'spelt political death', mostly for evoking the 'f-word', i.e. a federal statist quality of the Europolity, current activities resemble a 'political and intellectual stampede to embrace the idea of a constitution for Europe' (Weiler 2002: 563). The 'constitution is no longer a taboo' in integration discourse (Pernice 2001: 3–4) and the constitutionalization of the Treaties has become an accepted policy objective.[1] It is an expression of the constitutional turn in the Europolity. That is, supranational—European—integration has evolved from the pre-integration time of cooperation under anarchy and a long period of cooperation towards integration towards a new shared goal of constitution-building.

With this constitutional turn, the process of constitutionalizing the Europolity[2] enters into a qualitatively different phase. After supranational institution-building until the 1980s and the Europeanization of domestic institutions until the late 1990s, currently a process of 'late politicization' evolves (Wiener 2003: 136–8). Indeed, we argue that the constitutional turn that reflects both the historical process as well as the extensive scholarly literature since the 1990s, remains to a large extent undertheorized. The outcome and durability of this new quality of international cooperation therefore remains to be assessed.[3] The pressure of constitution-building raises the stakes of transnational politics—it may well turn into the make or break of the project of European integration. The following sections will first offer a comparative assessment of the different approaches to European integration presented in this volume ('Comparative perspective') and then map core issues and relevant research questions which European integration theories stand to elaborate more extensively in the future ('Outlook: towards the politicization of European integration').

## Comparative perspective

In the introduction, we suggested a comparison of the theoretical approaches to the analysis of European integration included in this volume along two dimensions, their purpose or function, and the specific area of integration they study. We also argued that the different approaches together would form a mosaic providing a multi-faceted and never complete picture of European integration and governance. To demonstrate this, we asked contributors to present a case that they thought 'their' approach is addressing particularly well ('best case'), as well as to apply 'their' approach to the 'test case' of enlargement. Our expectation was that contributors would select different aspects of European integration and governance as their 'best case', which they would analyse for different purposes. Furthermore, we expected that they would approach the analysis of EU enlargement from different angles, depending on the main purpose of 'their' approach, and focusing consequently on different aspects or areas of enlargement. If this was the case, the various approaches would neither be directly comparable or testable against each other, nor would they be incompatible. Instead, they could be seen as each shedding a different light on European integration and governance, and therefore adding another stone to the mosaic of integration theory.

Overall, the chapters in this volume have met our expectations, as the overview provided by Table 12.1 demonstrates. With a few exceptions, their 'best cases' differ widely, and where they overlap, such as in liberal intergovernmentalism's and neofunctionalism's attempt to explain outcomes of integration, they focus on different aspects of the integration process, which are not mutually exclusive, even though their relative importance can be tested empirically. Similarly, the ten approaches selected have very different things to say about enlargement, focusing on the explanation of enlargement, an analysis of the demands of enlargement on EU institutions, or a critical assessment of the effects of enlargement on the societies within the new member states—or admitting that they have little to contribute to this discussion, making such approaches appropriate for the analysis of deepening integration, but not of widening the territorial scope of membership.

Taking this 'test case' as an example, the emerging mosaic of enlargement is one that focuses first on the decision of the European Union to enlarge (Pollack, Risse, Wæver), proposing that norms and previous commitments were decisive in this respect. Generally, the decision to apply for EU membership by the candidate countries is seen as less problematic—the puzzle in the case of the EU is that rationalist explanations are ultimately not convincing. However, this does not mean that the membership candidacies are uncontested, or that there were no important bargaining processes between the EU and its current member states and the candidate countries, explaining the outcome of which is at the core of the liberal intergovernmentalist agenda (Schimmelfennig). Given the focus on explanation in their 'best cases' (see Table 12.1), surprisingly many contributors were concerned with the effect of enlargement. They predict, perhaps less surprisingly, that European governance and further integration will become more complicated: spill-over may be hindered (Schmitter); increased heterogeneity may lead to 'increasing regulatory competition and informality' (Jachtenfuchs and Kohler-Koch) the *acquis communautaire* will become further differentiated (Haltern); inexperienced civil servants may make decision-making more difficult, while reform of governance will be less likely due to the increased number of member states (Peterson); and path-dependency may dictate continued variation and therefore increased administrative complexity, while Europeanization may decrease this problem but only in the long run (Pollack). Given these complications, a federalist is, from a normative point of view, alarmed, and insists that the *acquis* cannot be jeopardized (Burgess). Finally, discourse analysis and gender studies add critical voices as to the terms on which enlargement proceeds (Wæver) and the effect it has on the women in the societies of the new member states (Hoskyns).

It should be obvious that such an account is incomplete in a double sense. First, it is a reflection of the most pressing questions that have been raised for European

**Table 12.1** Comparative perspective

| Chapter | Author | Approach | 'best case' | 'test case' (enlargement) |
|---|---|---|---|---|
| 2 | Burgess | Federalism | Normative: constitutional evolution | Normative: maintaining *acquis communautaire* |
| 3 | Schmitter | Neofunctionalism | Explaining integration outcomes (in cycles) | Predicting effects of enlargement on spill-over |
| 4 | Schimmelfennig | Intergovernmentalism | Explaining the consolidation of the Single Market | Explaining outcomes of bargaining in membership negotiations |
| 5 | Jachtenfuchs and Kohler-Koch | System Governance | Describing, explaining, assessing interplay of governance and polity | Predicting effects of increased heterogeneity on governance |
| 6 | Peterson | Network Governance | Explaining policy outcomes in CAP | Predicting effects of enlargement on policy networks |
| 7 | Pollack | Neo-institutionalism | Explaining executive, judicial and legislative politics | Explaining decision to enlarge, outcome of negotiations, and effect |
| 8 | Risse | Social Constructivism | Understanding the construction of European/national identity | Explaining the EU's decision to enlarge |
| 9 | Haltern | Integration through Law | Critical assessment of European citizenship laws | Critical assessment of effects of European law and the nature of the EU |
| 10 | Wæver | Discursive Approaches | Explaining/critically assessing policies towards integration | Critically assessing enlargement discourse; explaining decision to enlarge |
| 11 | Hoskyns | Gender Perspectives | Describing the role of gender in the *acquis*; critically assessing the EU's legitimacy | Critically assessing the effect of enlargement on women in new member states |

integration theory so far, but there will surely be others. It seems, for instance, quite likely that once the new member states have joined, competing explanations of the outcome of the negotiation processes can be put forward and assessed, and more specific questions about both domestic and EU Institutional effects of enlargement may be asked. Secondly, both the angle provided on enlargement by each author, as well as the selected 'best case' and how to approach it, do not necessarily cover all the work done from within one particular approach. Gender perspectives are presented in this volume, for instance, with a focus on the early days of gender analysis in the context of European integration. Thus, the phase of 'generating material' (Hoskyns) remains very often at a more descriptive level, e.g. stressing the observation of the widening scope of gender equality law within the EU, and the effects of integration on women more generally (see, e.g. Hoskyns 1996).[4] With this caveat in mind, Table 12.2 represents an attempt to approximate what might be most appropriately described as a 'mosaic of European integration theory' by filling in the boxes of Table 1.1 (see chapter 1). As a note of caution, this table is not intended to represent such a mosaic in itself, nor do we intend to offer a definitive answer to the question of how theoretical approaches relate to each other. According to the hermeneutic approach taken by the editors of this volume, we do, however, suggest that a debate about where one would preferably place each approach contributes to a better understanding both from the perspective of the editors and that of the readers.

**Table 12.2** The functions and areas of (integration) theory

|  | POLITY | POLICY | POLITICS |
|---|---|---|---|
| **EXPLANATORY/ UNDERSTANDING** | Neofunctionalism; Intergovernmentalism; Integration through Law | Policy Network Analysis; Discourse Analysis | Neoinstitutionalism; Social Constructivism |
| **ANALYTICAL/ DESCRIPTIVE** |  | Gender Perspectives |  |
| **CRITICAL/ NORMATIVE** | Federalism; (Critical) Integration through Law | Discourse Analysis | Gender Perspectives |

Three features of the above table immediately catch the eye and need to be addressed. The first and probably least problematic one is that both Integration through Law and Discourse Analysis appear twice, whereas the Governance Approach does not appear at all. The reason for the former appearing twice is that in both chapters, there is a clear differentiation between different strands that result in more radically different variations than in the case of, for example, neo-institutionalism. Within the Integration through Law chapter, we find the development from law as an explanatory factor of further integration towards law as a normative or critical reflection on current developments of the Europolity (as well as specific policies). Among the discursive approaches, there is a similar split between those trying to explain member states' policies towards integration and those problematizing the assumptions on which integration policies are based, although in practice both enterprises often go hand in hand. Governance approaches, in contrast, are not mentioned at all in the table. This omission is due to the fact that in their chapter, Jachtenfuchs and Kohler-Koch make a self-conscious attempt to bridge the different purposes as well as the different areas of theory, and therefore develop governance as a grand theory within which all other approaches can find their place. In a sense, this constitutes an alternative path of seeing the relationships between theoretical approaches to the one put forward by the editors. While Jachtenfuchs and Kohler-Koch propose a catch-all theory of overarching character, we argue that it is preferable to see integration theory as a mosaic in which different perspectives come together in their own right. Ultimately, the problem with the grand theory route, as we see it, is that it has to impose particular ontological and epistemological assumptions on the analytical possibilities included within the framework of the theory. Those closer to a narrow scientific understanding of theory may see this as a good thing, but it does not conform with the spirit of theoretical diversity, and doing justice to the purposes and areas of theory as set out in chapter 1.

The second and perhaps most obvious characteristic of Table 12.2 is—except for gender perspectives—the absence of entries in the 'analytical/descriptive' row. In chapter 1, we proposed that it was one of the functions of theory to provide new conceptualizations of particular social and political phenomena, and that this was particularly important in relation to the EU as a new kind of polity. We further argued that European integration theory evolved in phases, starting, after a period of normative pretheorizing, with an explanatory phase, which was then followed by an analytical phase as the EU was taken more seriously as a polity of its own right in the 1980s, and then by a renewed interest in normative questions, and, following the epistemological debates in the wider social sciences, in problematizing European integration and governance and particular policies.

A revised model of the three phases of theorizing would locate the approaches within the historical context of integration. From a hermeneutic standpoint, it is interesting to observe how these phases reflect distinct theoretical *foci* in relation to the relevance and place of institutions in theory and practice. Thus European integration theory develops gradually including the three phases of integration (explaining integration as supranational institution-building, Part I of this book), Europeanization (analyzing governance, Part II of this book), and politicization (constructing the polity, Part III of this book). Table 12.3 summarizes the three phases and their respective focus on institution-building.

As this book's contributions demonstrate, the first two phases are well developed sets of theoretical approaches. The third phase has just begun to shed light on substantial constitutional questions such as the legal status of the EU, the constitutional status of the Charter of Rights, the role of the church, and the application of Qualified Majority Voting in high politics such as Common Foreign and Security Policy.[5] These issues lead

**Table 12.3** Three phases of theorizing European integration

| Phase | Type | Place | Dynamic | Institutions |
|---|---|---|---|---|
| | *Normative pretheorizing* | World politics | | Hard |
| **1960–1985** | *Integration (more/less)* | Supranational level | *bottom-up* | Hard |
| **1985–** | *Europeanization (more/less)* | Domestic, regional level in member and candidate countries | *top-down* | Hard |
| **1993–** | *Politicization (more/less)* | Euro-polity | *trickle-across, bottom-up, top-down* | Hard/soft |

beyond the erstwhile considerably radical challenges of political relations beyond nation state boundaries, presented by the practice of pooling sovereignty as well as by the legal principles of supremacy and direct effect—and their potentially unintended consequences that have sunk in with social scientists only gradually (Craig and de Búrca 1998; see also Haltern in this volume).

A closer look at the governance approach, the policy network approach, and neo-institutionalism in Part II—Analysing European Governance demonstrates that they do take integration and the EU as a new kind of polity as a given, and therefore shift the emphasis from explaining or advocating integration to questions about how governance within this new polity works. Yet, it also emerges from these chapters that none of these approaches is content with the provision of new conceptualizations of governance alone, although this was an important contribution to the debate. Instead, they strive to explain specific phenomena within this system of governance, such as particular policies or particular aspects of its politics. While they are, in this sense, analysing governance rather than explaining integration as such, they are moving beyond the analysis of governance in the sense of a purpose of theory as set out in chapter 1.

As Table 12.2 highlights, the predominant purpose of theoretical approaches within European integration theory is to explain or understand either the process of integration and its outcomes, or particular aspects of European integration and governance. Even an approach such as discourse analysis, the roots of which can be traced to post-structuralism, is used at least by some in European integration theory to understand member states' policies towards integration, and although its usage of the term explanation is different from the usage, say, in liberal intergovernmentalism, the purpose is sufficiently similar to the latter's—indeed, Wæver (1998: 103–4) in his own work sets out explicitly to bridge the gap between critique and explanation. This heavy bias towards explanation may be seen as one symptom of the tendency to make claims beyond the scope of one's theory, which we have identified as problematic in our introduction. Be this as it may, the emphasis on the explanation of particular integration policies and outcomes in terms of polity has until recently led to a relative neglect of addressing the issue of politicization, both in the form of attempts to analyse the increasing politicization of integration and governance among societies, and in the form of contributing to a critical debate about the desired shape of the EU.

## Outlook: towards the politicization of European integration

How do integration theories fare fifty years on? What is the state of the discipline which has now developed an impressive corpus of texts, produced a stable research context based on international learned associations, and has, last not least, generated a widely acknowledged teaching profile? The discipline now encompasses a broad spectrum of theoretical approaches ranging from the period of normative preintegration theorizing that emerged largely from US-American IR theory (see, most prominently, Mitrany's as well as Deutsch's work) via grand theory debates (Hoffmann; Haas; Schmitter; Deutsch; Lindberg and Scheingold) to a more refined set of approaches in the early twenty-first century. This volume presents a selection of its core approaches. The overview of the past, present, and future of theorizing about European integration suggests that as an increasingly independent subfield in the social sciences, integration theory has come full circle *and* been able to move towards the proverbial higher plane. The following elaborates on this observation.

Given that in the early days of integration theory normative issues of integration were discussed within the framework of international relations theory, bringing in interest-oriented and institutional approaches to world politics, it appears that in the light of today's clearly discernable and distinguished, albeit interdisciplinary European studies discipline, theoretical approaches to integration have moved on. More specifically, the normative dimension of European integration is back on the table. However, the focus has changed. While in the 1950s the theoretical emphasis on explaining regional integration and supranational institution-building was put on the necessity and probability of enduring institutions in the international system of sovereign states with a view to constructing a civilised Kantian world community, today's normative approach is focused on the issue of democratic legitimacy (or the lack of it) under conditions of supranational constitutional integration. This shift from the former normative perspective on world politics that built on the idealist Grotian tradition in IR, to conditions of democratic governance in regionally integrated political orders, is embedded in a broad change in IR theories regarding the acceptance of institutions in world politics. Thus, institutional approaches developed both inside and outside European integration theories have contributed to a widely accepted role of—hard—institutions such as international organizations, treaties, conventions, and written agreements in world politics (March and Olsen 1989, 1998; Hall and Taylor 1996; Ruggie 1998; Onuf 2002). In particular, the various neo-institutionalisms have been able to sustain the role of institutions in world politics as enhancing cooperation among states, monitoring policy implementation, facilitating information, and safe-guarding norms (Keohane 1988; Garrett 1992; Goldstein and Keohane 1993; Pollack 1996; see also Pollack and Risse in this volume).

With its explicit focus on finality, community, and a constitutionalized polity, the dual process of enlargement and constitution-building presents a challenge to the majority of integration theories that study interests and institutions. The limit of such an exclusive focus compared with approaches that allow for a broader perspective on polity formation, governance, and constitutional principles is thus brought to the fore. This challenge is well presented by the choice of 'best' and 'test cases' by the contribu-tors of this volume, and the fact that far more contributors chose to focus on the effects of enlargement than on its explanation, while explanation dominated in the selection of 'best cases'. Surely, interests and institutions play a key role in explaining enlarge-ment. The pressure for institutional change which has been created by the massive enlargement process launched in Copenhagen 1993, affects member states and candi-date countries as well as the Europolity itself. Problematizing both institutional change and adaptation, on the one hand, as well as the interest in enlargement, on the other, can therefore be characterized as organic research objectives. Logically, they build on a long-standing tradition of explaining institution-building on the supranational level as well as institutional adaptation, or, Europeanization in the respective domestic member state contexts. Yet, different from previous enlargement rounds, this time constitutional reform has developed a much stronger momentum than previous Treaty revisions at intergovernmental conferences (Christiansen and Jørgensen 1999; Moravcsik and Nicolaïdes 1999; Falkner and Nentwich 2000; Wiener and Neunreither 2000; de Búrca and Scott 2002; Beaumont, Lyons, and Walker 2002; Bogdandy 2003; Weiler and Wind 2003).

Constitutional politics has therefore turned into a core political issue in the EU. More specifically, in distinction from states that cooperate under anarchy in world politics, on the one hand, and EU member states that have been cooperating towards integration, on the other (Wiener 2002), the current EU member states and, albeit to a limited extent, candidate countries have been cooperating towards a shared constitu-tional agreement. The constitutional turn has generated a new importance of constitu-tional norms, principles, and routinized practices. These so-called soft institutions have been addressed by a large and growing literature on constructivism in IR, that studied the influence of world views, principled beliefs, routinized practices, and norms to the fore (Kratochwil and Ruggie 1986; Koslowski and Kratochwil 1994; Ruggie 1998; Risse-Kappen 1996; Sikkink 1993; Katzenstein 1993, 1996). In European integration studies, the constructivist focus on soft institutions has offered a new inter-disciplinary perspective on European integration as a process that involves the consti-tutionalization of shared European norms, principles, and procedures including both law and the social sciences.

In sum, the constitutional turn in the 1990s raises deeper questions about the constitutive role of *social practices* and *(social) legitimacy* in supranational politics more generally. The EU is not a state yet evolves around and works on the basis of core constitutional norms, principles, and procedures akin to the central constitutional reference frame of national states such as the rule of law, fundamental and citizenship rights, and the principle of democracy (Art. 6, TEU) and some thus endorse the concept of European constitutional law.[6] These fundamental—constitutional—principles have evolved over time in interrelation with the fundamental constitutional principles and practices of the respective EU member states.[7] Their substance carries meaning created through a process from which candidate countries are by definition excluded. The routinized practices, procedures, and norms that have been constitutive for the constitutionalization of these fundamental principles therefore remain a foreign discourse with little meaning for candidate countries that were excluded from their constitution.[8] Politically speaking, different understandings generate issues of conflict. As a research theme, conflictive developments that are brought to the fore by the double process of enlargement and constitutional revision, raise different types of research questions, pending on the perspective, goal, and context from which the issue is assessed. Thus, for example, from a prescriptive analytical standpoint certain institutional conditions are necessary (types of constitution; political order; types of democracy; etc.). In turn, a normative analytical standpoint would focus on the question of whether it is possible, and if so, how to establish particular constitutional principles to keep such a diverse polity with its different understandings together.

## Conclusion

This volume's contributions have demonstrated that theorizing European integration involves at least *three main factors*. They include the choice of the *research object* (polity: supranational institution-building; policy: specific EU policies or member states' policies towards integration; politics: quality of integration), the analytical *research purpose* (explanatory/understanding; descriptive/analytical; normative/critical), and the *context* in which the research project has been designed (historical and disciplinary perspectives). The choice of research object and purpose does matter. It generates a distinct theoretical focus and impact which is highlighted by the book's organizational pattern presenting at least three core theoretical perspectives in three different phases of European integration. These phases are distinguished according to the respective analytical focus on explaining integration (Part I), analysing governance (Part II), and constructing the Europolity (Part III). In order to substantiate the main message of each approach, the contributors have been asked to choose a 'best case' scenario (quality of governance; market consolidation; labour market policy; human rights policy; committee governance; agricultural policy; constitutional policy and so forth) and then, in addition, apply their respective analytical perspective to the 'test case' scenario of enlargement.

The combination of best and test case scenarios in all contributions demonstrates nicely how research object and goal are subject to the choice of the individual researcher, yet, never under conditions of his or her own choosing. The clearly opposing views in each part sustain the point, including first, federalist, intergovernmentalist and neo-neofunctionalist views on how European integration is best explained; second institutionalist, network, and system-oriented approaches to analysing governance; and, third, social constructivist, gender-oriented and discursive perspectives on European integration. All offer telling cases for this understanding of context sensitive 'theorizing'.

While theoretical approaches do indeed raise general questions that are shared by a range of different approaches, for example the questions of how to explain institution-building above the state, how to account for governance as a process that develops across national boundaries, and how to assess the emergence of a socio-political system critically, their respective ways of addressing these questions are not necessarily *competitive*. They are first and foremost *complementary* in style.

These observations, above all, invite the student of European integration not to think in closed boxes and traditions, but creatively about theorizing European integration and governance, and not to dismiss other approaches all too easily. They also ask those engaged in this process of theorizing to perhaps be more humble than has been the case in the past, and to be aware of the scope of the approach proposed and its place in the overall mosaic of *European Integration Theory*. Finally, they propose to take a closer look at the issues involved in the linked processes of constitutionalization and politicization (see Table 12.3).

The mosaic of integration theory will never be finished. In order to keep providing fresh and relevant perspectives, however, it will have to be pushed forward by creativity, self-reflexivity, and the study of fundamental issues underlying the core debates of past, present, and future.

# Notes

1. See, for example, European Parliament, Committee of Institutional Affairs (2000), Report on the Constitutionalisation of the Treaties, Final A5–0289/2000, PE 286.949.

2. As Dieter Grimm notes '[W]hen a constitution for Europe is talked about today, what is meant is a basic legal order for the polity of the sort that arose at the end of the eighteenth century in the wake of two successful revolutions in America and in France . . .' (Grimm 1995: 284). For the discussion of the term see an overview with Schepel 2000, and an extensive discussion with Craig 2001.

3. However, the European constitutional debate is characterized by the absence of a shared constitutionalist approach. As Armin von Bogdandy notes '[T]he divergence in approach and even the lack in systematic approaches to European Union law render an assessment of key approaches, main directions, and plausible decisions in the constitutional debate, an enormously complex exercise' (Bogdandy 2000: 209). Indeed, to some it appears 'astonishing that so many scholars and politicians speak about the future constitution of Europe' (Zuleeg 2001: 1).

4. But see, for example, more analytical gender analysis by Elman 1996; Pollack and Hafner-Burton 2000; Liebert 1999; 2002; Locher 2002; Wobbe 2003; and Marx Ferree (forthcoming).

5. See the draft text of the Treaty that is to establish a 'Constitution' of the EU, and which was adopted by members of the *Convention on the Future of Europe*, Brussels, 13 June 2003. For the text see: Draft Convention Volume I including Part I and Part II (CONV 797/1/03) and Volume II including Parts III, IV, and V (CONV 805/03).

6. The existence of European constitutional law is usually derived from the constitutionalization of the Treaties going back to the process of 'integration through law', see also chapter 9

in this volume; for a few contributions to the burgeoning literature on the subject, see e.g. Pernice 1999; Bogdandy 1999; Weiler 1999; Craig 2000; Walker 2002; Beaumont, Lynn and Walker 2002; Bogdandy 2003; Stone Sweet 2002.

7. This interrelation between European and member state constitutional norms, values, and understandings is well encapsulated by the concept of 'multi-level constitutionalism' developed by Ingolf Pernice; see for details, Pernice 1999: 707–9.

8. In the legal literature the term 'constitutionalization' is applied with reference to the growing body of legal rules and procedures included in constitutional documents (Craig 2001; Schepel 2000).

# Bibliography

ABROMEIT, H. (1998), *Democracy in Europe. How to Legitimize Politics in a Non-State Polity* (Oxford: Berghahn).

ACKERS, L. (1998), *Shifting Spaces—Women, Citizenship and Migration Within the European Union* (Bristol: Policy Press).

ADLER, E. (1997), 'Seizing the Middle Ground: Constructivism in World Politics' *European Journal of International Relations* 3(3), 319–63.

—— (2002), 'Constructivism in International Relations', in Carlsnaes, W. et al. (eds.), *Handbook of International Relations* (London: Sage).

—— and BARNETT, M. (eds.) (1998), *Security Communities* (Cambridge: Cambridge University Press).

ALKER, H. (1996), *Rediscoveries and Reformulations: Humanistic Methodologies for International Relations* (Cambridge: Cambridge University Press).

ALLEN, A. (1996), 'Foucault on Power—a Theory for Feminists?', in Hekman, S. (ed.), *Feminist Interpretations of Michel Foucault* (University Park, PA: Penn State University Press), 265.

ALLOTT, P. (1991), 'The European Community is not the True European Community' *Yale Law Journal* 100(8), 2485–500.

ALTER, K. (1996), 'The European Court's Political Power' *West European Politics* 19(3), 458–87.

—— (1998), 'Explaining National Court Acceptance of European Court Jurisprudence: A Critical Evaluation of Theories of Legal Integration', in Slaughter, A.M., Stone Sweet, A., and Weiler, J. (eds.), 227–52.

—— (2001), *Establishing the Supremacy of European Law: The Making of an International Rule of Law in Europe* (New York: Oxford University Press).

—— and MEUNIER-AITSAHALIA, S. (1994), 'Judicial Politics in the European Community: European Integration and the Pathbreaking Cassis de Dijon Decision' *Comparative Political Studies* 26, 535–61.

ANDERSEN, S.S. and ELIASSEN, K.A. (eds.) (2001), *Making Policy in Europe* (London and Thousand Oaks, CA: Sage).

ANDERSON, B. (1991), *Imagined Communities. Reflections on the Origin and Spread of Nationalism*, rev. edn. (London and New York: Verso).

ANSELL, C.K., PARSONS, C.A., et al. (1997), 'Dual Networks in European Regional Development Policy' *Journal of Common Market Studies* 35(3), 347–75.

—— and WEBER, S. (1999), 'Organizing International Politics: Sovereignty and Open Systems' *International Political Science Review* 20(1), 73–93.

APELDOORN, B. VAN (2002), *Transnational Capitalism and the Struggle over European Order* (London: Routledge).

—— et al. (2003), 'Theories of European Integration: a Critique' in Cafruny, A. and Ryner, M. (eds.), *A Ruined Fortress? Neoliberal Hegemony and Tranformation in Europe* (Lanham, MD: Rowman and Littlefield), 17–45.

ARMSTRONG, K. and BULMER, S. (1998), *The Governance of the Single European Market* (New York: Manchester University Press).

ARTHUR, W.B. (1994), *Increasing Returns and Path Dependence in the Economy* (Ann Arbor: University of Michigan Press).

ASPINWALL, M.D. and SCHNEIDER, G. (1999), 'Same Menu, Separate Tables: The

Institutionalist Turn in Political Science and the Study of European Integration' *European Journal of Political Research* 38(1), 1–36.

—— and SCHNEIDER, G. (eds.) (2001), *The Rules of Integration: Institutionalist Approaches to the Study of Europe* (New York: Manchester University Press).

ATKINSON, T. (2002), 'Reassessing the Fundamentals: Social Inclusion and the European Union' *Journal of Common Market Studies* 40(4), 625–43.

AZOULAY, L. (2002), 'The Judge and the Community's Administrative Governance', in Dehousse, R. (ed.), *Good Governance in Europe's Integrated Market* (Oxford and New York: Oxford University Press), 107–37.

BACHE, I. (1998), *The Politics of European Union Regional Policy* (Sheffield: Sheffield Academic Press).

—— and GEORGE, S. (2001), *Politics in the European Union* (Oxford: Oxford University Press).

BAKKER, I. (ed.) (1994), *The Strategic Silence —Gender and Economic Policy* (London: Zed Books).

BALASSA, B.A. (1962), *The Theory of Economic Integration* (London: Allen and Unwin).

BALDWIN, R., BERGLÖF, E., GIAVAZZI, F., and WIDGRÉN, M. (2001), *Nice Try: Should the Treaty of Nice be Ratified?*, Monitoring European Integration 11 (London: Centre for Economic Policy Research). Consulted on-line on 3 October 2002 at www.cepr.org/pubs/books/P140.asp.

—— FRANCOIS, J., and PORTES, R. (1997), 'The Costs and Benefits of Eastern Enlargement: the Impact on the EU and Central Europe' *Economic Policy* 24, 125–76.

BANCHOFF, T. (1999), 'German Identity and European Integration' *European Journal of International Relations* 5(3), 259–90.

—— and SMITH, M. (eds.) (1999), *Legitimacy and the European Union: The Contested Polity* (London: Routledge).

BANERJEE, S. (1997), 'The Cultural Logic of National Identity Formation: Contending Discourses in Late Colonial India', in Hudson, V.M. (ed.), *Culture and Foreign Policy* (Boulder, CO: Lynne Rienner), 27–44.

BAŃKOWSKI, Z. and CHRISTODOULIDIS, E. (1998), 'The European Union as an Essentially Contested Project' *European Law Journal* 4, 341–54.

BARNETT, M.A. and FINNEMORE, M. (1999), 'The Politics, Power and Pathologies of International Organizations' *International Organization* 53(4), 699–732.

BARTELSON, J. (1995), *A Genealogy of Sovereignty* (Cambridge: Cambridge University Press).

BAUER, M.W. (2002), 'Limitations to Agency Control in European Union Policy-making: the Commission and Poverty Programmes' *Journal of Common Market Studies* 40(3), 381–400.

BAUMAN, Z. (1995), *Life in Fragments. Essays in Postmodern Morality* (Oxford/ Cambridge: Blackwell).

BEAUMONT, P., LYONS, C., and WALKER, N. (2002), *Convergence and Divergence in European Public Law* (Oxford and Portland, OR: Hart Publishing).

BEETHAM, D. and LORD, C. (1998), *Legitimacy and the European Union* (London: Longman).

BEHNKE, A. (2000), 'Inscriptions of Imperial Order: NATOs Mediterrenean Initiative' *International Journal of Peace Research* 5(1), available online at www.gmu.edu/ academic/ijps/vol5_1/behnke.htm (15 Oct. 2003).

BELLAMY, R. and CASTIGLIONE, D. (eds.) (1996), *Constitutionalism in Transforma-*

*tion: European and Theoretical Perspectives* (Oxford: Blackwell).

BENZ, A. (2003), 'Compound Representation in EU Multi-Level Governance', in Kohler-Koch, B. (ed.), *Linking EU and National Governance* (Oxford: Oxford University Press; under review) (in press).

BERGER, P.L. and LUCKMANN, T. (1966), *The Social Construction of Reality: A Treatise in the Sociology of Knowledge* (New York: Doubleday).

BERGER, T.U. (1996), 'Norms, Identity and National Security in Germany and Japan', in Katzenstein, P.J. (ed.), *The Culture of National Security: Norms and Identity in World Politics* (New York: Colombia), 317–56.

BIERSTEKER, T.J. (2002), 'Targeting Terrorist Finances: the Newe Challenges of Financial Market Globalization', in Dunne, T. (ed.), *Worlds in Collision: Terror and the Future of Global Order* (Basingstoke and New York: Palgrave).

BOGDANDY, A. VON (1999), 'The Legal Case for Unity: The European Union as a Single Organization with a Single Legal System' *Common Market Law Review* 36, 887–910.

—— (2000), 'Information und Kommunikation in der Europäischen Union. föderale Strukturen in supranationalem Umfeld', in Hoffmann-Riem, W. and Schmidt-Aßmann, E. (eds.), *Verwaltungsrecht in der Informationsgesellschaft* (Baden-Baden: Nomos), 133–94.

—— (2000a), 'A Bird's Eye View on the Science of European Law: Structures, Debates and Development Prospects of Basic Research on the Law of the European Union in a German Perspective' *European Law Journal* 6(3), 208–38.

—— (2000b), 'The European Union as a Human Rights Organization? Human Rights and the Core of the European Union' *Common Market Law Review* 37, 1307–38.

—— (2003), 'Links Between National and Supra-National Institutions. A Legal View of a New Communicative Universe', in Kohler-Koch, B. (ed.), *Linking EU and National Governance* (Oxford: Oxford University Press; under review).

—— (ed.) (2003), *Europäisches Verfassungsrecht. Theoretische und dogmatische Grundzüge* (Heidelberg: Springer).

BOMBERG, E. (1998), 'Issue Networks and the Environment: Explaining European Union Environmental Policy', in Marsh, D. (ed.), *Comparing Policy Networks* (Buckingham: Open University Press), 167–84.

—— and PETERSON, J. (1998), 'European Union Decision-Making: the Role of Sub-National Authorities' *Political Studies* 46(2), 219–35.

—— and STUBB, A. (eds.) (2003), *The European Union: How Does it Work?* (Oxford and New York: Oxford University Press).

BORNSCHIER, V. (ed.) (2000), *State-building in Europe: The Revitalization of Western European Integration* (Cambridge: Cambridge University Press).

BÖRZEL, T.A. (1997), 'Zur (Ir-)Relevanz der "postmoderne" für die Integrationsforschung: Eine Replik auf Thomas Diez's Beitrag "Postmoderne und europäische Integration"' *Zeitschrift für internationale Beziehungen* 4(1), 125–37.

—— (2001), 'Non-compliance in the European Union: Pathology or Statistical Artefact?' *Journal of European Public Policy* 8(5), 803–24.

—— (2002), *States and Regions in Europe. Institutional Adaptation in Germany and Spain* (Cambridge: Cambridge University Press).

—— (2002), Die Wirkung internationaler Institutionen: Von der Normanerkennung zur Normeinhaltung, in Jachtenfuchs, M. and Knodt, M. (eds.), *Regieren in internationalen Institutionen. Festschrift für Beate Kohler-Koch* (Opladen: Leske and Budrich), 141–81.

—— and Risse, T. (2000), 'When Europe Hits Home: Europeanization and Domestic Change' *European Integration on-line Papers* 4(15): http://eiop.or.at/eiop/texte/2000–015a.htm.

Boym, S. (2000), 'Leningrad into St. Petersburg: The Dream of Europe at the Margins', in Stråth, B. (ed.), *Europe and the Other and Europe as the Other* (Bruxelles: P.I.E.-Peter Lang), 311–24.

Branch, A.P. and Øhrgaard, J.C. (1999), 'Trapped in the Supranational—Intergovernmental Dichotomy: A Response to Stone Sweet and Sandholtz' *Journal of European Public Policy* 6(1), 123–43.

Bräuninger, T. and König, T. (2001), 'Voting Power in the Post-Nice European Union, Department of Politics and Management', University of Konstanz, manuscript consulted on-line on 3 October 2002 at www.uni-konstanz.de/FuF/Verwiss/koenig/manuskript1.pdf.

Bretherton, C. and Sperling, L. (1996), 'Women's Networks and the European Union—Towards an Inclusive Approach?' *Journal of Common Market Studies* 34(4), 487–508.

Browning, C. and Joenniemi, P. (forthcoming), 'Contending Discourses of Marginality: The Case of Kaliningrad'.

Bruter, M. (forthcoming), 'Civic and Cultural Components of a European Identity. A Pilot Model of Measurement of Citizens Levels of European Identity', in Herrmann, R.K. et al. (eds.), *Identities in Europe and the Institutions of the European Union*.

Bueno de Mesquita, B. and Stokman, F.N. (eds.) (1994), *European Community Decision Making: Models, Applications and Comparisons* (New Haven and London: Yale University Press).

Bulmer, S. (1994), 'The Governance of the European Union: A New Institutionalist Approach' *Journal of Public Policy* 13(4), 351–80.

Búrca, G. de (1995), 'The Language of Rights and European Integration', in Shaw, J. and More, G., 29–54.

—— (2001), 'Introduction', in de Búrca, G. and Weiler, J., 1–8.

—— and Weiler, J. (eds.) (2001), *The European Court of Justice* (Oxford: Oxford University Press).

Burgess, J.P. (1997a), 'On the Necessity and the Impossibility of a European Cultural Identity', in Burgess (ed.), *Cultural Politics and Political Culture in Postmodern Europe* (Amsterdam, Atlanta, GA: Postmodern Studies), vol. 24, 19–39.

—— (ed.) (1997b), *Cultural Politics and Political Culture in Postmodern Europe* (Amsterdam, Atlanta, GA: Postmodern Studies), vol. 24.

—— (2000), 'The Securitization of Economic Identity: Reason and Culture in the European Monetary Union', in Burgess, J.P. and Tunander, O. (eds.), *European Security Identities: Contested Understandings of EU and NATO* (Oslo: PRIO Report 2/2000), 57–80.

—— (2000), *Federalism and European Union: The Building of Europe, 1950–2000* (London: Routledge).

—— (ed.) (2001), *Culture and Rationality: European Frameworks of Norwegian Identity* (Kristiansund: Norwegian Academic Press).

Burgess, M. (1989), *Federalism and European Union: Political Ideas, Influences and Strategies in the European Community, 1972–1987* (London: Routledge).

BURLEY, A. and MATTLI, W. (1993), 'Europe before the Court: A Political Theory of Legal Integration' *International Organization* 47(2), 41–76.

BUZAN, B., WÆVER, O., and DE WILDE, J. (1998), *Security: A New Framework of Analysis* (Boulder, CO: Lynne Rienner).

CAFRUNY, A. and RYNER, M. (eds.) (2003), *A Ruined Fortress? Neoliberal Hegemony and Transformation in Europe* (Lanham, MD: Rowman and Littlefield).

CAMPBELL, D. (1992), *Writing Security: United States Foreign Policy and Politics of Identity* (Manchester: Manchester University Press).

CAMPBELL, J., HOLLINGSWORTH, J.R., and LINDBERG, L. (1992), *The Governance of the American Economy* (New York and Cambridge: Cambridge University Press).

CAPORASO, J. (1998), 'Regional Integration Theory: Understanding Our Past and Anticipating Our Future', in Sandholtz, W. and Stone Sweet, A., 334–51.

—— (1999), 'Toward a Normal Science of Regional Integration' *Journal of European Public Policy* 6(1), 160–4.

—— and KEELER, J.T.S. (1995), 'The European Union and Regional Integration Theory', in Rhodes, C. (ed.), *The State of the European Union*, vol. 3 (Boulder, CO: Lynne Rienner), 29–62.

CAPPELLETTI, M., SECCOMBE, M., and WEILER, J. (eds.) (1986a), *Integration Through Law. Europe and the American Federal Experience. vol. I: Methods, Tools and Institutions, Book 1: A Political, Legal and Economic Overview* (Berlin and New York: Walter de Gruyter).

——, ——, and —— (eds.) (1986b), *Integration Through Law. Europe and the American Federal Experience. vol. I: Methods, Tools and Institutions, Book 2: Political Organs, Integration Techniques and Judicial Process* (Berlin and New York: Walter de Gruyter).

——, ——, and —— (eds.) (1986c), *Integration Through Law. Europe and the American Federal Experience. vol. I: Methods, Tools and Institutions, Book 3: Toward a European Identity* (Berlin and New York: Walter de Gruyter).

——, ——, and —— (1986d), 'Integration Through Law: Europe and the American Federal Experience. A General Introduction' in Cappelletti, M., Seccombe, M., and Weiler, J. (1986a), 3–68.

CARDOZO, R. (1987), 'The Project for a Political Community, 1952–54', in Pryce, R. (ed.), *The Dynamics of European Union* (London: Croom Helm), 49–77.

CARPENTER, D.P., ESTERLING, K.M., et al. (1998), 'The Strength of Ties in Lobbying Networks: Evidence from Health-Care Policies in the United States' *Journal of Theoretical Politics* 10(4), 417–44.

CASSIRER, E. (1953), *Philosophie der symbolischen Formen*, 3 vols., 2nd edn. (Darmstadt: Wissenschaftliche Buchgesellschaft).

CASTELLS, M. (1998), *End of Millennium* (Oxford and Malden, MA: Blackwell).

CEDERMAN, L.-E. (ed.) (2001), *Constructing Europe's Identities: The External Dimension* (Boulder, CO: Lynne Rienner).

CHECKEL, J.T. (2001), 'Constructing European Institutions', in Aspinwall, M. and Schneider, G. (eds.), *The Rules of Integration: The Institutionalist Approach to European Studies* (Manchester: Manchester University Press), 19–39.

CHECKEL, J. (2001), 'International Institutions and Socialization in the New Europe', paper presented at the IDNET Conference on International Institutions and Socialization in the New Europe, European University Institute, Florence, 18–19 May.

—— (2001a), 'Social Construction and Integration', in Christiansen, T., Jørgensen, K.E., and Wiener, A. (eds.), *The Social Construction of Europe* (London: Sage), 50–64.

—— (2001b), 'Why Comply? Constructivism, Social Norms, and the Study of International Institutions'. *International Organization*.

—— and MORAVCSIK, A. (2001), 'A Constructivist Research Program in EU Studies?' *European Union Politics* 2(2), 219–49.

CHILTON, P. (1996), *Security Metaphors: Cold War Discourse from Containment to Common House* (Berne and New York: Peter Lang Publishing).

—— and ILLYIN, M. (1993), 'Metaphor in Political Discourse: the Case of the "Common European House"', *Discourse and Society* 4(1), 7–31.

CHRISTIANSEN, T. (2001), 'Introduction', in Christiansen, T. et al. (eds.), *The Social Construction of Europe* (London: Sage), 1–19.

—— and JØRGENSEN, K.E. (1999), 'The Amsterdam Process: A Structurationist Perspective on EU Treaty Reform' *European Integration Online Papers* 3, 23.

—— and KIRCHNER, E. (eds.) (2000), *Administering the 'New Europe'. Committees in the European Union* (Manchester: Manchester University Press).

——, JØRGENSEN, K.E. and WIENER, A. (eds.) (1999), 'The Social Construction of Europe' *Journal of European Public Policy* 6(4).

CHOULIARAKI, L. and FAIRCLOUGH, N. (1999), *Discourse in Late Modernity: Rethinking Critical Discourse Analysis* (Edinburgh: Edinburgh University Press).

CITRIN, J. and SIDES, J. (forthcoming), 'Is it the Nation, Europe, or the Nation and Europe? Trends in Political Identities at Century's End', in Herrmann, R.K. et al. (eds.), *Identities in Europe and the Institutions of the European Union* (Lanham, MD: Rowman and Littlefield).

COCKBURN, C. (1998), *The Space Between Us: Negotiating Gender and National Identities in Conflict* (London: Zed Books).

COLEMAN, W.D. (2001), 'Policy Networks, Non-State Actors and Internationalized Policy-Making: A Case Study of Agricultural Trade', in Wallace, W. (ed.), *Non-State Actors in World Politics* (Basingstoke and New York: Palgrave), 93–112.

—— and PERL, A. (1999), 'Internationalized Policy Environments and Policy Network Analysis' *Political Studies* 47(4), 691–709.

COLLINS, R. and SKOVER, D. (1996), *The Death of Discourse* (Boulder, CO: Westview Press).

CONROY, P. (1997), 'Ten Questions on Economic and Monetary Union', Paper to ETUC Conference on Building the Equality Dimension to EMU and the IGC. Lisbon, February 1997.

COOTER, R.D. and GINSBURG, T. (1996), 'Comparative Judicial Discretion' *International Review of Law and Economics* 16(3), 295–313.

COPPEL, J. and O'NEILL, A. (1992), 'The European Court of Justice: Taking Rights Seriously?' *Common Market Law Review* 29(4), 669–92.

COSS, S. (2002), 'Knight of the Realms: Albert Bore' *European Voice* 10.

COUDENHOVE-KALERGI, R.G. (1971), *Weltmacht Europa* (Stuttgart: Seewald).

COWLES, M.G., CAPORASO, J., and RISSE, T. (eds.) (2001), *Transforming Europe: Europeanization and Domestic Change* (Ithaca, NY: Cornell University Press).

CRAIG, P. (2001), 'Constitutions, Constitutionalism, and the European Union' *European Law Journal* 7, 125–50.

—— and DE BÚRCA, G. (1998), *EU Law. Text, Cases, and Materials*, 2nd edn. (Oxford: Oxford University Press).

—— and —— (eds.) (1999), *The Evolution of EU Law* (Oxford: Oxford University Press).

CRAM, L. (2001), 'Governance "to Go": Domestic Actors, Institutions and the Boundaries of the Possible' *Journal of Common Market Studies* 39(4), 595–618.

CROMBEZ, C. (1997), 'The Co-Decision Procedure in the European Union' *Legislative Studies Quarterly* 22(1), 97–119.

DAHL, R.A. (1989), *Democracy and Its Critics* (New Haven, CT: Yale University Press).

DAUGBJERG, C. (1999), 'Reforming the CAP: Policy Networks and Broader Institutional Structures' *Journal of Common Market Studies* 37(3), 407–28.

—— and MARSH, D. (1998), 'Explaining Policy Outcomes: Integrating the Policy Network Approach with Macro-Level and Micro-Level Analysis', in Marsh, D. (ed.), *Comparing Policy Networks* (Buckingham: Open University Press).

DAVID, P. (1985), 'Clio and the Economics of QWERTY' *American Economic Review* 75(2), 332–7.

DAVIS, S.R. (1978), *The Federal Principle: A Journey Through Time in Quest of a Meaning* (London: University of California Press).

DEHOUSSE, R. (1997), 'Regulation by Networks in the European Community: the Role of European Agencies' *Journal of European Public Policy* 4(2), 246–61.

—— (2002), 'Misfits: EU Law and the Evolution of European Governance', in Dehousse, R. (ed.), *Good Governance in Europe's Integrated Market* (Oxford and New York: Oxford University Press), 207–30.

DELANTY, G. (1995a), *Inventing Europe: Idea, Identity, Reality* (London: Macmillan).

—— (1995b), 'The Limits and Possibility of a European Identity: A Critique of Cultural Essentialism' *Philosophy and Social Criticism* 21(4), 15–36.

—— (1998), 'Social Theory and European Transformation: Is there a European Society?' *Sociological Research Online* 3(1) www.socresonline.org.uk/socresonline/3/1/1.html.

DELGADO MOREIRA, J.M. (2000), 'Cohesion and Citizenship in EU Cultural Policy' *Journal of Common Market Studies* 38(3), 449–70.

DEN BOER, P., BUGGE, P., and WÆVER, O. (1995 [1993]), *The History of the Idea of Europe* (London: Rouledge; originally: Open University Press 1993).

DEPPE, F. (ed.) (1976), *Arbeiterbewegung und westeuropäische Integration* (Cologne: Pahl-Rugenstein).

——, FELDER, M., and TIDOW, S. (2003), 'Structuring the State—The Case of European Employment Policy', in Kohler-Koch, B. (ed.), *Linking EU and National Governance* (Oxford: Oxford University Press; under review).

DERRIDA, J. (1974 [1967]), *Of Grammatology* (Baltimore, MD: Johns Hopkins University Press).

—— (1978 [1967]), 'Structure, Sign and Play in the Discourses of the Human Sciences', in *Writing and Difference* (London: Routledge and Kegan Paul), 278–93.

—— (1992 [1991]), *The Other Heading: Reflections on Today's Europe* (Bloomington, IN: Indiana University Press).

DEUTSCH, K.W., et al. (1957), *Political Community and the North Atlantic Area: International Organization in the Light of Historical Experience* (Princeton, NJ: Princeton University Press).

DEUTSCH, K.W., et al. (1967), *France, Germany and the Western Alliance: A Study of Elite*

*Attitudes on European Integration and World Politics* (New York: Scribner's Sons).

DEWANDRE, N. and LENOBLE, J. (eds.) (1992), *L'Europe au soir du siècle: identité et démocratie* (Paris: Editions Esprit).

DICEY, A.V. (1915), *Introduction to the Study of the Law of the Constitution* (London: Macmillan).

DIEZ, T. (1995), *Neues Europa, altes Modell: Die Konstruktion von Staatlishckeit im politischen Diskurs zur Zukunft der europäischen Gemeinshaft* (Frankfurt/M: Haag+Herchen).

—— (1996), 'Postmoderne und europäische Integration: Die Dominanz des Staatsmodells, die Verantwortung gegenüber dem Anderen und die Konstruktion eines alternativen Horizonts' *Zeitschrift für internationale Beziehungen* 3(2), 255–81.

—— (1997), 'International Ethics and European Integration: Federal State or Network Horizon' *Alternatives* 22(3), 287–312.

—— (1998), 'Perspektivenwechsel. Warum ein "postmoderner" Ansatz für die Integrationsforschung doch relevant ist' *Zeitschrift für internationale Beziehungen* 5(1), 139–48.

—— (1999a), 'Speaking "Europe": the politics of integration discourse' *Journal of European Public Policy* 6(4), 598–613.

—— (1999b), *Die EU lesen: Diskursive Knotenpunkte in der britischen Europadebatte* (Opladen: Leske und Budrich).

—— (1999), 'Riding the AM-Track through Europe. Or: The Pitfalls of a Rationalist Journey through European Integration' *Millennium: Journal of International Studies* 28(2), 355–69.

—— (2001), 'Europe as a Discursive Battleground: Discourse Analysis and European Integration Studies' *Cooperation and Conflict* 36(1), 5–38.

DOGAN, R. (2000), 'A Cross-sectoral View of Comitology: Incidence, Issues and Implications', in Christiansen, T. and Kirchner, E. (eds.), *Committee Governance in the European Union* (New York: St. Martin's Press), 45–61.

DOWDING, K. (1995), 'Model or metaphor? A Critical Review of the Policy Network Approach' *Political Studies* 43(1), 136–58.

—— (2000), 'Institutionalist Research on the European Union: A Critical Review' *European Union Politics* 1(1), 125–44.

—— (2001), 'There must be an End to Confusion: Policy Networks, Intellectual Fatigue, and the Need for Political Science Methods Courses in British Universities' *Political Studies* 49(1), 89–105.

DREYFUS, H.L. and RABINOW, P. (1982), *Michel Foucault: Beyond Structuralism and Hermeneutics* (New York: Harvester Wheatsheaf).

DUCHESNE, S. and FROGNIER, A.-P. (1995), 'Is There a European Identity?', in Niedermayer, O. and Sinnott, R. (eds.), *Public Opinion and Internationalized Governance* (Oxford: Oxford University Press), 194–226.

DUNN, J.A. and PERL, A. (1994), 'Policy Networks and Industrial Revitalization: High Speed Rail Initiatives in France and Germany' *Journal of Public Policy* 14(3), 311–43.

EDER, K. (2003), 'Öffentlichkeit und Demokratie', in Jachtenfuchs, M. and Kohler-Koch, B. (eds.), *Europäische Integration*, 2nd edn. (Opladen: Leske und Budrich), 85–120.

—— and GIESEN, B. (eds.) (1999), *European Citizenship and the National Legacies* (Oxford: Oxford University Press).

EISENSTADT, S.N. and GIESEN, B. (1995), 'The Construction of Collective Identity' *European Journal of Sociology* 36, 72–102.

EISING, R. (2003), 'Europäisierung und Integration. Konzepte in der EU-Forschung', in Jachtenfuchs, M. and Kohler-Koch, B. (eds.), *Europäische Integration*, 2nd edn. (Opladen: Leske und Budrich), 379–426.

—— and KOHLER-KOCH B. (1999), 'Introduction: Network Governance in the European Union', in Eising, R. (ed.), *The Transformation of Governance in the European Union* (London: Routledge), 1–29.

EL-AGRAA, A.M. (1982), 'The theory of economic integration', in El-Agraa, A.M. (ed.), *International Economic Integration* (Basingstoke: Macmillan), 10–27.

ELAZAR, D.J. (1987), *Exploring Federalism* (Tuscaloosa, AL: University of Alabama Press).

ELMAN, R.A. (ed.) (1996), *Sexual Politics and the European Union: The Feminist Challenge* (Oxford: Berghahn).

ELSTER, J. (1989), *Nuts and Bolts for the Social Sciences* (Cambridge: Cambridge University Press).

ENLOE, C. (1989), *Making Feminist Sense of International Politics: Bananas, Beaches, Bases* (London: Pandora Press).

EPSTEIN, D. and O'HALLORAN, S. (1999), *Delegating Powers: A Transaction Cost Politics Approach to Policy Making under Separate Powers* (New York: Cambridge University Press).

EPSTEIN, R. (2001), 'The EU, EBRD, and NATO: Persuasion, Coercion, and De-politization in Post-Communist Poland' paper presented in the framework of the 2001–2002 European Forum, 'Europe in the World: The External Dimensions of Europeanization', Robert Schuman Centre for Advanced Studies, European University Institute, 6 December.

ERIKSEN, E.O. and FOSSUM, J.E. (eds.) (2000), *Democracy in the European Union: Integration through Deliberation?* (London: Routledge).

ETZIONI, A. (1965), *Political Unification: A Comparative Study of Leaders and Forces* (New York: Holt, Rinehart and Winston).

EUROPEAN COMMISSION (1992), *Europe and the Challenge of Enlargement* (Agence Europe, Europe Documents 1790).

—— (1992), 'The Principle of Subsidiarity', SEC(92)1990 final, 27 October 1992.

—— (2000), The Commission and Non-Governmental Organisations. Building a Stronger Partnership, Discussion Paper, Brussels, 17/03/2000.

—— (2001), *European Governance. A White Paper*, COM(2001)428 final, Brussels, 25 July 2001.

EUROPEAN WOMEN'S LOBBY (2002), 'Convention on the Future of Europe: Where are the Women?' Press release, 26 February 2002.

EVERSON, M. (1995), 'The Legacy of the Market Citizen', in Shaw, J. and More, G. (eds.), *New Legal Dynamics of the European Union*, 73–89.

—— (1998), 'Beyond the Bundesverfassungsgericht: On the Necessary Cunning of Constitutional Reasoning' *European Law Journal* 4(4), 389–410.

FAIRCLOUGH, N. (1992), *Discourse and Social Change* (Cambridge: Polity Press).

—— (1995), *Critical Discourse Analysis: The Critical Study of Language* (London: Longman).

FALKNER, G. (1999), 'European Social Policy: Towards Multi-Level and Multi-Actor Governance', in Eising, R., *The Transformation of Governance in the European Union* (London and New York: Routledge), 83–97.

—— (2000), 'Policy Networks in a Multi-Level System: Convergence Towards Moderate Diversity?' *West European Politics* 23(4), 94–120.

—— (2000), 'The Council or the Social Partners? EC Social Policy Between Diplomacy and Collective Bargaining' *Journal of European Public Policy* 7, 705–24.

—— et al. (2002), Interessendurchsetzung im Mehrebenensystem am Beispiel der EU-Sozialpolitik, conference paper, Mannheim, 4–5 July 2002.

—— and M. NENTWICH (2000), 'Enlarging the European Union: The Short-Term Success of Incrementalism and De-Politicisation', Cologne, Max-Planck-Institut für Gesellschaftsforschung, MPIfG Working Paper 00/4, July 2000.

FEARON, J.D. and WENDT, A. (2002), 'Rationalism and Constructivism in International Relations Theory', in Carlinaes, W., Risse, T., and Simmons, B.A. (eds.), *Handbook of International Relations* (London: Sage), 52–72.

FELSENTHAL, D. and MACHOVER, M. (2001), 'The Treaty of Nice and Qualified Majority Voting' London School of Economics, paper consulted on-line on 4 October 2002 at www.lse.ac.uk/Depts/cpnss/projects/VPPpdf/niceqmv.pdf.

FIERKE, K.M. and WIENER, A. (1999), 'Constructing Institutional Interests: EU and NATO Enlargement' *Journal of European Public Policy* 6(5), 721–42.

—— and —— (2001), 'Constructing Institutional Interests: EU and NATO Enlargement' in Christiansen, T., Jørgensen, K.E., and Wiener, A. (2001), 121–39.

FORSYTH, M. (1981), *Unions of States: The Theory and Practice of Confederation* (Leicester: Leicester University Press).

FOUCAULT, M. (1972 [1969?]), *The Archeology of Knowledge* (London: Pantheon).

—— (1991), 'Politics and the Study of Discourse', in Burchell, G. et al. (eds.), *The Foucault Effect. Studies in Govern-*

*mentality* (Hemel Hempstead: Harvester Wheatsheaf), 53–72.

FRANCHINO, F. (2000), 'Control of the Commission's Executive Functions: Uncertainty, Conflict and Decision Rules' *European Union Politics* 1(1), 63–92.

FRASER, N. (1995), 'What's Critical About Critical Theory?', in Meehan, J., *Feminists Read Habermas* (New York and London: Routledge), 21–55.

FRIEDRICH, C.J. (1969), *Europe. An Emergent Nation?* (New York: Harper and Row).

FRIIS, L. and MURPHY, A. (2000), in Kelstrup, M. and Williams, M.C. (eds.), *International Relations Theory and the Politics of European Integration. Power, Security and Community* (London: Routledge), 226–49.

FROWEIN, J., SCHULHOFER, S., and SHAPIRO, M. (1986), 'The Protection of Fundamental Human Rights as a Vehicle of Integration', in Cappelletti, M., Seccombe, M., and Weiler, J. (1986c), 231–344.

GAL, S. and KLIGMAN G. (2000), *The Politics of Gender After Socialism* (Princeton, NJ: Princeton University Press).

GARCÍA, S. (ed.) (1993), *European Identity and the Search for Legitimacy* (London: Pinter).

GARRETT, G. (1992), 'International Cooperation and Institutional Choice: The European Community's Internal Market' *International Organization* 46(2), 533–60.

—— (1995), 'The Politics of Legal Integration in the European Union' *International Organization* 49(1), 171–81.

—— and TSEBELIS, G. (1996), 'An Institutional Critique of Intergovernmentalism' *International Organization* 50(2), 269–99.

—— and WEINGAST, B. (1993), 'Ideas, Interests, and Institutions: Constructing the European Community's Internal Market' in Goldstein, J. and Keohane, R.

(eds.), *Ideas and Foreign Policy* (Ithaca, NY: Cornell University Press), 173–206.

——, KELEMEN, R.D., and SCHULZ, H. (1998), 'The European Court of Justice, National Governments, and Legal Integration in the European Union' *International Organization* 52(1), 149–76.

GALEOTTI, M. (2001), 'Non-State Actors in World Politics', in Wallace, W., *Non-State Actors in World Politics* (Basingstoke and New York: Palgrave).

GEERTZ, C. (1973), *The Interpretation of Cultures. Selected Essays* (New York: Basic Books).

GENSCHEL, P. (2002), *Steuerharmonisierung und Steuerwettbewerb in der Europäischen Union* (Frankfurt/M.: Campus).

GHECIU, A. (2002), 'Security Institutions as Agents of Socialization? NATO and Post-Cold War Central and Eastern Europe' Paper prepared for the ARENA/IDNET Third Project Workshop, European University Institute (22–23 February).

GIDDENS, A. (1982), 'Hermeneutics and Social Theory', in Giddens, A. (ed.), *Profiles and Critiques in Social Theory* (Berkeley, CA: University of California Press), 1–17.

—— (1984), *The Constitution of Society: Outline of a Theory of Structuration* (Cambridge: Polity).

GIESEN, B. (1993), *Die Intellektuellen und die Nation. Eine deutsche Achsenzeit* (Frankfurt/M.: Suhrkamp).

—— (1999), *Kollektive Identität. Die Intellektuellen und die Nation 2* (Frankfurt/M.: Suhrkamp).

GLARBO, K. (2001), 'Reconstructing a Common European Foreign Policy', in Christiansen, T. et al. (eds.), *The Social Construction of Europe* (London: Sage), 140–57.

GOETZ, K.H. (2001), 'European Integration and National Executives. A Cause in Search of an Effect', in Goetz, K.H. and Hix, S. (eds.), *Europeanised Politics. European Integration and National Political Systems* (London: Frank Cass), 211–31.

—— and HIX, S. (eds.) (2000), *Europeanised Politics? European Integration and National Political Systems. Special Issue of 'West European Politics'* 4th edn. vol. 23 (Ilford: Frank Cass).

GOLDSTEIN, J. and KEOHANE, R.O. (1993), 'Ideas and Foreign Policy: An Analytical Framework', in Goldstein, J. and Keohane, R.O. (eds.), *Ideas and Foreign Policy: Beliefs, Institutions, and Political Change* (Ithaca, NY: Cornell University Press), 3–30.

GOLUB, J. (1996), 'The Politics of Judicial Discretion: Rethinking the Interaction between National Courts and the European Court of Justice' *West European Politics* 19, 360–85.

GRABBE, H. and HUGHES, K. (1998), *Enlarging the EU Eastwards* (London: Pinter).

GRANDE, E. (1996), 'The State and Interest Groups in a Framework of Multi-Level Decision-Making. The Case of the European Union' *Journal of European Public Policy* 3, 318–38.

GRANOVETTER, M.S. (1973), 'The Strength of Weak Ties' *American Journal of Sociology* 78(5), 1360–80.

GRANT, W. (1997), *The Common Agricultural Policy* (Basingstoke and New York: Palgrave).

GRIMM, D. (1995), 'Does Europe Need a Constitution?' *European Law Journal* 1, 282–302.

GSTÖHL, S. (2002), *Reluctant Europeans. Norway, Sweden, and Switzerland in the Process of European Integration* (Boulder, CO: Lynne Rienner).

HAAHR, J.H. (2003), '"Our Danish Democracy": Community, People and

Democracy in the Danish Debate on the Common Currency' *Cooperation and Conflict* 38(1), March, 27–47.

HAAS, E.B. (1958), *The Uniting of Europe: Political, Social, and Economic Forces 1950–57* (Stanford, CA: Stanford University Press).

—— (1961), 'International Integration: the European and the Universal Process' *International Organization* 15(3), 366–92.

—— (1964), 'Technocracy, Pluralism, and the New Europe', in Graubard, S.R. (ed.), *A New Europe?* (Boston: Hougton Mifflin), 62–88.

—— (1967), 'The "Uniting of Europe" and the "Uniting of Latin America"' *Journal of Common Market Studies* 5(2), 315–43.

—— (1968), 2nd edn., *The Uniting of Europe: Political, Social and Economic Forces 1950–1957* (Stanford, CA: Stanford University Press).

—— (1970), 'The Study of Regional Integration: Reflections on the Joy and Anguish of Pretheorizing' *International Organization* 24(4), 607–46.

—— (1975), *The Obsolescence of Regional Integration Theory* (Berkeley, CA: University of California, Institute of International Studies, Research Series, No. 25).

—— (2001), Does Constructivism Subsume Neofunctionalism?, in Christiansen, T. et al. (eds.), *The Social Construction of Europe* (London: Sage), 22–31.

—— and SCHMITTER, P.C. (1964), 'Economics and Differential Patterns of Political Integration: Projections About Unity in Latin America' *International Organization* 18(4), 705–37.

HAAS, P.M. (1992), 'Epistemic Communities and International Policy Coordination' *International Organization* 46(1), 1–35.

—— (1999), 'Compliance with EU Directives: Insights from International Relations and Comparative Politics'
*Journal of European Public Policy* 5(1), 17–37.

HABERMAS, J. (1981), *Theorie des kommunikativen Handelns*, 2 vols. (Frankfurt/M.: Suhrkamp).

—— (1992), *Faktizität und Geltung. Beiträge zur Diskurstheorie des Rechts und des demokratischen Rechtsstaats* (Frankfurt/M.: Suhrkamp).

—— (1992), 'Citizenship and National Identity: Some Reflections on the Future of Europe' *Praxis International* 12, 1–19.

—— (1994), 'Staatsbürgerschaft und nationale Identität', in Dewandre, N. and Lenoble, J. (eds.), *Projekt Europa. Postnationale Identität: Grundlage für eine europäische Demokratie* (Berlin: Schelzky und Jeep), 11–29.

—— (1996), 'Der europäische Nationalstaat—Zu Vergangenheit und Zukunft von Souveränität und Staatsbürgerschaft' in Habermas, J., *Die Einbeziehung des Anderen* (Frankfurt/M.: Suhrkamp), 154–84.

HAGEN, J. (1996), 'The Political Economy of Eastern Enlargement of the EU', in Ambrus-Lakatos, L. and Schaffer, M. (eds.), *Coming to Terms with Accession* (London: CEPR, Institute for East-West Studies), 1–41.

HALL, P.A. (1986), *Governing the Economy: The Politics of State Intervention in Britain and France* (New York: Oxford University Press).

—— and TAYLOR, R.C.R. (1996), 'Political Science and the Three New Institutionalisms' *Political Studies* 44(5), 936–57.

HALTERN, U. (2001), 'Europe Goes Camper. The EU Charter of Fundamental Rights From a Consumerist Perspective' *Constitutionalism Web-Papers, ConWEB No. 3/2001*, http://les1.man.ac.uk/conweb/.

—— (2003), 'Pathos and Patina: The Failure and Promise of Constitutionalism in the

European Imagination' *European Law Journal* 9(1), 14–44.

HANSEN, L. (1997), 'Nation Building on the Balkan Border' *Alternatives* 21, ss. 473–96.

—— (2001), 'Sustaining Sovereignty: the Danish approach to Europe', in Hansen, L. and Wæver, O. (eds.), *European Integration and National Identity: The Challenge of the Nordic States* (London: Routledge), 50–87.

—— (forthcoming), *Security as Practice: Discourse Analysis and the Bosnian War* (London: Routledge).

—— and WÆVER, O. (eds.) (2002), *European Integration and National Identity: The Challenge of the Nordic States* (London: Routledge).

—— and WILLIAMS, M.C. (1999), 'The Myths of Europe: Legitimacy, Community and the "Crisis" of the EU' *Journal of Common Market Studies* 37(2), 233–49.

HARDING, C. (2000), 'The Identity of European Law: Mapping Out the European Legal Space' *European Law Journal* 6(2), 128–47.

HARTLEY, T.C. (1999), *Constitutional Problems of the European Union* (Oxford: Hart Publishing).

HASSNER, P. (1997), 'The European Nation State versus Transnational Forces', in Tunander, O. et al. (eds.), *Geopolitics in Post-Wall Europe* (London: Sage), 45–58.

HAY, C. and ROSAMOND, B. (2002), 'Globalization, European integration and the discursive construction of economic imperatives' *Journal of European Public Policy* 9(2), 147–67.

HAY, D. (1968), *Europe. The Emergence of an Idea*, 2nd edn. (Edinburgh: Edinburgh University Press) (1st edn. 1957).

HAYES-RENSHAW, F., LEQUESNE C., and MAYOR LOPEZ, P. (1992), 'The Permanent Representations of the Member States to the European Communities' *Journal of Common Market Studies* 28(2), 119–37.

HECLO, H. (1978), 'Issue Networks and the Executive Establishment', in King, A., *The New American Political System* (Washington, DC: American Enterprise Institute), 87–124.

HÉRITIER, A. (1999), *Policy-Making and Diversity in Europe: Escape from Deadlock* (Cambridge and New York: Cambridge University Press).

—— (2001), 'Differential Europe. The European Union Impact on National Policymaking', in Héritier, A. et al., *Differential Europe. The European Union Impact on National Policymaking* (Lanham, MD: Rowman and Littlefield), 1–21.

—— (2002), 'New Modes of Governance in Europe. Policy-Making Without Legislating?', in Héritier, A. (ed.), *Common Goods. Reinventing European and International Governance* (Lanham, MD: Rowman and Littlefield), 185–206.

—— and KNILL, C. (2001), 'Differential Responses to European Policies. A Comparison', in Héritier, A. et al., *Differential Europe. The European Union Impact on National Policymaking* (Lanham, MD: Rowman and Littlefield), 257–94.

——, et al. (2001), *Differential Europe—New Opportunities and Restrictions for Policy Making in Member States* (Lanham, MD: Rowman and Littlefield).

HERRMANN, R.K. et al. (eds.) (forthcoming), *Identities in Europe and the Institutions of the European Union.*

HIX, S. (1994), 'The Study of the European Community: the Challenge to Comparative Politics' *West European Politics* 17(1), 1–30.

—— (1999), *The Political System of the European Union* (Basingstoke: Macmillan).

—— (2001), 'Legislative Behaviour and Party Competition in EP: An Application of Nominate to the EU' *Journal of Common Market Studies* 39(4), 663–88.

HIX, S. and LORD, C. (1997), *Political Parties in the European Union* (New York: St. Martin's).

HODSON, D. and MAHER, I. (2000), 'The Open Method as a New Mode of Governance. The Case of Soft Economic Policy Co-ordination' *Journal of Common Market Studies* 39, 719–46.

HOFFMAN, M. (1987), 'Critical Theory and the Inter-Paradigm Debate' *Millennium* 16(2), 231–49.

HOFFMANN, S. (1966), 'Obstinate or Obsolete? The Fate of the Nation-State and the Case of Western Europe' *Daedalus* 95, 862–915.

—— (1982), 'Reflections on the Nation-State in Western Europe Today' *Journal of Common Market Studies* 21(1)–(2), 21–37.

—— (1995), *The European Sisyphus. Essays on Europe, 1964–1994* (Boulder, CO: Westview Press).

HOLLAND, S. (1980), *UnCommon Market: Capital, Class and Power in the European Community* (London: Macmillan).

HOLLIS, M. and SMITH, S. (1990), *Explaining and Understanding International Relations* (Oxford: Clarendon).

HOLM, U. (1992), *Det Franske Europa* (Aarhus: Aarhus Universitetsforlag).

—— (1997), 'The French Garden is not what it used to be', in Jørgensen, K.-E. (ed.), *Reflective Approaches to European Governance* (London: Macmillan), 128–46.

HOOGHE, L. and MARKS, G. (2001), *Multi-Level Governance and European Integration* (Lanham, MD: Rowman and Littlefield).

HOSKYNS, C. (1985), 'Women's Equality and the European Community' *Feminist Review* 20, 71–88.

—— (1996), *Integrating Gender: Women, Law and Politics in the European Union* (London: Verso).

HOWE, P. (1995), 'A Community of Europeans: The Requisite Underpinnings' *Journal of Common Market Studies* 33(1), 27–46.

HOWSE, R. and NICOLAÏDIS, K. (2002), '"This is my Utopia": the EU, the WTO, Global Governance and Global Justice' *Journal of Common Market Studies* 40(4), forthcoming.

HRBEK, R. (1972), *Die SPD—Deutschland und Europa: Die Haltung der Sozialdemokratie zum Verhältnis von Deutschland-Politik und West-Integration* (Bonn: Europa Union).

HUBER, J. and SHIPAN, C. (2000), 'The Costs of Control: Legislators, Agencies, and Transaction Costs' *Legislative Studies Quarterly* 25(1), 25–52.

INSTITUT FÜR EUROPÄISCHE POLITIK AND TRANS EUROPEAN POLICY STUDIES ASSOCIATION (1998), *Enlargement/Agenda 2000—Watch. Pilot Issue* (www.tepsa.be).

IPSEN, H.P. (1972), *Europäisches Gemeinschaftsrecht* (Tübingen: J.C.B. Mohr).

JACHTENFUCHS, M. (1995), 'Theoretical Perspectives on European Governance' *European Law Journal* 1, 115–33.

—— (2001), 'The Governance Approach to European Integration' *Journal of Common Market Studies* 39(2), 245–64.

—— (2002), *Die Konstruktion Europas. Verfassungsideen und institutionelle Entwicklung* (Baden-Baden: Nomos).

—— and KOHLER-KOCH, B. (1996), 'Einleitung: Regieren im dynamischen Mehrebenensystem', in Jachtenfuchs, M. and Kohler-Koch, B. (eds.), *Europäische Integration* (Opladen: Leske und Budrich), 15–444.

——, DIEZ, T., and JUNG, S. (1998), 'Which Europe? Conflicting Models of a Legitimate European Political Order' *European Journal of International Relations* 4(4), 409–46.

JOERGES, C. (1996), 'Taking the Law Seriously: On Political Science and the Role of Law in the Process of European Integration' *European Law Journal* 2(2), 105–35.

—— (2002), '"Deliberative Supranationalism"—Two Defences' *European Law Journal* 8(1), 133–51.

—— (2002), 'The Law in the Process of Constitutionalizing Europe', EUI Working Paper LAW No. 2002/4.

—— (2002), 'The Law's Problems with the Governance of the European Market', in Joerges, C. and Dehousse, R. (eds.), *Good Governance in Europe's Integrated Market* (Oxford: Oxford University Press), 3–31.

—— and NEYER, J. (1997a), 'Transforming Strategic Interaction into Deliberative Problem–Solving: European Comitology in the Foodstuffs Sector' *Journal of European Public Policy* 4(4), 609–25.

—— and —— (1997b), 'From Intergovernmental Bargaining to Deliberative Political Process: The Constitutionalization of Comitology' *European Law Journal* 3(3), 273–99.

—— and VOS, E. (eds.) (1999), *EU Committees. Social Regulation, Law and Politics* (Oxford and Portland, OR: Hart).

JOHANSEN, A. (1997), 'Fellowmen, Compatriots, Contemporaries: On the Formation of Identity within the Expanding "Now" of Communication', in Burgess, J.P. (ed.), *Cultural Politics and Political Culture in Postmodern Europe* (Amsterdam and Atlanta, GA: Postmodern Studies), 24, 169–209.

JÖNSSON, C., et al. (2000), *Organizing European Space* (London: Sage).

JORDAN, G. (1981), 'Iron Triangles, Woolly Corporatism and Elastic Nets: Images of the Policy Process' *Journal of Public Policy* 1(1), 95–123.

—— and SCHUBERT, K. (1992), 'A Preliminary Ordering of Policy Network Labelling' *European Journal of Political Research* 21 (special issue), 7–28.

JØRGENSEN, K.E. (1997), 'PoCo: the Diplomatic Republic of Europe', in Jørgensen, K.E. (ed.), *Reflective Approaches to European Governance* (Basingstoke: Macmillan), 167–80.

—— (2000), 'Continental IR Theory: the Best Kept Secret' *European Journal of International Relations* 6(1), 9–42.

JOSSELIN, D. and WALLACE, W. (eds.) (2001), *Non-State Actors in World Politics*. (Basingstoke and New York: Palgrave).

JUNG, S. (1999), *Europa, made in France. Eine Analyse des politischen Diskurses Frankreichs zur Zukunft der Europäischen Gemeinschaft—von den Anfängen bis heute* (Baden-Baden: Nomos).

JUPILLE, J. and CAPORASO, J.A. (1999), 'Institutionalism and the European Union: Beyond International Relations and Comparative Politics' *Annual Review of Political Science* 2, 429–44.

——, ——, and CHECKEL, J. (2003), 'Integrating Institutions. Rationalism, Constructivism, and the Study of the European Union' *Comparative Political Studies* 36(1)–(2), 7–40.

KADAYIFEI, A. (1996), *Discourse Analysis and Conflict: Turkish Identity Creation* (Ph.D. University of Kent at Canterbury).

KADELBACH, S. (2003), 'Europäisches Bürgerrecht', in Bogdandy, A. von (ed.), *Europaeisches Verfassungsrecht: Theoretische und dogmatische Grundzuege* (Berlin: Springer), 539–82.

KAHN, P.W. (1997), *The Reign of Law. Marbury v. Madison and the Construction of America* (New Haven, CT and London: Yale University Press).

—— (1999), *The Cultural Study of Law. Reconstructing Legal Scholarship* (Chicago, IL and London: Chicago University Press).

—— (2003), *Multiculturalism. Putting Liberalism in Its Place* (manuscript, Yale).

KASSIM, H. (1993), 'Policy Networks, Networks and European Union Policy-Making: a Sceptical View' *West European Politics* 17(4), 15–27.

KATZENSTEIN, P. (1993), 'Coping with Terrorism: Norms and Internal Security in Germany and Japan', in Goldstein, J. and Keohane, R.O. (eds.), *Ideas & Foreign Policy. Beliefs, Institutions, and Political Change* (Ithaca, NY: Cornell University Press), 265–95.

—— (ed.) (1996), *The Culture of National Security* (New York: Columbia University Press).

KAZAN, I. (1994), *Omvendt Osmannisme og Khanaternes Kemalisme: Tyrkiets udenrigspolitik—en diskurs udfordret af EFs integration og Sovjetunionens opløsning*, Speciale, Institut for Statskundskab, Københavns Universitet.

KECK, M.E. and K. SIKKINK (1998), *Activists Beyond Borders: Advocacy Networks in International Politics* (Ithaca, NY and London: Cornell University Press).

KELSTRUP, M. (1998), 'Integration Theories: History, Competing Approaches and New Perspectives', in Wivel, A. (ed.), *Explaining European Integration* (Copenhagen: Copenhagen Political Studies Press), 15–55.

—— and WÆVER, O. (1993), 'Europe and its Nations', in Wæver, O. et al. (eds.), *Identity, Migration and the New Security Agenda in Europe* (London: Pinter).

—— and WILLIAMS, M.C. (eds.) (2000), *International Relations Theory and the Politics of European Integration: Power,*

*Security and Community* (London: Routledge).

KEOHANE, R. (1984), *After Hegemony. Cooperation and Discord in the World Political Economy* (Princeton, NJ: Princeton University Press).

—— (1988), 'International Institutions: Two Approaches' *International Studies Quarterly* 32, 379–96.

—— (2001), 'Governance in a Partly Globalized World' *American Political Science Review* 95, 1–13.

—— and HOFFMANN, S. (eds.) (1991), *The New European Community: Decision-making and Institutional Change* (Boulder, CO and Oxford: Westview).

—— and NYE, J. (1977), *Power and Interdependence. World Politics in Transition* (Boston: Little, Brown).

KIELMANSEGG, P.G. (1996), 'Integration und Demokratie', in Jachtenfuchs, M. and Kohler-Koch, B. (eds.), *Europäische Integration* (Opladen: Leske und Budrich), 47–71.

KILROY, B. (1999), *Integration Through Law: ECJ and Governments in the EU* (Ph.D. dissertation, UCLA).

KING, G., KEOHANE, R.O., and VERBA, S. (1994), *Designing Social Inquiry: Scientific Inference in Qualitative Research* (Princeton, NJ: Princeton University Press).

KISSINGER, H.A. (1957), *A World Restored: Castlereagh, Metternich and the Restoration of Peace, 1812–1822* (Boston: Houghton Mifflin).

KNILL, C. (2001), *The Europeanisation of National Administrations. Patterns of Institutional Change and Persistence* (Cambridge: Cambridge University Press).

KNOKE, D. (1998), 'Who Steals My Purse Steals My Trash: the Structure of Organizational Influence Reputation' *Journal of Theoretical Politics* 10(4), 507–30.

KOFMAN, E., PHIZACKLEA, A. et al. (2000), *Gender and International Migration in Europe* (London: Routledge).

KOHLER-KOCH, B. (1993), 'Die Welt regieren ohne Weltregierung', in Böhret, C. and Wewer, G. (eds.), *Regieren im 21. Jahrhundert. Zwischen Globalisierung und Regionalisierung. Festgabe für Hans-Hermann Hartwich zum 65. Geburtstag* (Opladen: Leske und Budrich), 109–41.

—— (2000), 'Framing: the Bottleneck of Constructing Legitimate Institutions' *Journal of European Public Policy* 7(4), 513–31.

—— (2001), 'On Networks, Travelling Ideas, and Behavioural Inertia', in Conzelmann, T. and Knodt, M. (eds.), *Regionales Europa—Europäisierte Regionen* (Frankfurt/M.: Campus Verlag), 87–103.

—— (2002), 'Linking EU and National Governance', paper presented at the ECPR Conference on European Union Politics, Bordeaux, 26–28 September 2002.

—— and EISING, R. (eds.) (1999), *The Transformation of Governance in the European Union* (London: Routledge).

KÖNIG, T. (1998), 'Introduction: Modeling Policy Networks' *Journal of Theoretical Politics* 10(4), 387–8.

KOOIMAN, J. (ed.) (1993), *Modern Governance. New Government-Society Interactions* (London: Sage).

KOREMENOS, B., LIPSON, C., and SNIDAL, D. (2001), 'The Rational Design of International Institutions' *International Organization* 55(4), 761–99.

KOSLOWSKI, R. (2001), 'Understanding the European Union as a Federal Polity', in Christiansen, T. et al. (eds.), *The Social Construction of Europe* (London: Sage), 32–49.

—— and KRATOCHWIL, F. (1994), 'Understanding Change in International Politics: The Soviet Empire's Demise and the International System' *International Organization* 48, 215–47.

KOSTAKOPOULOU, T. (1997), 'Why a "Community of Europeans" Could be a Community of Exclusion: A Reply to Howe' *Journal of Common Market Studies* 35(2), 301–14.

—— (2001), *Citizenship, Identity, and Immigration in the European Union: Between Past and Future* (Manchester: Manchester University Press).

KRASNER, S.D. (1983), 'Structural Causes and Regime Consequences. Regimes as Intervening Variables', in Krasner, S.D. (ed.), *International Regimes* (Ithaca, NY and London: Cornell University Press), 1–21.

KRATOCHWIL, F. (1989), *Rules, Norms, and Decisions* (Cambridge: Cambridge University Press).

—— and RUGGIE, J.G. (1986), 'International Organization: A State of the Art on an Art of the State' *International Organization* 40, 753–75.

KREHBIEL, K. (1991), *Information and Legislative Organization* (Ann Arbor, MI: University of Michigan Press).

KREPPEL, A. (1999), 'The European Parliament's Influence over EU Policy Outcomes' *Journal of Common Market Studies* 37(3), 521–38.

—— and TSEBELIS, G. (1999), 'Coalition Formation in the European Parliament' *Comparative Political Studies* 32(8), 933–66.

KRUGMAN, P. (1991), 'History and Industry Location: The Case of the Manufacturing Belt' *American Economic Review* 81(1), 80–3.

KUHN, T.S. (1964), *The Structure of Scientific Revolutions* (Chicago, IL: University of Chicago Press).

LACLAU, E. (1993), 'Discourse', in Gooding and Pettir (eds.), *The Blackwell Compan-*

*ion to Contemporary Philosophy* (Oxford: Blackwell), 431–37.

—— and MOUFFE, C. (1985), *Hegemony and Socialist Strategy: Towards a Radical Democratic Politics* (London: Verso).

LADEUR, K.-H. (1997), 'Towards a Legal Theory of Supranationality—the Viability of the Network Concept 1' *European Law Journal* 3(1), 33–54.

LAFFAN, B. (1996), 'The Politics of Identity and Political Order in Europe' *Journal of Common Market Studies* 34(1), 81–102.

—— (forthcoming), 'The European Union and its Institutions as "Identity Builders"', in Herrmann, R.K. et al. (eds.), *Identities in Europe and the Institutions of the European Union.*

—— et al. (2000), *Europe's Experimental Union. Rethinking Integration* (London: Routledge).

LARSEN, H. (1997a), *Foreign Policy and Discourse Analysis: France, Britain, and Europe* (London: Routledge).

—— (1997b), 'British Discourses on Europe: Sovereignty of Parliament, Instrumentality and the Non-Mythical Europe', in Jørgensen, K.-E. (ed.), *Reflective Approaches to European Governance* (London: Macmillan), 109–27.

—— (1999), 'British and Danish European Policies in the 1990s: A Discourse Approach' *European Journal of International Relations* 5(4), 451–83.

—— (2000), 'Danish CFSP Policy in the Post-Cold War Period: Continuity or Change' *Cooperation and Conflict* 35(1), 37–64.

LE GALÈS, P. and THATCHER, M. (eds.) (1995), *Les Reseaux de Politique Publique* (Paris: L'Harmattan).

LEGRO, J.W. and MORAVCSIK, A. (1999), 'Is Anybody Still a Realist?' *International Security* 24(2), 5–55.

LEHMBRUCH, G. (2000), *Parteienwettbewerb im Bundesstaat. Regelsysteme und Spannungslagen im Institutionengefüge der Bundesrepublik Deutschland*, 3rd edn. (Wiesbaden: Westdeutscher Verlag).

LEHNING, P.B. and WEALE, A. (eds.) (1997), *Citizenship, Democracy and Justice in the New Europe* (London and New York: Routledge).

LEIBFRIED, S. and PIERSON, P. (2000), 'Social Policy. Left to Courts and Markets?', in Wallace, H. and Wallace, W. (eds.), *Policy-Making in the European Union*, 4th edn. (Oxford: Oxford University Press), 267–92.

LEWIS, J. (1998), 'Is the "Hard Bargaining" Image of the Council Misleading? The Committee of Permanent Representatives and the Local Elections Directive' *Journal of Common Market Studies* 36(4), 479–504.

LIJPHART, A. (1979), 'Religious vs. Linguistic vs. Class Voting. The "Crucial Experiment" of Comparing Belgium, Canada, South Africa and Switzerland' *American Political Science Review* 73, 442–58.

LINDBERG, L.N. (1963), *The Political Dynamics of European Economic Integration* (Stanford, CA: Stanford University Press).

—— and SCHEINGOLD, S.A.(1970), *Europe's Would-Be Polity: Patterns of Change in the European Community* (Englewood-Cliffs, NJ: Prentice Hall).

—— and —— (1971), *Regional Integration: Theory and Research* (Cambridge, MA: Harvard University Press).

LOCHER, B. (2002), *Trafficking in Women in the European Union. A Norm-based Constructivist Approach* (University of Bremen, unpubl. Ph.D. dissertation).

LOVENDUSKI, J. (1981), 'Towards the Emasculation of Political Science—the Impact of Feminism', in Spender, D.

(ed.), *Mens' Studies Modified* (London: Pergamon), 83–97.

—— (1986), *Women and European Politics* (London: Wheatsheaf Books).

LOWI, T. (1964), 'American Business, Public Policy, Case Studies, and Political Theory' *World Politics* 16, 677–715.

LOWNDES, V. (1996), 'Varieties of New Institutionalism: a Critical Appraisal' *Public Administration* 74(2), 181–97.

LUCKHAUS, L. (1990), 'Changing Rules, Enduring Structures—Equal Treatment and Social Security' *Modern Law Review* 53(5).

LUHMANN, N. (1973), 'Politische Verfassungen im Kontext des Gesellschaftssystems' *Der Staat* 12, 1–22 and 165–82.

LÜTZ, S. (2002), *Der Staat und die Globalisierung von Finanzmärkten. Regulative Politik in Deutschland, Großbritannien und den USA* (Frankfurt/M.: Campus Verlag).

MACCORMICK, N. (1999), *Questioning Sovereignty. Law, State, and Nation in the European Commonwealth* (Oxford: Oxford University Press).

MCCUBBINS, M. and SCHWARTZ, T. (1987), 'Congressional Oversight Overlooked: Police Patrols versus Fire Alarms', in McCubbins, M. and Sullivan, T. (eds.), *Congress: Structure and Policy* (New York: Cambridge University Press), 426–40.

MCDONALD, M. (2000), 'Identities in the European Commission', in Nugent, N. (ed.), *At the Heart of the Union: Studies of the European Commission* (Basingstoke: Macmillan), 49–70.

MCGLYNN, C. (2000), 'Ideologies of Motherhood in European Community Sex Equality Law' *European Law Journal* 6(1), 29–44.

MCKELVEY, R. (1976), 'Intransitivities in Multidimensional Voting Models and Some Implications for Agenda Control' *Journal of Economic Theory* 12(4), 472–82.

MCNAMARA, K.R. (2002), 'Managing the Euro: the European Central Bank', in Shackleton, M. (ed.), *The Instiutions of the European Union* (Oxford: Oxford University Press), 164–85.

MACRAE, H. (2001), 'Engendering Europe: the What, Why and How of a Feminist Perspective on European Integration' (Paper presented at the ISA Convention 2001, Chicago, IL).

MADURO, M.P. (2002), 'Where To Look For Legitimacy?', paper presented at the Arena Annual Conference, Oslo.

MAIR, P. (2000), 'The Limited Impact of Europe on National Party Systems' *Western European Politics* 23(4), 27–51.

MAJONE, G. (1998), 'Europe's "Democracy Deficit": the Question of Standards' *European Law Journal* 4(1), 5–28.

—— (2001), 'Two Logics of Delegation: Agency and Fiduciary Relations in EU Governance' *European Union Politics* 2(1), 103–21.

—— (2002), 'Functional Interests—European Agencies', in Shackleton, M., Peterson, J. (eds.), *The Institutions of the European Union* (Oxford: Oxford University Press), 299–325.

MALMBERG, M. and STRÅTH, B. (eds.) (2002), *The Meaning of Europe* (Oxford: Berg).

MALMVIG, H. (2002), *Sovereignty Intervened: Constitutions of State Sovereignty during Interventionary and Non-Interventionary Practices in Kosovo and Algeria* (University of Copenhagen: unpubl. Ph.D. dissertation).

MANDEL, E. (1967), 'International Capitalism and "Supra-Nationality"' *Socialist Register*, 27–41.

MARCH, J.G. and OLSEN, J.P. (1984), 'The New Institutionalism: Organizational

Factors in Political Life' *American Political Science Review* 78(3), 734–49.

—— (1989), *Rediscovering Institutions: The Organizational Basis of Politics* (New York: Free Press).

—— (1998), 'The Institutional Dynamics of International Political Orders' *International Organization* 52, 943–69.

MARCUSSEN, M. (1999), 'The Dynamics of EMU Ideas' *Cooperation and Conflict* 34(4), 383–413.

MARCUSSEN, M. (2000), *Ideas and Elites. Danish Marco-Economic Policy Discourse in the EMU Process* (Aalborg: Aalborg University Press).

——, et al. (1999), 'Constructing Europe. The Evolution of French, British, and German Nation-State Identities' *Journal of European Public Policy* 6(4), 614–33.

MARKS, G. (1992), 'Structural Policy and Multi-level Governance in the EC', in Rosenthal, G.G. (ed.), *The State of the European Community II* (Boulder, CO and Ilford: Lynne Rienner and Longman), 390–410.

—— and McADAM, D. (1996), 'Social Movements and the Changing Structure of Political Opportunities in the EU', in Marks, G., Scharpf, F.W., Schmitter, P.C., and Streeck, W. (eds.), *Governance in the EU* (London: Sage), 95–120.

—— HOOGHE, L., and BLANK, K. (1996), 'European Integration from the 1980s: State-Centric v. Multi-level Governance' *Journal of Common Market Studies* 34(3), 341–78.

—— SCHARPF, F.W., SCHMITTER, P.C., and STREECK, W. (1996), *Governance in the European Union* (London: Sage).

MARSH, D. (ed.) (1998), *Comparing Policy Networks* (Buckingham: Open University Press).

—— and RHODES, R.A.W. (eds.) (1992), *Policy Networks in British Government* (Oxford: Clarendon Press).

—— and SMITH, M. (2000), 'Understanding Policy Networks: Towards a Dialectical Approach' *Political Studies* 48(1), 4–21.

—— and —— (2001), 'There is More than One Way to do Political Science: on Different Ways to Study Policy Networks' *Political Studies* 49(3), 528–41.

MARTINOTTI, G. and STEFFANIZZI, S. (1995), 'Europeans and the Nation-State', in Niedermayer, O. and Sinnott, R. (eds.), *Public Opinion and Internationalized Governance* (Oxford: Oxford University Press), 163–89.

MARX FERREE, M. (forthcoming), *Gender Politics in the European Union: Forging Transnational Feminism in the New Europe* (University of Wisconsin-Madison, Ms).

MATTLI, W. (1999), *The Logic of Regional Integration. Europe and Beyond* (Cambridge: Cambridge University Press).

—— and SLAUGHTER, A.-M. (1995), 'Law and Politics in the European Union: A Reply to Garrett' *International Organization* 49(1), 183–90.

—— and —— (1998), 'Revisiting the European Court of Justice' *International Organization* 52(1), 177–209.

—— and —— (1999), *The Logic of Regional Integration* (Cambridge: Cambridge University Press).

—— and —— (1998), 'The Role of National Courts in the Process of European Integration: Accounting for Judicial Preferences and Constraints', in Slaughter, A.-M., Stone Sweet, A., and Weiler, J. (eds.), 253–76.

MAURER, A., MITAG, J., and WESSELS, W. (2003), 'National Systems' Adaptation to the EU System. Trends, Offers and Constraints', in Kohler-Koch, B. (ed.), *Linking EU and National Governance* (Oxford: Oxford University Press; under review).

MAZEY, S. and RICHARDSON, J. (eds.) (1993), *Lobbying in the European Community*

(Oxford and New York: Oxford University Press).

MEARSHEIMER, J.J. (1990), 'Back to the Future: Instability in Europe after the Cold War' *International Security* 15(1), 5–56.

MEEHAN, E. (1993), *Citizenship and the European Community* (London: Sage).

MERLINGEN, M. (2001), 'Identity, Politics and Germany's Post-TEU Policy on EMU' *Journal of Common Market Studies* 39(3), 463–83.

METCALFE, L. (2000), 'Reforming the Commission: Will Organizational Efficiency Produce Effective Governance?' *Journal of Common Market Studies* 38(5), 817–41.

MILLIKEN, J. (1999), 'The Study of Discourse in International Relations: A Critique of Research and Methods' *European Journal of International Relations* 5(2), 225–54.

MILNER, H.V. (1998), 'Rationalizing Politics: The Emerging Synthesis of International, American, and Comparative Politics' *International Organization* 52(4), 759–86.

MILWARD, A.S. (1992), *The European Rescue of the Nation-State* (London: Routledge).

MITRANY, D. (1943), *A Working Peace System: An Argument for the Functional Development of International Organization* (London: Royal Institute of International Affairs).

—— (1966), 'The Prospect of Integration: Federal or Functional' *Journal of Common Market Studies* 4(2), 119–49.

MOE, T. (1984), 'The New Economics of Organization' *American Journal of Political Science* 28(4), 739–77.

MONNET, J. (1978), *Memoirs* (New York: Doubleday).

MORAVCSIK, A. (1991), 'Negotiating the Single European Act: National Interests and Conventional Statecraft in the European Community' *International Organization*, 45, 19–56.

—— (1993), 'Preferences and Power in the European Community: A Liberal Intergovernmentalist Approach' *Journal of Common Market Studies* 31, 473–524.

—— (1994), 'Why the European Community Strengthens the State: Domestic Politics and International Cooperation', Center for European Studies, Working Paper Series No. 52 (Harvard University).

—— (1997), 'Taking Preferences Seriously: A Liberal Theory of International Politics' *International Organization* 51(4), 513–53.

—— (1997), 'Warum die Europäische Union die Exekutive stärkt: Innenpolitik und internationale Kooperation', in Wolf, K. (ed.), *Projekt Europa im Übergang? Probleme, Modelle und Strategien des Regierens in der Europäischen Union* (Baden-Baden: Nomos), 211–69.

—— (1998), 'Federal Ideals and Constitutional Realities in the Treaty of Amsterdam' *Journal of Common Market Studies*, Annual Review, 36, 13–38.

—— (1998), *The Choice for Europe. Social Purpose and State Power From Messina to Maastricht* (Ithaca, NY: Cornell University Press).

—— (1999a), 'The Choice for Europe: Current Commentary and Future Research: A Response to James Caporaso, Fritz Scharpf, and Helen Wallace' *Journal of European Public Policy* 6(1), 168–79.

—— (1999b), 'A New Statecraft? Supranational Entrepreneurs and International Cooperation' *International Organization* 53(2), 267–306.

—— (1999c), 'The Future of European Integration Studies: Social Science or Social Theory' *Millennium: Journal of International Studies* 28(2), 371–91.

—— (2001), 'Federalism in the European Union: Rhetoric and Reality', in Nicolaidis, K. and Howse, R. (eds.), *The Federal Vision: Legitimacy and Levels of Governance in the United States and the European Union* (Oxford: Oxford University Press), 161–87.

—— (2001a), 'Bringing Constructivist Integration Theory Out of the Clouds: Has it Landed Yet?' *European Union Politics* 2(2), 226–40.

—— (2001b), 'Constructivism and European Integration: A Critique', in Christiansen, T. et al. (eds.), *The Social Construction of Europe* (London: Sage), 176–88.

MORAVCSIK, A. (2002), 'In Defence of the Democratic Deficit: Reassessing Legitimacy in the European Union' *Journal of Common Market Studies* 40(4), 603–24.

—— (2003), 'Reassessing Legitimacy in the European Union' *Journal of Common Market Studies* 40(4), 603–24.

—— and NICOLAIDIS, K. (1998), 'Keynote Article: Federal Ideals and Constitutional Realities in the Treaty of Amsterdam' *Journal of Common Market Studies* 36, 13–38.

—— and VACHUDOVA, M.A. (2002), 'Bargaining Among Unequals: Enlargement and the Future of European Integration' *EUSA Review* 15(4), 1, 3–5.

—— and —— (2003), 'National Interests, State Power, EU Enlargement' *East European Politics and Societies* 17(1), 42–57.

MOSER, P. (1996a), 'The European Parliament as an Agenda-Setter: What are the Conditions? A Critique of Tsebelis' *American Political Science Review* 90(4), 834–8.

—— (1996b), 'A Theory of Conditional Influence of the European Parliament in the Cooperation Procedure' *Public Choice* 91(3), 333–50.

—— (1997), 'The Benefits of the Conciliation Procedure for the European Parliament: Comment to George Tsebelis' *Aussenwirtschaft* 52(1), 57–62.

—— and TRUBEK, D. (2003), 'EU Governance, EU Employment Policy, and the European Social Model' *Journal of Common Market Studies* 41(1), forthcoming.

MÜLLER, H. (1994), 'Internationale Beziehungen als kommunikatives Handeln. Zur Kritik der utilitaristischen Handlungstheorien' *Zeitschrift für Internationale Beziehungen* 1(1), 15–44.

MUMMENDEY, A. and WENZEL, M. (1999), 'Social Discrimination and Tolerance in Intergroup Relations: Reactions to Intergroup Difference' *Personality and Social Psychology Review* 3, 224–49.

NELSEN, B.F. and STUBB, A. C.-G. (1994), *The European Union: Readings on the Theory and Practice of European Integration* (Boulder, CO: Lynne Rienner).

NEUMANN, I.B. (1996), *Russia and the Idea of Europe: A Study in Identity and International Relations* (London: Routledge).

—— (1996), 'Self and Other in International Relations' *European Journal of International Relations* 2(2), 139–74.

—— (1998a), 'European Identity, EU Expansion, and the Integration/Exclusion Nexus' *Alternatives* 23, 397–416.

—— (1998b), *Uses of the Other: the 'East' in European Identity Formation* (Manchester: Manchester University Press).

—— (2001), 'This Little Piggy Stayed at Home: Why Norway is Not a Member of the EU', in Hansen and Wæver (eds.), *European Integration and National Identity: The Challenge of the Nordic States* (London: Routledge), 88–129.

NEYER, J. (2002), 'Politische Herrschaft in nicht-hierarchischen Mehrebenensystemen' *Zeitschrift für Internationale Beziehungen* 9(1), 9–38.

—— and WOLF, D. (2003), 'Horizontal Enforcement in the EU. The BSE Case and the Case of State Aid Control', in Kohler-Koch, B. (ed.), *Linking EU and National*

*Governance* (Oxford: Oxford University Press; under review).

NORTH, D.C. (1990), *Institutions, Institutional Change and Economic Performance* (Cambridge: Cambridge University Press).

NUNAN, F. (1999), 'Policy Network Transformation: the Implementation of the EC Directive on Packaging and Packaging Waste' *Public Administration* 77(3), 621–38.

OECD (ed.) (2001), *Governance in the 21st Century* (Paris: OECD).

ØHRGAARD, J.C. (1997), 'Less than Supranational, More than Intergovernmental: European Political Cooperation and the Dynamics of Intergovernmental Integration' *Millennium: Journal of International Studies* 26(1), 1–29.

O'LEARY, S. (1995), 'The Relationship Between Community Citizenship and the Protection of Fundamental Rights in Community Law' *Common Market Law Review* 32, 519–54.

—— (1996), *The Evolving Concept of Community Citizenship: From the Free Movement of Persons to Union Citizenship* (The Hague: Kluwer).

OLSEN, J.P. (2001), 'Four Faces of Europeanization' (Oslo: ARENA (paper)).

—— (2002), 'Reforming European Institutions of Governance' *Journal of Common Market Studies* 40, 581–602.

ONUF, N. (1989), *World of Our Making: Rules and Rule in Social Theory and International Relations* (Colombia, SC: University of South Carolina Press).

—— (2002), 'Institutions, Intentions and International Relations' *Review of International Studies* 28, 211–28.

OPTEM (2000), *Perceptions of the European Union. A Qualitative Study of the Public's Attitudes to and Expectations of the European Union in the 15 Member States and in 9 Candidate Countries,* http://europa.eu.int/comm/governance/areas/studies/optem-report_en.pdf.

ORDESHOOK, P.C. and SCHWARTZ, T. (1987), 'Agenda and the Control of Political Outcomes' *American Political Science Review* 81(1), 179–200.

PAGDEN, A. (ed.) (2002), *The Idea of Europe: From Antiquity to the European Union* (Cambridge: Cambridge University Press).

PANTEL, M. (1999), 'Unity-Diversity: Cultural Policy and EU Legitimacy', in Banchoff, T. and Smith, M. (eds.), *Legitimacy and the European Union* (London: Routledge), 46–65.

PARKER, N. (2002), 'Differentiating, Collaborating, Outdoing: Nordic Identity and Marginality in the Contemporary World' *Identities: Global Studies in Culture and Power*, 9, Autumn 2002, 355–81.

PARSONS, C. (2000), 'Domestic Interests, Ideas and Integration: Lessons from the French Case' *Journal of Common Market Studies* 38(1), 45–70.

PATEMAN, C. (1988), *The Sexual Contract* (Cambridge: Polity Press).

PEDERSEN, T. (1998), *Germany, France and the Integration of Europe: A Realist Interpretation* (London: Pinter).

PENTLAND, C. (1973), *International Theory and European Integration* (London: Faber and Faber).

PERNICE, I. (1999), 'Multilevel Constitutionalism and the Treaty of Amsterdam: European Constitution-Making Revisited?' *Common Market Law Review* 36, 703–50.

—— (2001), 'The European Constitution', 16th Sinclair-House Talks in Bad Homburg, 11–12 May 2001.

PETERS, B.G. (1996), *The Future of Governing: Four Emerging Models* (Lawrence, KS: University Press of Kansas).

—— (1998), 'Policy Networks: Myth, Metaphor and Reality', in Marsh, D. (ed.), *Comparing Policy Networks* (Buckingham: Open University Press), 21–32.

—— (1999), *Institutional Theory in Political Science* (London and New York: Continuum).

PETERSON, J. (1991), 'Technology Policy in Europe: Explaining the Framework Programme and EUREKA in Theory and Practice' *Journal of Common Market Studies* 29(1), 269–90.

—— (1995), 'Decision-making in the European Union: Towards a Framework for Analysis' *Journal of European Public Policy* 2(1), 69–93.

—— (1995), 'EU Research Policy: the Politics of Expertise', in Mazey, S., *The State of the European Union Vol. 3: Building a European Polity?* (Boulder, CO and Ilford: Lynne Rienner and Longman), 391–412.

—— (1997), 'The European Union: Pooled Sovereignty, Divided Accountability' *Political Studies* 45(3), 559–78.

—— (2001), 'The Choice for EU Theorists: Establishing a Common Framework for Analysis' *European Journal of Political Research* 39(3), 289–318.

—— and BOMBERG, E. (1999), *Decision-making in the European Union* (Basingstoke and New York: Palgrave).

—— and —— (2000), 'The European Union After the 1990s: Explaining Continuity and Change', in Smith, M. *The State of the European Union, vol. 5: Risks, Reform, Resistance and Revival* (Oxford and New York: Oxford University Press), 19–41.

—— and JONES, E. (1999), 'Decision Making in an Enlarging European Union', in Sperling, J., *Two Tiers or Two Speeds? The European Security Order and the Enlargement of the European Union and*

*NATO* (Manchester and New York: Manchester University Press), 25–45.

—— and O'TOOLE JR., L.J. (2001), 'Federal Governance in the United States and the European Union: a Policy Network Perspective', in Howse, R., *The Federal Vision: Legitimacy and Levels of Governance in the United States and the European Union* (Oxford and New York: Oxford University Press), 300–34.

—— and SHACKLETON, M. (2002), 'Conclusion', in Shackleton, M., *The Institutions of the European Union* (Oxford: Oxford University Press), 347–67.

—— and SHARP, M. (1998), *Technology Policy in the European Union* (Basingstoke: Macmillan).

PIERSON, P. (1996), 'The Path to European Integration: a Historical Institutionalist Analysis' *Comparative Political Studies* 29(2), 123–63.

—— (1998), 'The Path to European Integration: A Historical-Institutionalist Analysis', in Sandholtz, W. and Stone Sweet, A., *European Integration and Supranational Governance* (Oxford: Oxford University Press), 27–58.

—— (2000), 'Increasing Returns, Path Dependence, and the Study of Politics' *American Political Science Review* 94(2), 251–67.

PINDER, J. (1992), *European Community: The Building of a Union* (Oxford: Oxford University Press).

—— (ed.) (1998), *Altiero Spinelli and the British Federalists* (London: Federal Trust).

POCOCK, J.G.A. (1991), 'Deconstructing Europe' *London Review of Books*, 19 December, 6–10.

POLLACK, M.A. (1996), 'The New Institutionalism and EU Governance: The Promise and Limits of Institutionalist Analysis' *Governance* 9(4), 429–58.

—— (1997), 'Delegation, Agency and Agenda Setting in the European Community' *International Organization* 51(1), 99–135.

—— (2001), 'International Relations Theory and European Integration' *Journal of Common Market Studies* 39(2), 221–44.

—— (2002), *The Engines of European Integration: Delegation, Agency and Agenda-Setting in the EU* (New York: Oxford University Press).

—— and HAFNER-BURTON, E. (2000), 'Mainstreaming Gender in the European Union' *Journal of European Public Policy* 7(4), 432–56.

PRZEWORSKI, A. and TEUNE, H. (1982), *The Logic of Comparative Social Inquiry* (Malabar, FL: Krieger).

PUCHALA, D.J. (1972), 'Of Blind Men, Elephants and International Integration' *Journal of Common Market Studies* 10(3), 267–84.

PUTNAM, R.D. (1988), 'Diplomacy and Domestic Politics: The Logic of Two-Level Games' *International Organization* 42(3), 427–60.

RADAELLI, C.M. (1999), *Technocracy in the European Union* (Harlow and New York: Addison-Wesley Longman).

—— (2000), 'Wither Europeanization? Concept Stretching and Substantive Change', in European Integration Online Papers, http://eiop.or.at/eiop/texte/2000–008.htm.

RANDALL, V. (1987), 2nd edn. *Women and Politics* (London: Macmillan).

RASMUSSEN, H. (1986), *On Law and Policy in the European Court of Justice* (Dordrecht: Martinus Nijhoff).

RAUNIO, T. (1997), *The European Perspective: Transnational Party Groups in the 1989–1994 European Parliament* (Aldershot: Dartmouth).

REIF, K. and SCHMITT, H. (1980), 'Nine Second-Order National Elections. A Conceptual Framework for the Analysis of European Election Results' *European Journal of Political Research* 8, 3–45.

RHODES, R.A.W. (1990), 'Policy Networks: a British Perspective' *Journal of Theoretical Politics* 2(2), 293–317.

—— (1997), *Understanding Governance. Policy Networks, Governance, Reflexivity and Accountability* (Buckingham: Open University Press).

RICHARDSON, J. (ed.) (1982), *Policy Styles in Western Europe* (London: Allen and Unwin).

—— (2000), 'Government, Interest Groups and Policy Change' *Political Studies* 48(5), 1006–25.

RIKER, W. (1980), 'Implications from the Dis-equilibrium of Majority Rule for the Study of Institutions' *American Political Science Review* 74(3), 432–47.

RISSE-KAPPEN, T. (1996), 'Exploring the Nature of the Beast: International Relations Theory and Comparative Policy Analysis Meet the European Union' *Journal of Common Market Studies* 34(1), 53–80.

RISSE, T. (2000), ' "Let's Argue!" Communicative Action in International Relations' *International Organization* 54(1), 1–39.

—— (2001), 'A European Identity? Europeanization and the Evolution of Nation-State Identities', in Cowles, M.G. et al. (eds.), *Transforming Europe. Europeanization and Domestic Change* (Ithaca, NY: Cornell University Press), 198–216.

—— (forthcoming), 'European Institutions and Identity Change: What Have We Learned?', in Herrmann, R.K. et al. (eds.), *Europeanization: Institutions and the Evolution of Social Identities*.

—— and ENGELMANN-MARTIN, D. (2002), 'Identity Politics and European Integration: The Case of Germany', in Pagden, A.

(ed.), *The Idea of Europe* (Cambridge: Cambridge University Press), 287–316.

—— and WIENER, A. (2001), 'The Social Construction of Social Constructivism', in Christiansen, T. et al. (eds.), *The Social Construction of Europe* (London: Sage), 199–205.

—— et al. (1999), 'To Euro or Not to Euro. The EMU and Identity Politics in the European Union' *European Journal of International Relations* 5(2), 147–87.

ROSAMOND, B. (1995), 'Mapping the European Condition: the Theory of Integration and the Integration of Theory' *European Journal of International Relations* 1(3), 391–408.

—— (1999), 'Discourses of Globalization and the Social Construction of European Identities' *Journal of European Public Policy* 6(4), 652–68.

—— (2000), *Theories of European Integration* (Basingstoke: Macmillan).

—— (2001), 'Discourses of Globalisation and European Identities', in Christiansen, T. et al. (eds.), *The Social Construction of Europe* (London: Sage), 158–73.

Ross, G. (1995), *Jacques Delors and European Integration* (Cambridge: Polity).

RUBERY, J. et al. (eds.) (1998), *Women and European Employment* (London: Routledge).

RUGGIE, J.G. (1993), 'Territoriality and Beyond: Problematizing Modernity in International Relations' *International Organization* 47(1), 139–74.

—— (1997), 'The Past as Prologue? Interest, Identity, and American Foreign Policy' *International Security* 21(4), 89–125.

—— (1998), 'What Makes the World Hang Together? Neo-Utilitarianism and the Social Constructivist Challenge' *International Organization* 52(4), 855–85.

RYNER, M., OVERBEEK, H., and HOLMAN, O. (eds.) (1998), *Neoliberal Hegemony and the Political Economy of European Restructuring,* special issue of *International Journal of Political Economy* 21(1)–(2).

RYTKØNEN, H.L. (2002), 'Europe and its "Almost-European" Other: A Textual Analysis of Legal and Cultural Practices of Othering in Contemporary Europe', (Stanford University: unpubl. Ph.D. dissertation).

SABATIER, P.A. (1993), 'Policy Change Over a Decade or More', in Jenkins-Smith, H.C., *Policy Change and Learning: An Advocacy Coalition Approach* (Boulder, CO and Oxford: Westview), 1–19.

—— (1998), 'The Advocacy Coalition Framework: Revisions and Relevance for Europe' *Journal of European Public Policy* 5(1), 98–130.

—— and JENKINS-SMITH, H.C. (eds.) (1993), *Policy Change and Learning: an Advocacy Coalition Approach* (Boulder, CO and Oxford: Westview).

SANDHOLTZ, W. (1996), 'Membership Matters: Limits of the Functional Approach to European Institutions' *Journal of Common Market Studies* 34(3), 403–29.

—— and STONE SWEET, A. (eds.) (1998), *European Integration and Supranational Governance* (Oxford: Oxford University Press).

—— and ZYSMAN, J. (1989), '1992: Recasting the European Bargain' *World Politics* 42(1), 99–128.

SBRAGIA, A. (1992), 'Thinking about the European Future: the Uses of Comparison', in Sbragia, A. (ed.), *Euro-Politics: Institutions and Policy-Making in the New European Community* (Washington, DC: The Brooking Institution), 257–91.

—— (2001), 'Italy Pays for Europe: Political Leadership, Political Choice, and Institutional Adaptation', in Cowles, M.G. et al. (eds.), *Transforming Europe. Europeanization and Domestic Change* (Ithaca, NY: Cornell University Press), 79–98.

SCHARPF, F.W. (1988), 'The Joint-Decision Trap: Lessons from German Federalism and European Integration' *Public Administration* 66(3), 239–78.

—— (1994), 'Community and Autonomy. Multi-Level Policy-Making in the European Union' *Journal of European Public Policy* (1), 219–42.

—— (1996), 'Negative and Positive Integration in the Political Economy of European Welfare States', in Gary, M., Scharpf, F.W., Schmitter, P.C., and Streeck, W. (eds.), *Governance in the European Union* (London: Sage), 15–39.

—— (1997), *Games Real Actors Play. Actor-Centered Institutionalism in Policy Research* (Boulder, CO: Westview).

—— (1999), *Governing in Europe: Effective and Democratic?* (Oxford and New York: Oxford University Press).

—— (1999), 'Selecting Cases and Testing Hypotheses' *Journal of European Public Policy* 6(1), 164–8.

—— (2002), 'Regieren im europäischen Mehrebenensystem. Ansätze zu einer Theorie' *Leviathan* (30), 65–92.

—— (2002), 'The European Social Model: Coping with the Challenges of Diversity' *Journal of Common Market Studies* 40(4), 645–69.

SCHELLING, T.C. (1960), *The Strategy of Conflict* (Cambridge, MA: Harvard University Press).

SCHEPEL, H. (1998), 'Legal Pluralism in the European Union', in Fitzpatrick, P. and Bergeron, H.J. (eds.), *Europe's Other: European Law Between Modernity and Postmodernity* (Aldershot: Ashgate Dartmouth), 47–66.

—— (2000), 'Reconstructing Constitution-alization: Law and Politics in the European Court of Justice' *Oxford Journal of Legal Studies* 20, 457–68.

SCHERPEREEL, J. (2002), 'Between State Socialism and European Union: Remaking the Czech and Slovak States' paper presented at the Transatlantic Graduate Workshop on EU Politics, European University Institute, Florence, 7–8 June.

SCHIMMELFENNIG, F. (1997), 'Rhetorisches Handeln in der internationalen Politik' *Zeitschrift für Internationale Beziehungen* 4(2), 219–54.

—— (2000), 'International Socialization in the New Europe: Rational Action in an Institutional Environment' *European Journal of International Relations* 6(1), 109–39.

—— (2000), *NATO's Enlargement to the East: An Analysis of Collective Decision-making*, EAPC-NATO Individual Fellowship Report 1998–2000; www.nato.int/acad/fellow/98–00/schimmelfennig.pdf.

—— (2001), 'Liberal Norms, Rhetorical Action, and the Enlargement of the EU' *International Organization* 55(1), 47–80.

—— (2001a), 'The Community Trap: Liberal Norms, Rhetorical Action, and the Eastern Enlargement of the European Union' *International Organization* 55(1), 47–80.

—— (2001b), 'Conditionality, Cost, and Commitment: Explaining the Uneven International Socialization of Central and Eastern European Countries', paper presented at the IDNET Conference on International Institutions and Socialization in the New Europe, European University Institute, Florence, 18–19 May.

—— (2003), 'Strategic Action in a Community Environment: The Decision to Enlarge the European Union to the East' *Comparative Political Studies* 36(1)–(2), 156–83.

—— (forthcoming), *Rules and Rhetoric. The Eastern Enlargement of NATO and the*

*European Union* (Cambridge: Cambridge University Press).

—— and SEDELMEIER, U. (2002), 'Theorizing EU Enlargement: Research Focus, Hypotheses, and the State of Research' *Journal of European Public Policy* 9(4), 500–28.

SCHLESINGER, P. (1991) *Media, State and Nation: Political Violence and Collective Identities* (London: Sage).

SCHMALZ-BRUNS, R. (1999), 'Deliberativer Supranationalismus. Demokratisches Regieren jenseits des Nationalstaats' *Zeitschrift für Internationale Beziehungen* 6, 185–244.

SCHMIDT, S.K. (1997), 'Sterile Debates and Dubious Generalisations: European Integration Theory Tested by Telecommunications and Electricity' *Journal of Public Policy* 16(3), 233–71.

SCHMITTER, P.C. (1969), 'Three Neo-Functional Hypotheses about International Integration' *International Organization* (Winter), vol. 23, no. 0, 562–64.

SCHMITTER, P.C. (1970), 'A Revised Theory of Regional Integration' *International Organization* (Autum), 836–68. Also published in Lindberg, L. and Scheingold, S. (eds.), *Regional Integration: Theory and Research* (Cambridge, MA: Harvard University Press, 1971), 232–65.

—— (1996), 'Imagining the Future of the Euro-Polity with the Help of New Concepts', in Marks, G., Scharpf, F.W., Schmitter, P.C., and Streeck, W. (eds.), *Governance in the European Union* (London: Sage), 121–50.

—— (2000a), *How to Democratize the European Union . . . and Why Bother?* (London, MD: Roman and Littlefield).

—— (2000b), 'Federalism and the Euro-Polity' *Journal of Democracy*, Tenth Anniversary Issue, vol. 11, no. 1 (January), 40–7.

SCHNEIDER, H. (1977), *Leitbilder der Europapolitik I: Der Weg zur Integration* (Bonn: Europa Union).

SCHNEIDER, V. (2001), 'Institutional Reform in Telecommunications: The European Union in Transnational Policy Diffusion', in Cowles, M.G. et al. (eds.), *Transforming Europe. Europeanization and Domestic Change* (Ithaca, NY: Cornell University Press), 60–78.

SCULLY, R.M. (1997a), 'Policy Influence and Participation in the European Parliament' *Legislative Studies Quarterly* 22(2), 233–52.

—— (1997b), 'The EP and the Co-Decision Procedure: A Reassessment' *Journal of Legislative Studies* 3(3), 57–73.

—— (1997c), 'The EP and Co-Decision: A Rejoinder to Tsebelis and Garrett' *Journal of Legislative Studies* 3(3), 93–103.

—— (1997d), 'Positively My Last Words on Co-Decision' *Journal of Legislative Studies* 3(4), 144–6.

SEDELMEIER, U. (1998), 'The European Union's Association Policy towards the Countries of Central and Eastern Europe: Policy Paradigms and Collective Identities in a Composite Policy' (Ph.D. dissertation, Contemporary European Studies, University of Sussex, Sussex).

—— (2000), 'East of Amsterdam: The Implications of the Amsterdam Treaty for Eastern Enlargement', in Neunreither, K. and Wiener, A. (eds.), *European Integration After Amsterdam: Institutional Dynamics and Prospects for Democracy* (Oxford: Oxford University Press), 218–38.

—— (2000), 'Eastern Enlargement: Risk, Rationality, and Role-Compliance', in Green Cowles, M. and Smith, M. (eds.), *State of the European Union Volume 5: Risk, Reforms, Resistance, and Revival* (Oxford: Oxford University Press), 164–85.

—— and WALLACE, H. (2000), 'Eastern Enlargement. Strategy or Second Thoughts?', in Wallace, H. and Wallace, W. (eds.), *Policy-Making in the European Union*, 4th edn. (Oxford: Oxford University Press), 427–60.

SHAW, J. (1995), 'Introduction', in Shaw, J. and More, G. (eds.), *The New Legal Dynamics of European Union*, 1–14.

—— (1996a), *Law of the European Union*, 2nd edn. (Houndmills: Macmillan).

—— (1996b), 'European Union Legal Studies in Crisis? Towards a New Dynamic' *Oxford Journal of Legal Studies* 16(2), 231–53.

—— (1997), 'Citizenship of the Union: Towards Post-National Membership?' *Harvard Jean Monnet Working Paper No. 6/97.*

—— (1999), 'Postnational Constitutionalism in the European Union' *Journal of European Public Policy* (6), 579–97.

—— (2000), 'Importing Gender: the Challenge of Feminism and the Analysis of the EU Legal Order' *Journal of European Public Policy* 7(3), 406–31.

—— (2001), 'European Union Governance and the Question of Gender: a critical comment', in Meny Joerges, M. and Weiler, J., *Mountain or Molehill?* www.jeanmonnetprogramme.org.papers/01/010601.

—— (2001), 'Postnational Constitutionalism in the European Union', in Christiansen, T., Jørgensen, K.E., and Wiener, A. (2001), 66–84.

—— and MORE, G. (eds.) (1995), *New Legal Dynamics of European Union* (Oxford: Clarendon).

SHEPSLE, K.A. (1979), 'Institutional Arrangements and Equilibrium in Multidimensional Voting Models' *American Journal of Political Science* 23(1), 27–60.

—— (1986), 'Institutional Equilibrium and Equilibrium Institutions', in Weisberg, H. (ed.), *Political Science; The Science of Politics* (New York: Agathon), 51–81.

—— and WEINGAST, B.R. (1984), 'Uncovered Sets and Sophisticated Voting Outcomes with Implications for Agenda Control' *American Journal of Political Science* 28(1), 49–74.

SHIELDS, R. (1992), 'The Individual, Consumption Cultures and the Fate of Community', in Shields, R. (ed.), *Lifestyle Shopping. The Subject of Consumption* (London and New York: Routledge), 99–113.

SHORE, C. (2000), *Building Europe. The Cultural Politics of European Integration* (London and New York: Routledge).

SIKKINK, K. (1993), 'The Power of Principled Ideas: Human Rights Policies in the United States and Western Europe', in Goldstein, J. and Keohane, R. (eds.) *Ideas & Foreign Policy. Beliefs, Institutions, and Political Change* (Ithaca, NY: Cornell University Press), 139–70.

SLATER, D. (1997), *Consumer Culture and Modernity* (Cambridge: Polity Press).

SLAUGHTER, A.-M. and MATTLI, W. (1995), 'Law and Politics in the European Union: A Reply to Garrett' *International Organization*, 49(1), 183–90.

——, STONE SWEET, A., and WEILER, J. (1998) (eds.), *The European Courts and National Courts. Doctrine and Jurisprudence. Legal Change in Its Social Context* (Oxford: Hart Publishing).

SMITH, A.D. (1992), 'National Identity and the Idea of European Unity' *International Affairs*, vol. 68(1), 55–76.

SMITH, D.L. and RAY, J.L. (1993), 'European Integration: Gloomy Theory Versus Rosy Reality', in Smith, D.L. and Ray, J.L. (eds.), *The 1992 Project and the Future of Integration in Europe* (Armonk, NY: Sharpe), 19–44.

SMITH, M.J. (1990), *The Politics of Agricultural Support in Britain* (Aldershot and Brookfield, VT: Dartmouth).

SMITH, S. (2000), 'International Theory and European Integration', in Kelstrup, M. and Williams, M.C., *International Relations Theory and the Politics of European Integration* (London, Routledge), 33–56.

—— (2000), 'Wendt's World' *Review of International Studies* 26(1), 151–63.

SNYDER, F. (1990), *New Directions in European Community Law* (London: Weidenfeld and Nicolson).

—— (1993), 'The Effectiveness of European Community Law. Institutions, Processes, Tools and Techniques' *Modern Law Review* (56), 19–54.

SOYSAL, Y. (1994), *Limits of Citizenship: Migrants and Postnational Citizenship in Europe* (Chicago, IL and London: University of Chicago Press).

SPINELLI, A. (1966), *The Eurocrats—Conflict and Crisis in the European Community* (Baltimore, MD: The Johns Hopkins Press).

STARK, D. (1992), 'Path Dependence and Privatization Strategies in East Central Europe' *East European Politics and Society* 6(1), 17–54.

STAVRAKAKIS, Y. (forthcoming), 'Passions of Identification: Discourse, Enjoyment and European Identity', in Howarth, D. and Torfing, J. (eds.), *Discourse Theory and European Politics* (Basingstoke: Palgrave).

STEIN, E. (1981), 'Lawyers, Judges, and the Making of a Transnational Constitution' *American Journal of International Law* 75(1), 1–27.

STETSON, D.M. and MAZUR, A.G. (eds.), *Comparative State Feminism* (Newbury Park, CA: Sage).

STEUNENBERG, B., KOBOLDT, C., and SCHMIDTCHEN, D. (1996), 'Policymaking, Comitology, and the Balance of Power in the European Union' *International Review of Law and Economics* 16(2), 329–44.

——, —— and —— (1997), 'Beyond Comitology: A Comparative Analysis of Implementation Procedures with Parliamentary Involvement' *Aussenwirtschaft* 52(1), 87–112.

STINCHCOMBE, A.L. (1968), *Constructing Social Theories* (New York: Harcourt, Brace and World).

STONE SWEET, A. (1998), 'Constitutional Dialogues in the European Community', in Slaughter, A.-M., Stone Sweet, A., and Weiler, J. (eds.), 305–30.

—— (2000), *Governing with Judges: Constitutional Politics in Europe* (Oxford: Oxford University Press).

—— (2003), 'European Integration and the Legal System', in Börzel, T. and Cichowski, R. (eds.), *Law, Politics, and Society* (The State of the European Union 6) (Oxford: Oxford University Press), 18–47.

—— and BRUNELL, T.L. (1998), 'Constructing a Supranational Constitution: Dispute Resolution and Governance in the European Community' *American Political Science Review* 92(1), 63–81.

—— and —— (2000), 'The European Court, National Judges, and Legal Integration: A Researcher's Guide to the Data Set on Preliminary References in EC Law, 1958–98' *European Law Journal* 6(2), 117–27.

—— and CAPORASO, J.A. (1998), 'From Free Trade to Supranational Polity: The European Court and Integration', in Sandholtz, W. and Stone Sweet, A. (eds.), *European Integration and Supranational Governance* (New York: Oxford University Press), 92–133.

—— and SANDHOLTZ, W. (1997), 'European Integration and Supranational Governance' *Journal of European Public Policy* 4(3), 297–317.

—— and —— (1998), 'Integration, Supranational Governance, and the Institutionalization of the European Polity', in Sandholtz, W. and Stone Sweet, A. (1998), 1–26.

——, ——, and FLIGSTEIN, N. (eds.) (2001), *The Institutionalization of Europe* (Oxford: Oxford University Press).

STRAEHLE, C., WEISS, G., WODAK, R., MUNTIGL, P., and SEDLAK, M. (1999), 'Struggle as Metaphor in European Union Discourses on Unemployment' *Discourse and Society*, 10(1), 67–100.

STRÅTH, B. (2000a), 'Introduction: Europe as a Discourse' in Stråth, B. (ed.), *Europe and the Other and Europe as the Other* (Brussels: P.I.E.-Peter Lang), 13–44.

—— (2000b), 'Multiple Europes: Integration, Identity and Demarcation to the Other', in Stråth, B. (ed.), *Europe and the Other and Europe as the Other* (Brussels: P.I.E.-Peter Lang), 385–420.

TALLBERG, J. (1999), *Making States Comply: The European Commission, the European Court of Justice and the Enforcement of the Internal Market* (Lund, Sweden: Lund Political Studies 09, Department of Political Science, Lund University).

—— (2000), 'The Anatomy of Autonomy: An Institutional Account of Variation in Supranational Influence' *Journal of Common Market Studies* 38(5), 843–64.

THATCHER, M. (1998), 'The Development of Policy Network Analyses: From Modest Origins to Overarching Frameworks' *Journal of Theoretical Politics* 10(4), 389–416.

—— and STONE SWEET, A. (2002), *The Politics of Delegation: Non-Majoritarian Institutions in Europe*, special issue of *West European Politics*, 25(1), 1–219.

THELEN, K. (1999), 'Historical Institutionalism in Comparative Politics' *Annual Review of Political Science* 2, 369–404.

—— and STEINMO, S. (1992), 'Introduction', in Thelen, K. and Steinmo, S. (eds.), *Structuring Politics: Historical Institutionalism in Comparative Politics* (New York: Cambridge University Press), 1–32.

THOMPSON, G., FRANCES, J. et al. (eds.) (1991), *Markets, Hierarchies and Networks: the Coordination of Social Life* (Buckingham and London: Open University Press and Sage).

TITSCHER, S., MEYER, M., WODAK, R., and VETTER, E. (2000), *Methods of Text and Discourse Analysis* (London: Sage).

TOOLEY, M.J. (ed.) (1955), *Six Books of the Commonwealth* (Oxford: Basil Blackwell).

TORFING, J. (1999), *New Theories of Discourse: Laclau, Mouffe and Zizek* (Oxford: Blackwell).

TORREBLANCA, J. (2001), *The Reuniting of Europe: Promises, Negotiations and Compromises* (Aldershot: Ashgate).

TRANHOLM-MIKKELSEN, J. (1991), 'Neofunctionalism: Obstinate or Obsolete? A Reappraisal in the Light of the New Dynamism of the European Community' *Millennium: Journal of International Studies* 20(1), 1–22.

*Treaties Establishing The European Communities (ECSC, EEC, EAEC)* (abridged edn.) (1987), (Luxembourg: Office for Official Publications of the EC).

TSEBELIS, G. (1994), 'The Power of the European Parliament as a Conditional Agenda Setter' *American Political Science Review* 88(1), 129–42.

—— (1995), 'Conditional Agenda Setting and Decision-Making *Inside* the European Parliament' *Journal of Legislative Studies* 1(1), 65–93.

—— (1996), 'More on the European Parliament as a Conditional Agenda-Setter: Response to Moser' *American Political Science Review* 90(4), 839–44.

—— (1997), 'Maastricht and the Democratic Deficit' *Aussenwirtschaft* 52(1), 29–56.

—— and GARRETT, G. (1997a), 'Agenda Setting, Vetoes, and the European Union's Co-Decision Procedure' *Journal of Legislative Studies* 3(3), 74–92.

—— and —— (1997b), 'More on the Co-Decision Endgame' *Journal of Legislative Studies* 3(4), 139–43.

—— and —— (2001a), 'Legislative Politics in the European Union' *European Union Politics* 1(1), 9–36.

—— and —— (2001b), 'The Institutional Foundations of Intergovernmentalism and Supranationalism in the European Union' *International Organization* 55(2), 357–90.

—— and KALANDRAKIS, A. (1999), 'European Parliament and Environmental Legislation: The Case of Chemicals' *European Journal of Political Research* 36(1), 119–54.

——, JENSEN, C.B., KALANDRAKIS, A., and KREPPEL, A. (2001), 'Legislative Procedures in the European Union' *British Journal of Political Science* 31(4), 573–99.

UGREŠIĆ, D. (1998), 'Nice People Don't Mention Such Things' *European Journal of Women's Studies* (5), 297–310.

ULLRICH, H. (2002), 'The Impact of Policy Networks in the GATT Uruguay Round: the Case of US-EC Agricultural Negotiations' *Government and International Relations* (London: London School of Economics).

UNITED NATIONS (2000), United Nations Millennium Declaration, A/Res/55/2.

URRY, J. (1995), *Consuming Places* (London and New York: Routledge).

VACHUDOVA, M.A. (2001), 'The Leverage of International Institutions on Democratizing States' EUI Working Paper No. 2001/33, consulted on-line at: www.iue.it/RSC/WP-Texts/01_33.pdf.

VAN DIJK, T.A. (ed.) (1997), *Discourse Studies: A Multidisciplinary Introduction* (vol. 1: Discourse as Structure and Process; vol. 2: Discourse as Social Interaction) (London: Sage).

VAN SCHENDELEN, M.P.C. (ed.) (1998), *EU Committees as Influential Policymakers* (Aldershot and Brookfield, VT: Ashgate).

WÆVER, O. (1989), 'Ideologies of Stabilization—Stabilization of Ideologies: Reading German Social Democrats', in Harle, V. and Sivonen, P. (eds.), *Europe in Transition: Politics and Nuclear Strategy* (London: Frances Pinter), 110–39.

—— (1990), 'Three Competing Europes: German, French, Russian' *International Affairs* 66(3), 477–93.

—— (1991) 'Det tyske problem i 1990erne' (The German Problem in the 1990s) *Internasjonal Politikk* (Oslo), 1991(4), 401–19.

—— (1994), 'Resisting the Temptation of Post Foreign Policy Analysis', in Carlsnaes, W. and Smith, S. (eds.), *European Foreign Policy: The EC and Changing Perspectives in Europe* (ECPR/Sage), 238–73.

—— (1995), 'Power, Principles and Perspectivism: Understanding Peaceful Change in Post-Cold War Europe', in Patomäki, H. (ed.), *Peaceful Changes in World Politics* (Tampere: TAPRI), 208–82.

—— (1996a), '"The Struggle for Europe": A Discourse Analysis of France, Germany and European Union', Center for International Studies, School of International Relations, University of Southern California, 'Re-thinking Security' Seminar Paper No. 11, 23 October 1996 (62 pages).

—— (1996b), 'The Rise and Fall of the Inter-paradigm Debate', in Smith, S., Booth, K., and Zalewski, M. (eds.), *International Theory: Positivism and Beyond* (Cambridge: Cambridge University Press), 149–85.

—— (1996c), 'European Security Identities' *Journal of Common Market Studies* 34(1), March, 103–32.

—— (1998a), 'The Sociology of a Not so International Discipline: American and European Developments in International Relations' *International Organization* 52(4), 687–727.

—— (1998b), 'Explaining Europe by Decoding Discourses', in Wivel, A. (ed.), *Explaining European Integration* (Copenhagen: Political Studies Press), 100–46.

—— (2000), 'The EU as a Security Actor: Reflections from a Pessimistic Constructivist on Post-sovereign Security Orders', in Kelstrup, M. and Williams, M.C. (eds.), *International Relations Theory and the Politics of European Integration. Power, Security and Community* (London: Routledge), 250–94.

——, HOLM, H. and LARSEN, H. (1991), *The Struggle for Europe: French and German Concepts of State, Nation and European Union* (unpublished book ms).

WALDRON, J. (1999), 'How to Argue for a Universal Claim' *Columbia Human Rights Law Review* (30), 305–14.

WALKER, N. (2002), 'The Idea of Constitutional Pluralism' *The Modern Law Review* (65), 317–59.

WALLACE, H. (2000), 'Analysing and Explaining Policies', in Wallace, W., *Policy-Making in the European Union* (Oxford: Oxford University Press), 65–81.

—— (2000), 'EU Enlargement: A Neglected Subject', in Green Cowles, M. and Smith, M. (eds.), *State of the European Union Volume 5: Risk, Reforms, Resistance, and Revival* (Oxford: Oxford University Press), 149–63.

—— (2000), 'The Institutional Setting. Five Variations on a Theme', in Wallace, H. and Wallace, W. (eds.), *Policy-Making in the European Union* (Oxford: Oxford University Press), 3–37.

—— (2002), 'Experiments in European Governance', in Jachtenfuchs, M. and Knodt, M. (eds.), *Regieren in internationalen Institutionen* (Opladen: Leske und Budrich), 255–69.

—— (2003), 'Contrasting Images of European Governance', in Kohler-Koch, B. (ed.), *Linking EU and National Governance* (Oxford: Oxford University Press; under review).

WALLACE, W. (1996), 'Truth and Power, Monks and Technocrats: Theory and Practice in International Relations' *Review of International Studies* 22(3), 301–21.

WALTERS, W. (2002), 'The Power of Inscription: Beyond Social Construction and Deconstruction in European Integration Studies' *Millennium* 31(1), 83–108.

WALTZ, K.N. (1979), *Theory of International Politics* (New York: McGraw-Hill).

WARD, I. (2001), 'Beyond Constitutionalism: The Search for a European Political Imagination' *European Law Journal* 7(1), 24–40.

WARD, S. and WILLIAMS, R. (1997), 'From Hierarchy to Networks? Sub-central Government and EU Urban Environment Policy' *Journal of Common Market Studies* 35(3), 439–64.

WATSON, P. (2000), 'Politics, Policy and Identity: EU Eastern Enlargement and East/West Differences' *Journal of European Public Policy* 7(3), 369–84.

WEATHERILL, S. (1995), *Law and Integration in the European Union* (Oxford: Clarendon).

WEBER, M. (1978), *Economy and Society. An Outline of Interpretive Sociology* (Berkeley, CA and London: University of California Press).

WEILER, J. (1981), 'The Community System: The Dual Character of Supranationalism' *Yearbook of European Law* (1), 267–306.

—— (1982), 'Community, Member States and European Integration: Is the Law Relevant?' *Journal of Common Market Studies* (21), 39–56.

—— (1986), 'Eurocracy and Distrust: Some Questions Concerning the Role of the European Court of Justice in the Protection of Fundamental Human Rights Within the Legal Order of the European Communities' *Washington Law Review* (61), 1103–42.

—— (1987a), 'The European Court at a Crossroads: Community Human Rights and Member State Action', in Capotorti, F. et al. (eds.), *Du droit international au droit de l'intégration* (Baden-Baden: Nomos), 821–42.

—— (1987b), 'The Court of Justice on Trial' *Common Market Law Review* (24), 555–89.

—— (1991), 'The Transformation of Europe' *Yale Law Journal* 100(8), 2405–83.

—— (1992), 'Thou Shalt Not Oppress a Stranger: On the Judicial Protection of the Human Rights of Non EC Nationals—A Critique' *European Journal of International Law* 3(1), 65–91.

—— (1993), 'Journey to an Unknown Destination: A Retrospective and Prospective of the European Court of Justice in the Arena of Political Integration' *Journal of Common Market Studies* 31(4), 417–46.

—— (1994), 'A Quiet Revolution: The European Court of Justice and Its Interlocutors' *Comparative Political Studies* 26(4), 510–34.

—— (1995), 'The State "über alles": Demos, Telos, and the German Maastricht Decision', in Due, O. et al. (eds.), *Festschrift für Ulrich Everling* (Baden-Baden: Nomos), 1651–88.

—— (1998a), 'Epilogue. The European Courts of Justice: Beyond "Beyond Doctrine" or the Legitimacy Crisis of European Constitutionalism', in Slaughter, A.-M., Stone Sweet, A., and Weiler, J. (eds.), 365–91.

—— (1998b), 'Bread and Circus: The State of the European Union' *Columbia Journal of European Law* 4, 223–48.

—— (1998c), 'Europe: The Case Against the Case for Statehood' *European Law Journal* 4(1), 43–62.

—— (1999), *The Constitution of Europe. 'Do the New Clothes Have an Emperor?' and Other Essays on European Integration* (Cambridge: Cambridge University Press).

—— (1999a), 'Epilogue. "Comitology" as Revolution. Infranationalism, Constitutionalism and Democracy', in Joerges, C. and Vos, E. (eds.), *EU Committees. Social Regulation, Law and Politics*, 339–50.

—— (2000), 'Epilogue: Towards a Common Law of International Trade', in Weiler, J. (ed.), *The EU, the WTO and the NAFTA. Towards a Common Law of International Trade* (Oxford: Oxford University Press), 201–32.

—— (2001), 'Epilogue: The Judicial Après Nice', in de Búrca, G. and Weiler, J. (2001), 215–26.

—— (2002), 'A Constitution for Europe? Some Hard Choices' *Journal of Common Market Studies* 40, 563–80.

—— and LOCKHART, N. (1995), ' "Taking Rights Seriously" Seriously: The European Court and Its Fundamental Rights Jurisprudence', *Common Market Law Review* 32, 51–94, 579–627.

—— and WIND, M. (eds.) (2003), *European Constitutionalism Beyond the State* (Cambridge: Cambridge University Press).

——, HALTERN, U., and MAYER, F. (1995), 'European Democracy and its Critique: Five Uneasy Pieces' *West European Politics* 18(3), 4–39.

WEISE, C., BRÜCKER, H., FRANZMEYER, F., LODAHL, M., MÖBIUS, U., SCHULTZ, S.,

SCHUMACHER, D., and TRABOLD, H. (1997), *Ostmitteleuropa auf dem Weg in die EU—Transformation, Verflechtung, Reformbedarf* (Berlin: Duncker und Humblot).

WENDT, A. (1999), *Social Theory of International Politics* (Cambridge: Cambridge University Press).

WESSELS, W. (2000), *Die Öffnung des Staates. Modelle und Wirklichkeit grenzüberschreitender Verwaltungspraxis 1960–1995* (Opladen: Leske und Budrich).

WIENER, A. (1998), *'European' Citizenship Practice: Building Institutions of a Non-State* (Boulder, CO: Westview).

—— (2000), 'Explaining Unintended Consequences of Institution-Building: The Case of Union Citizenship', Paper prepared for presentation at the annual meeting of the *International Studies Association*, 14–19 March 2000, Los Angeles, CA.

—— (2001), 'The Constitutional Significance of the Charter of Fundamental Rights', *German Law Journal*, 2, 18, 01 December 2001.

—— (2002), 'Finality vs. Enlargement. Opposing Rationales and Constitutive Practices towards a New Transnational Order' *Jean Monnet Working Paper 8/02, NYU School of Law*.

—— (2003), 'Institutionen', in Bogdandy, A. von (ed.), *Europäisches Verfassungsrecht. Theoretische und dogmatische Grundzüge* (Heidelberg: Springer), 121–47.

—— and NEUNREITHER, K. (2000), 'Introduction: Amsterdam and Beyond', in Neunreither, K. and Wiener, A. (eds.), *European Integration After Amsterdam* (Oxford: Oxford University Press), 1–11.

WIGHT, C. (2002), 'Philosophy of Science and International Relations', in Carlsnaes, W. et al. (eds.), *Handbook of International Relations* (London: Sage), 23–51.

WILKINSON, J.D. (1981), *The Intellectual Resistance in Europe* (Cambridge, MA: Harvard University Press).

WILLIAMS, F. (2003), 'Contesting "Race" and "Gender" in the European Union', in Hobson, B. (ed.), *Recognition Struggles and Social Movements: Contested Identities, Agency and Power* (Cambridge: Cambridge University Press).

WILLIAMS, M.C. and NEUMANN, I.B. (2000), 'From Alliance to Security Community: NATO, Russia, and the Power of Identity', *Millennium: Journal of International Studies* 29(2), 357–87.

WINCOTT, D. (1995a), 'Institutional Interaction and European Integration: Towards an Everyday Critique of Liberal Intergovernmentalism', *Journal of Common Market Studies* 33(4), 597–609.

—— (1995b), 'Political Theory, Law, and European Union', in Shaw, J. and More, G. (eds.), 293–311.

—— (1998), 'Does the European Union Pervert Democracy? Questions of Democracy in New Constitutionalist Thought on the Future of Europe', *European Law Journal* 4(4), 411–28.

WIND, M. (1992), 'Eksisterer Europa? Reflektioner over forsvar, identitet og borgerdyd i et nyt Europa', in Sørensen, C. (ed.), *Europa Nation-Union: efter Minsk og Maastricht* (Copenhagen: Fremad), 23–81.

—— (2001), *Sovereignty and European Integration. Towards a Post-Hobbesian Order* (London and New York: Palgrave (Macmillan)).

WITTE, B. DE (1999), 'Direct Effect, Supremacy, and the Nature of the Legal Order', in Craig, P. and de Búrca, G. (eds.), 177–213.

WOBBE, TH. (2003), 'From Protecting to Promoting: Evolving EU Sex Equality Norms in an Organisational Field', *European Law Journal* 9, 88–108.

WODAK, R. and WEISS, G. (2000), 'The Globalization Rhetoric in Discourses of the European Union', in Suess, A. (ed.), *Globalisierung: Ein wissenschaftlicher Diskurs?* (Vienna: Passagen), 209–39.

WOODS, N. (1996), 'The Uses of Theory in the Study of International Relations', in Woods, N. (ed.), *Explaining International Relations since 1945* (Oxford: Oxford University Press), 9–31.

WRIGHT, M. (1988), 'Policy Community, Policy Network and Comparative Industrial Policies', *Political Studies* 36(2), 593–612.

YOUNG, O.R. (1999), *Governance in World Affairs* (Ithaca, NY and London: Cornell University Press).

YUVAL-DAVIS, N. (1997), *Gender and Nation* (London: Sage).

ŽIŽEK, S. (1999), 'Carl Schmitt in the Age of Post-Politics', in Mouffe, C. (ed.), *The Challenge of Carl Schmitt* (London and New York: Verso), 18–37.

ZULEEG, M. (2001), 'Comment' *German Law Journal* 2(2).

ZÜRN, M. (1998), *Regieren jenseits des Nationalstaates. Globalisierung und Denationalisierung als Chance* (Frankfurt/M.: Suhrkamp).

—— and WOLF, D. (1999), 'European Law and International Regimes. The Features of Law Beyond the Nation State' *European Law Journal* 5, 272–92.

# Index